PAINTING LANDSCAPES
in
Watercolour

PAINTING LANDSCAPES
in
Watercolour

TAKING YOUR ART TO THE NEXT LEVEL

OLIVER PYLE

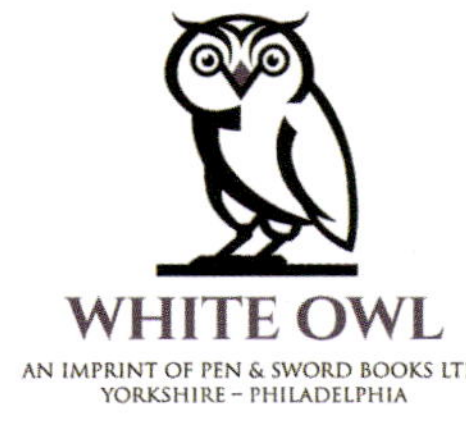

WHITE OWL

AN IMPRINT OF PEN & SWORD BOOKS LTD.
YORKSHIRE – PHILADELPHIA

First published in Great Britain in 2024 by
White Owl
An imprint of
Pen & Sword Books Ltd.
Yorkshire - Philadelphia

ISBN 978 1 39908 487 1

A CIP catalogue record for this book is available from the British Library.

Typeset by SJmagic DESIGN SERVICES, India.

Printed and bound in India by Replika Press Pvt. Ltd.

Pen & Sword Books Ltd. incorporates the imprints of Pen & Sword Books: After the Battle, Archaeology, Atlas, Aviation, Battleground, Discovery, Family History, History, Maritime, Military, Politics, Select, Transport, True Crime, Fiction, Frontline Books, Leo Cooper, Praetorian Press, Seaforth Publishing, Wharncliffe and White Owl.

For a complete list of Pen & Sword titles please contact:

PEN & SWORD BOOKS LIMITED
George House, Beevor Street, Off Pontefract Road, Hoyle Mill, Barnsley, South Yorkshire, England, S71 1HN.
E-mail: enquiries@pen-and-sword.co.uk
Website: www.pen-and-sword.co.uk

or

PEN AND SWORD BOOKS
1950 Lawrence Rd, Havertown, PA 19083, USA
E-mail: uspen-and-sword@casematepublishers.com
website: www.penandswordbooks.com

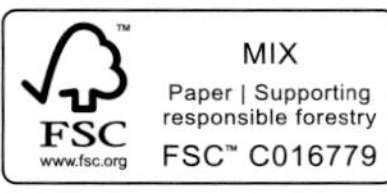

CONTENTS

FOREWORD

"'If you could say it in words, there would be no reason to paint" – Edward Hopper. The more you understand painting, the more profound these words by the great artist become; artist Oliver Pyle certainly understands these words. Working in the often misunderstood medium of watercolour, he proves it daily – image by strikingly beautiful image. Mr Pyle's speciality is landscape painting – a study of his work will demonstrate just how completely he understands that a watercolour painting can capture the ephemeral essence of a place far more effectively than any other painting medium or photographic process. The reasons for this are many, but Pyle's seemingly effortless ability to speak fluently in the wordless vocabulary of watercolour goes a long way toward an explanation. A mastery of edges, rich fluidity, transparency and complementary tonality are all within easy reach of Pyle's inspired brush.

But perhaps more importantly, Pyle's work demonstrates something even more crucial for a successful landscape painting – a palpable sense of place. Ironically, this emerges less from the expert rendition of what is seen – a line of trees or outcropping of rock perhaps – but rather from what is not seen, only felt; often, the power of a brilliant watercolour painting can be found in what is not painted more than in what is painted. The contours of negative space, pure atmosphere, and the endless complexities of light – these are what wordlessly define Oliver Pyle's emotive landscape painting.'

Thomas Wells Schaller
New York City, December 2023

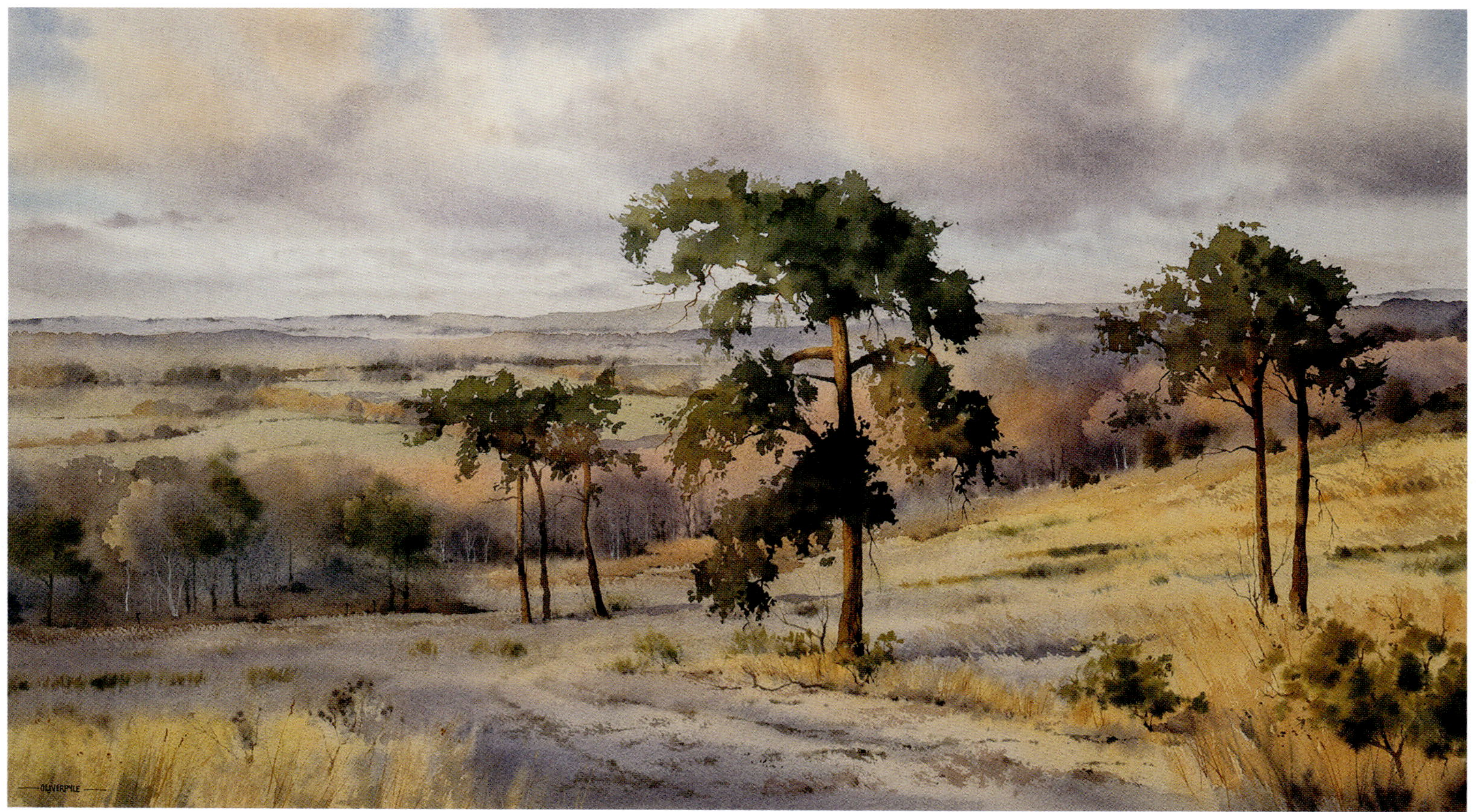

Winter Light near Wren's Warren – 72cm x 45cm

The Ashdown Forest in Sussex is the perfect place to start, and this painting conveys much of what I love about painting the landscape: soft-edged clouds and distant trees set against the rugged, hard-edged detail of majestic Scots Pines; winter sunshine throwing contrasting blankets of cool shadows and warm highlights across the heathland landscape; a suggestive pathway, inviting us to explore the distant woodland of beech and birch trees. It is impossible not to be excited by subjects like this.

INTRODUCTION

A small library could be filled with books about landscape painting and a good number of those would include instruction on how to do so using the medium of watercolour. The obvious question is, do we really need another one? My challenge in approaching this subject has been to find new angles and fresh insight that will contribute positively to these already crowded shelves. Surprisingly, the task has not been as daunting as you might imagine. My years of study, teaching and immersion in the subject has revealed a notable point of interest: in the landscape painting library most books focus on the technicalities of painting, but not many promote the importance of a rich understanding of the subject – the landscape. Perhaps this is just the way it has developed and reflects the optimal way to learn; or is there an alternative perspective? I believe so.

The purpose of this book is to direct those with experience of painting in watercolour along the path to progress and success in becoming accomplished landscape painters. The map that I provide is a little different: success as a landscape painter is more about landscape than it is about painting. In this book our time will be spent considering landscape 'whys' as opposed to 'hows'. Instead of providing you with pages of step-by-step guides to follow, which can often be counterproductive, we will be spending our time in the landscape, understanding it, experiencing it, learning from it. You will be shown strategies and techniques enabling you to make both simple and complex landscape paintings with consistent results and I will take you with me into the landscape, where we learn to look, observe, sketch and paint the places and moments that inspire us. Instead of supplying you with a list of technical exercises, the important learning points from this book are illustrated by examples from my own paintings.

In recent times the genre of landscape art has undergone something of a transformation. Traditionally, an experienced landscape painter developed a deep connection to their subjects, returning time and again to witness new moments, changing atmospherics and alternative compositions. Finding it impossible to convey their experiences using words – either written or spoken – the art of painting seemed the only available method of communicating their feelings and landscape encounters. Viewers of their paintings were able engage with the artist's

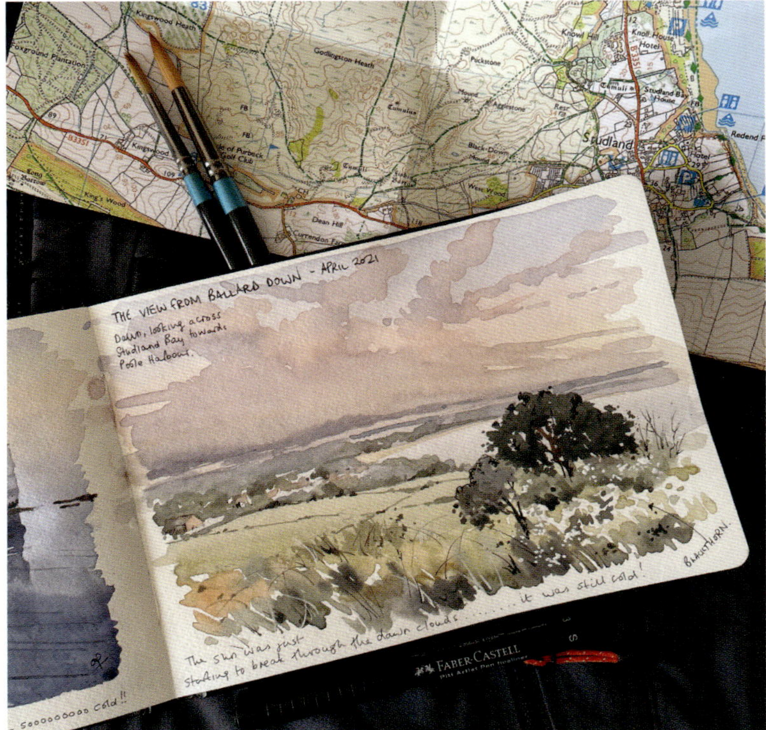

A sketch from an early morning walk on Ballard Down, Dorset.

With today's access to the internet, social media platforms have increasingly become the go-to venue for learning whatever it is that inspires and motivates us. In some respects, this is a positive development and one that I have benefited from on many occasions. It can also act as a springboard for self-promotion and quick money-making, encouraging the formation of unhelpful ideas. Instead of being inspired by their subject – the landscape – many are now inspired by an artist that they follow online and their style of painting. Instead of expressing vision and emotion by making their own instinctive marks and through their own decision making, many painters have fallen into the trap of emulating the work of more established artists, often their tutors. They become illustrators of landscape paintings, not landscape painters themselves. Of course, this has happened throughout the history of landscape art in varying degrees, but the recent explosion of available tutorial content online has amplified this significantly. Painting is an expressive, creative activity and to ultimately succeed as a landscape painter you must develop your own ways of communicating your vision and feelings, with the brush and on the paper. Much of today's teaching runs the risk of replacing creativity with technical competence and it is why this book is different; it is my ambition to provide some balance and encourage a return to the traditional attributes of landscape painting, primarily the inspiration that comes from our connection with being outdoors and in nature. I only paint when I respond to my subject, the landscape, in an emotional way. Having established that connection I can then respond in a critical, academic and technical way. An emotional connection must come first though, or there seems to be little reason to paint.

You will find the instruction in the first two sections is weighted heavily in favour of understanding the landscape, providing you with a range of ideas that will act as a tool kit to help you develop the skills you need to paint the landscapes you want, with an identity that is your own. Paint your way, using the brushstrokes that feel natural to you, in colours that resonate with your vision of the landscape and how you

moods and motivation, as well as enjoying their aesthetic presentation of the landscape, which together gave a clear insight into what it was like to be there at that moment in time. Knowing that, added a weight of significance and substance to the quality of their work; this is where the attraction of a good landscape painting truly lies.

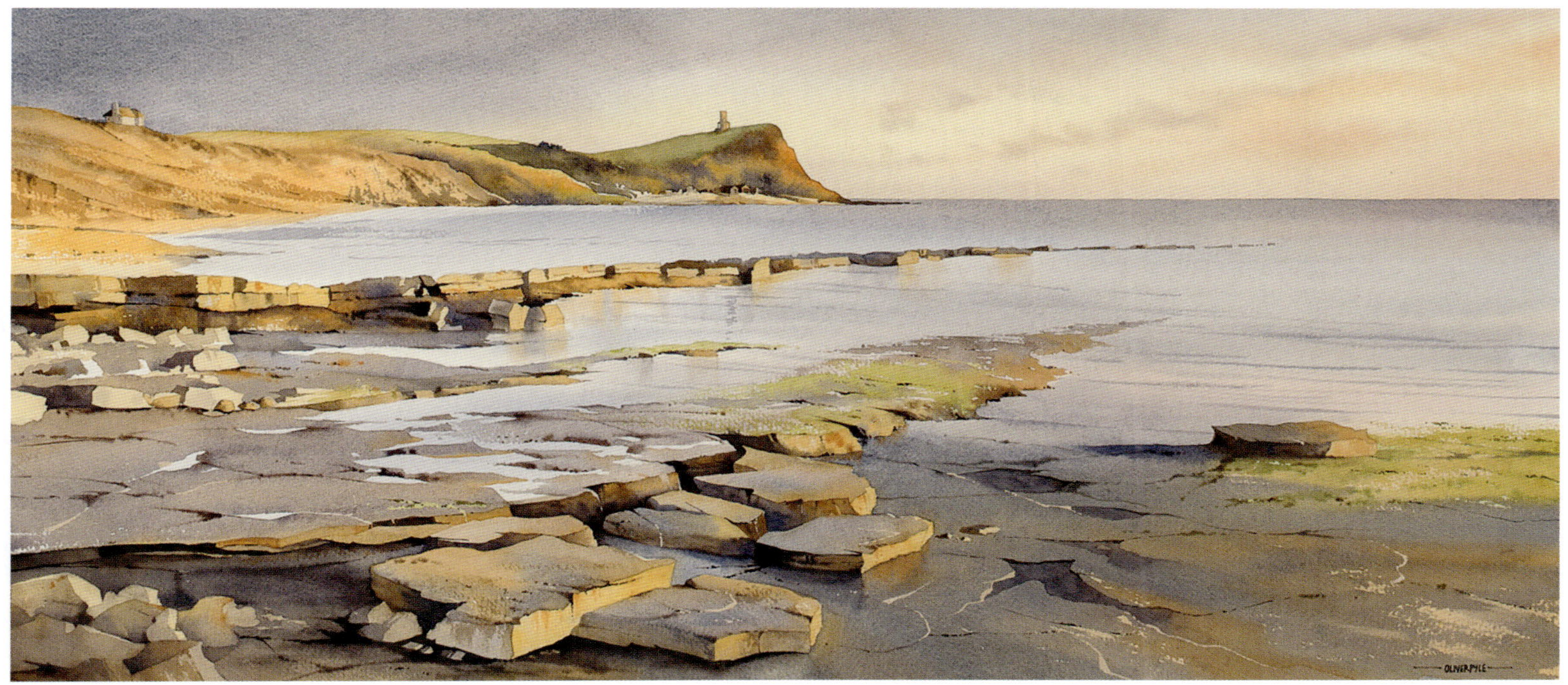

The Last Days of Summer, Kimmeridge Bay – 70cm x 36cm
Without my knowledge and experience of places – over decades in many cases – I would struggle to paint compelling landscapes. Painting these ledges, sunlit in places, shaded in others, stretching into the shimmering sea, requires technical skill, but it is my familiarity with this beautiful, rugged bay in Dorset that is the secret to success.

feel when you are in it. Learning 'landscape-looking' and how to be inspired by nature seems to be curiously missing from the agenda these days, particularly in the watercolour tuition that I see online. This book reflects my commitment to see landscape itself return to the top of the landscape painting curriculum once more.

So please bear with me as I attempt to fire your inspiration, perhaps weaning some of you off the sticky diet of the online world. Join me on the journey as we put landscape ahead of painting, why before how, experience as well as aesthetic. Once we have reached that point, I will show you the Three Cs: Colour, Contrast and Composition – and

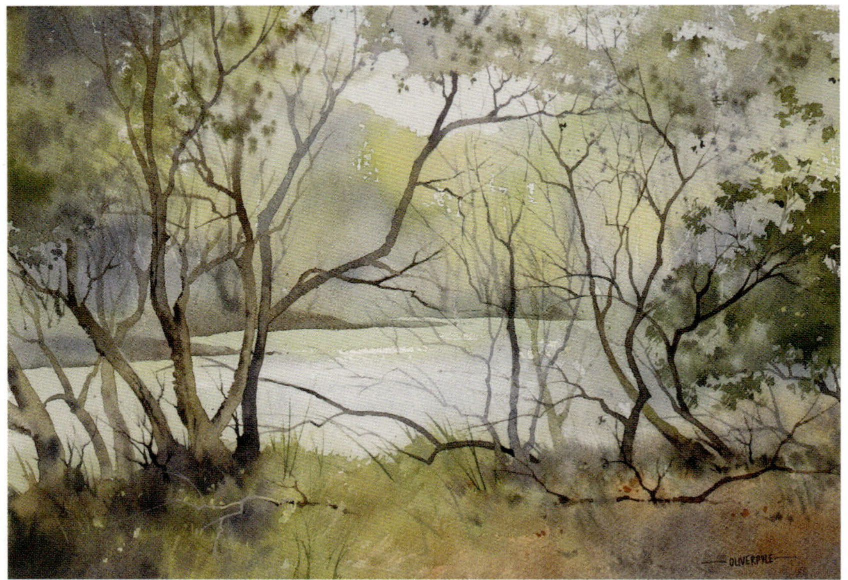

The Pond Beyond – 39cm x 29cm
Often, all it takes is a quick stroll through the woods on a camping holiday; you glance through the trees and there's your next subject. Be alert – inspiration is everywhere.

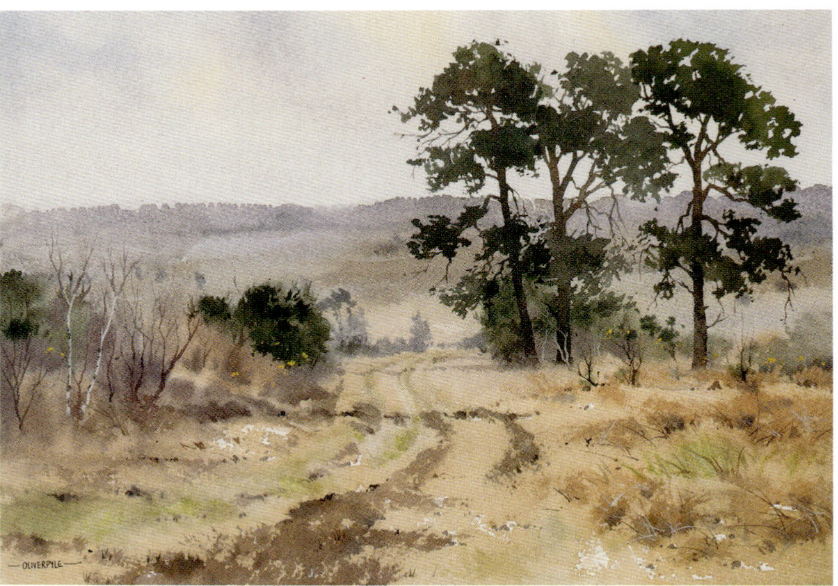

December, Ashdown Forest – 39cm x 29cm
A well-trodden path in a favourite heathland landscape. Following paths, physically or metaphorically is satisfying. Negotiate the undulations, the twists and turns and they will take you to the places you want to be.

how these are central to assessing subjects and creating visual interest in your work. We will visit the Four Ds: Decisions, Development, Definition, Detail – and how to use this structure to approach any painting, increasing your skills in manging the unmanageable medium of watercolour. Allow me to take you on several field trips, each one demonstrating a specific element of the landscape or the skills required to paint it: we will spend time on the South Downs in Sussex, the Purbeck coast in Dorset and the River Thames in London and I will show you how my deep knowledge of these places has enabled me to paint them convincingly. At the end of the path, my hope is that you will have increased your inspiration for landscape painting as a genre and enhanced your understanding of watercolour as a medium. We will part ways with a reflection on how I made the leap from a hobby painter to a full-time artist, with the hope that there might be some useful learning points that you can use, should you be considering a similar transition.

LANDSCAPE – 'TAKING PART IN THE EXISTENCE OF THINGS'

Before we start to explore the skills required to paint the landscape, we need to take a little time to understand our subject; it may seem an obvious question, but what exactly is 'landscape'? It is easy to think of it as a countryside view, stretched out in front of us and loved by the painter, walker and photographer. Or just a collection of hills, valleys, streets and woodlands through which we pass or inhabit. It is all these things, yet infinitely more; a rich tapestry of sounds, sights, smells and textures, woven on the looms of nature and human enterprise. The rasping call of a pheasant. Soft, curving lines of downland fields and the sharp, jagged interference of a gorse bush. The organised irregularity of a dry-stone wall or the silver uniformity of an urban canal. Think of the landscape not so much as a place to go or see, but more a place in which to be; expansive vistas to admire, nature's details to experience and our history to consider.

Unspoilt natural places in Britain are almost impossible to find now; the landscapes that we see and experience today have been defined by millennia of human activity; mining, coppicing, grazing, reclaiming, harvesting, travelling, defending, worshipping. We have benefited greatly from all of these and the landscape remains the most elegant document we have that records our collective endeavours, our imagination, ambitions, fears, our best work but also our worst. It is the richest record we have of the past. Our feeling of connection to nature, the countryside and urban spaces is no mystery – after all, we have shaped these spaces ourselves for generations. The role of the landscape artist is not so much to paint pretty pictures of these places but rather to explore our experiences of them and our involvement in them. The art we make then becomes a visual appendix to this elegant document. As a landscape painter, my engagement with the landscape is inescapable and the motivation for my work is always the landscape,

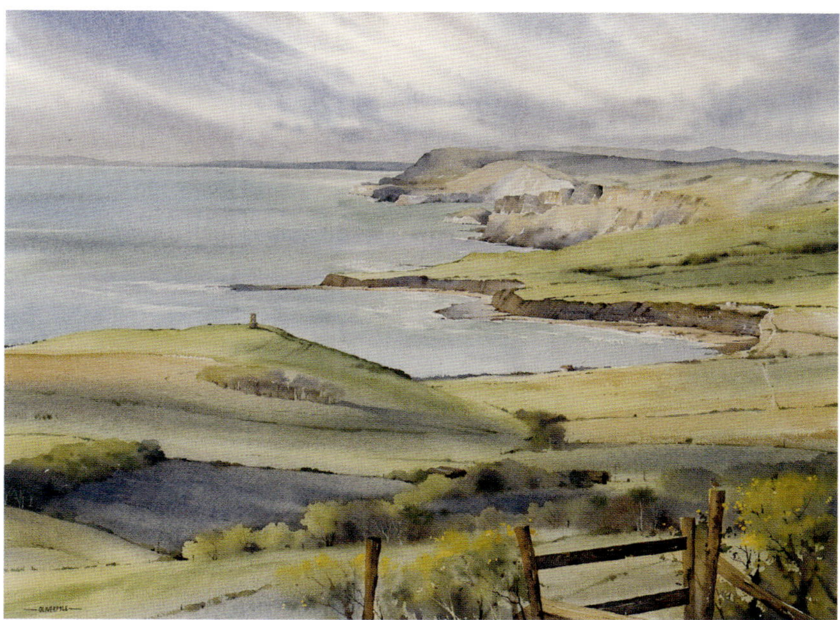

Signs of Spring, Swyre Head – 60cm x 48cm
Landscape elements-a-plenty here – 'Soft, curving lines of downland fields and the sharp, jagged interference of a gorse bush'.

not the painting. I want to be there, seeing the views, experiencing the details and living the moments. Drawing, painting and sketching encourages me to observe and concentrate on my surroundings and allows me to record and share my experiences. Through each painting or sketch that I make I always hope that by viewing them you will come with me, through the beautiful ancient woodland, up onto the cliff top, through the heathland heather, and along the city streets. You can scan distant horizons, focus on the structure of a leaf, or maybe appreciate the impact of industrial infrastructure. The landscape is a multi-dimensional space: somewhere for us to learn, observe, touch, smell, taste, imagine, dream, laugh and cry. Alone or together. It is a stadium in which we can walk, run, jump, ride and swim. A playroom, a school and a workplace. Somewhere we can escape to and be still.

The more time the artist invests in the landscape, the greater the reward; it promotes an awareness of details, intricacies and phenomena that a more superficial engagement will miss. As the tide recedes around Britain, do we realise that it reveals a total area that is greater than all the land that has been concreted over? Why is it that the distant hills,

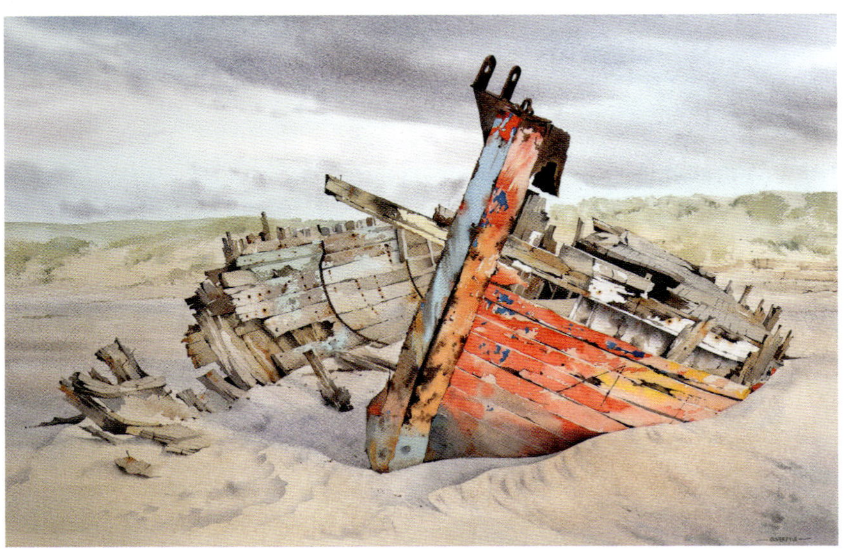

A Colourful Retirement – 50cm x 34cm
Very little remains today of this old vessel, neglected in its retirement at Crow Point, the estuary meeting place of the rivers Taw and Torridge in North Devon. I'm glad that I visited here some years earlier, as the peeling, coloured paint and rotting timbers created a strong visual statement, presenting an opportunity for me to indulge my passion for painting colour and detail.

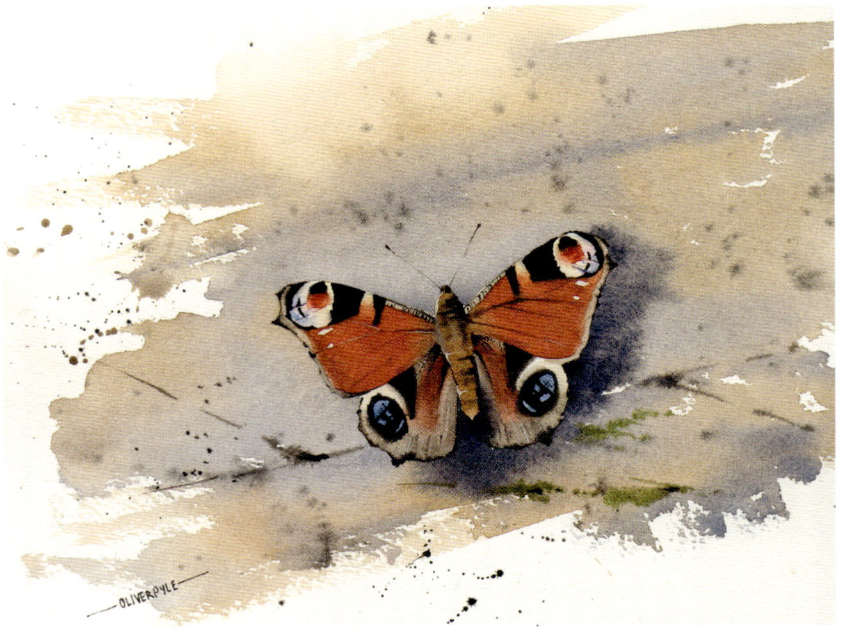

Proud as a Peacock – 20cm x 15cm
The simplest of brushstrokes for the background, gestures almost, allows the stunning markings on this magnificent creature to jump from the page. Give your subjects the best chance to make an impact – balancing detail is a good way to achieve that.

covered in green grass and trees, yellow gorse, and warm ochre fields of wheat look the coolest tint of blue? Have you stopped to notice the visible entropy of rust, carving beautiful shapes as it slowly pulls apart the rotting hull of a retired fishing boat on the estuary mudflats? Consider the landscape's inhabitants: the Peacock butterfly – a transition from the grey, papery prison of a chrysalis into a riot of vivid colour and movement. As a landscape artist, take time to reflect on the places, the feelings, the aesthetics that inspire you and find ways to get into those landscapes, recording moments and experiences that you can pass on and share with others. Experience is everything; any appraisal of my own work can never be based purely on my assessment of its aesthetic or technical results; for it to be a successful landscape painting it must ultimately convey an experience of time, place and senses to those that view it. Despite its utility as a method of practice, a nice painting of a never-experienced location from a third-party photograph has very little to do with a thoughtful understanding of landscape painting.

Above all, take time to be in the landscape; observe it, learn from it, respect it and find ways to express your experience of it. By being in the landscape we are, as the Romantic poet John Keats beautifully expressed it, 'taking part in the existence of things.'

A Walk to Firle Beacon

It might be tempting to think that easy access to high quality landscape photography on Google Images, Shutterstock, Pinterest et al has come as a rich blessing to landscape painters seeking inspiration and subjects to paint. Nothing could be further from the truth.

As part of my working routine, I often use photographs – my photographs. Photographs of the places I have been to and know well; photographs of moments I have experienced. The inspiration for my paintings has already come from the place and moments captured in these images, not the photographs themselves. They simply act as a useful point of reference for detail, colour and tone when I am back in the studio. Many amateur landscape painters believe that painting outdoors is too difficult (it is difficult) and so they assume that their inspiration will need to be

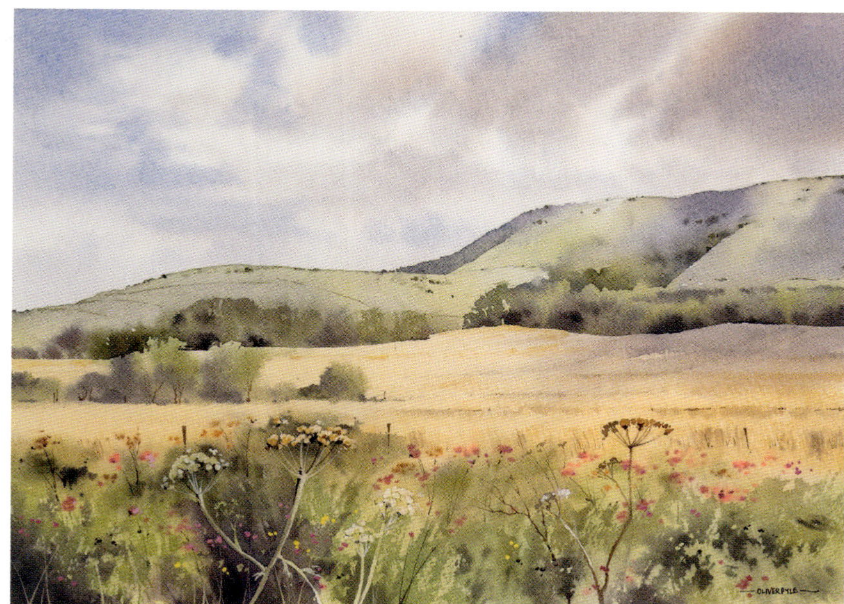

Harvest Colours on the South Downs – 39cm x 29cm
The soft light and shade catching the escarpment is cool, compared to the warm wheat field, awaiting imminent harvest. It helps to push the Downs into the distance, despite their relative proximity. Warmer hues and crips details in the foreground meadow contribute further to the illusion of depth.

found elsewhere, often online or in books, copying the composition and inspirational moments of other photographers and artists. Consequently, they never venture into the landscape expecting to be inspired, looking for potential subjects, with or without their paints and sketchpads. If that could be you, come with me for a pleasant summer walk on the South Downs in Sussex if you will; let me help you find inspiration in the places you love, without your paints, and how to use that inspiration to create paintings, using your photographs as a useful aide-memoire.

We have woken up to a beautiful sunny morning in August and the weather could not be any more conducive for a walk along the South Downs Way. I am meeting Jeremy, a friend and teammate at my cricket club and the plan is to walk west from the hamlet of Berwick, along the ridge of the South Downs to Firle Beacon, circling back for a spot of lunch at – believe it or not – The Cricketers' Arms; a 10-mile walk, or thereabouts. The South Downs is a unique and historic chalk landscape, a ridge of gently undulating hills that runs like a horizontal spine across the south coast of England, from Sussex in the east to Hampshire in the west. Designated as one of Britain's fifteen National Parks and an Area of Outstanding Natural Beauty this landscape has always provided a backbone to my life: seen on most days from anywhere in Sussex as a distant, pale-blue cardboard cut-out; a looming presence at some beautiful cricket grounds in charming villages, tucked under the steep escarpments on the north side; a place of family bank holiday memories; a muse for the skilled brushstrokes of Eric Ravilious and Frank Wootton; a retreat for the inspired writings of Jane Austen and Virginia Woolf.

It would be unreasonable to expect anyone to wait for regular twenty-minute interludes while I stop to sketch the Sussex countryside, but I know that from start to finish, my powers of observation will be whirring away like an old ciné camera, taking in vistas, compositions, moments and details. I am tuned-in to the sounds and smells and make sure that I take time to appreciate the textures, all helping to paint a sensory picture. It is impossible to be uninspired in this familiar and much-loved landscape, and today I am happy allowing my memory and camera to capture what I may need to rely on later for reference.

Following a wrong turn, adding half a mile to our walk, we make our way up an ever-steepening path onto the ridge. Chalk dust, wildflowers, rolling golden wheatfields, a coincidental meeting with an old friend, long views, Wealden vistas, bees and butterflies, buzzards, dragonflies; the South Downs throws them all at you, and more. The view looking east, back down the South Downs Way and out towards Pevensey is a natural composition; the dusty track winding through the scene creates

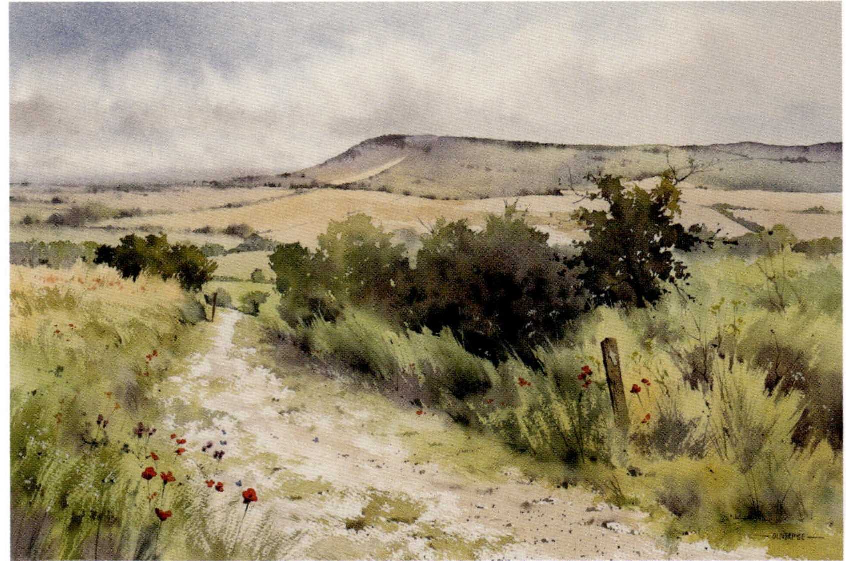

The South Downs Way, Near Firle – 50cm x 34cm
The chalk path, winding its way downhill, connects the eye to a zig-zag of distant trees and wooded areas on the left, taking us across the wheat field to the foot of the Downs.

a helpful leading line and then a zig-zag of distant trees and woodlands lead the eye towards the foot of the Downs near Alfriston. Looking at my photo of this a few days later, there is no distant zig-zag, it has been compressed by the wide-angle lens of my camera-phone and this happy compositional accident is no longer there. Photographs are helpful, but do not rely on them to accurately present you with a record of what you have seen – use them together with observation, memory and sketches for a more accurate representation.

Our walk takes us several miles along the ridge to Firle Beacon, 200 metres above sea level with a stunning 360° view: Eastbourne to the east, Newhaven to the south, Brighton to the west and a beautiful countryside patchwork of fields, woodlands and villages to the north; the Sussex Weald. Sheep chew what grass is available; this landscape's lawnmowers, responsible for maintaining the Downs' close-cropped chalk grasslands for centuries (although the ubiquitous rabbits might have something to say about that).

Light cloud and a pleasant breeze are keeping the temperature manageable. The pace is even, the company is good: Jeremy is an engaging interlocutor, equally at home discussing the political and economic impacts of inflation as he is proposing the optimal temperature for a

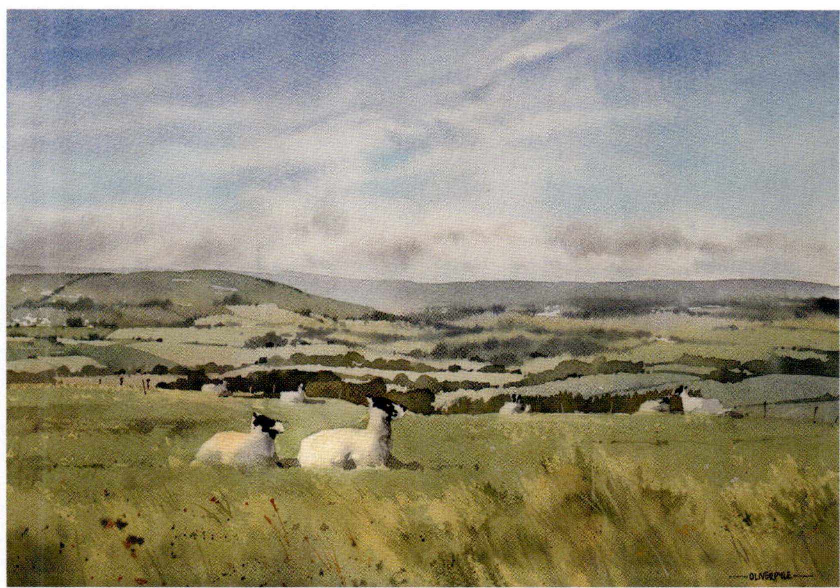

Wealden Views From Firle Beacon – 36cm x 26cm
Sweeping vistas are not the easiest subjects to paint, as they can never compete with the spectacle of reality. By including a point of interest, either near or far, it helps the painting to read better – in this case, that role is played by the sheep.

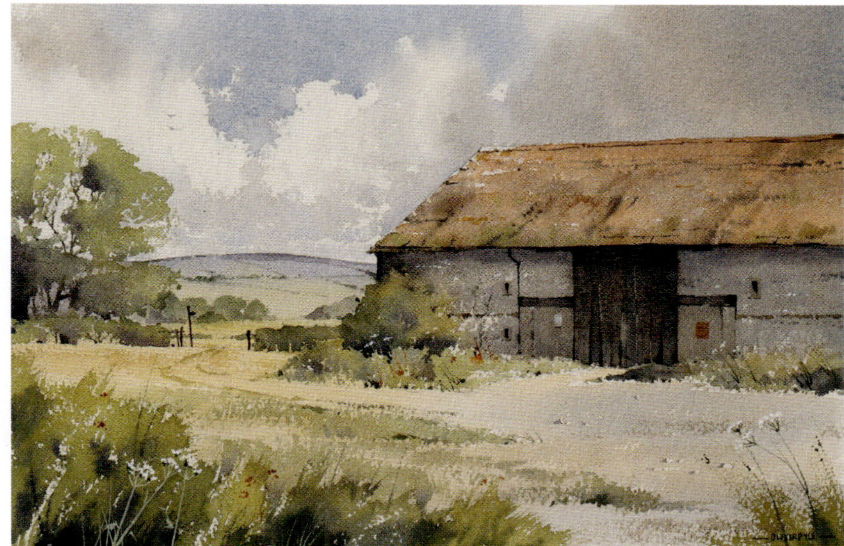

The Old Flint Barn, Near Firle – 36cm x 26cm

well-kept pint of ale. The unmistakable hum of a Rolls-Royce Merlin engine is audible above. 'A Spitfire' points out a gentleman walking in the opposite direction, at pains to tell us how he regularly walks these paths in his mid eighties. This icon of British military history (aeroplane, not man) disappears into the distance. Enjoyable as this distraction is, we inadvertently walk past the path that takes us to the foot of the Downs and back to Berwick. Add a couple more to our 9-mile walk.

Eventually we wend our way back, passing a lovely old Sussex barn, its walls studded with flints. A path – not ours – winds its way around the side of the barn. You will see later in the book on our visit to Dancing Ledge in Dorset that paths around barns lead to good places… I want to follow this one too, but perhaps another day.

Arriving at Berwick, I have enjoyed 11 miles of Sussex summer splendour. I have been painting without paints. The simple act of being in the landscape, walking, talking, experiencing it, provides me with much inspiration for future work. I will be able to use my photographs to provide me with a visual reference, but their value lies in being able to recall the moments at these places. Landscape painting is not about finding a beautiful image online and simply changing the medium from pixels to paint. There may be some value in the technical practice, but other than that there is little meaning to the result, no matter how good. The art of landscape painting lies in creativity, not just technical skill. Next time you are in the landscape, go there with the objective of being inspired and be constantly on the lookout for possible compositions and perspectives – something I call Landscape Looking. Take photos and use them, and when you come to paint and sketch there will be a genuine artistic quality to your work, inspired by experience and informed by your observational awareness.

Lunch at The Cricketers' Arms comes at just the right time and is ideal fare for walkers, particularly those careless enough to have paid insufficient attention to their maps and signposts! The Harveys ale has been well kept, and a cool pint is the most welcome refreshment; Jeremy thinks it should be a touch warmer.

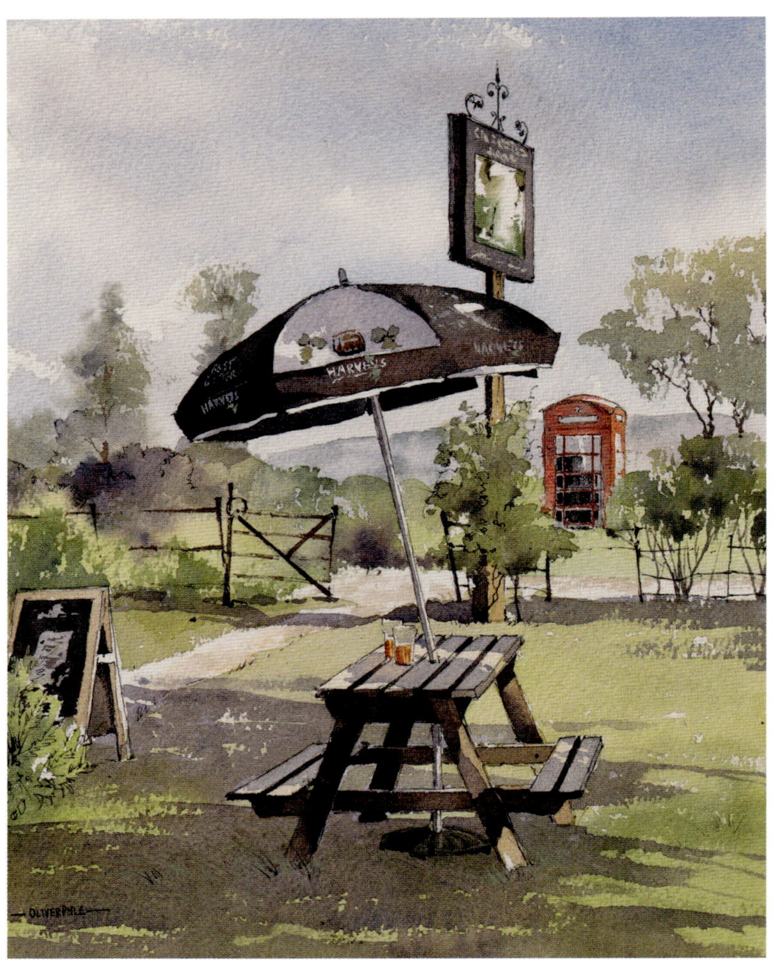

A Pint of Harveys at The Cricketers' Arms – 25cm x 35cm

WHY WATERCOLOUR?

Much has been written about the relative merits of the different painting media and this has often been partisan: oils are better than watercolour for landscape painting, acrylics are more user-friendly than oils, mixed media offers greater flexibility to the painter, and so on. I tend to avoid these discussions as they have a habit of elevating our choice of medium to a place of greater importance than the subject we are trying to paint. The clue is in the word – 'medium', a conduit through which our sensory impressions of the subject are able to flow. I see watercolour as nothing more than that, simply a substance that helps me to convey what I am trying to communicate about the landscape. The paints, the brushes, the paper are just the tools I use to do that. I must engage in this discussion for a short time, however, so that you can appreciate the reasons behind my decision to work in watercolour, and encourage your engagement with the medium.

The simple equipment required to start painting in watercolour hides an inconvenient truth – it is perhaps the most difficult painting medium to master.

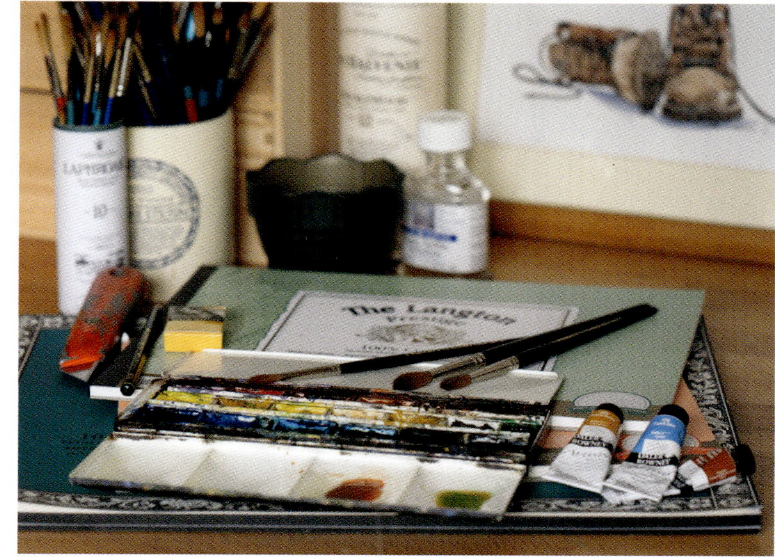

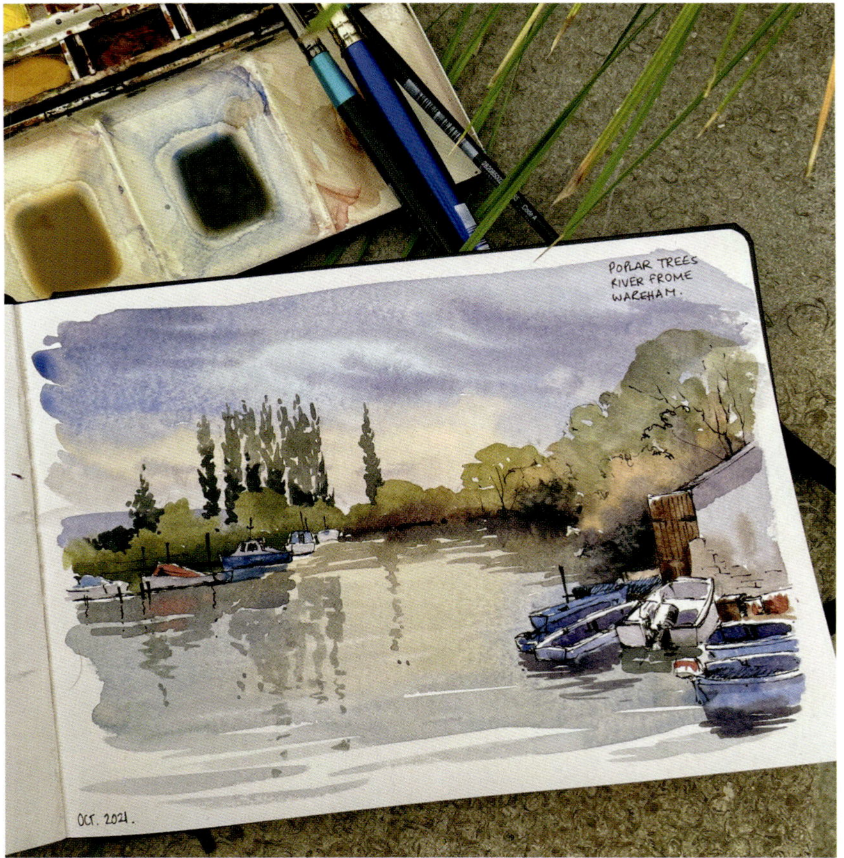

A quick sketch on the River Frome, Wareham
The minimal equipment required and the ease with which it can be used, cleaned up and packed away, makes watercolour the perfect medium for working quickly on location.

Having tried all the different media at one point or another, I settled on watercolour as my medium of choice at an early stage. There were various reasons for this: I enjoyed the delicate look of watercolour paintings; the simplicity of equipment required was a great help for painting and sketching outdoors; the unpredictable nature of the watery paint presented a challenge that I relished; the flow and application of paint to paper was a process that I preferred to the thicker, plasticky application of oil and acrylic, or the dusty nature of pastels.

There are two characteristics that are unique to watercolour and understanding them is essential to becoming a capable exponent of the medium:

1) It is transparent. To make a colour paler, it is diluted with water as opposed to the addition of white paint. This creates transparency and when the paint is applied, the whiteness of the paper is able to shine through. This gives a watercolour painting its distinctive, delicate appearance, helping to capture the subtle tones and hues of the landscape. It can also create a problem for the inexperienced painter – watercolour's transparent nature makes it an unforgiving medium, where previously painted areas (including mistakes)

This simple exercise of painting a red and yellow stripe across an area of blue that has already dried, clearly demonstrates the transparent nature of the medium; yellow and blue combining to create a green intersection, red and blue creating purple.

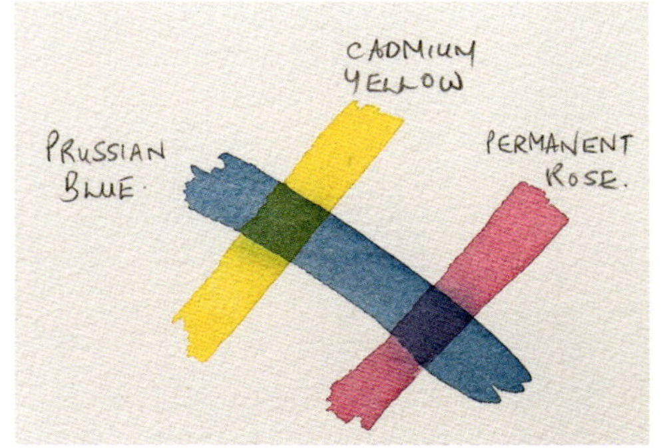

will show through any washes painted over the top. Using the medium well requires a considered and strategic approach, where the planning and sequence of applying watercolour washes to the paper is important in achieving a successful outcome.

2) When working with damp paper or painting into wet areas in a painting, the marks that we make will not stay where we put them on the paper. Pigments flow and mix, suspended in the water, in varying degrees. This often leads to unpredictable results and frustration in the hands of inexperienced painters but confers benefits to the skilful artist who is able to use the medium's fluidity to blend colours and edges softly, with subtle transitions that can be more challenging to achieve when using other media.

While both attributes can present difficulties when learning how to paint in watercolour, making it the most difficult medium to master, they offer

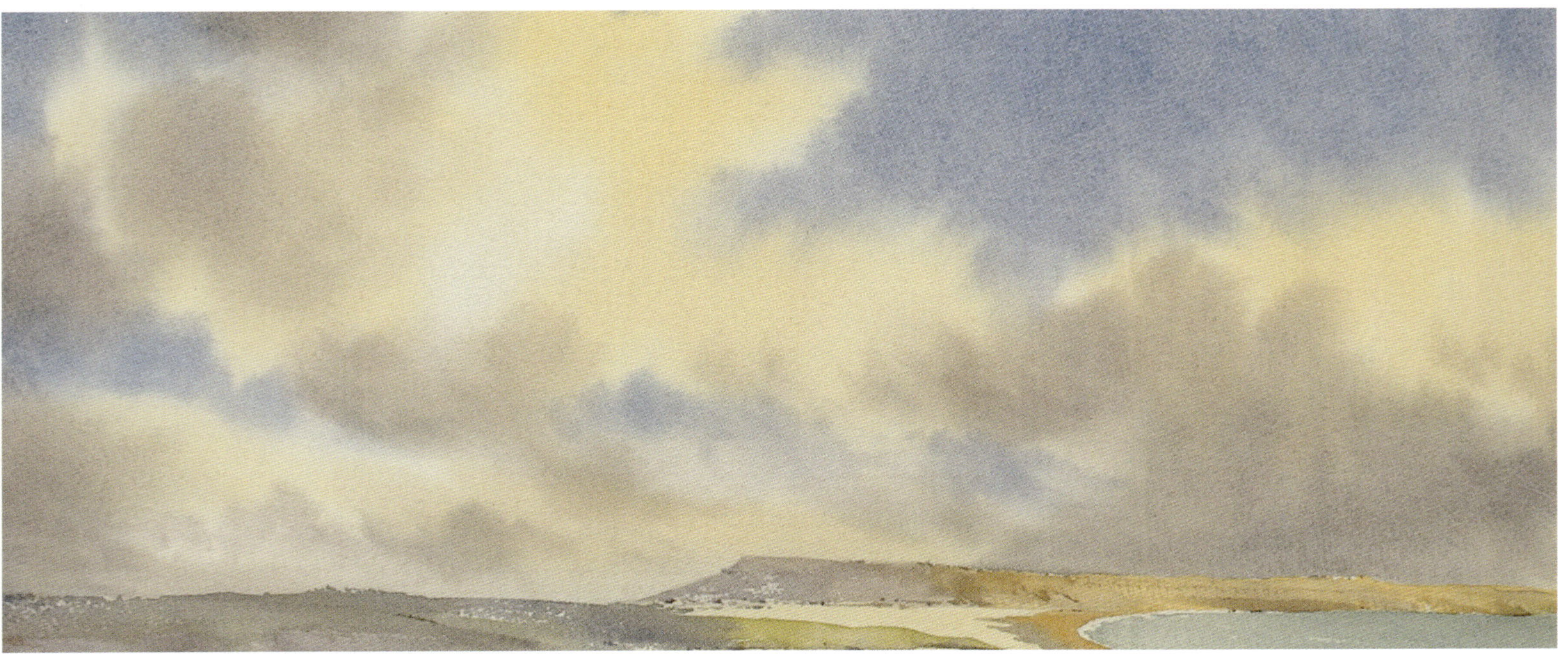

This sky has been painted by dropping the colours onto a piece of paper that has been pre-wet with clear water. It allows the areas of blue sky, cloud highlights and shadows to merge together, the soft transitions between them being blended with a damp brush.

me a painting experience that I find compelling. Watercolour provides me with the ability to capture the subtle colour gradations in the landscape unlike any other medium and its transparency, allowing the paper to shine through, offers a unique luminosity to my paintings that I have been unable to replicate when using other media. It is a look that I love seeing in my work and I always feel a sense of excitement and achievement when I have finished a painting that displays these characteristics. It is challenging and fulfilling and at this stage of my painting career I find no reason to paint the landscapes I love in anything other than watercolour. It is a medium that allows me to communicate accurately how I feel about the landscape, describing my experience of place and moment; that is all I need it to do.

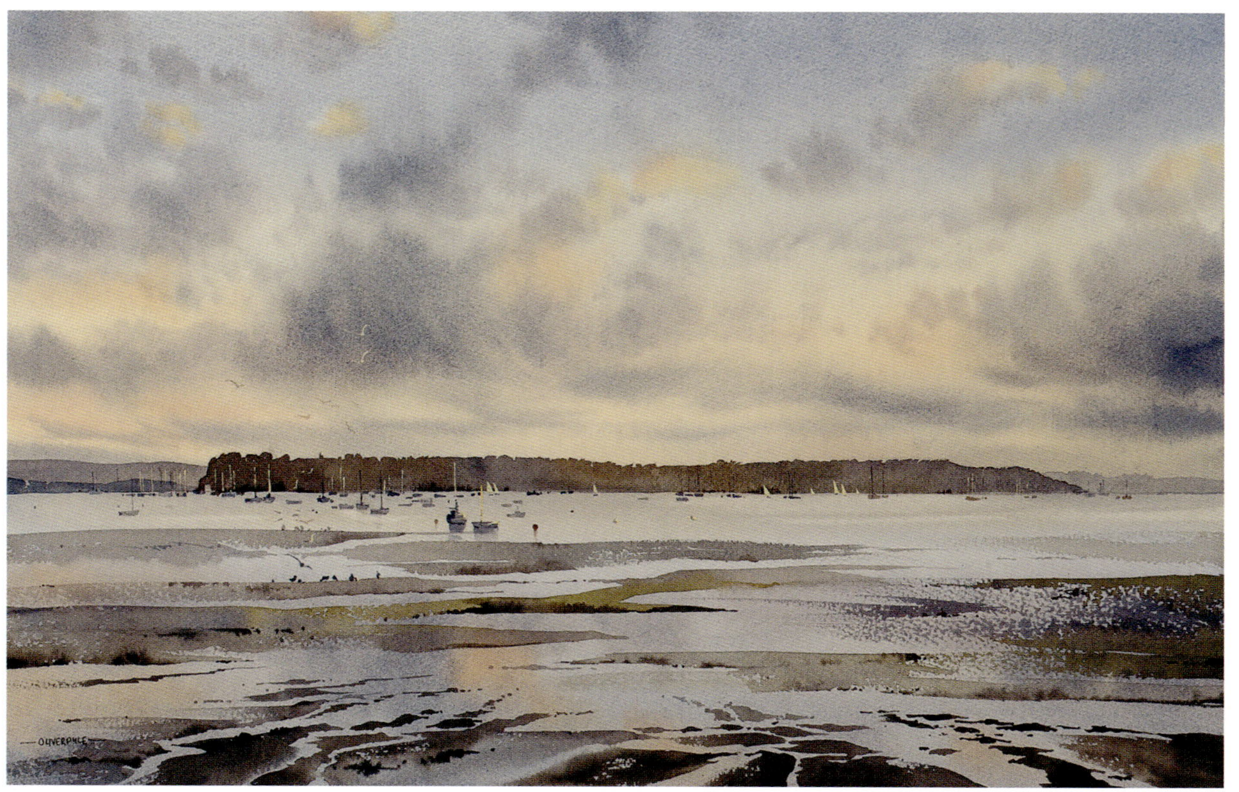

Sailing at Sunset, Brownsea Island – 50cm x 34cm
The transparent nature of watercolour allows the white of the paper to shine through, creating a luminous feel to the sea and sky. By dropping darker cloud tones into the sky while the initial wash is wet, the shapes take on a soft, characteristic lightness. It is an exciting but challenging way to paint, as the wet shapes decide where to settle; it takes experience and some gentle control to achieve a satisfactory result.

When painting on location, the quick-drying nature of watercolour and the minimal equipment required offers me the ability to respond to a subject with speed and spontaneity. This direct interface between me, the place and the moment, allows me to capture an immediate, instinctive impression of the landscape. I have not experienced another medium that enables me to express colour and tone with such simplicity and candour. The beauty of watercolour lies in its tendency to stay quiet, to allow the work to be about the experience, not the medium; instead of jumping up and down, shouting for attention it just whispers 'This is what Oliver saw, this is all he needed to say.' It is the impact of the scene and the reality of the experience that is allowed to do all the talking.

If you are considering using watercolour as a medium, then the following section detailing what you will need is a good place to start. If you have experience of painting in watercolour, you should find this helpful too in considering what will help you to refine your work. If you are thinking that we are about to take a deep dive into the world of paint, paper and brushes, you will be disappointed: the character attributes that you need (and can develop) will have far more impact on your progress as a painter than a trip to the nearest art store. For those that are interested, a list of the equipment that I use is available on my website, details of which can be found at the end of the book.

ATTRIBUTES

Patience

We live in a time where immediacy and quick results are expected and often demanded. This approach to life and learning finds its way into everything these days and landscape painting and the watercolour medium are not immune from this. Courses and tutorial programs offer rapid results, with a swift progression from beginner to experienced

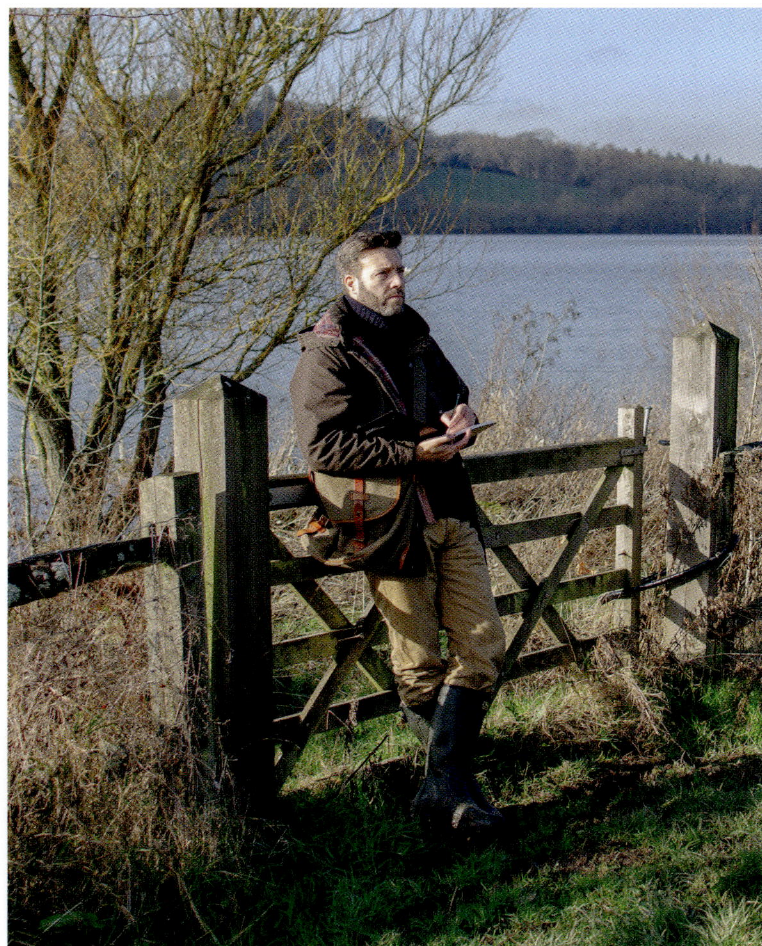

The author sketching at Ardingly Reservoir in Sussex.

painter, with the tempting hook that you will 'paint like a pro' on completion of the program. You won't – avoid these programs.

Visual art and the creativity required to produce it are not rules-based and are therefore difficult to teach. While there are important principles and techniques that can be learned and practiced, many of which I cover in this book, it is learning through individual experimentation and observation that yields the best results. Your ability to create compelling landscape paintings through your skilful deployment of the watercolour medium is reliant on a little instruction, but primarily practice and patience. Let me illustrate this by identifying three technical skills required by the watercolourist that are difficult to teach:

1) **Timing.** Understanding when to apply more paint to an area of the painting that is still wet, or when the paper is damp, is a difficult skill to master. It requires an accurate assessment of how wet or dry the paper is, how concentrated the paint to be applied is, how much of that paint is held by the brush and how quickly that brush interacts with the paper. Bringing these four variables together to create the marks and shapes that you are hoping for is not an easy concept to explain and teach, and something that students struggle with when starting their watercolour journeys. Even the most lucid explanation will only take you so far – you will learn far more by practicing, observing the results, identifying what went wrong and exploring the remedies. This takes time – often years – and requires patience.

2) **Colour tone.** It is good practice to understand the relationship of lights and darks in a painting by making a monochrome sketch or value study that explores these tonal values. A question I am regularly asked is 'How do I then take those tonal values and know how light or dark to mix my colours so they correspond

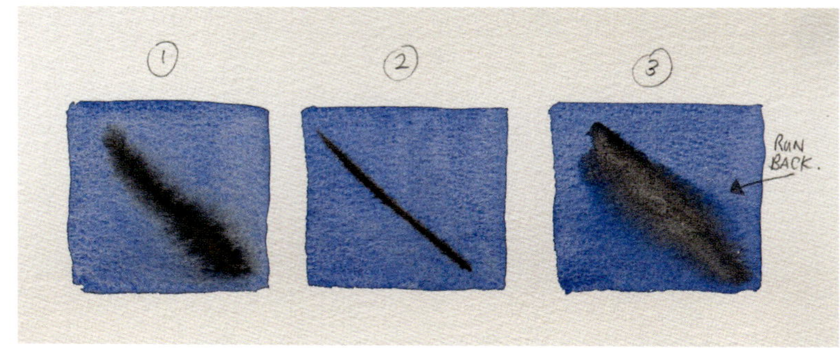

In this simple example, a brushstroke of dark, concentrated pigment has been painted into each blue square in an attempt to create a well-defined stripe that has soft edges. In No. 1 the blue was still very wet and so the dark stripe didn't hold its position, bleeding out into the blue area. In No. 2 the blue had dried significantly allowing the dark stripe to 'grip' creating the stripe required – well pronounced, but retaining soft edges. The blue square in No. 3 was just damp, as it was in No. 2, but the dark stripe was made with a weaker mix of paint, too wet for the damp blue area. The result is an ugly mess where the weaker dark stripe disturbs the blue pigment that has not yet dried, creating blooms of pigment where they are unwanted. Understanding timing – combining the correct concentration of paint with the dampness of the paper to achieve the effect you want – is an essential technical skill for the watercolourist.

to my value study?' There have been several suggestions over the years, none of which I have found to be wholly satisfactory in the context of landscape painting: making charts of endless tonal gradations for each colour, or equating the viscosity of your colour mixes to different substances – water, milk, tea, soup, cream etc. These can work well for some, but don't offer an ideal solution for me. I prefer to judge the tone of my colour mixes instinctively, based on how the paint feels on the surface of my palette and in the hairs of my brush. Even after thirty years of experience with the medium, I can feel that my ability to accurately hit the tone I need continues to improve. No one has taught me this; my own experience and observation of what I am doing has informed it. This takes time – often years – and requires patience.

3) **Broken brushstrokes.** The swift movement of a brush across the paper, often carrying a limited amount of paint, referred to sometimes as drybrush, is a way to create texture and suggest detail in a painting. Using dynamic brushstrokes like this is important and I can teach a student methods for holding the brush, how to load it with paint and how to move it to achieve these types of marks. Having taught this, I often see mechanical-looking, unnatural results. Is this a flaw in my teaching or is something else

Brushstroke 1 is a traditional dry brushstroke, where very little paint is picked up on the brush and it is moved quickly across the paper, its texture helping to achieve a hit-and-miss look. This is not quite the same as the area painted for brushstroke 2, where the brush is loaded with plenty of wet paint and then flexed quickly in different directions to achieve broken edges, perfect for describing areas such as tree foliage or foreground grass and hedgerows. The dexterity required for these brushstrokes comes from much practice and developing a feel for when the brush's hairs interact with the surface. Teaching this only takes a student so far – it is their own craft that ultimately achieves satisfying results.

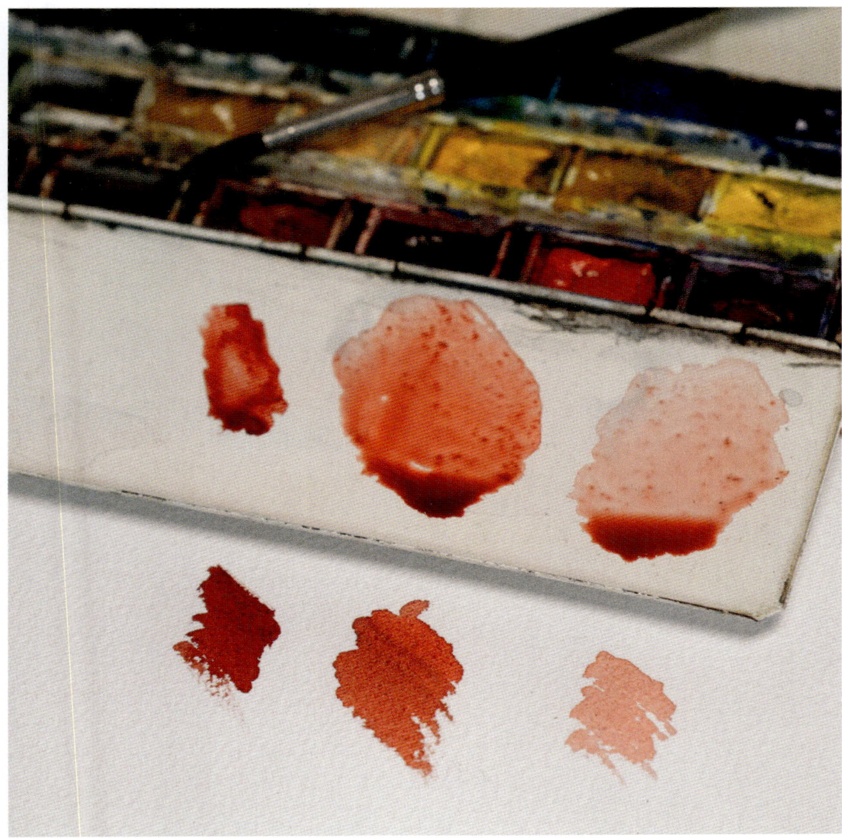

Judging the consistency of your paint mixes is not easy. I find that observing the flow and movement on the palette and the ease with which the residual paint forms a pool or bead is the best way to assess the tonal strength of a colour or mix, while maintaining the ability to paint quickly and instinctively. Experience is required to make accurate judgements.

going on? Making a brushstroke involves a motor skill, where the speed of movement and application of pressure will have a direct impact on the outcome. To achieve the look that is often admired in watercolour paintings, where the detail of a distant village has been described in a single deft brushstroke, a lesson doesn't need to be learned but a skill needs to be developed. I hear regularly from subscribers to my YouTube channel, remarking on how easy it looks when I paint trees using this method. It also looks easy when an Italian nonna produces tray after tray of perfectly hand-formed tortellini. The swing of a top golfer exudes an air of effortless simplicity. While of course there may have been some helpful instruction along the way, these results were not immediate and did not come from an instruction manual or by signing up for some online tutorials. These skills take time – often years – and require patience. The apparent simplicity is misleading.

Patience is also an essential element of the painting process. As a painting develops there will be times where you may want to rush ahead to put

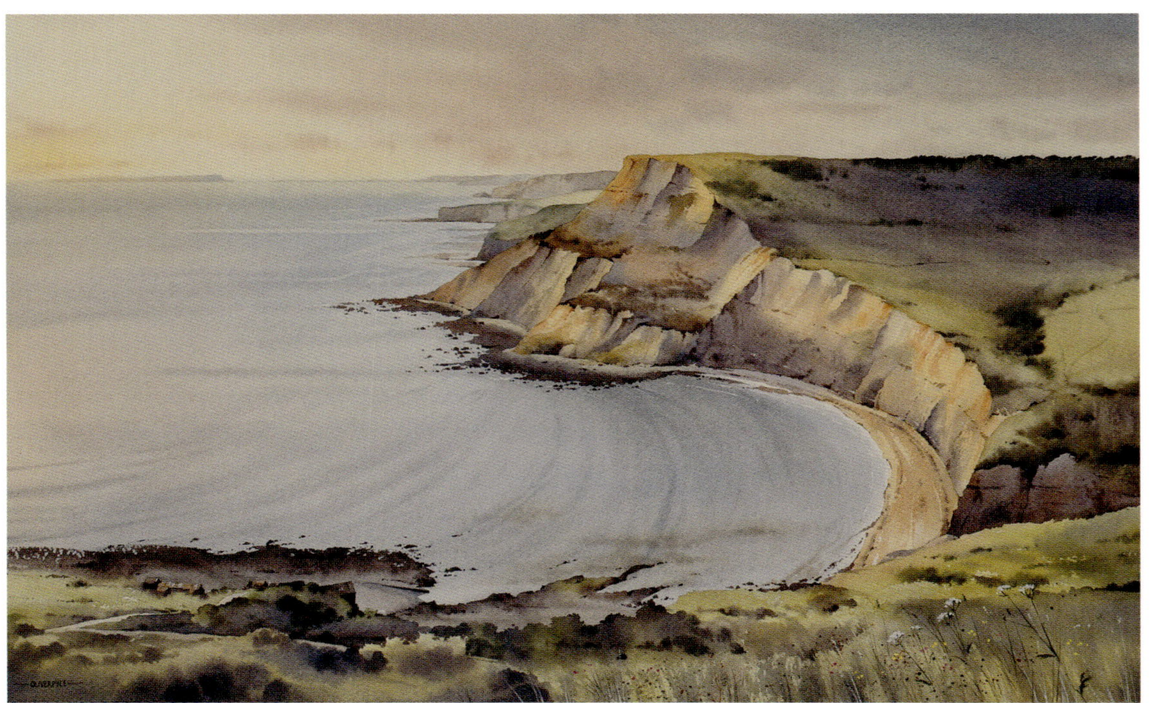

Dusk at Chapmans Pool – 72cm x 52cm
The numerous ripples in the bay, suggesting the incoming tide, needed to be painted with soft edges to prevent them from being too prominent. Waiting for the perfect moment to paint these requires patience to achieve the correct timing: if the area of sea is still too wet, the ripple marks will bleed out and be lost; if the area is too dry, the ripple marks will hold their shapes, but the edges will be too strongly defined. Learning this skill requires patience too – you won't perfect it first time round, nor the second…

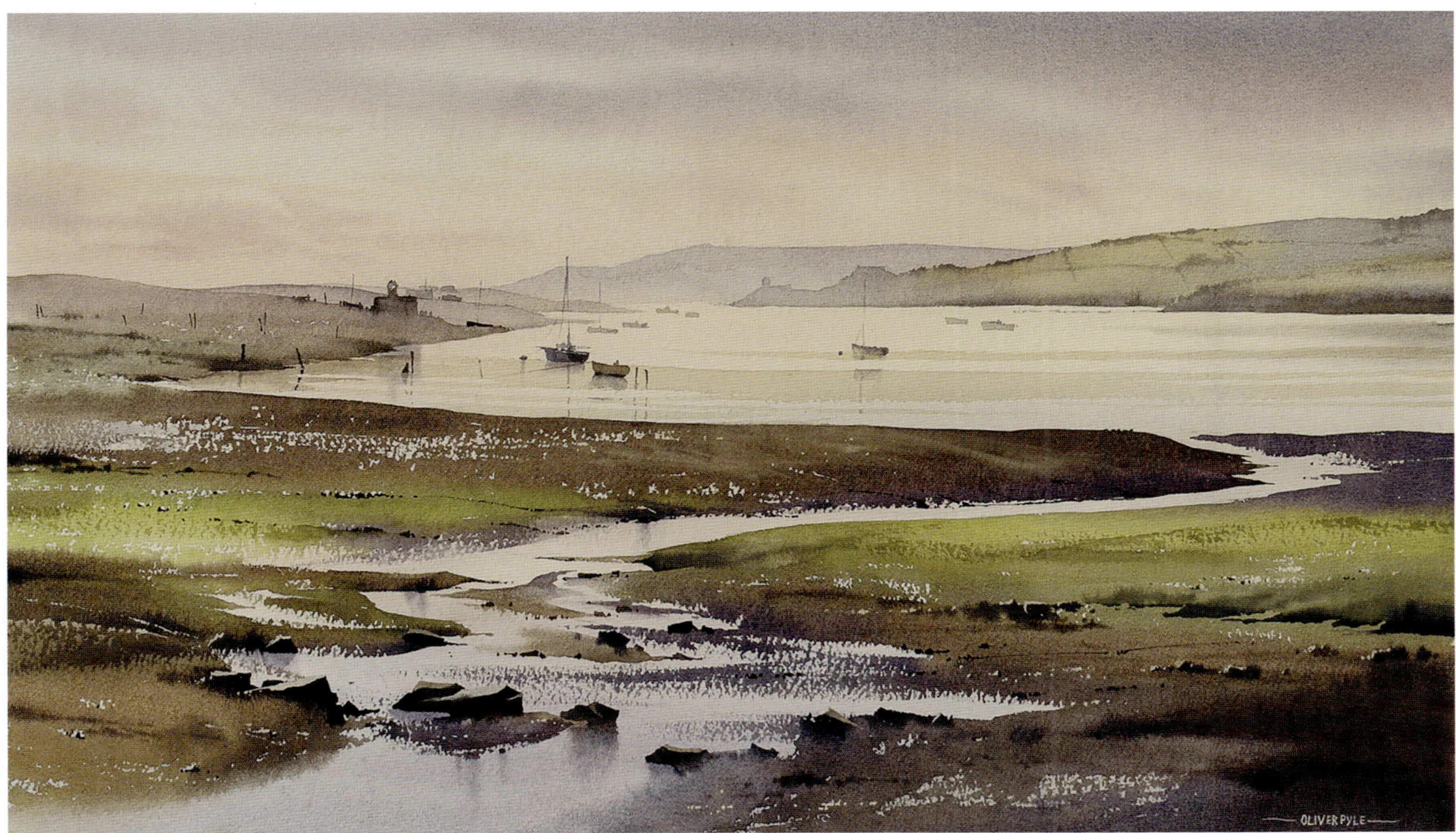

Winter Sunset, Fleet Lagoon – 50cm x 34cm
The broken brushstrokes that suggest light catching the mudflats and small stones at the water's edge often look easy when watching an experienced artist use them. They are difficult to achieve and come with patient practice. Try to hone this technique on pieces of scrap paper (a rough surface ideally).

some detail into your centre of interest or add some additional work into a wet wash. There will also be a temptation to write off your work as a failure before the painting is finished; caught in a moment of chaos where a brushstroke fails or a colour mix clashes, we often forget to take a step back and keep in mind our vision of the finished painting. Be a patient painter.

Confidence

Watercolour is regarded by many as the most demanding of media with little margin for error, those errors being difficult to rectify when they inevitably arise. In its purest form, watercolour is the expression of an expert and confident hand, capable of controlling washes and applying details with apparent ease and simplicity. Such control however does not come quickly or easily; it is the result of many years of careful application and dedication through which there are no shortcuts, and where experimentation and practice is the only possible pathway. Practice ultimately breeds confidence, an attribute that the successful watercolour painter cannot be without. Taking time to comprehend the possibilities and peculiarities that watercolour presents allows the painter to witness common problems and outcomes, and then practice the skills to cope with these. Having confidence when painting a watercolour landscape, knowing that the unusual flows and patterns developing on your paper are ones that you have witnessed before and are capable of managing, will result in a work that has energy and vitality. A timid approach to the medium, where brushstrokes and tonal work is restrained by a lack of confidence rarely makes for satisfying results but tends to produce paintings that are tentative and lacking in expression, with a muddy, overworked look to the washes. Fresh and vibrant watercolours can only be painted when the washes are applied with a confident hand and not repeatedly worked over. It allows the pigment to be suspended in the water and then settle gently onto the fibres of the paper as it dries. It is not a way of painting that comes naturally, where there is a tendency to want to 'work' the paint as is required with other media (or when painting the garden fence).

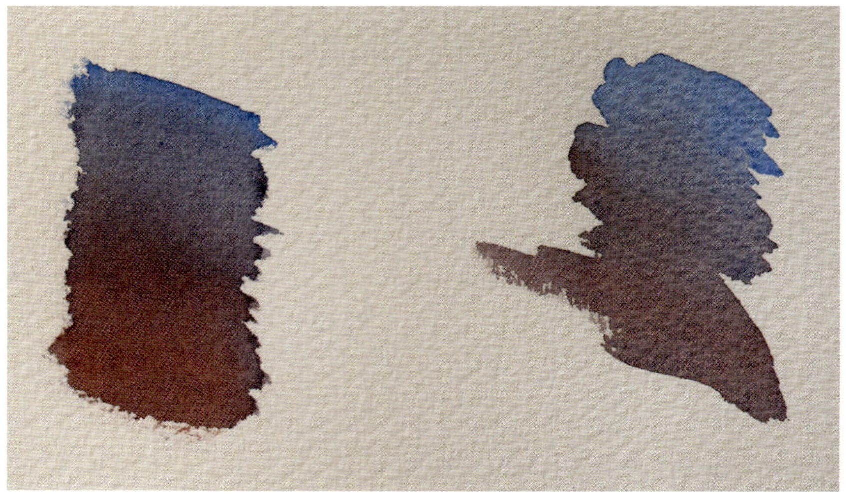

There is a subtle, but important, point of difference between the two shapes illustrated here. On the left the variegated wash of blue and red has been painted with many tight, laboured brushstrokes, overpainting the area while still wet. It has the effect of repeatedly driving the pigment particles into the damp paper. The result is a dull, heavy looking wash that lacks the freshness and transparency that watercolour should have. On the right, the same wash has been made with a larger brush full of wet paint and making as few strokes as possible, with no going back over the wet painted area. The pigment floats on the surface of the paper and dries with a fresher, more transparent presentation of the colours. The difference between these two examples is often the result of painting with confidence, or lack thereof – we tend to tighten up, exert too much control and over-paint when we are unsure of our skills and lacking in confidence. Many inexperienced painters (and tutors!) will blame the paints they are using, their transparency ratings, or the use of single/multiple pigments as the cause of dull muddy paintings; these are rarely at fault, when it is our heavy-handed, confidence-lacking technique that is usually to blame.

The quickest way of building confidence is to work on technical skills and exercises that will enable you to focus on the behaviour of the medium and the interaction of paint with paper. Every time you confront a beautifully stretched half-sheet of expensive, pristine white paper, goading you and tugging at your insecurities, the stakes are immediately raised, confidence wanes and you say to yourself 'I must complete a successful painting.' Take the pressure off by regularly filling sheets of paper with a range of brushstrokes, colour mixes, or wet-on-wet shapes. You will find that your confidence in handling the medium increases rapidly. People say to me that to do so would be a waste of good paper

Beneath the Branches, Petworth Park –
72cm x 52cm
In a large, detailed painting such as this, much is at stake. Time has been taken to accurately draw Petworth House, the sky has been painted successfully and the detailed branches need to be painted on top. There is not a second chance to get these right – they need to be painted with a confidence that comes from years of painting trees. The tree shadows running across the park must also be painted wet-on-wet, with one or two bold, confident brushstrokes; any over-painting or corrections and the effect will lose its clarity. Practice breeds confidence.

but will then spend four times the amount on an online course, teaching a fraction of what they will learn themselves: a false economy indeed.

Flexibility

If you were to fill three glasses with water and then tip the contents onto the floor, I can guarantee that the resulting pools of water would not be the same shape. Far from it, and this is what we are up against with watercolour; the insistence of water to flow where it wants is one of the medium's idiosyncrasies, presenting us with a constant challenge. Our role as watercolour painters is to find the right balance between active control and passive involvement. The very nature of painting a landscape, no matter how abstract your approach and results may be, requires a decisive approach where you will have expectations of the resulting shapes and colours. The more experienced you become, the easier it is for you to achieve those expectations, but the erratic nature of water-flow will require you to continually maintain a flexible approach; failure to do so will lead to disappointment and a likely disillusionment with watercolour will set in.

There are a couple of things you can do to help you develop a flexible mindset. The first is to embrace the unpredictable nature of watercolour, seeing it as your friend, not your enemy. The medium wants to help you to create a beautiful landscape painting so give it a little more responsibility, instead of thinking that it's always trying to trip you up. When a brushstroke you apply to the paper dries in a way that you hadn't intended, suggesting some distant trees for example, then go with that. If the addition of very wet paint makes streaks in your foreground, giving the appearance

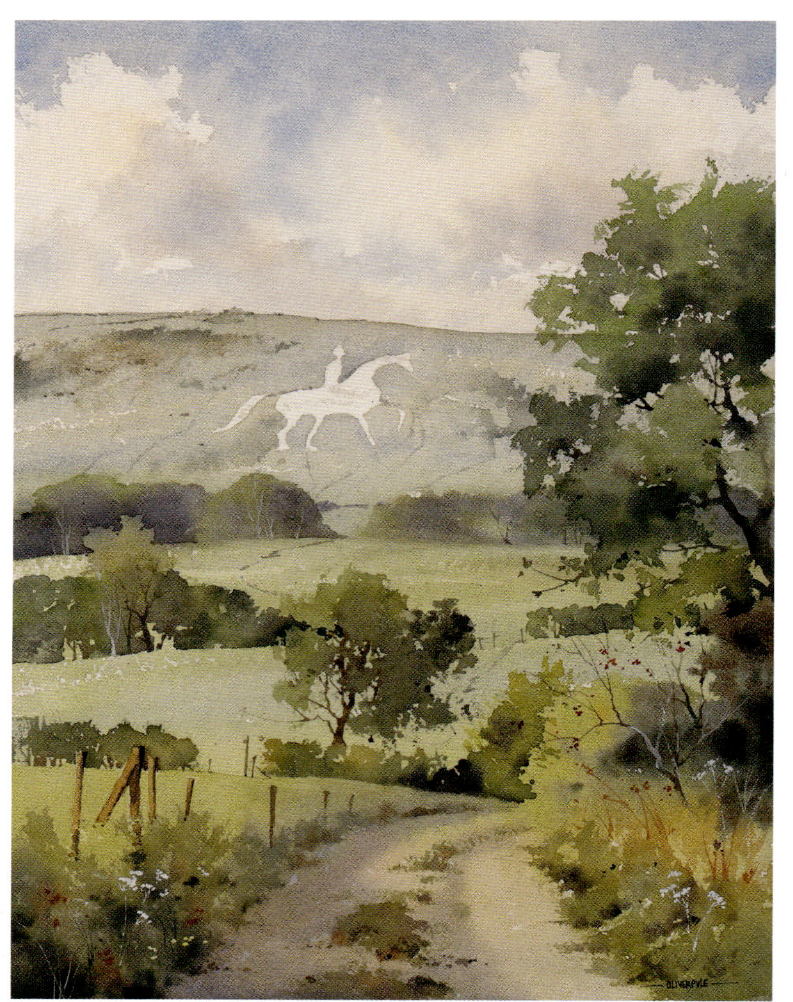

RIGHT: The Path to Osmington White Horse – 41cm x 31cm
The shapes that appeared in the foreground of this painting to define the verge and hedgerows on either side of the path had more to do with luck than judgement. I allowed broken brushstrokes to define the areas, and then worked with the shapes that evolved. I find that adopting a flexible approach helps to promote a more natural feel to areas such as these.

of long meadow fescue grass, thank the medium for helping you out and add one or two well defined blades to give this some further definition. If your brushstroke leaves a few white chips of unpainted paper as you paint across the beach, consider the extent to which these could become stones or shells on the seashore. Always keep an eye out for these unplanned occurrences – the nature of the medium and your own fallibilities will present these to you on a regular basis. Be ready to welcome them, if you can. Secondly – and this helps with what I have just mentioned – there will be passages in your painting where it pays to keep your focus on the painting, not your subject. Foregrounds are an excellent example of this and though you may look at my paintings and say that an area of grass and wildflowers must be an accurate representation of my subject, the reality is that it is simply an impression. I know from looking at my subject that there is an area of long grass, with some hogweed, brambles, fallen leaves, but that is as far as my engagement with the subject takes me. Instead, I prefer to make combinations of loose washes – broken brushstrokes and glazes – that are approximate to what I know to be there. All the time my focus remains on the painting, watching the shapes that the brush wants to make as I move it quickly across the paper and the colours that blend as the washes merge together. I have no need to accurately replicate the blades of grass and the position of leaves but will make some final marks to define and describe the area, making sense of what has developed on the paper, as opposed to rigidly following the subject or reference image.

There is a contradiction, a tension that lies at the heart of watercolour painting: from a technical perspective we must be able to control the medium; from an aesthetic perspective we need to be able to relax our control of it. Once you accept that watercolour has a mind of its own and can welcome its unpredictable contributions, you will find a new enjoyment of the medium and your flexibility will be rewarded with paintings that have a loose and instinctive feel to them. Continue to fight it, and you will soon become irritated by the medium, finding yourself browsing through the oil paint section on your next visit to

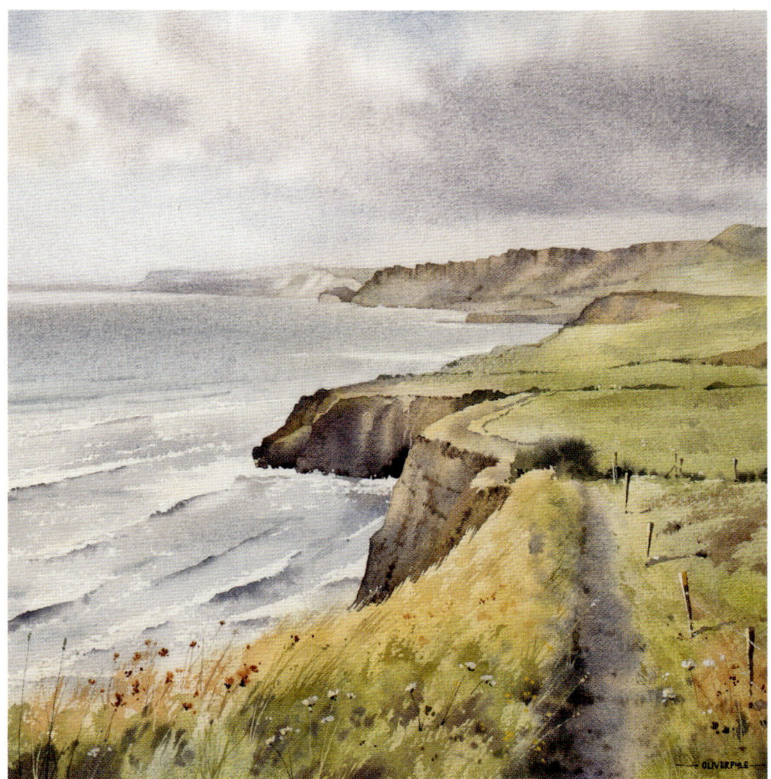

The Coast Path Near Rope Lake Head – 30cm x 30cm
I had intended to paint the large thicket of brambles and hawthorn, appearing to block the path, with a hard edge once the green wash on the field behind had dried. Not fully concentrating, I started to paint while the wash underneath was still damp – the dark green shape fuzzed into the background, creating a soft edge that is a far better outcome than the one I had planned. Be flexible and adapt if you need to.

the art shop. Experienced watercolour painters are able to manage the medium with a light touch, giving it the freedom to flow and develop without a continual need to correct the passages that appear different to the subject or their expectations. Creating a compelling impression of the landscape in watercolour cannot be achieved without flexibility.

EQUIPMENT

Although there is much in this book that will help those that are new to landscape painting and watercolour, it has been written primarily for

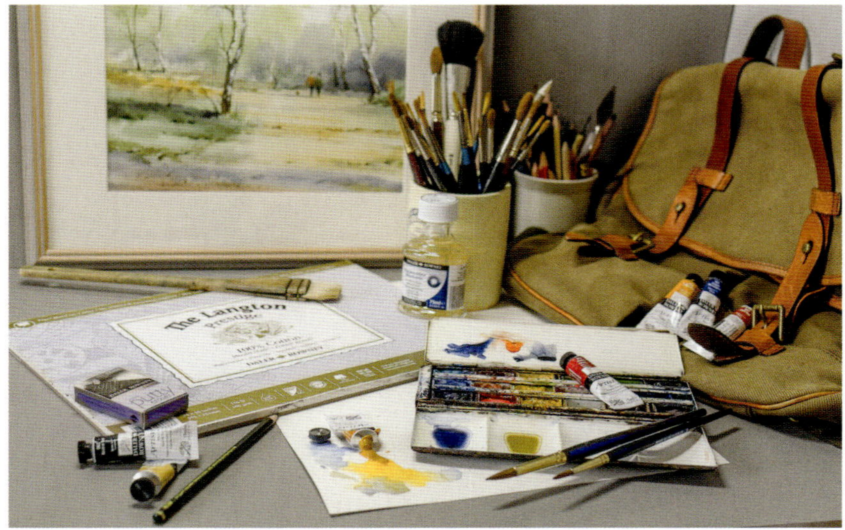

Equipment is important – experiment by all means, but settle on a combination of paper, paint and brushes that delivers consistent results for the way that you like to paint.

those of you that already have experience of both subject and medium and are looking to take your art to the next level. You will already have a collection of equipment that hopefully you have become familiar with and helps you to paint those special landscape moments.

There seems to be little merit in taking you through an extensive list of the paints, paper and brushes that I use, but for those that are interested I have included an Appendix at the end of the book and links to these items can be found on my website. For many amateur painters, equipment is elevated to a position where it becomes more important in their minds than inspiration, technique and practice, and so my attempt to divert your focus from another discussion on the merits of cotton versus cellulose papers, or a laboured analysis of pigment numbers, is quite deliberate. I can recount instances where I have given demonstrations and during a break, delegates have come up to look at the development of the painting – or so I thought – only to walk past it, to say 'Oh, I've been waiting to see what brushes you use!' In Q&A sessions at workshops, emails from students and comments on my social media pages, the vast majority relate to equipment, not technique, as if there is some esoteric combination of paint and paper that I should be encouraged to divulge, or that perhaps my brushes didn't come from an art supplies store, but from Ollivander's wand shop. There are no secrets, it is simply equipment that I have used for years and I trust to deliver consistent results with the quality expected by purchasers of my work. The equipment that you choose is, and should be, based on personal preference and will suit the way in which you like to paint. As I have mentioned previously, your equipment is simply a collection of tools that you use to get the job done. Always try to purchase the best equipment you can afford, but don't rely on it to make dramatic improvements to your skills as a painter. Just a quick glance at my painting checklist later in the book will make it abundantly clear that equipment has a minimal role to play in the successful outcome of your paintings.

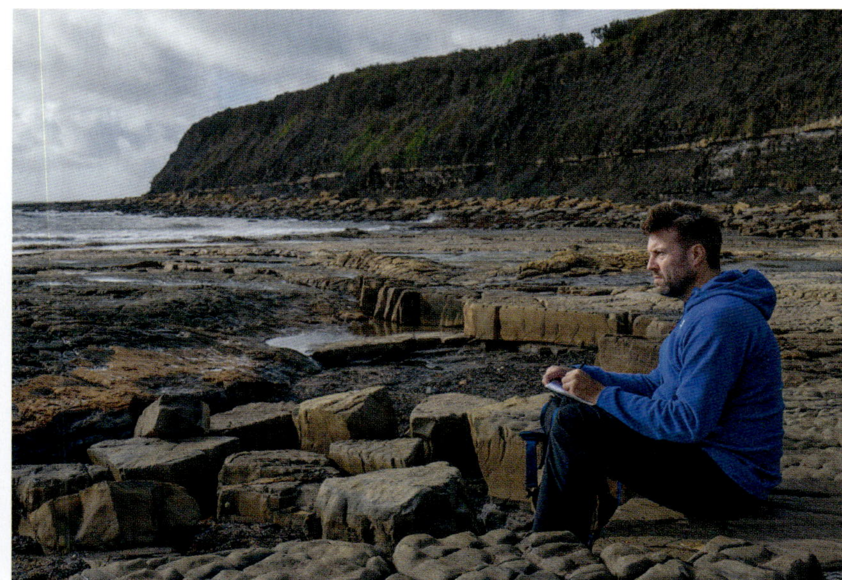

The simplest sketching equipment, thrown quickly into your backpack is often all that's required to make an immediate impression of the landscape. Here, the author works quickly to capture the fast-changing light and waves rolling in at Kimmeridge Bay in Dorset.

The equipment that you need to paint on location is often overlooked, however, and getting this right is important. Having placed an emphasis on being in the landscape as the key to unlocking your ability to paint it, I think some guidance on the equipment that will make this easier is sensible. I have witnessed artists painting on location with an astonishing array of equipment: elaborate easels, large comfortable chairs, imperial-sized painting boards, camping stoves for a mid-morning brew. These all have their place, but often such a collection of paraphernalia can act as an obstacle to painting outdoors and will certainly restrict the painter's ability to seek out locations that are more than 100 paces from where the car was parked. You will not arrive at the beautiful vista in a calm, creative frame of mind if you have just walked half a mile, laden down like a pack-horse. I have three different set-ups for painting outdoors that enable me to respond quickly to different situations. Think about whether these could help you to spend more time in the landscape, not just with the frequency of your visits, but your ability to start painting quickly on arrival at a location, being more productive while you are there.

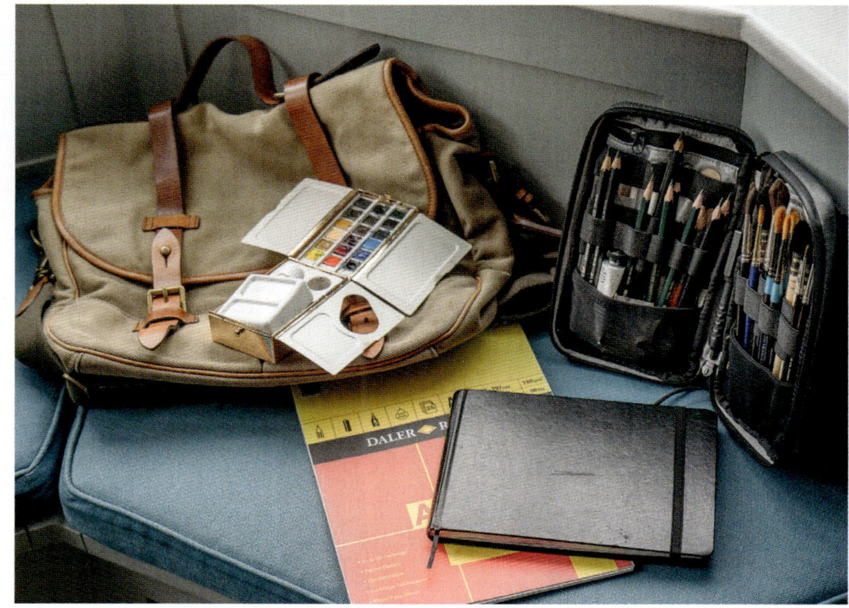

My Quick Sketch set-up. The key here is to think 'less is more'.

Set-Up One – The Quick Sketch

Keeping a bag or small backpack ready with the most basic of painting equipment enables you to respond quickly to an opportunity for painting on location. A small watercolour travel set is an excellent idea, especially if you can find one that includes paint, palette, water bottle and water pot. It will enable you to make a few simple washes, which is often all you need to sketch a quick impression. Throw in a couple of sketch pads and a case to hold brushes, pens and pencils and you will have everything you need. The countryside is often generous in providing a range of seating options: fences, gates, fallen tree trunks, rock ledges. If you can't find one, a small pack-away sheet that you can throw onto a soft tussock of grass is more than adequate. Balance your pad on your knees, set your paints down and you're all good. Grab-and-go painting.

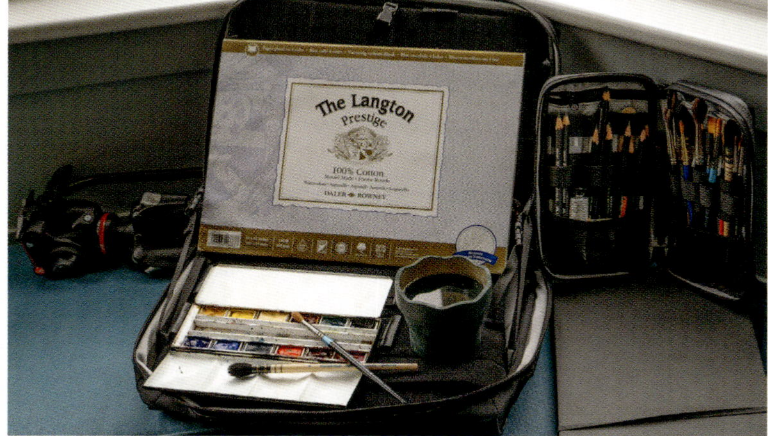

The Etchr Satchel is a versatile solution to painting outdoors, able to support a water pot and larger palette for mixing. You will see that my Etchr Field Case comes with me on all of my painting excursions.

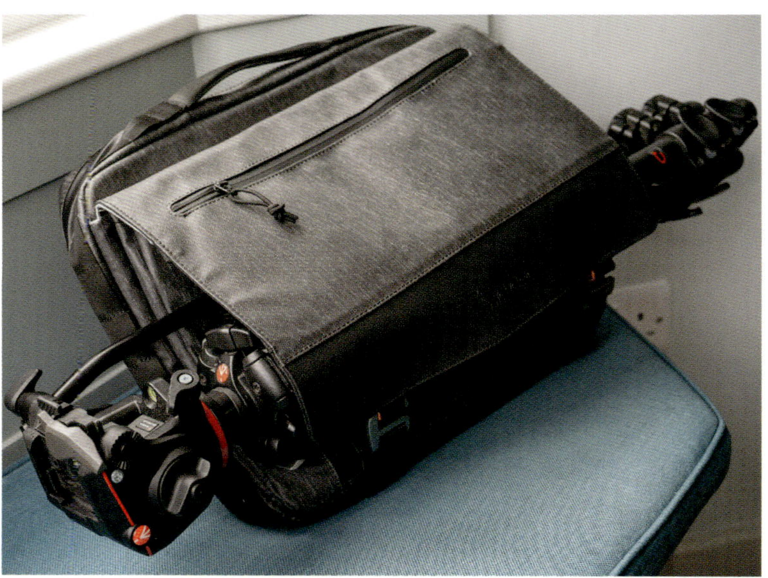

Straps can be conveniently placed to allow your tripod to be carried comfortably, if you choose to use one – the satchel can be supported in a variety of other ways.

Set-Up Two – The Plein Air Painting

When I have planned to make a more considered painting outdoors, my equipment requirements change. My demand for simplicity and portability remains, and I have found an excellent solution provided by a company called Etchr. Their Art Satchel is an expandable, weatherproof and modular system designed to adapt to your preferred way of working. It's perfect for either digital or traditional media and it can be used as a backpack or a sling bag.

I can use it to carry my tripod which then acts as a support for the Art Satchel, creating an easel. It holds paints, brushes, water, sketch pads and watercolour blocks and is a versatile solution for the plein air painter. It is expensive, but it is high quality, built like a tank and will last for years.

My trusty Osprey daypack is more than sufficient for carrying all the kit I need for a day's painting on location, and is not only weather resistant, but supremely comfortable too.

Set-Up Three – The Long Trek

Sometimes the subjects that I paint will require a walk, or a hike even, to reach. In these situations, I may be outdoors for most of the day and so a different approach is required. Painting equipment needs to be as light and

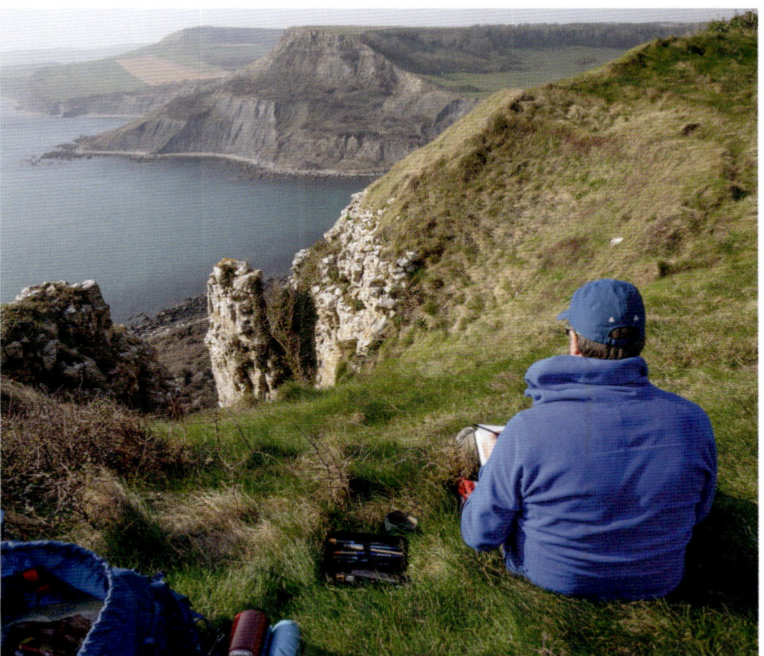

ABOVE AND OVERLEAF: A coastal walk from Worth Matravers to Chapmans Pool, with some dramatic elevation changes along the way, requires minimal sketching equipment. It is not the time to be carrying elaborate easels and comfortable chairs; a soft clump of grass and a sketchbook on the knees is more than adequate.

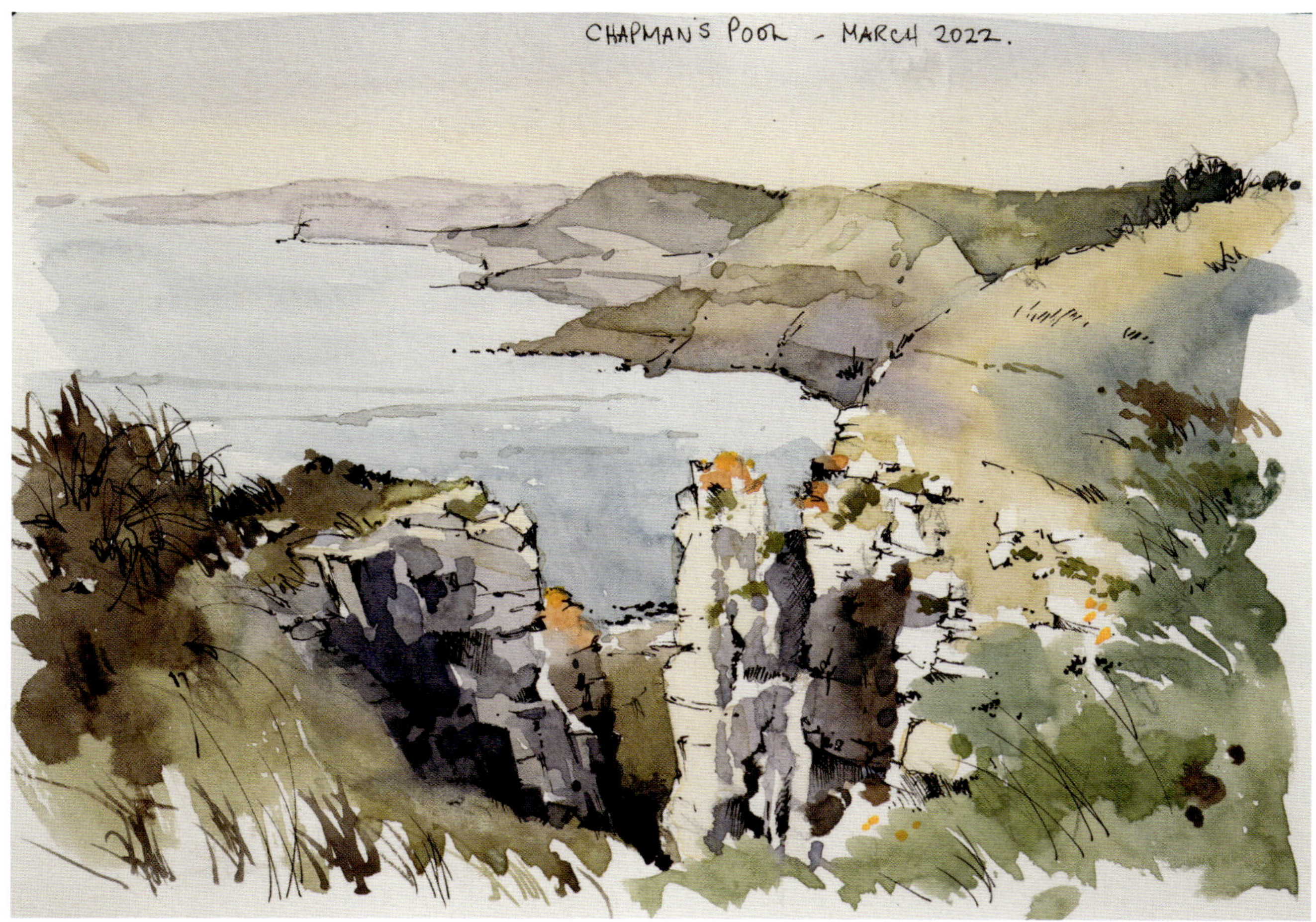

I have fond memories of making this pen and wash sketch: the weather was beautiful, and sitting on the breezy cliff top in the soft grass gave me strong sense of connection to the landscape.

portable as possible; you will need a comfortable, medium/large daypack (mine is 48 litre) so you can include a couple of additional clothing layers if needed, food and drink, safety equipment such as compass, first aid kit and maps. I also have room for my camera and a small collapsible stool and table. The last thing you need in these situations is to be weighed down by too much equipment that will inevitably persuade you that the location you want to paint is out of reach. Pack light, invest in some quality hiking gear and you will find the obstacles to painting outdoors are easily removed. The satisfaction of a good walk, an afternoon of painting and sketching, accompanied by a flask of tea is difficult to beat; it is a wonderful way to spend time in the landscape.

Understanding and organising your equipment is essential for the landscape painter. Over the years there will always be experimentation with new equipment and ideas, but try to settle on a combination that complements the way that you paint and provides you with the flexibility to optimise your time in the landscape.

FIELD TRIP – THE IMPORTANCE OF SKETCHING
The River Thames at Richmond

There are many different elements that have influenced our landscapes, one of the strongest contenders being rivers. Carving their winding, watery pathways from source to sea, they are perhaps more responsible for the development of our familiar landscape components than anything else: hills and valleys, cliffs and gorges, wetlands and marshes, lakes and reservoirs, towns and cities. In the United Kingdom our capital cities of Belfast, Edinburgh, Cardiff and London are all situated on major rivers: Lagan, Forth, Taff and Thames respectively. In his outstanding and thorough book, *The Making of The British Landscape*, Nicholas Crane charts a fascinating insight into the evolution of London from a trading outpost

to a global financial centre, all brought about by the utility, access and transport of the River Thames. Having worked in central London for several years I was always impressed by the river's vital energy; its ability to set the pace, promote activities and develop communities. It is out-of-town however, that the river has greater appeal to me today; the river of Jerome K. Jerome's *Three Men in a Boat*. As it ambles its way through the Home Counties from its source in Gloucestershire, its influence on the landscapes through which it flows makes for never-ending sources of artistic inspiration: bridges and barges, locks, old mills, rowing regattas, weeping willow trees, historic houses and houseboats, church spires reflected in the river, swans, sluice gates, pleasure boats and picnics. In many ways, there is nothing more enjoyable than sitting on a riverbank, watching the comings and goings of tides, people, wildlife, nature. If you have a sketchbook to hand, then so much the better.

The River Arun in Sussex is a popular haunt of mine, but I have made a conscious decision recently to return to the Thames. My sisters Jennifer and Chloe both live in West London and it seemed like a good opportunity to meet up for the day in the elegant borough of Richmond-upon-Thames. I would sketch a few scenes, they would supply me with coffee and cake, and we would engage in traditional sibling chat (understandable to us, but meaningless to anyone that cared to listen in). Helpfully, they acted as my photographers for the day too.

Sketching is the engine room of landscape painting. The artist that sketches regularly from nature will sharpen their observation skills, assessing and editing scenes in a way that is simply not possible indoors. Sketching allows me to make quick impressions of scenes, where the speed of working dictates that only the immediate impact of a place or moment can be recorded. In the three-dimensional outdoors there is simply too much detail to be observed and captured and so the sketch becomes an essential editing tool, enabling larger paintings to be made in the studio, based more on feelings than information. This process will help your work to develop from being prosaic and illustrative to expressive and evocative.

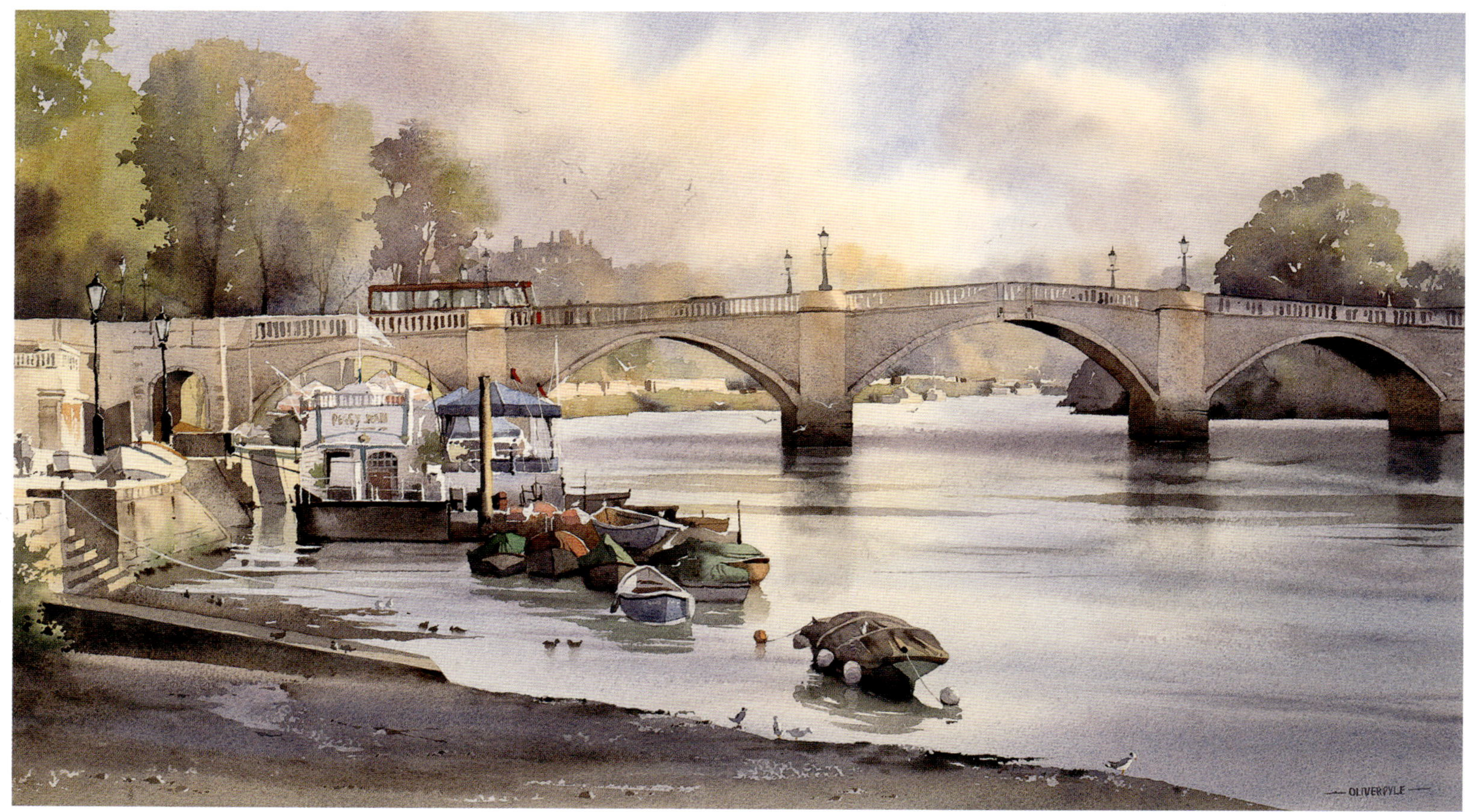

An Autumn Afternoon, Richmond-upon-Thames – 72cm x 36cm
One of my favourite Thames views, this scene is difficult to beat; full of colour and detail, with a natural composition. The preeminent skill required to paint a scene like this is to allow the quiet areas of the painting to be heard: river, sky, background. By including too much noise (detail) in these areas, the painting would become a cacophony, full of discord.

It was important to be able to quickly grab my Etchr satchel and tripod, then jump on the 8.50am train to London as the weather and our diaries synchronised; it is a fundamental aspect of my approach to painting on location; think ahead, be prepared, then move fast. It was a stunning November morning, surprisingly warm for the time of year and the low angle of the sun helped to render boats and bridges as semi-silhouettes against the sparkling river, looking upstream. It was pleasant

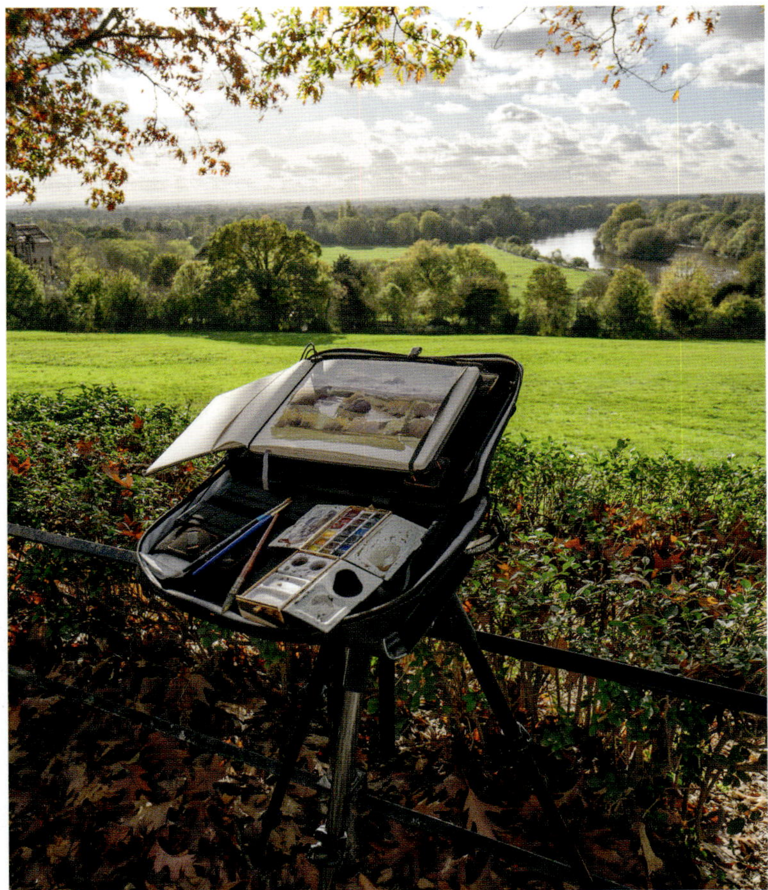

The Etchr Satchel – an excellent addition to my outdoor kit. Highly portable, versatile and easy to customise, it allows me to paint on location with minimal equipment. I like to think that JMW Turner esq. would have enjoyed using this set-up.

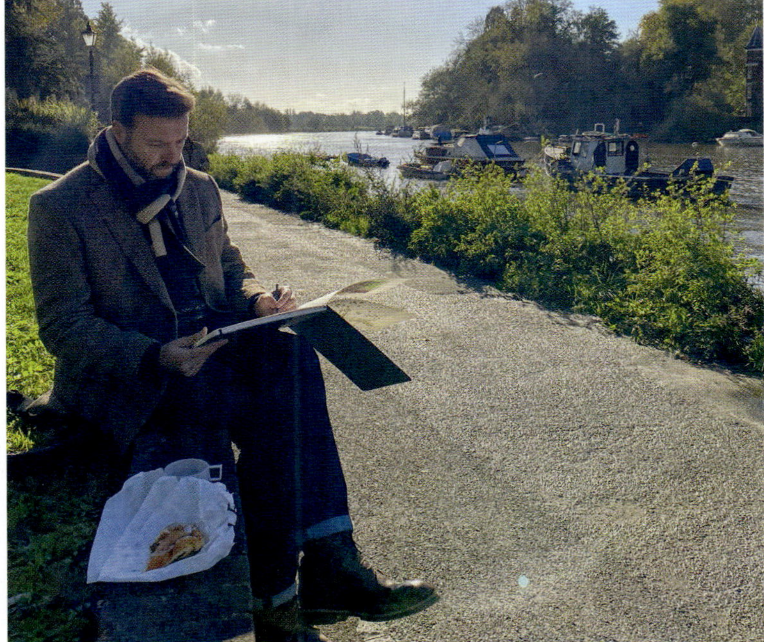

The wall on the tow path made for a perfect seat, the sketchbook on the knees a perfect easel. Simplification is the answer to everything you do on location: simplify your equipment, simplify the scenes as you sketch them.

beyond words to sit on the riverside wall on a clear morning, sketching in delightful company with some remarkably tasty Cinnamon Social cake (an unctuous, sticky, sharing pastry dreamed up by a Danish bakery).

Downstream, the sun's spotlight enhanced the colourful pleasure boats moored by the bank, while warming up the autumnal colours and allowing the London buses crossing Richmond Bridge to announce their presence in the strongest possible terms.

As a landscape painter it is impossible to be in Richmond without taking a stroll through the Terrace Gardens to the viewing point on Richmond Hill frequented and painted two centuries earlier by one of my most inspirational painters – Joseph Mallord William Turner RA. During stays at his country residence in Twickenham, the great man would visit this place, sketchbook in-hand, laying the foundations for some of his grand works, including *Thomson's Aeolian Harp* and *Richmond Hill on the Prince Regent's Birthday*. Looking across the Terrace Field toward Glover's Island that sits on the bend in the river, the scene today is less open with both banks and the island more heavily wooded than in Turner's time. It is a beautiful scene that seems almost improbable given its proximity to central London and despite a little gathering of distant cloud, the Thames slid through the scene like a silver serpent among the warm autumnal hues shrouding it's banks. A quick watercolour painting is the perfect way capture a moment like this: it

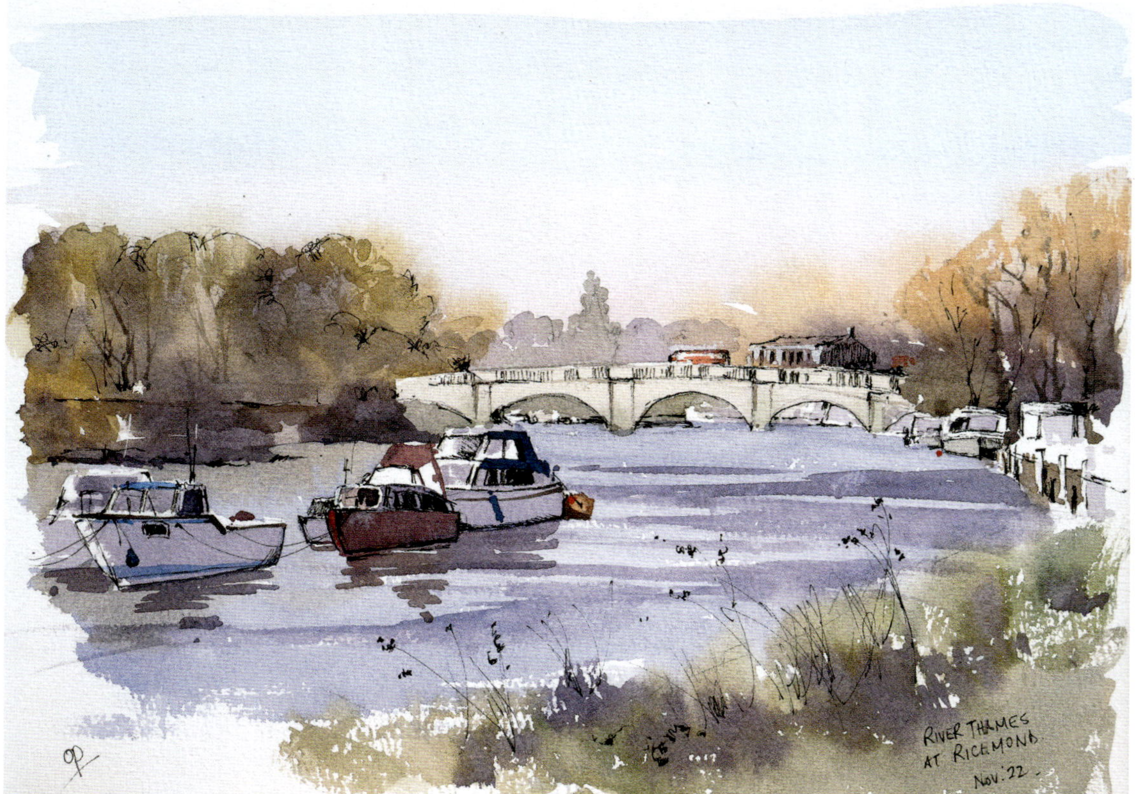

November, Richmond Bridge Pen and Wash Sketch

Simple washes are painted first, without too much concern for tidiness. Working over the top with a fine ink pen pulls the washes together. It is the perfect way to record complex scenes quickly when working outdoors.

has an immediate freshness to it that is often difficult to replicate in the studio. Chatting to passers-by, keeping an eye on the changing light, seeing the oak, beech and maple leaves falling now and then in the gentle breeze, all helped to sharpen the senses, encouraging a way of looking that combined vitality and simplicity.

With a day's sketching planned, it is simply not possible to make a sketch of everything that inspires you. In Richmond, new details and interesting perspectives were hiding around every corner, and so I resolved to make as many sketches as time would permit, but don't think that the fun stopped there; on return to the studio, I continued sketching out ideas while the impressions and feelings of the day remained fresh in my mind. As we walked down to the riverbank in the morning, I remarked on the convenient red telephone boxes, complementing the green shop façade on Richmond Green; I took a quick photo and resolved to make a pen and wash painting of this in due course. All morning I was aware of the dramatic tonal contrasts on the river and a day or so later, I decided to make an experimental sketch with some walnut ink and Prussian blue to explore how

these contrasts played out with the hire boats, moored by Richmond Bridge. Sketching, based on memories and feelings, is a way of working that is familiar to me and helps me to consolidate my experiences of places and moments. I will do this regularly when I have been unable to commit a scene to a sketchbook at the time – a few simple marks and

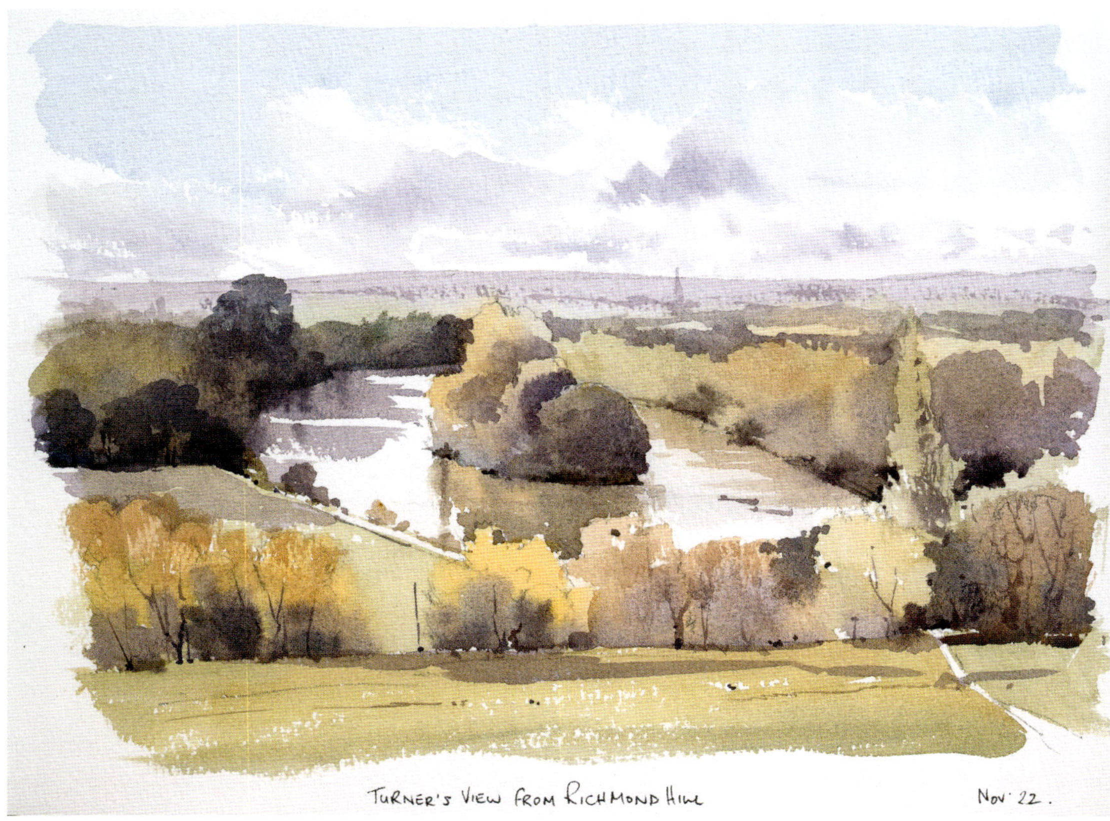

A quick watercolour painting of the River Thames, viewed from Richmond Terrace; a scene much loved by Turner.

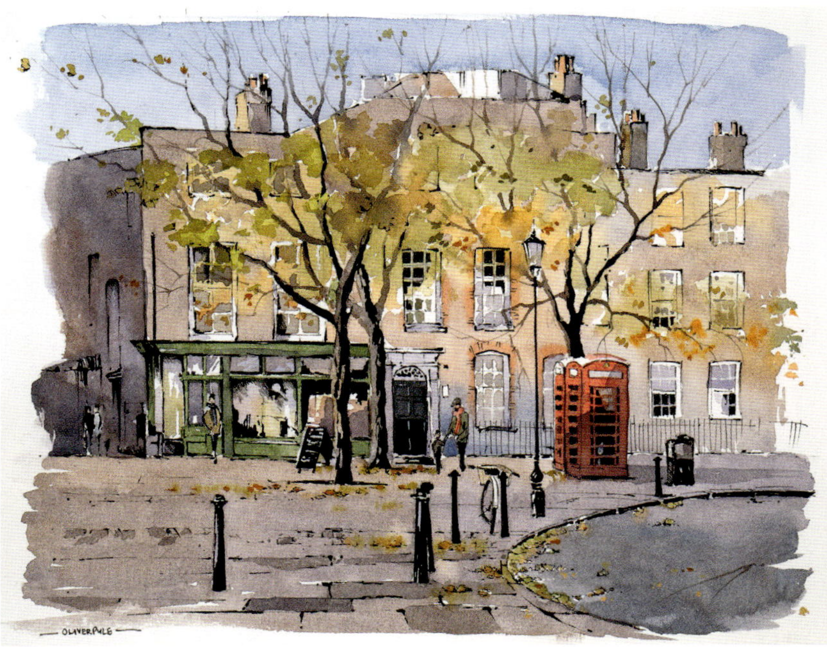

Falling Leaves, Richmond Green – 35cm x 25cm

Pen and wash doesn't need to be reserved only for the sketchbook; I see it as a wonderful extension of the watercolour medium and a much underrated technique – this has just as much right to be considered a 'grown up' painting as anything else in this book. If you are finding your paintings becoming too tight and fiddly, use this technique – it's a great way to loosen up.

quick washes is often all that is required. There is never a time to stop sketching; the day you do, your landscape paintings will start to descend the slippery slope to mediocrity. Sketch; spend time with family; eat cake. It is a winning combination.

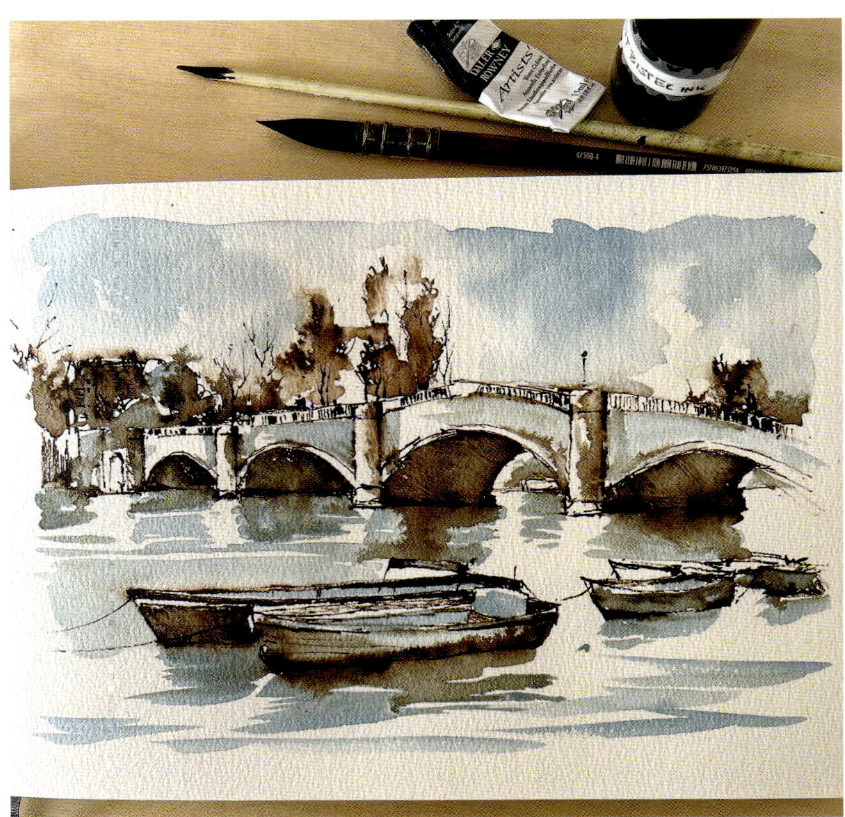

Boat Hire, Richmond – bister and watercolour sketch

This quick study explores the tonal values on the Thames – glaring highlights on the river and deep shadows under the bridge, and on the boats' hulls. Drawn loosely with a sharpened stick, in bister (walnut ink) the addition of loose washes of cool Prussian Blue creates a lovely contrast. Be prepared for the medium to dictate and control you if you use this technique – it's liberating.

ACCEPTING THE CHALLENGE

easons for painting the landscape are varied, the most prosaic being that we simply don't know what else to paint. While there's nothing wrong with that per se, it is more likely that we are inspired by places, experiences and our memories of them and are motivated to record and recreate them in some way. As a painter, you may keep the resulting work in a sketchpad, folder or drawer. You may sell them; you may give them away. It is likely that you will enjoy sharing your experiences through different outlets, particularly online and for those that have enjoyed a degree of success with their work, wider commercial opportunities may have already presented themselves. Whatever your motivation for painting and wherever your results may end up, all landscape painters are confronted with a fundamental challenge: our subject is spacious and three dimensional, yet our paintings are restricted and two dimensional. In teaching the art of landscape painting it is easy to focus on equipment, colours, brushstrokes and techniques, however many a poorly painted landscape is the result of misunderstanding the challenge of translating three-dimensional space into two-dimensional confinement; the clumsy application of the

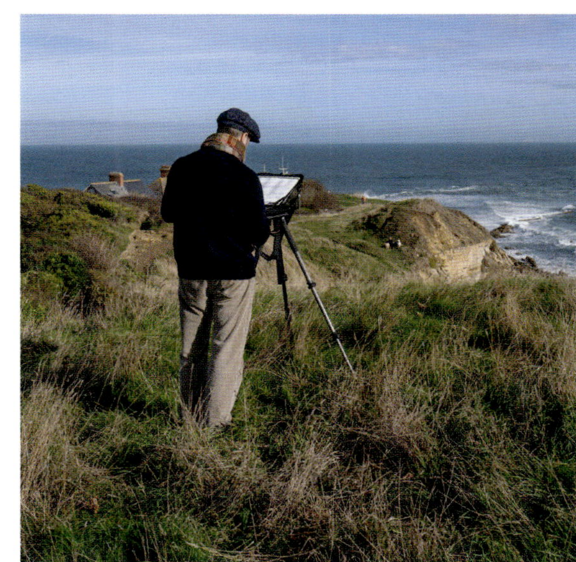

At some point, the ambitious landscape painter will need to confront their subject head-on, with all the discomfort and inconvenience that may be involved. Here, the author paints on the cliff top at Peveril Point, Swanage, the stiff breeze testing his tripod's stability.

'wrong' colour or a misplaced brushstroke are less likely to be at fault. This is a point of fundamental importance in the creation of successful landscape art and in this section I will show you three areas of practice or discipline that will help you to accept and overcome the challenge of landscape painting: be Outdoors, be Obsessed, be Observant. You may feel tempted to skip ahead to the next section, the fun bit that provides you with more technique and less theory. To do so would be a mistake: this section is unapologetically the first and it is the most important.

BE OUTDOORS

A choice confronts the landscape painter: paint in the comfort of home and studio, or paint outdoors, on location. The ease and comfort of the studio has evident merits: a fixed reference point from which to work, easy access to equipment, freedom from interruptions and a comfortable work-station. The benefits of this way of working should not be underestimated – they allow the painter to concentrate on their work with a high degree of focus, particularly helpful for those learning to paint. Mastering technical skills just seems to be easier indoors.

The unpredictable practice of painting outdoors does not offer such comforts. The artist must tackle a number of unhelpful elements: transient light, awkward access to locations, pared-down equipment, inquisitive livestock, interested members of the public and the vagaries of the weather. It is not the optimal environment in which to practice skills and fine-tune techniques. However, it offers an immediate interface with our subject, allowing us a full sensory experience to inform our work. It also provides a spatial experience, helping to develop a way of looking at the landscape that is visceral and simply not possible in the studio. Painting outdoors confers benefits that are of tremendous importance in our progress as artists, enabling us to get to grips with the challenge of landscape painting:

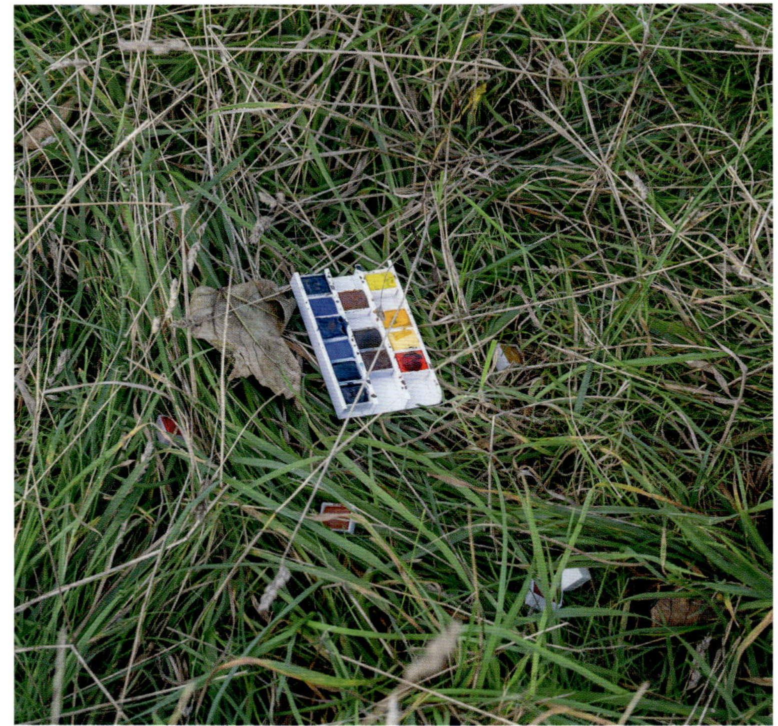

Retrieving half-pans from the long grass – just one of the joys of painting on location.

1) Time spent outdoors allows us to build up a mental sketchbook, full of images, reference points and details, gained simply through observation. I have often said to students that when I'm outdoors in the landscape I never really stop painting, even though paper, paints and palettes may be back in the studio. The greatest skill

required for landscape painting is observation and no equipment is required for that. Be outdoors in a woodland and take time to stop and observe carefully. You will notice how shadows cast by the large oak tree define the undulations of the ground from which it grows and how the evening sun brushes across the trunk, revealing a texture of cracks and canyons on the bark. As you walk along the riverbank you will see the reflections falling vertically into the river while the ripples on the surface run horizontally. Through observation you learn that the reflected darks seem paler and the reflected lights appear darker than their respective objects on the bank. My friends and family will tell you that our conversations outdoors are regularly punctuated by a wandering gaze to the treetops, glowing in the late evening sun, or expressions of excitement at the wet sand on the shore, shining unbearably bright like the purest mirror. Irritating for others, essential for me. If you have a sketch pad with you to record all your experiences and observations then so much the better, but the reality is that it's often not the case, or social circumstances may prevent you from taking time out to sketch. It matters little – just by being there and observing your surroundings carefully you are building up an invaluable treasure chest of information about the landscape. You are learning the landscape and experiencing new ways of looking; you are learning to observe.

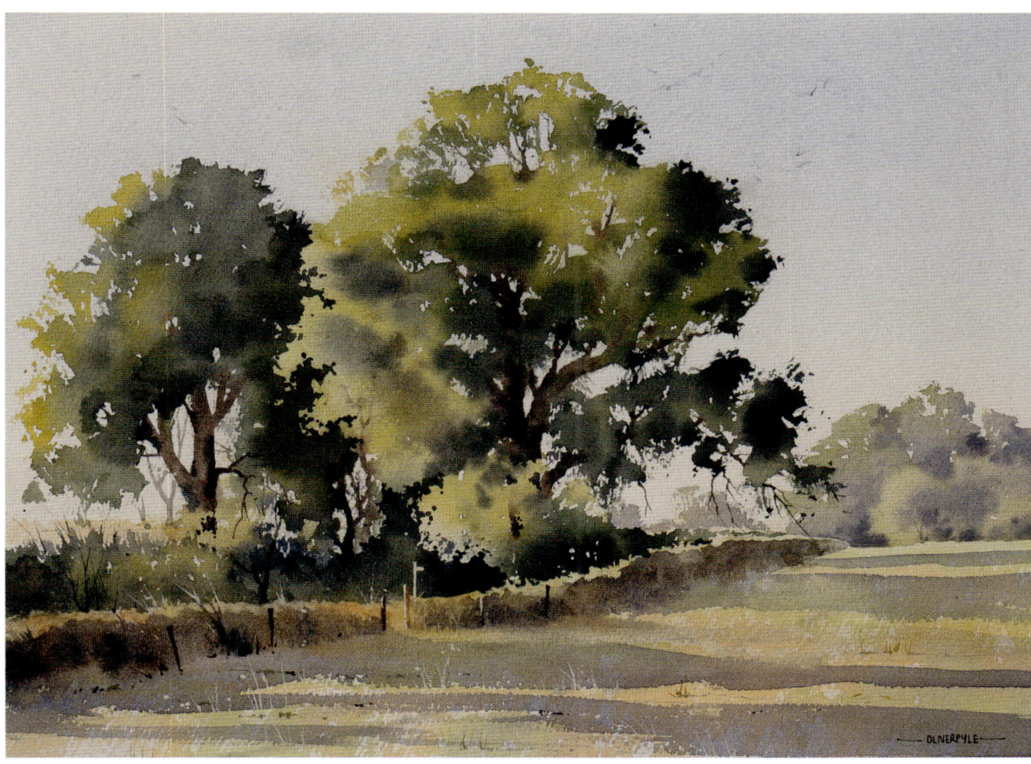

A Summer Evening, Sussex – 39cm x 29cm
I have walked through this field many times, normally to secure a view of the Ouse Valley Viaduct and the trains that run thereon. This evening, the stunning oaks that always command a presence couldn't be ignored. It's a quick painting that captures the essence of a much-loved place at a favourite time of the day.

2) We are able to see space in a way that is simply not possible by looking at a photograph. Particularly with today's smart phones, cameras come with wide angle lenses that distort perspectives and photographs have a general tendency to flatten middle distance space, compressing the sense of depth within a scene. Furthermore, the dynamic range between lights and darks that a camera can capture is significantly less than that which the human eye observes. The algorithms that process images captured by a camera's digital sensor are designed to shrink the dynamic range, so that we can see details in both lights and darks, based on average values. While this can be useful for the photographer, it is not a true representation of how our eyes work and respond to light in the landscape. Photographs can be a useful resource that enable us to record fleeting moments, particularly in rapidly changeable weather and the lighting conditions at either end of the day and can provide an important reference point for detail – just be aware of their limitations.

3) All our senses are engaged in our surroundings. Not only can we view the landscape but we can hear, touch and smell it. While no trickery exists to transfer these sensory experiences to a piece of paper in an interactive way, they impact our ability to understand and interpret a landscape scene, informing our work with profound insight that is not available from simply downloading a picture from Google Images of a location we have never been to. The chatter of tree branches rustling in the breeze,

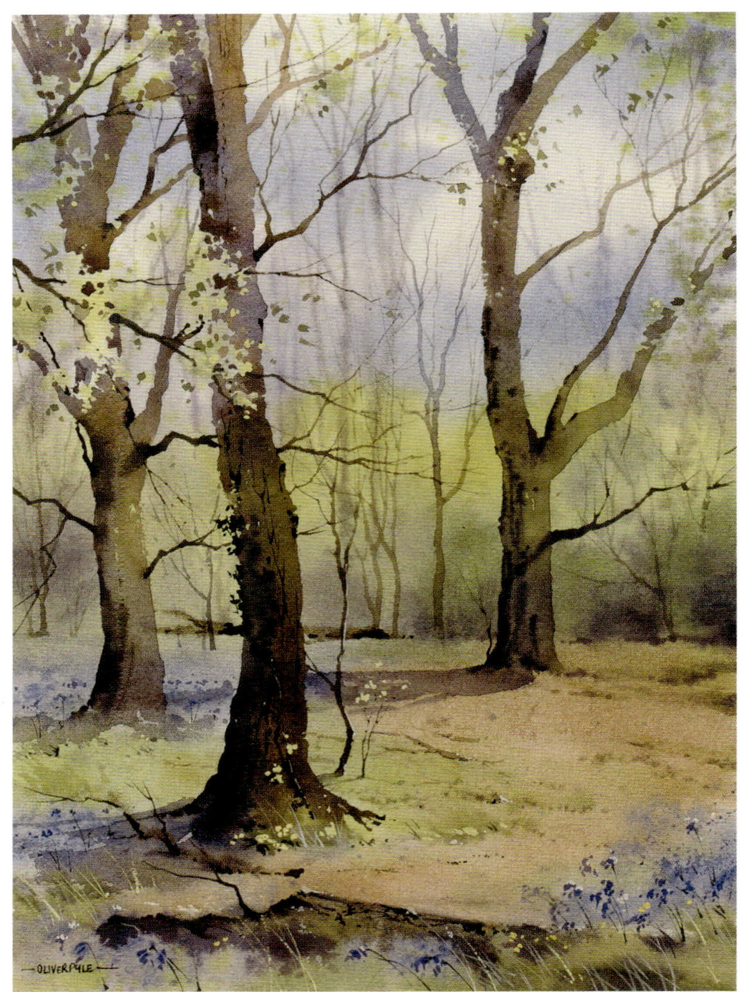

Bluebell Season, Sussex – 29cm x 39cm
The sights, smells and sounds of the Sussex woodlands in which I spent large chunks of my childhood, and still frequent as often as possible today, will never leave me: soft blue carpets in spring, their fragrance lingering on the breeze that gently knocks branches and clatters twigs in the canopy above. Always beautiful.

the feel of pebbles, cold and smooth to the touch from the sea's relentless polishing, the salty smell of fresh seaweed deposited on the wrack line – all have a subconscious impact on our experience of a place and enable us to convey a deeper experience of the landscape for the viewer. How many times have we heard a viewer comment on a beautiful painting and say 'It feels like I'm there – the atmosphere reminds me of times that I have spent there with my family?' The reason is, the artist was there! I know that all my best paintings are of the places that I know intimately. I simply cannot convey the same sense of engagement with the landscape for a place that I don't know; the intangible quality of these sensory experiences simply does not exist and cannot inform my work.

4) Painting and sketching on location provides the artist with a continually evolving scene, not just a static image, frozen in time. Although this may seem inconvenient as the light changes, or boats in the harbour are continually on the move as you try to paint them, it forces you to respond quickly and dynamically to the scene in front of you and allows you to provide a wider experience of the subject. Most of my location sketches portray a period of time spent in the landscape rather than a snapshot of a moment; a couple of horses wander down to the river bank, old branches and leaves float past with the changing tide; all are included in the sketch. The scene continually evolves and consequently portrays a broader, richer experience of the place.

5) Inspiration comes easily outdoors. As a young amateur painter I often found it difficult to find subjects to paint, relying heavily on photographs for inspiration and reference. Without well-developed skills of observation and experience I fell into the trap of painting from a photograph that looked like it would make

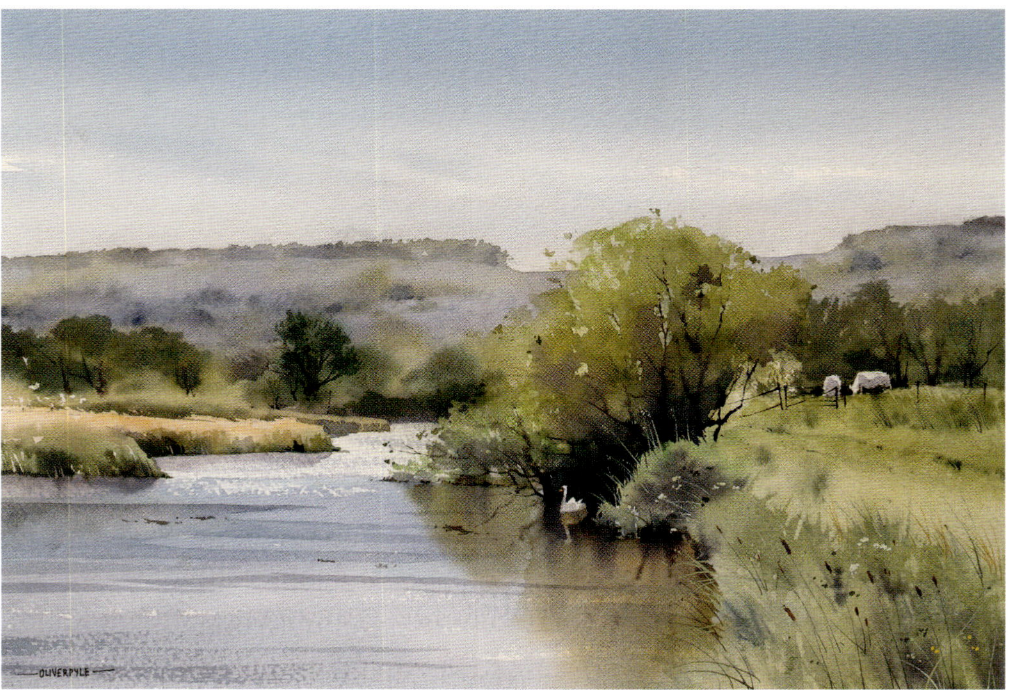

Summer Sparkle on the Arun – 39cm x 29cm
I painted this scene on location for a YouTube demonstration and then made this version on return to the studio. It captures everything that is so wonderful about a summer's day in Sussex. Warm vibrant greens and cool blues combine well to create a feeling of afternoon heat.

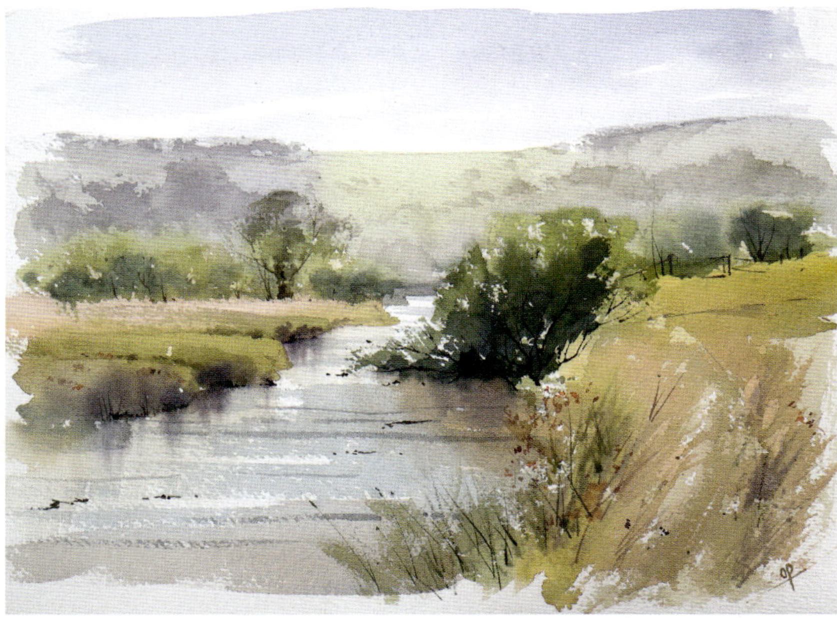

The quick painting I made on location has a wonderful freshness and sense of immediacy to it. It can often be difficult to recreate the same feeling and spontaneity later in the studio.

the perfect watercolour, with colours, composition and contrasts already taken care of. It is an easy trap to fall into and an important one to avoid. I soon found that such reference images were scarce and very quickly the inspiration dried up. Being outdoors, finding inspiration is never the problem, in fact trying to whittle down your choices of what to paint in a limited time is more of a challenge. When I am on location I no longer look for the 'killer scene' but find so much inspiration from my surroundings

that it gives me a wide array of interesting subjects to paint, there and then, but also later in the studio. Expansive vistas of rolling hills, old barns, or simply some cow parsley in the hedgerow – inspiration is easy. If you are finding that the subjects you want to paint are few and far between, then move away from Pinterest and Google, pick up a sketch pad and go for a walk. You will be confronted each time by a number of decisions that have not been made for you by a photographer: where should the focal point be; are there elements you can include or exclude to improve the composition; are there subtle colour variations that you can play with to enhance the sense of atmosphere in the painting? By undertaking this visual editing process yourself, your work will improve rapidly and you will become an increasingly versatile painter, able to find inspiration and see subjects almost anywhere.

Creative art is one of life's activities where right and wrong ought not to exist, yet it is surprising how often a dogmatic approach finds its way into the teaching of art. Landscape painting and watercolour are not immune from this and one of the unhelpful observations that exists relates to painting outdoors: 'your landscape paintings lack validity and meaning unless they are painted on location.' While the points I have outlined above are certainly important, such a statement misrepresents the nature of the genre and ignores a rich history of studio-based work.

Don't worry if the bulk of your work is painted indoors – it is often necessary, especially for larger, more complex paintings – but let's make sure that we are finding our inspiration from the right place, from the landscape itself. You will often find that the best botanical painters have a herbaceous border, crammed with blooming dahlias, hydrangeas and ornamental grasses, or simple flower pots on the patio with lovingly curated displays of geraniums and petunias. Inevitably, such green-fingered individuals make the best botanical artists. In the same way, those that find fascination in those around them, and the rich

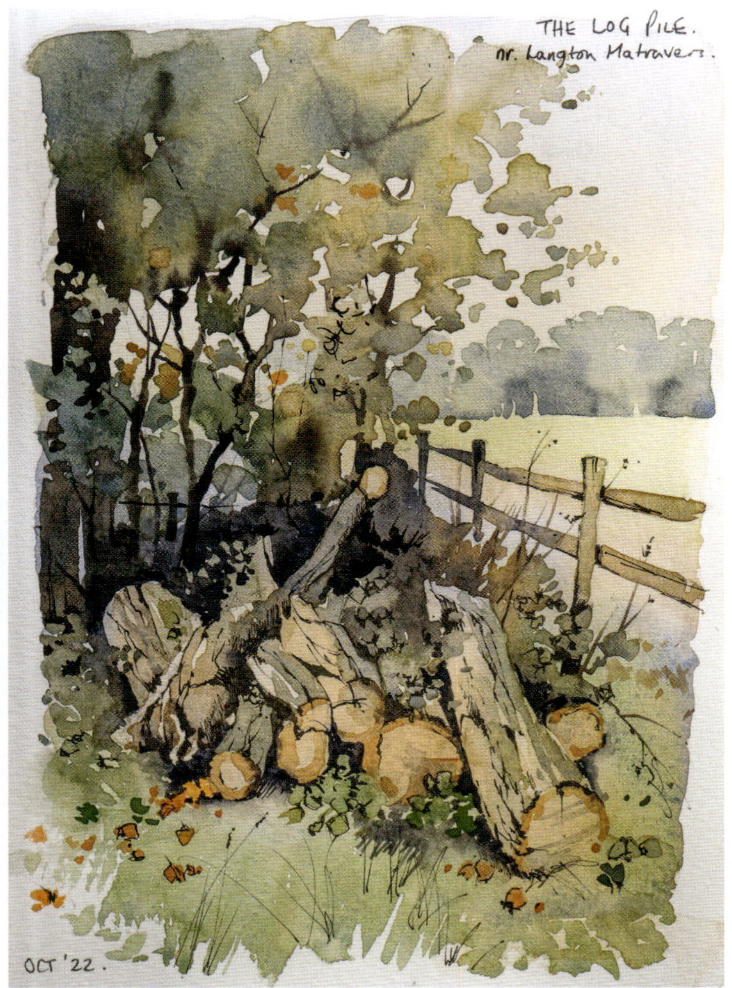

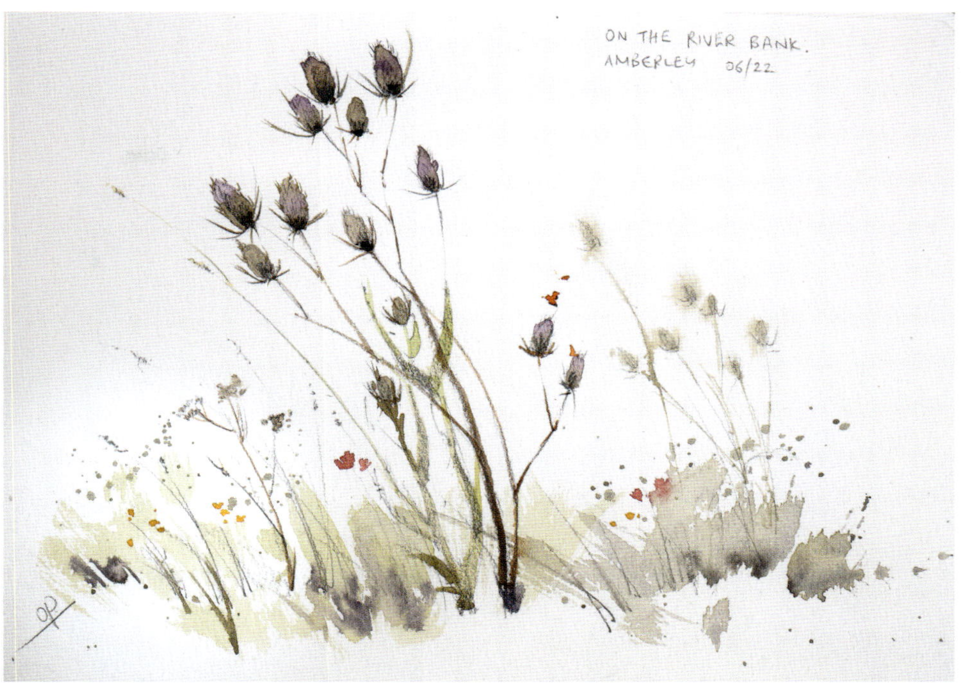

ABOVE: No sweeping vistas here, just a simple, quick study of some riverbank teasels (one of my favourite wildflowers) near Amberly, Sussex. Don't ignore landscape details – they make for wonderful subjects.

LEFT: There was no intention to sketch a pile of logs while I was out for a walk, and it's not a subject that I would normally entertain, but such is the nature of inspiration – it is a visitor that can come knocking when you least expect it. Be ready to welcome it when it does.

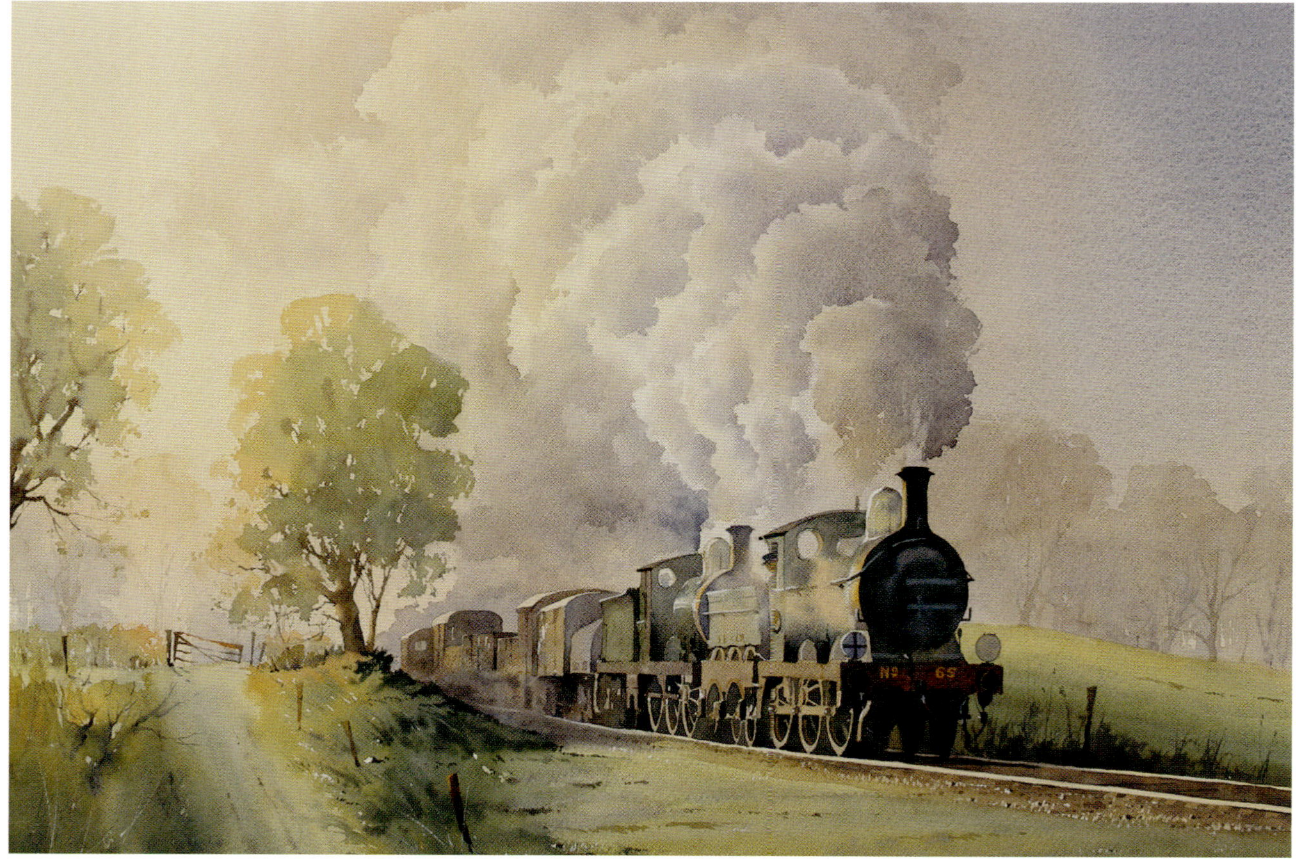

Sun, Steam, Sussex – 72cm x 54cm
The detail and complex shapes and perspectives involved with a moving subject like this are better handled in the comfort of the studio. This was a large painting of the Bluebell Railway in Sussex, commissioned by Andrew, a long-time school friend of mine. Sadly, he is no longer with us and it's nice to keep his memory alive. Top bloke.

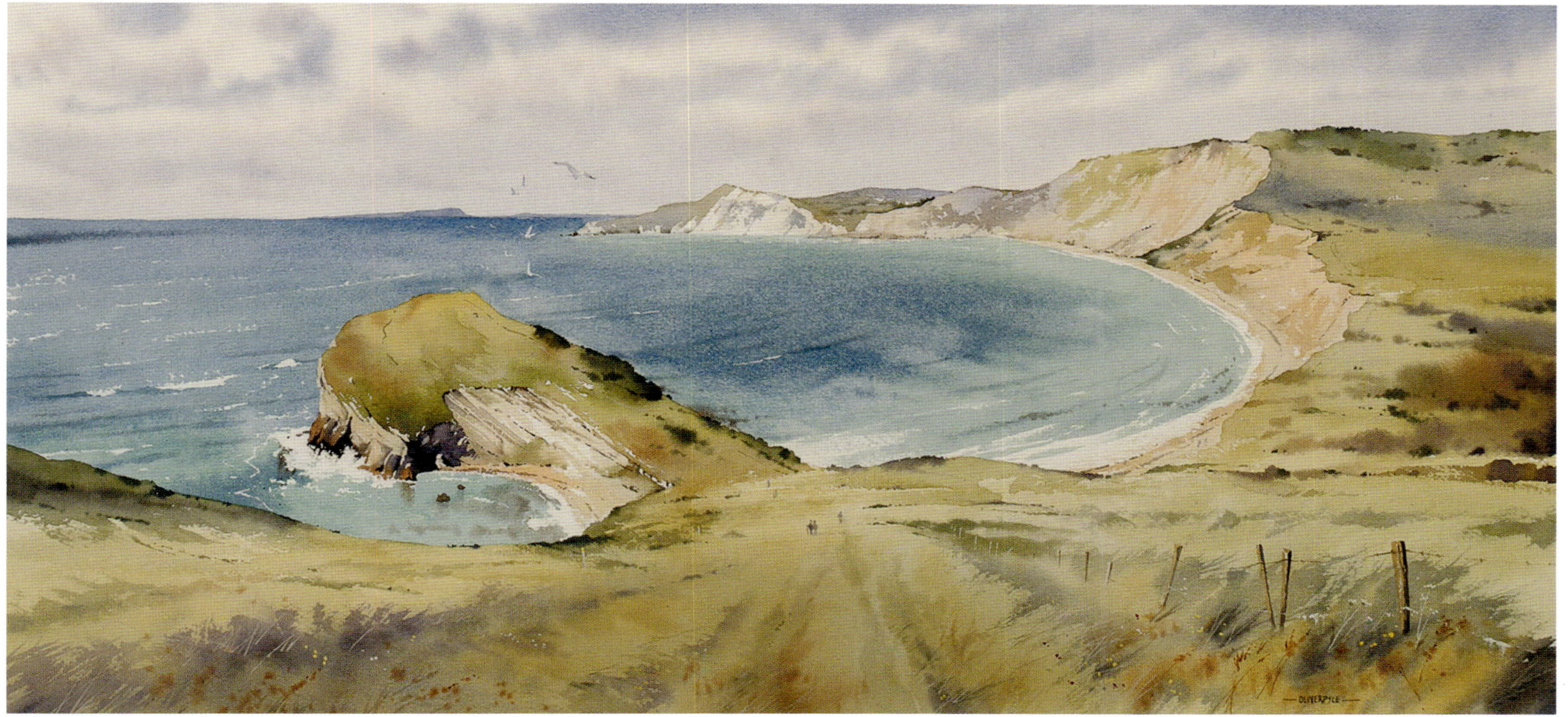

A Blustery Walk to Worbarrow Bay – 72cm x 36cm
I remember it well: a brisk walk from the abandoned village of Tyneham; a strong onshore wind trying its best to persuade us not to descend the steep coast path to the bay; seagulls screeching, free-wheeling. Activity + scenery + memories = painting inspiration.

spectrum of human behaviour and experience, will often make the best portrait painters. It seems inconceivable that the stunning, evocative portraits that are displayed in the galleries, stately homes and corporate collections around the world were created by misanthropic artists, with little or no experience of their subjects. If you want to be a successful landscape painter, you will need a similar rapport with your subject. You will be outdoors, walking through country lanes, sitting on cliff tops, running in a city park, swimming in the sea; observing, sketching, painting, enjoying, being. Allow yourself to absorb the landscape and it will inspire you.

BE OBSESSED

Being in the landscape is a good place to start and whether it's a daily walk with the dog, or a favourite Sunday afternoon stroll, you will start to build up a level of expertise in the landscapes you experience. There is a consensus that in life, generally, a broad experience of many things is preferable to a deep experience of one or two. My advice to those aspiring to progress with their landscape painting is to favour the latter; focus on and deepen your experience of the landscapes you love. Most successful landscape painters return time and again to a small handful of favoured locations, each time creating fresh and dynamic work: Turner – Isle of Thanet and Petworth; Rowland Hilder – Shoreham Valley and Chichester Harbour; Monet – Argenteuil, Giverny and the River Thames; Andrew Wyeth – Chadds Farm and Cushing; David Curtis – Staithes and Langdale, just to name a few.

Although I paint a range of different landscapes and locations it is reasonable to say that 85 per cent of my work features both my home county of Sussex, with the South Downs, Ashdown Forest, Arundel and Chichester Harbour being my favoured subjects and

an area of Dorset from Poole Harbour, along the coast to Abbotsbury. The reason for painting Sussex is simple – I live there and it is where I have walked, driven, played, laughed, cried, been a child, grown up, experienced the people and places for most of my life. Dorset – specifically the Isle of Purbeck – was where we spent our annual family holiday each year and its landscapes, coastline, villages and available activities captivated me from the age of 9 years old. I return there many times each year and now own a gallery in the town of Swanage.

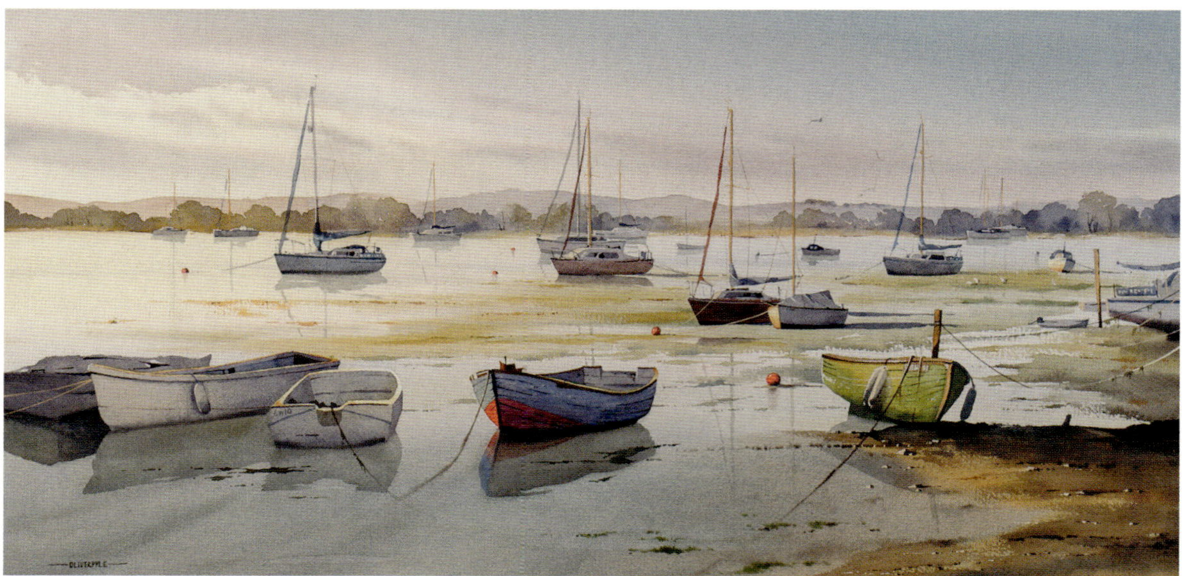

Still Waters, Dell Quay – 72cm x 36cm
It's not difficult to understand why Chichester Harbour has been such an inspiration to artists over the years. It is a wonderful place to paint, full of small pleasure craft jostling for position as the tide ebbs and flows, framed by the inescapable South Downs. Delicate glazes and transparent washes are key to creating the illusion of a fluid surface and a sense of evening tranquillity at low tide.

The affection that I have for these places and my affinity with them provides me with a never-ending source of inspiration. By knowing and understanding these landscapes so intimately, I feel well placed to express my experiences of them through my paintings in a way that resonates with those that view and collect my work. Some might say that I should broaden my horizons, but there is only so much we can experience and paint and I firmly believe that by coming to know these places so closely my vision and artistic expression is deepened, not limited. Beyond any doubt, as my relationship with the landscape grows stronger, so does my motivation for painting it, leading me on to new ideas, perspectives and interpretations.

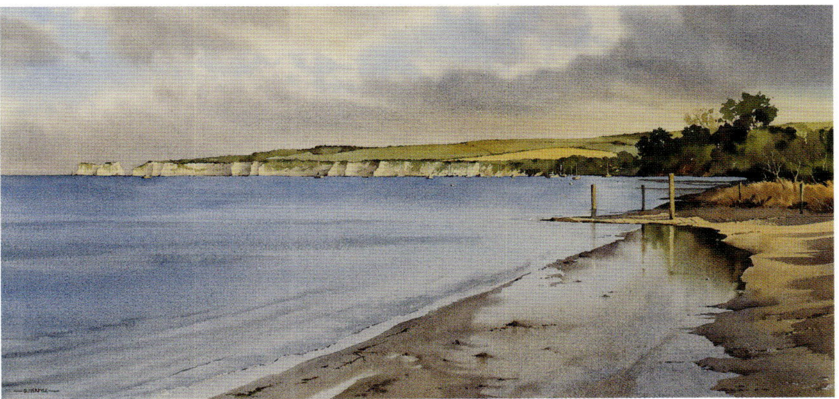

After the Storm, Studland – 72cm x 36cm

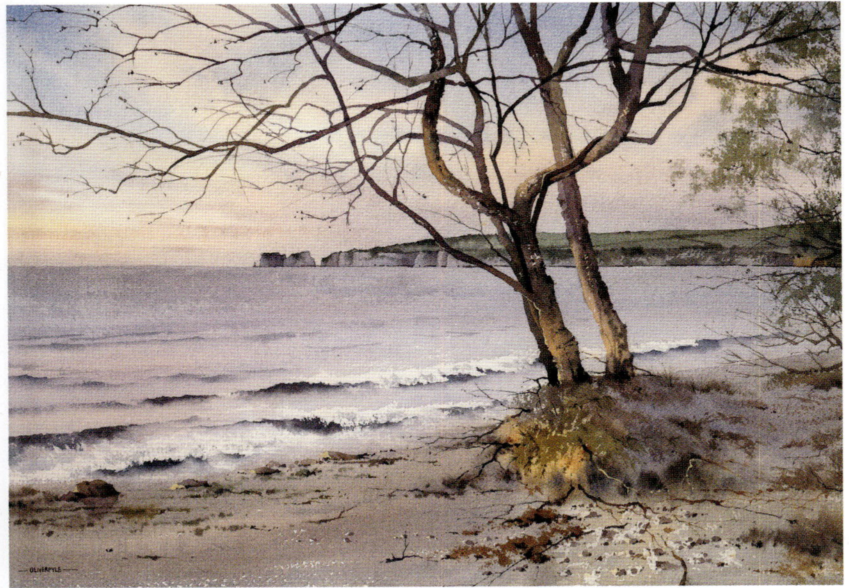

Root and Branch – Middle Beach, Studland – 50cm x 34cm

Take Studland in Dorset, for example. It is a small village on the Purbeck coast with a beautiful, east-facing bay, comprising three separate beaches: Knoll, Middle and South. It is sheltered from the winds of the south and the west by the Purbeck Hills, creating a headland that ends at Handfast Point. Here, coastal erosion to the chalk cliffs has created an iconic arrangement of stacks – Old Harry Rocks – that are visible from all vantage points in the bay. Behind the beaches lies a nature reserve of dunes, topped with cushions of heather (glorious in their covering of summer purple), marram grass and fiery yellow gorse.

It is a biodiverse home to Britain's heathland reptiles, birds and butterflies and lends a wonderfully natural feel to the environment. I have sat on these beaches for more times than I can recount and without a doubt Studland is the subject that I have painted most frequently. My time spent there and the work I have produced has created a visual memory for me that enables me to make paintings that are informed by experience and knowledge. I understand how the dune grasses move

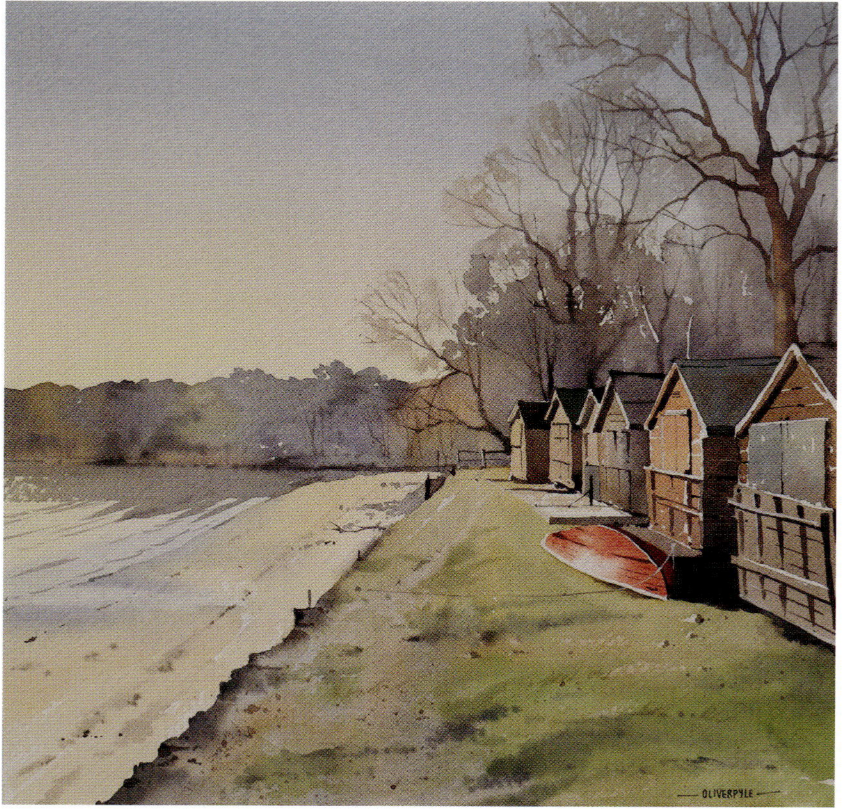

Winter Morning, South Beach – 30cm x 30cm

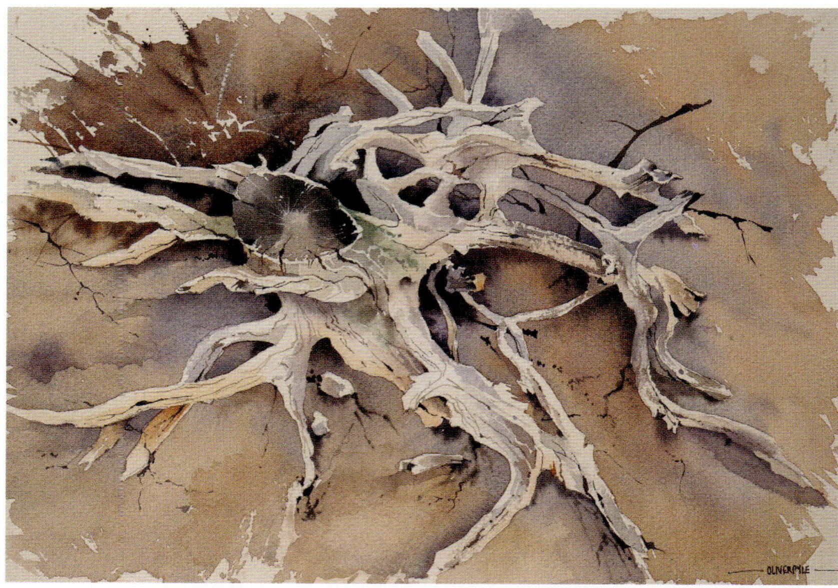

Almost Driftwood – 36cm x 26cm
There it sat, abandoned by the retreating sand: a giant arboreal arachnid, mutated by tide and time. I was fascinated by this old tree root on Middle Beach, and it made for an excellent subject to practice my negative painting technique; a method of describing a light-toned shape by the painting of its darker-toned surroundings.

in the breeze, how the sea often seems to come to a standstill such is the sheltered nature of the bay and how the shadows move across the headland during the day to create challenging tonal patterns on the cliff face. I am drawn to the wide views that work so well in a panoramic 2:1 format, yet find equal fascination in the landscape detail: old tree roots, sanded smooth by the lapping tide, but clinging on for dear life as the same tide scoops away their surroundings; a small shard of light on the wet foreshore, glowing in the soft dawn light; boats and beach huts huddled together to form interesting patterns.

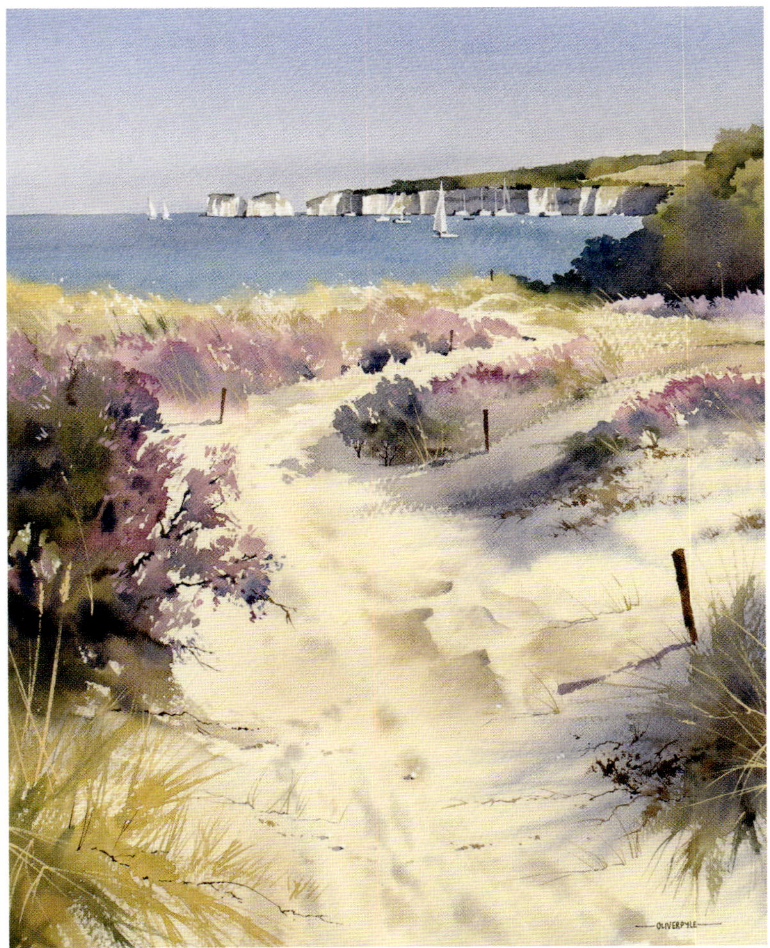

Summer Heather, Studland – 34cm x 50cm

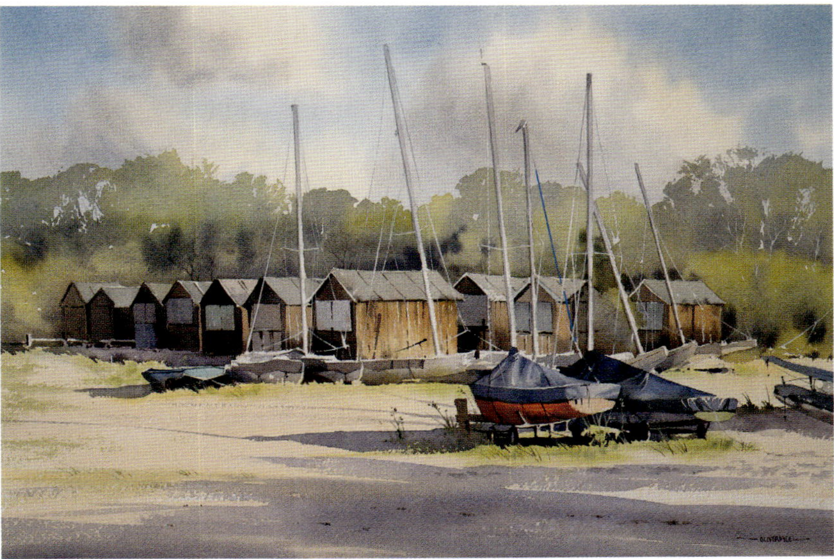

Boats and Beach Huts, Studland – 50cm x 34cm

Inevitably there will be places that you hold firmly in your affections and in terms of inspiration and an endless source of painting subjects these are a good place to start. Visit them as often as you can – at different times of the day when the combination of light and shade will reveal different shapes, forms and tonal arrangements. Take your camera, take your sketchpad or simply a notebook and become skilled at observing these subtle changes that occur throughout the day. As you become more familiar with how the light has an impact on your subject, make visits at different times of the year. In the UK we benefit from four distinct seasons, each having a significant impact on how I approach my paintings, often bringing different colours on my palette into play. But I'm not happy to stop there. For example, I know that the Ashdown Forest in

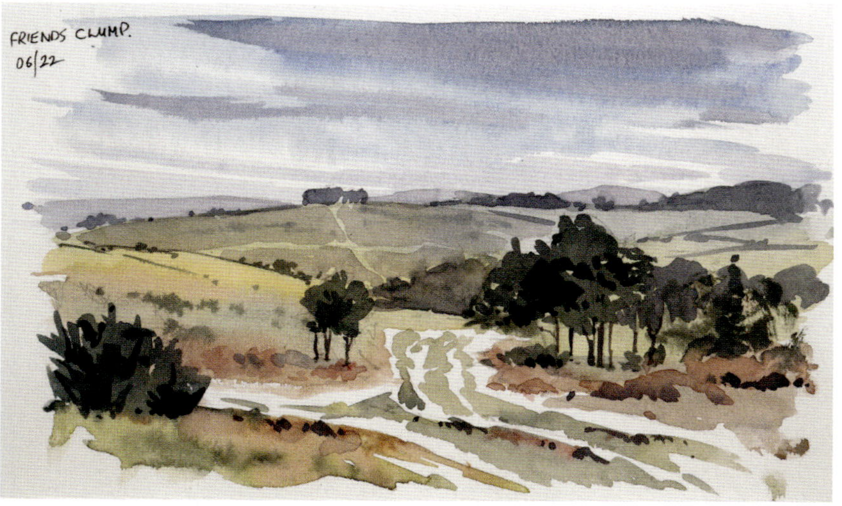

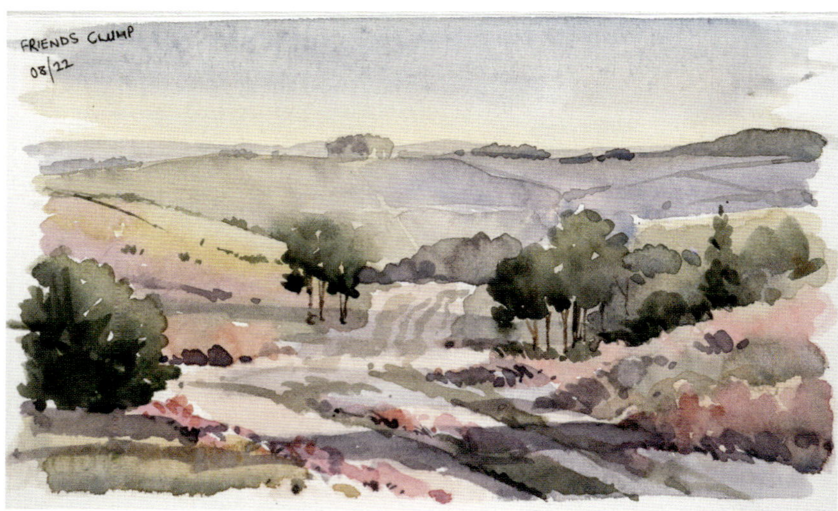

June and August (both summer months in the UK) offer entirely different opportunities: verdant vistas in June, replaced by pink and purple carpets of heather in August, as these sketches of Friends Clump demonstrate.

Once you start to increase your familiarity with a place, by default you will start to look closer at the landscape, observing carefully. In the process you will start to find that instead of running out of 'watercolour-ready' images on the internet, you will become more preoccupied with where you will find the time to paint all these amazing subjects and ideas. You will start looking at weather forecasts, sunrise charts and tide times. You will seek out books that not only illustrate your landscapes but provide you with written detail and the experiences of those who have gone before and have shared your passion for the place. Your family and friends may remark 'you're obsessed!' and it's at that point that you are well on your way to becoming a serious landscape painter.

To illustrate the point, this painting of Kimmeridge Bay was only possible through an obsessive focus on the combination of weather and tide times and my knowledge of the topography. Join me in the rock pools and I will talk you through the process.

FIELD TRIP – CONNECTING WITH THE LANDSCAPE
Evening Light at Kimmeridge Bay

Kimmeridge Bay in Dorset has been a popular muse of mine in recent years. While its beauty is impossible to ignore it cannot be said that it is the most compliant of subjects, often turning up to a sitting in a drab overcoat of browns and greys, constantly fidgeting with the ebb and flow

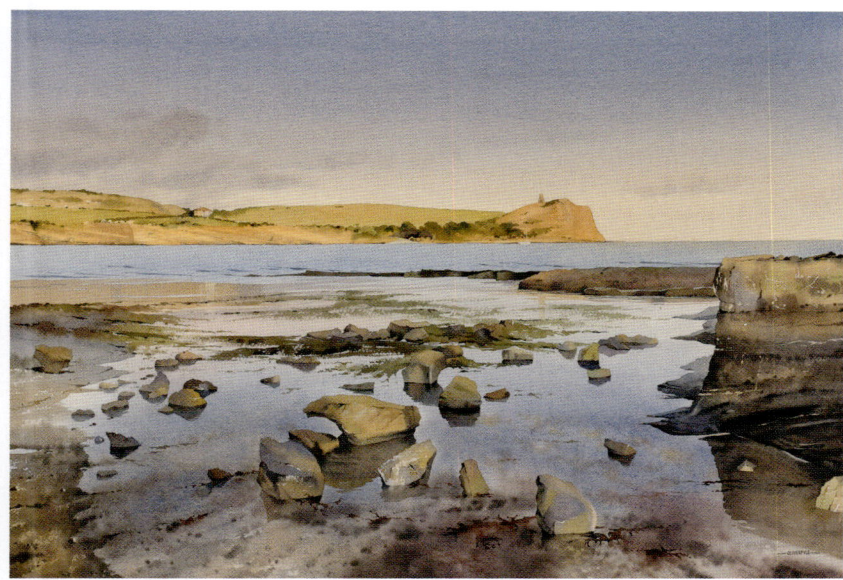

A Calm Summer Evening, Kimmeridge Bay – 72cm x 52cm

couple of hours after high tide, a natural composition reveals itself; the colours are balanced naturally between warm and cool, and the chaotic arrangement of the rocks and seaweed becomes a pleasing juxtaposition against the calm, orderly nature of the landscape as a whole. With the complexity of the subject and the light changing quickly, as it does at the end of the day, I knew that I would need to work fast. I kept an eye on both weather and tide times hoping for the right combination to present itself and when it did, I headed down to the coast. If truth be told, the tide was a fraction too high when I arrived, so I had to set up my camera tripod in the shallows of the rock pool to achieve the composition that I wanted – a low perspective, emphasising the ledge on the right, leading out to the sea with the central boulders tucked inside it. It just works; everything points conveniently towards the headland while the wide angle of vision helps to create an illusion that the viewer is almost standing in the foreground (with wet feet!) being inexorably lured into the painting. With the light disappearing in a matter of minutes there was no time to paint on location, but I knew that I had the image I was looking for and could work from it back in the comfort of the studio. With reference to the photo, I then made a few thumbnail sketches to resolve some outstanding issues; the positioning of several rocks, the tonal tension between them, their reflections, and in the rock pool the extent to which I could dial up the red colouring in the submerged seaweed without compromising the harmonious feeling of evening calm.

Being outdoors, collecting ideas and inspiration is a central pillar of landscape painting. Despite the painting being completed in the studio, it was only possible as a result of my connection with the place and my knowledge of it and the variable conditions that influence it. As I painted, I was experiencing that warm summer evening again: feeling the gentle sea breeze and listening to the faint clatter of small pebbles and slate shards tumbling down the cliff face behind me; smelling the brackish odour of seaweed, pleasantly pungent in the clear air; the golden glow of the headland starting to recede rapidly as the sun called time on another day.

of the tide. But I have been in the bay before when it has looked glowing and memorable and I wanted to make a painting that captured that; to do so I needed to draw on my knowledge and prior experience of the place. Having spent so much time in this beautiful, natural bay I know where the best view points are, the times of day at which they are their most presentable, and the ideal weather conditions to set them off. The trick is to be there just before the sun goes down, shining like a golden spotlight to reveal the warm siennas and ochres of the headland. This needs to be carefully timed however, as neither low tide nor high present the optimal configuration of ledges and rock pools from this vantage point on the west side of the bay. With the strong August sun low in the sky and a

BE OBSERVANT

The most important attribute required to make credible and compelling landscape paintings has nothing to do with the mechanics of painting itself – brushstrokes, colour mixing, wash techniques – but rather the discipline of careful observation. By far the most common answer that I give to those who ask 'What's the best way to paint…' is very simply

'Paint what you see.' It may sound a little patronising and dismissive, but it points to an important truth for those learning to paint: they don't paint what they see, but what their mind tells them they see. The reason for this is simply that learned behaviour from our most common experiences and logical thought processes tends to override the image that we are observing. For example, if you hold up your thumb at arm's length and compare its size to a large picture on the other side of the room, your thumb appears larger than the picture. That's how it should be drawn, but often our mind interferes in the recording process and whispers 'Wrong – you know your thumb is smaller than the picture. You must draw it that way!' It is surprising how often the mind gets its own way, evidenced by the many poorly drawn objects and scenes we see and have indeed made ourselves.

This eye-mind tension can be understood and overcome by considering two different challenges that present themselves. Firstly, translating the three-

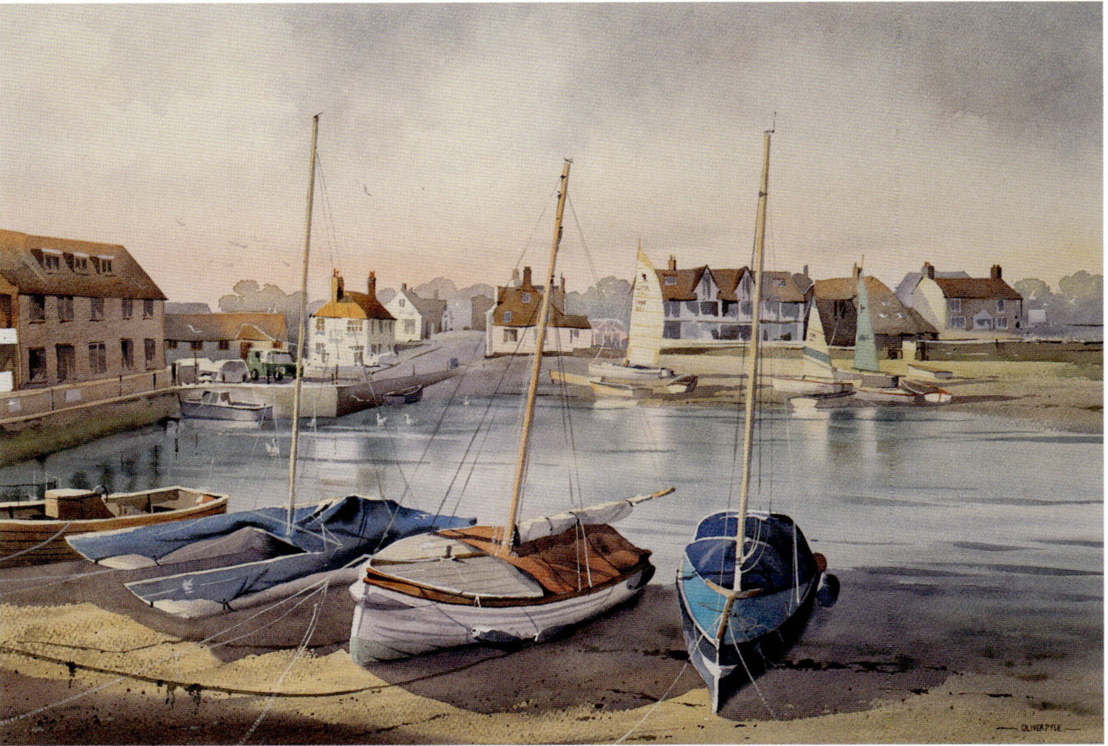

Evening Light, Emsworth Harbour –
60cm x 40cm
It just doesn't seem right to paint blue trees, but to accentuate the depth in this painting it is important to do so. The extreme difference in scale between foreground boats and those in the background, while seemingly illogical, is required to achieve an accurate sense of perspective throughout the scene.

dimensional reality of a landscape into a two-dimensional painting requires us to understand the optical illusions evident in nature and physics. Secondly, the imposition of necessary frames and boundaries around what we paint, which are absent from our subject in nature, poses problems for us; I refer to this as spatial constraint. Let's take a look at each one in turn and then in Section 3, Understanding The Principles, I will show you how the use of colour, contrast and composition all combine to make sense of these illusions and constraints.

Optical Illusions

We have spent enough time outdoors to know that grass is green and wheat fields are golden. We also know that one end of a railway line is the same width as the other. We can see that a new post and rail fence marking a field's boundary has been installed with precision by the farmer, each post equidistant from the next. Our experience tells us that there is a crisp definition to the edges of tree trunks and branches on the distant hillside. Across the valley is a farmhouse, recently painted white, in stark contrast to the black doors of the old barn next to it. We know all of this with a high degree of confidence. However, depending on our proximity to these things, or our viewpoint of them, our eyes are likely to tell us an entirely different story. These are optical illusions that we commonly refer to with the catch-all term of 'perspective'. Nothing has greater ability to glaze the eyes of workshop participants or destroy the atmosphere in painting demonstrations than mentioning the 'P' word. It is seen as a necessary evil in our quest for drawing accurately and achieving

realism in our artwork yet understanding its impact on the way we communicate our observations is vital. Without this understanding we make flat, unrealistic landscape paintings that convey no sense of depth, reinforcing, instead of remedying, the two-dimensional nature of our work.

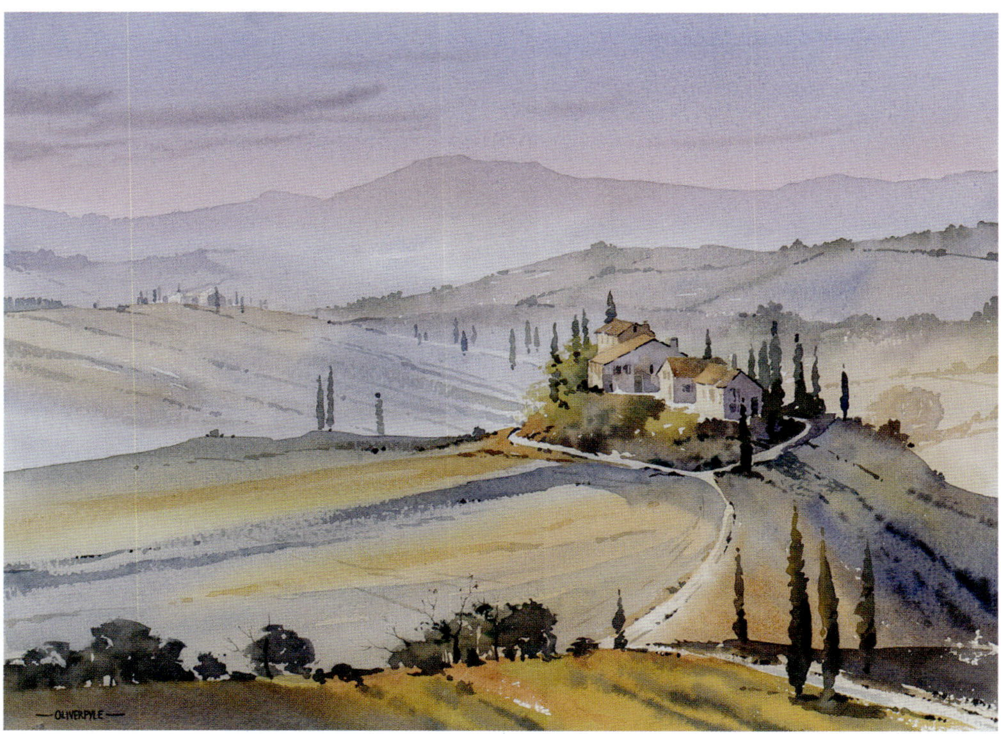

The Colours of Tuscany – 39cm x 29cm
The optical illusions of perspective are evident in this painting: narrowing paths, reduced detail in distant buildings and cypress trees, a tighter tonal range in the distance and a cooling of colour temperature from front to back. These all contribute to an illusion of three dimensions on a two dimensional surface.

The optical illusions that we refer to as perspective can be grouped into three variants: linear perspective, aerial perspective and chromatic perspective. Let's take a look at each of them in turn.

1) Linear Perspective

Return with me to the railway line – a well-travelled example. Despite our learned experience that both rails must remain parallel for the length of the line, watching it disappear into the distance it appears that both lines converge to a point. Roads, roof lines, fences, pathways – we see this phenomenon repeatedly in the landscape without giving it a second thought, yet the moment we put pencil to paper our logic and intuition takes over and we start to ignore what we observe. Many excellent resources exist to assist us with the technical aspects of linear perspective, providing a formulaic approach through the establishment of horizon lines and vanishing points and I can hear a collective sigh of relief as I tell you that it is not the purpose of the book to repeat this.

One element of linear perspective that is often overlooked, pushed aside by the more ubiquitous railway line example, is the reduction in space between vertical, equidistant objects and their diminishing size. I previously mentioned the post and rail fence for a reason: I often see fences painted, tailing off into the distance but with the same gap between each fence post. Accurate observation will show you that these reduce dramatically in size as they become more distant, as does the width and height of each post. The organised rendition of a fence never looks good in a landscape painting and should normally be avoided, but it looks even worse if the principles of linear perspective have not been correctly applied.

A Distinguished Guest, Corfe Castle –
72cm x 52cm
Linear perspective comes at you from every angle in this painting. Careful drawing is essential for a subject like this and tedious though it may seem, a credible sense of depth in the painting cannot be achieved without it.

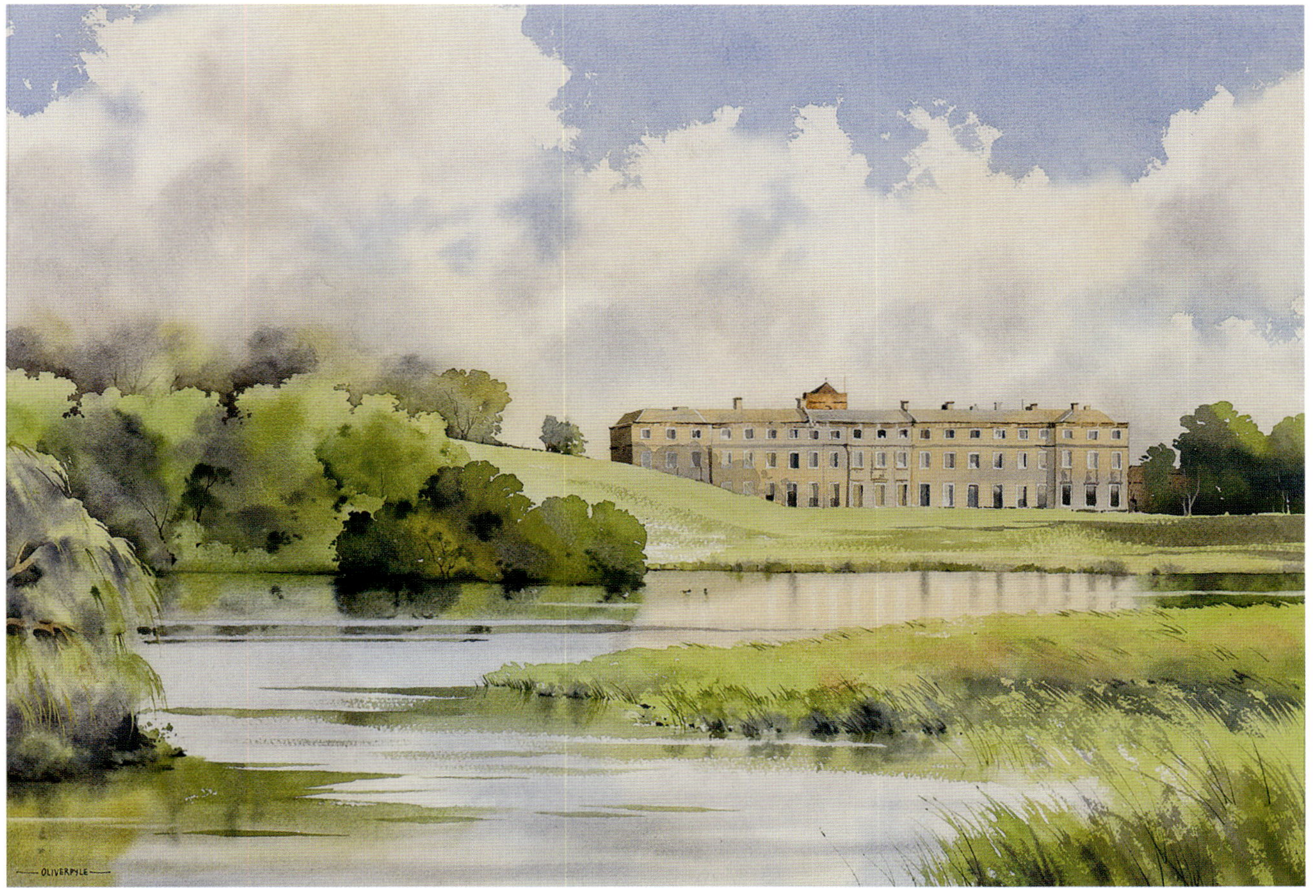

Bright Intervals, Petworth House – 50cm x 34cm
The treatment of the grass in this painting helps to create the illusion of depth in the painting. In the foreground, we see several blades painted individually, then moving closer to the house these are simply suggested in increasingly diminished broken brushstrokes, which conveys detail without explicitly rendering it.

In much of my work, straight lines and organised spaces are few and far between, often intentionally, however it does not mean that I can play fast and loose with the concepts of linear perspective. When I paint a foreground field or hedgerow, full of wildflowers and grasses it is important to move through the painting from front to back reducing the definition in the grass or the size of each head of cow parsley, for example. It may sound obvious and simple but you would be surprised at how many paintings I have seen where a little attention to detail in areas like this would have led to a more compelling painting, with a greater feeling of depth.

2) Aerial Perspective

There are other optical illusions that become more apparent the further away we are from objects in the landscape. I mentioned the tree branches with their hard edges, evident to us as we view them closely, wonderful subjects for paintings and excellent study subjects in their own right. Despite our knowledge of their composition and structure we find that the crisp definition that we see so closely becomes harder to see when we look at the same trees on a distant hillside. Instead of a mass of intricate branches, twigs and leaves, all we see is a simple, soft-edged shape. The effects of airborne particles between the viewer and a distant object renders them with far less definition and it is important that we capture this in our landscape painting. Of course, the temptation exists to include hard-edged detail since we know that it exists, but it isn't

Glorious Purbeck – 34cm x 50cm
Contrast the different treatment given to the trees in three areas of this painting. In the foreground we have detail showing on the trunk's bark, individual leaves and branches. The copse in the middle distance simply shows shapes and trunks, and in the distance, near the castle, they are just a soft smudge, painted wet-on-wet to suggest their presence. This phasing-out of detail throughout a scene is often overlooked, but is essential in creating a sense of depth and realism.

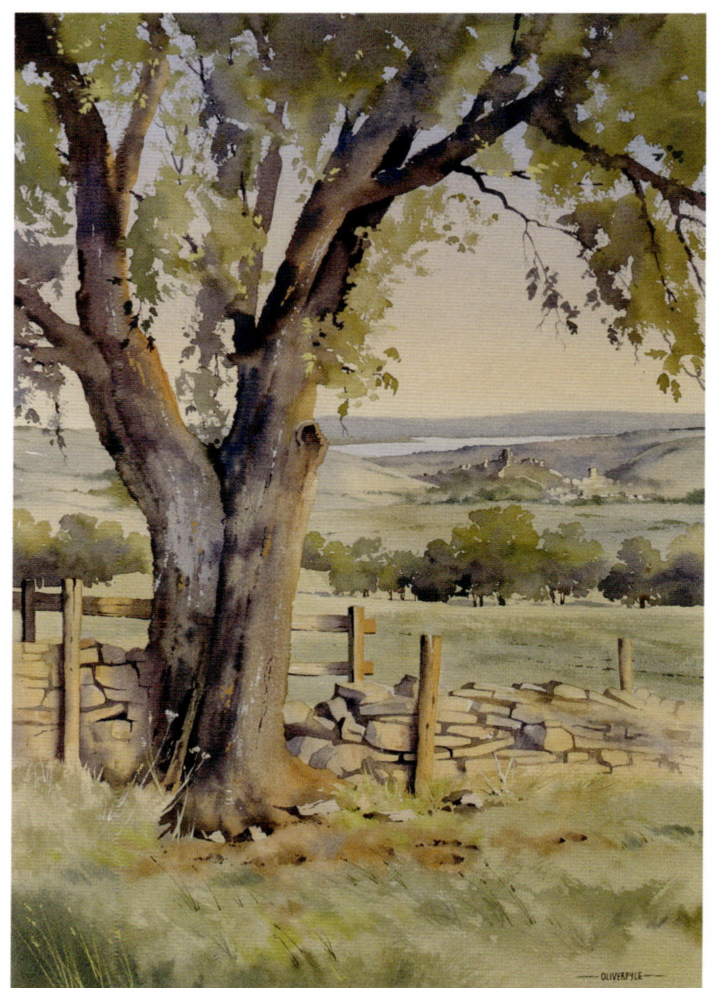

what we see and so we must resist this. Often the simplest mark with a brush, painted wet-on-wet can convey the reality of what we observe. The more we paint hard edges in distant areas, the more difficult it becomes to create the illusion of a third dimension, depth.

In a similar way, the further away that objects are, the less tonal contrast becomes apparent. Consider the white farmhouse and the black doors of the barn, that I mentioned previously – viewed closely, it is the strongest tonal contrast possible. When viewed from across the valley, it is essential that we forget this dynamic and simply record what we see: the white of the farmhouse will look darker while the black doors appear paler. The greater the space between us and distant landscape objects, the more compressed their tonal range becomes, often to the extent that the contrast becomes almost imperceptible. It is important that we observe this carefully and paint it accordingly.

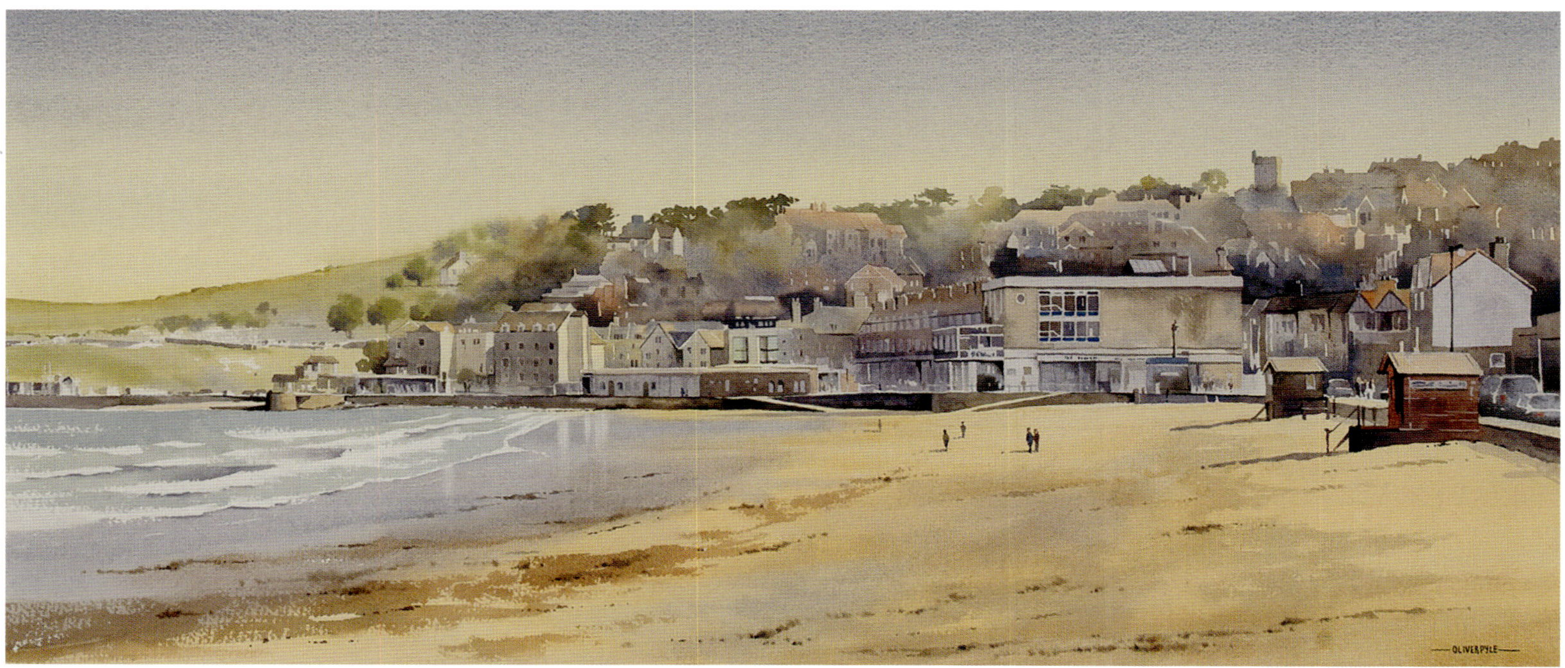

A Crisp Spring Day, Swanage – 72cm x 33cm
As the buildings move further away, up the hill, their tonal range becomes tighter – lights are not quite as bright, and darks have lightened up a little. In comparison with the more dramatic tonal range on the seafront, a sense of depth is created in the scene.

3) Chromatic Perspective

Grass is green and wheat fields are yellow, but seen from a distant viewpoint these colours tend to fade and almost disappear, being replaced by blue. As we know from listening well in our physics lessons, white light splits into rays of different colour, with blue being the shortest wavelength (well, violet actually). Blue light is released in a greater quantity though and our eyes find it easier to detect than violet, which is why the sky appears blue, its short wavelength being disrupted and scattered by atmospheric particles. The further away an object is, the greater the quantity of blue light there is to see between it and us. Distant grass becomes blue, distant wheat fields become blue; the problem is that we know this to be an illusion and it feels counter-intuitive to paint what we see, so we tend to paint what logic and experience tells us instead. In doing so, these distant areas in a painting suddenly jump forward, destroying any sense of depth to the painting.

This is the reason behind the commonly taught notion that cool colours (blues, greys, purples) should be kept in the background and as we move closer to the foreground, colours become warmer (yellows, oranges, reds). Observing this as a general principle helps to promote a three-dimensional feeling to our landscape painting, creating the illusion of space and depth. Of course, there are occasions where this doesn't always play out: a deep shadow falling across the foreground, while the sun picks out a distant headland for example.

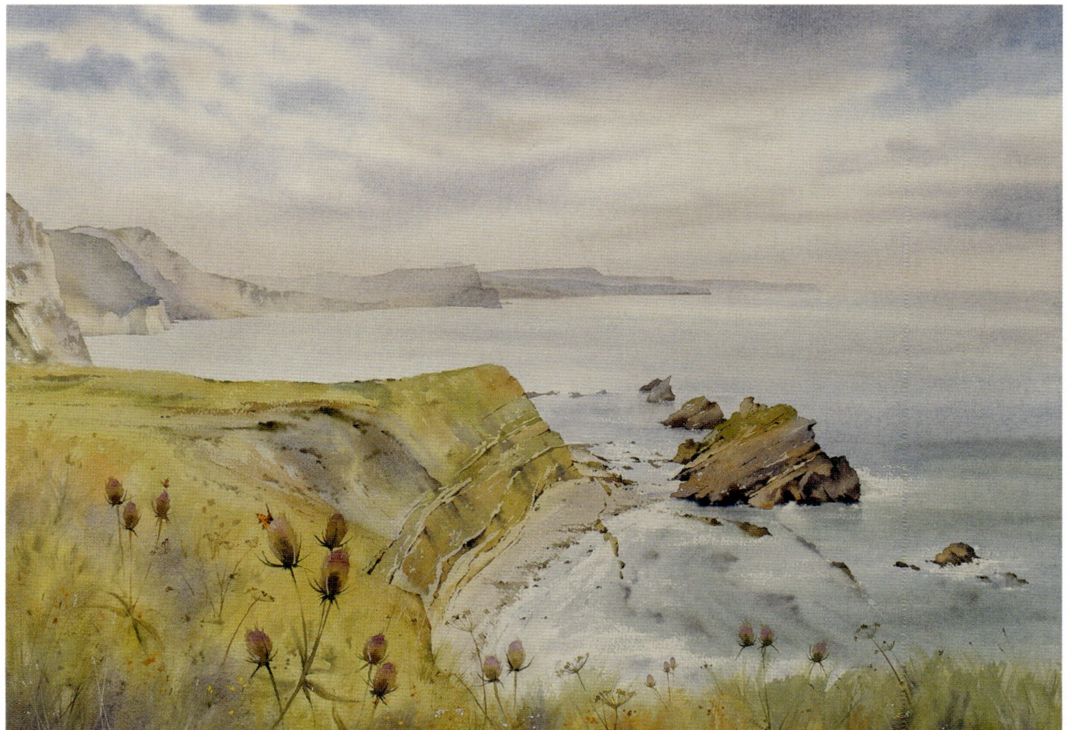

A Peaceful Afternoon, Mupe Bay –
72cm x 52cm
The warm colours of the foreground cliffs at Mupe Bay and Bacon Hole are to be found all the way along the coastline to St Aldhelm's Head in the distance. To paint them that way would be a mistake – chromatic perspective renders these areas progressively cooler as they recede into the distance, demanding a palette of greys and blues where yellows and greens exist in reality.

In addition to these three different iterations of perspective, the sense of depth within a painting is also promoted by the placement of overlapping elements. Two trees that are placed side by side on a two-dimensional plane give us very little clues that one may be closer than the

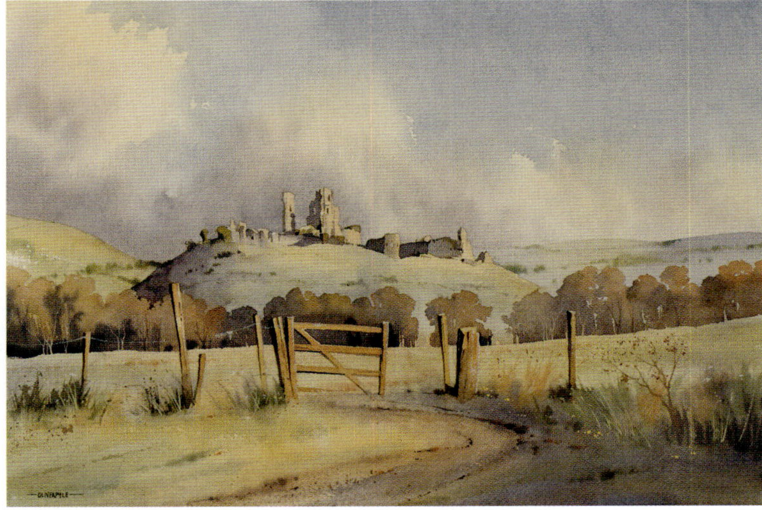

ABOVE: Autumnal Colours, Corfe Castle – 50cm x 34cm
I liked the combination of elements in this scene, but from my vantage point, the top of the fence posts fell below the trees at the foot of the castle mound. By taking a lower angle of view, the fence overlapped the trees which helped to push them and the castle further back.

RIGHT: Shadows and Arches – 34cm x 50cm
With little difference in the colour temperature from front to back, given the relative proximity of the different elements, overlapping the branches of the oak tree in front of the Ouse Valley Viaduct really helps to create an illusion of three dimensions.

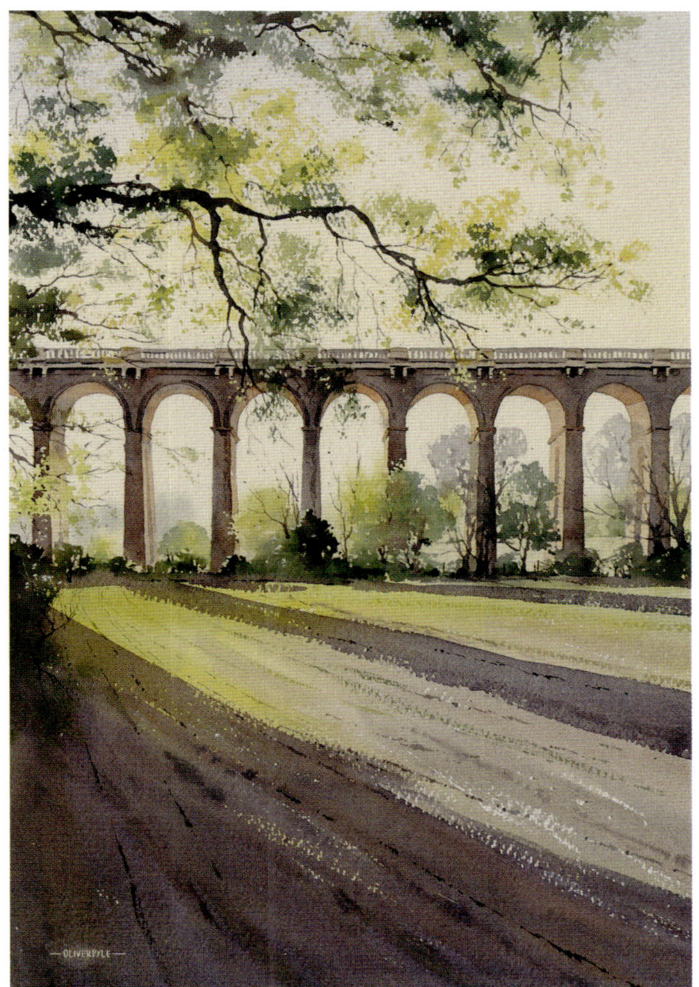

other. However, if the branches of one tree fall across the other tree, then we are able to perceive a sense of depth. Look for opportunities in your compositions where you can arrange some elements to overlap others and you will find that it works wonders in promoting the illusion of depth.

Spatial Constraint

Framing

As my experience as a landscape painter has developed, I have become increasingly engaged with the subject of composition, one of the most fundamental and early-taught artistic disciplines: what is the optimal arrangement of components within a landscape painting that will provide the viewer with the most satisfying aesthetic experience? This consideration is important and in the next section of the book we will take a closer look at some principles to help us improve the compositions in our landscape paintings; conversely, it may not necessarily be as important as we often consider it to be. For now though, let's take a step back and think about why composition is an issue in the first place, especially when you consider the extent to which this discipline is irrelevant once you are outdoors in the landscape, seeing the views for yourself. I don't think we would stop the car at a roadside vantage point in the countryside, step out to admire the view and immediately fill our minds with thoughts of the Golden Ratio, Rule of Thirds, sight lines, repeating shapes and focal points. We simply observe and enjoy the experience. Our heads and eyes move: left to right, up and down, close-focus, distant-

focus. We are not constrained by the imposition of boundaries to what can be seen. As we walk into a room with a beautiful view through the window beyond, we rarely stop in the centre of the room and satisfy ourselves with the small vignette that has been chosen for us by the window frame. No, we walk up to the window, peer around the frame and allow ourselves to take in a fuller, broader perspective.

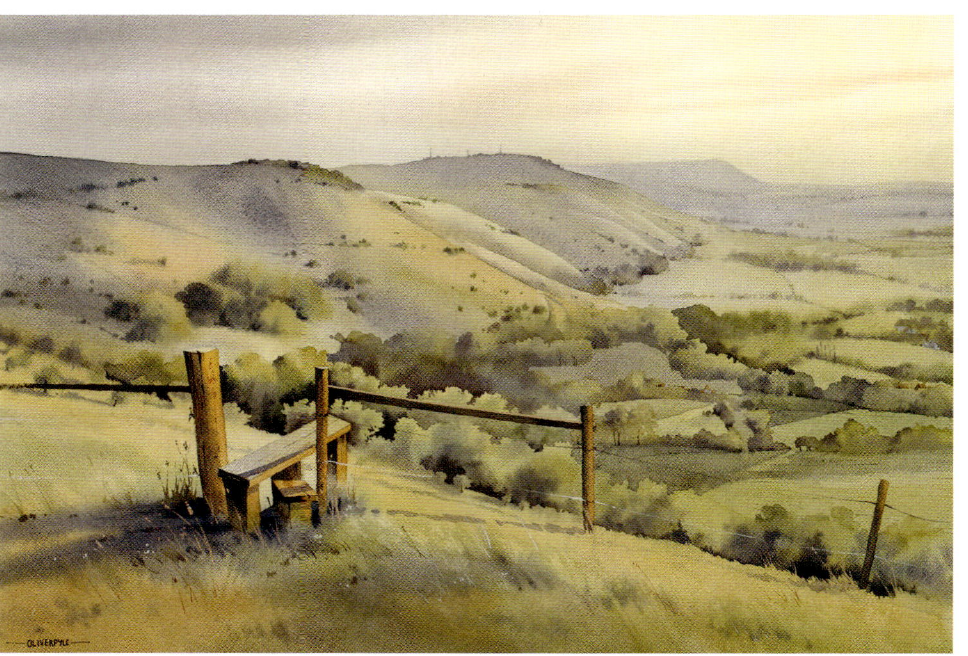

Soft Shadows at Fulking Escarpment – 50cm x 34cm
The views across Sussex from the South Downs are expansive and stunning. From this viewpoint at Devil's Dyke, there are expansive vistas across the Weald, but only so much can be included within the paper's boundary. It is the artist's job to edit visually and present what they want you to see.

As we move outdoors, there is no limit to what we can see (subject to natural obstructions and phenomena) but in the studio or on the gallery wall that freedom is repressed, coming in the form of a frame, a border, a mount and a matt. These artificial frontiers, absent when we are in the landscape, represent the ultimate challenge to even the most seasoned landscape painter. Unable to present a viewer with a full, immersive experience of being in the landscape, the artist's craft is to identify and select combinations of elements, angles of view and points of interest that communicate what initially inspired them to paint the scene. The skill of being able to provide this insight – creating the illusion of expansion within contraction – is the fulcrum on which a successful landscape painting career is balanced.

Focus

Imagine you are standing in the churchyard of St James's Church in Kingston, Dorset. In front of you are the overhanging branches of a beech tree. You look at them, observing the familiar shapes of the leaves and twigs, detailed and in crisp focus. Through the branches and in your peripheral vision are distant hills, roof tops, Poole Harbour, and the unmistakable presence of Corfe Castle. With your focus on the foreground branches, these distant elements are fuzzy and blurred, showing no detail. You allow your gaze to wander and suddenly you notice the red ridge tiles on the roof and the distant castle, the shapes of its ruins defined by the sunlight, even down to the windows on what remains of the old keep. In a role-reversal the detail of the beech tree's branches is now in your peripheral vision, rendered as little more than abstract lines and blobs across the detail of the background landscape. This is how our eyes work when we are outdoors; the laws of physics prevent us from being able to keep everything in focus all the time. However – and this is an important 'however' – as we return home and reflect on our time in the woodland we remember the leaves on the branches and we recall the impressive ruins of the distant castle. When

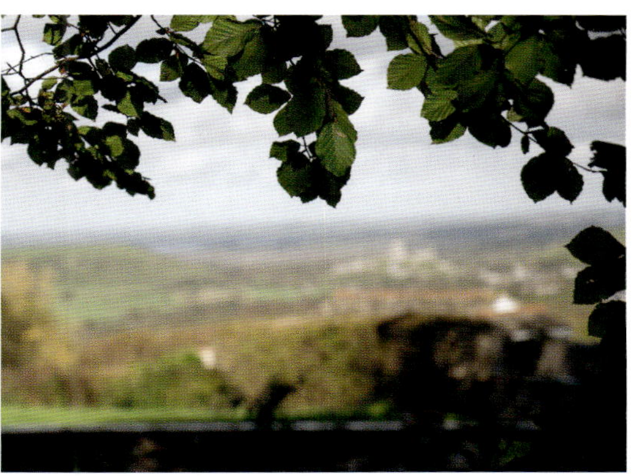

RIGHT: Focus on the overhanging tree renders the peripheral background as a collection of blurred shapes.

BELOW: Focussing on the distant castle has the reverse effect of rendering the nearby leaves as out-of-focus shapes.

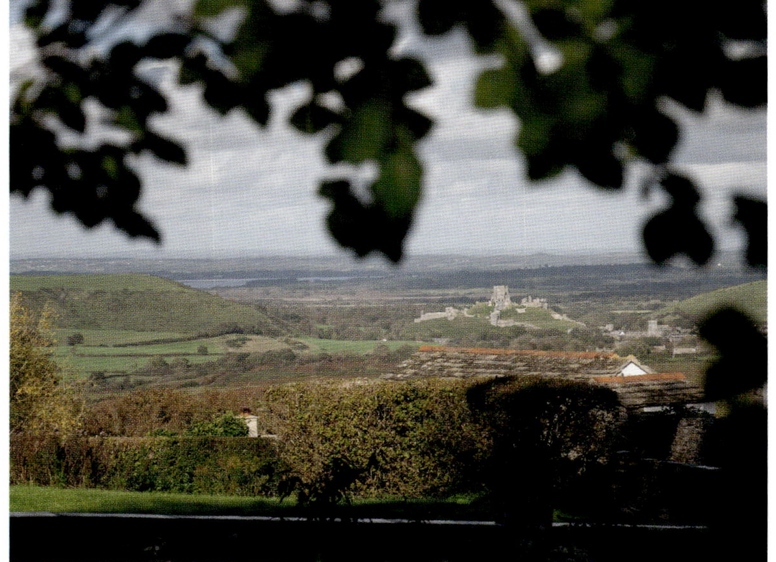

we are outdoors and engaged by our subject our eyes scan the landscape and we build up a lasting image with multiple focal points, a composite of each different view that we stopped to observe.

A traditional discipline in landscape photography is to ensure that as much of a photograph is in focus as possible, achieving crisp front-to-back detail in an expansive scene. With the realism that photography can present, this concept, called depth-of-field, is a way of capturing and presenting the way that we would have viewed the scene had we been there ourselves, as our eyes moved around the scene, building up and recording a composite picture of everything we observed. As landscape painters, our finished work will always have a greater degree of abstraction than a photograph, no matter how hyper-realistic our style may be; we simply cannot record the level of detail that is possible with a pin-sharp camera lens and a small aperture. We need to make decisions that communicate our vision of a place and what we want our viewers to experience, so the careful identification of a focal point is essential. A painting that inevitably lacks the high detail available in reality or a photograph starts to look rather unusual when the limited detail that we paint is evenly distributed throughout the scene. Pick the focal point that communicates the story you are trying to tell and concentrate your detail around that point in the painting; our inability to present what

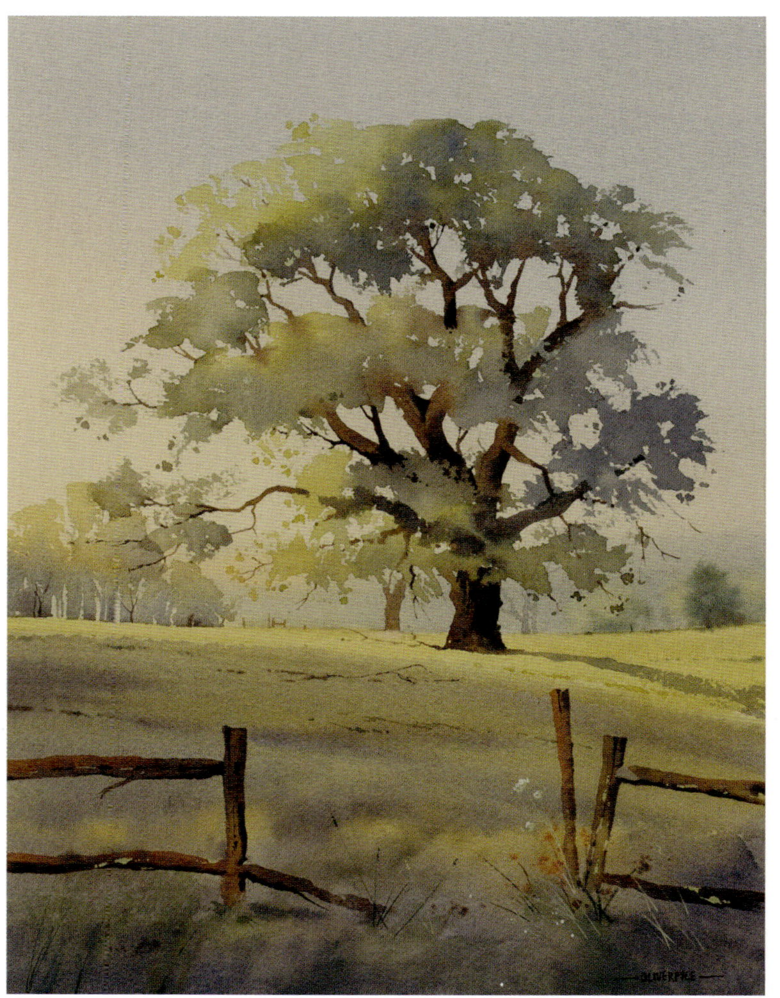

Sussex Oak – 29cm x 39cm
This is one of my favourite trees, just a short walk from home. It stands impressively alone in the field with a woodland backdrop. A chestnut post-and-rail fence runs in front of it, creating a barrier to the eye if it were to be included in the painting. My idea of 'landscape looking' is to see scenes and situations as potential paintings, and consider what needs to be done to communicate the place and moment in a way that will resonate with those that see the painting. Here, it's a case of breaking down the fence to allow the eye to move into the scene, playing down the distant woodland and allowing the focal point, this gracious old oak tree, to take centre stage.

we witnessed on location – a broad, detailed experience without spatial constraints – requires us to adopt this approach.

As our outdoor observation skills improve, we begin to realise the extent of our challenge in presenting an expansive three-dimensional space, while reducing it to the constraints of a two-dimensional image. This understanding is critical if we are to develop techniques and methods that will enable us to meet and overcome the challenge. Carefully observing the optical illusions that the laws of nature and physics present and being aware of the limitations and demands of spatial constraint, we start to train ourselves to make a thoughtful analysis of the scene in front of us; we develop the skill

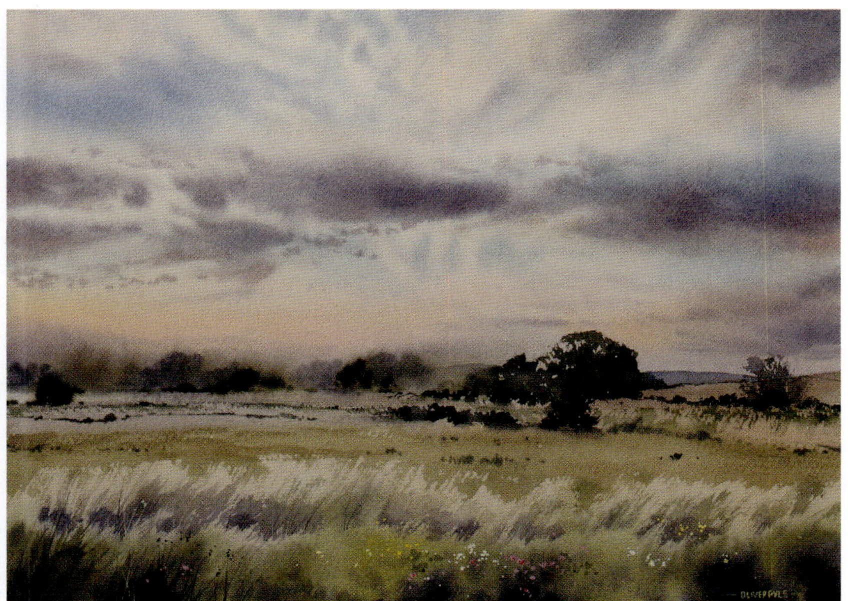

Last Light, Amberley – 39cm x 29cm

of landscape-looking. In this trip to Abbotsbury, I want to introduce some counter-balance to this, a little thought provocation, if you will.

Views of Abbotsbury

Overcoming and working with the limitations of spatial constraint has turned my eyes to rectangles; wandering through the landscape I must now remind myself to see the views, not just the pictures. The impediment of restricted viewing leads me, and indeed many other landscape painters, to search out subjects that have single points of interest or detail: country stiles, significant trees, boats, dry-stone walls, flowers, animals, geological forms, church spires, country lanes, fence posts. They provide visual anchor points and help nullify the natural tendency for our eyes to want more and roam across the landscape. For that reason and despite its obvious beauty, I tend to shy away from painting scenes like this magnificent view at Abbotsbury in Dorset (overleaf). It is a scene where there is no apparent subject or focal point, rather a cast of contenders: the village itself, the English Channel, Chesil Beach, The Fleet, Portland in the distance. With a view this striking, none of these elements carry enough significance to be the subject of the painting; the view is the subject. Being unable to present such a vista in all its spectacular dimensions and details and ultimately working within a boundary, the voice suggesting that you will never do it justice is hard to ignore. In essence we are trying to beat the landscape at its own game, a daunting challenge to even the most capable landscape painter. The challenge, however, must be accepted.

This view takes the eye across foreground fields, through trees to the village. Beyond, rolling hills, fields, hedges and farms blend into an undulating carpet of soft shapes, muted colours and gentle tones. Portland, the wedge-shaped promontory in the distance, sits on the

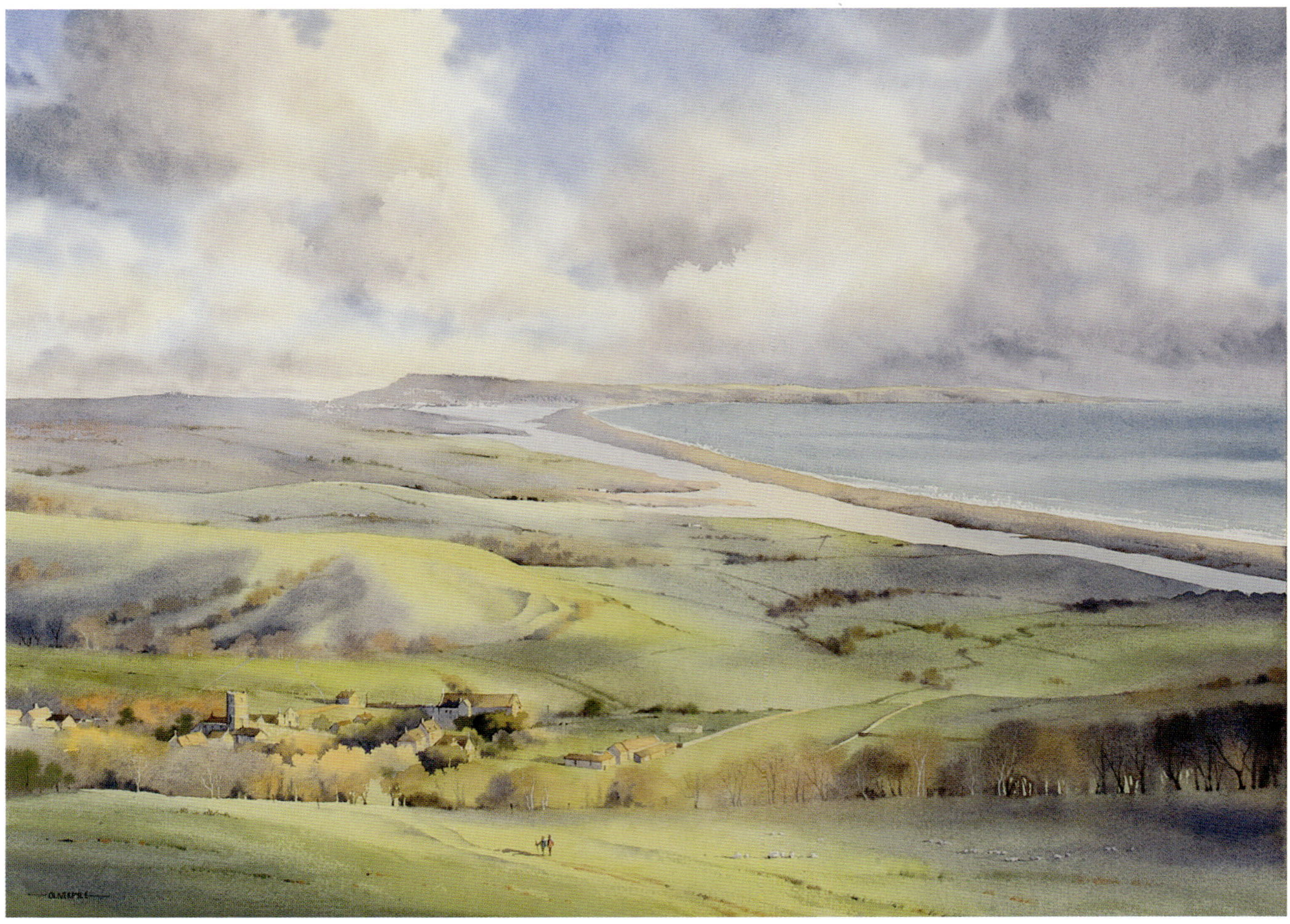

'Simply Stunning!' – Coastal Views from Abbotsbury – 72cm x 52cm

horizon. It would be a wonderful scene as it is, but its proximity to the coast and the inescapable presence of Chesil Beach, a tremendous shingle bank that stretches 16 miles from Portland to West Bay, creates a landscape view that is truly spectacular, undeserving of framed limitations. To capture its scope and impact, attempting to present the sweeping view from the hillside, it seemed to me that an equal treatment of all the elements – land, sea, sky, trees, village – would be important. In the painting, despite the village being rendered in more detail, I have tried to ensure that all the elements have equal prominence and combine to define the subject – the view. It is difficult to achieve; often the inability to limit detail to a specific focal point leads to everything becoming over-complicated. This painting was a constant struggle against my proclivity for painting detail – ultimately it is for you to judge if that struggle has been successful. In the painting I have employed a few compositional techniques that help to capture a sense of both time and place. Painting on a full sheet (76cm x 56cm) immediately enhances the sense of space – big view, big painting. The walkers provide a sense of scale to the foreground area and as they walk away from us, taking in the view, we are encouraged to do the same. The dark shadows across fields and trees on the right hand side, together with the heavy clouds, help us to move our eye through the scene and towards the light, moving along the strong diagonal line of Chesil Beach. The energetic sky provides a nice balance to the dynamic nature of the landscape beneath.

The quickest of sketches allows me to focus on the main components of the view and their relationship to each other, mapping out some simple compositional ideas. With the car parked on the B3157 and a stunning view unfolding beneath my vantage point on Abbotsbury Hill, my reluctance to engage with thoughts of composition is strong; this is the landscape painter's challenge – compositional considerations are important, but this process of selective looking and editing is never a substitute for the overwhelming, unrestrained reality of the landscape that you are in. Often, my urge is to simply paint my immediate impression without any thought for framing and format. Is this a more honest and visceral approach to landscape painting? We will explore this idea in a little more depth in the section on Composition.

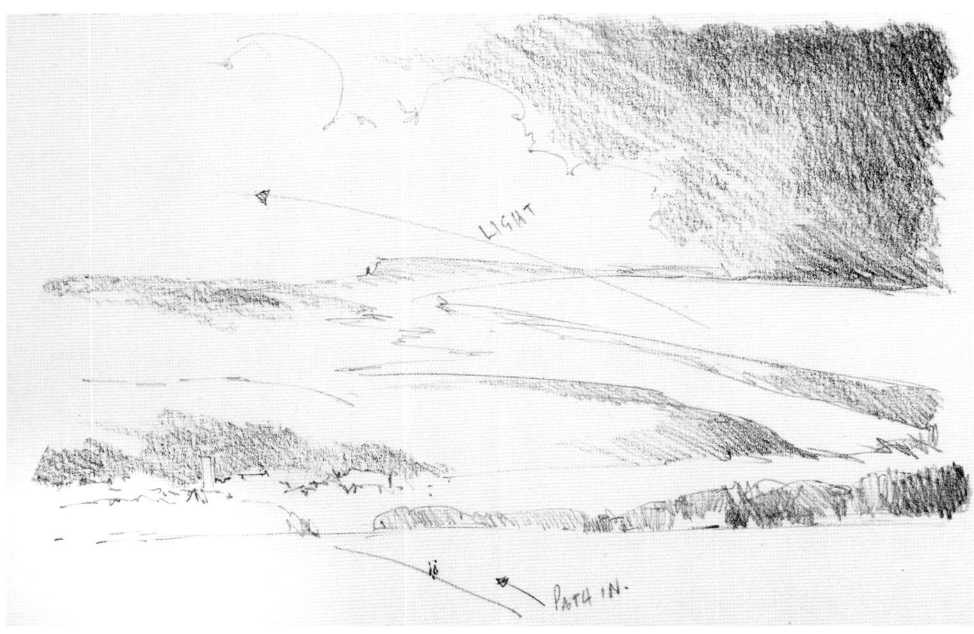

Observation, planning and a quick sketch often help to resolve compositional issues.

UNDERSTANDING THE PRINCIPLES

While it is essential that you are inspired by your subject — and all good landscape painters are — inspiration alone will not elevate your work to a place on the gallery wall and more is required than simply understanding the challenges laid out in the previous section, vital as they are to our progression in the genre of landscape art. Over the years, I have organised my technical observations and thoughts into three main principles, pillars if you like, that provide structure and competence to my work; an awareness of, and ability to practice these concepts will help your work to become dynamic and impactful. The three principles are Colour, Contrast and Composition and I will unpack each one in turn. By understanding their impact in a successful painting, you will

Evening Light, Portland Bill – 50cm x 34cm
This painting – a favourite of mine – relies on the three principles of colour, contrast and composition to deliver impact. The soft muted colour palette, including the duck-egg hue of the beach hut shutters, sits well alongside the splash of red on the lighthouse. The strong tonal contrast between the sky and beach hut adds a soft glow to the light. The strong inverted L-shape formed by the boat and beach hut creates a pleasing composition.

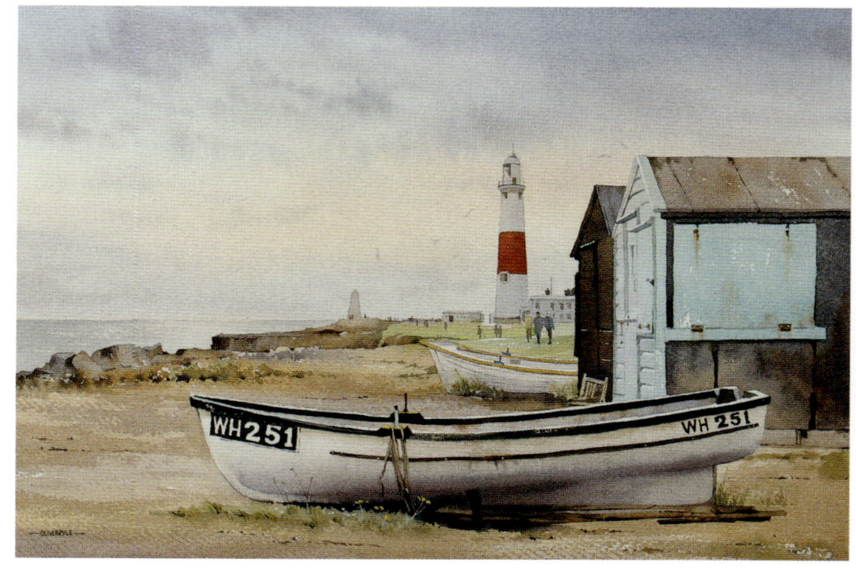

be able to use these considerations as design tools when you approach and assess new subjects, ideas and inspiration for your work.

The ability to create landscape paintings that convey a sense of time and place doesn't happen by accident. Whether your technique is hyper-realistic, impressionistic or abstract, there is a range of ideas and disciplines that can be practiced and deployed to ensure that the landscape that inspired you is captured dynamically and has an impact on the viewer. To many, the ability to make good art is shrouded in mystery as if there is an elusive, transcendent quality, or set of skills that you either have, or you don't. There may be a small element of that, but I am of the firm belief that if something can be observed and practised – and landscape painting certainly can – then anyone can be successful at it, in varying degrees. You will have experienced, for we all have, the feeling of being inspired to paint a scene that looks dynamic and has impact, yet you seem unable to capture it as your initial vision becomes lost in a blur of technical inadequacies. I hear regularly from people saying that they're uninspired and don't know what to paint. More often than not, they do know what to paint and have found a subject that inspires them;

what they really mean is 'I've found a subject that inspires me, but I don't have the technical skills to be able to paint it.' It is much easier to feign a lack of inspiration, than admit to technical shortcomings, and is something that we are all guilty of. Gain familiarity with the Three Cs: Colour, Contrast and Composition – put the ideas into practice and I am sure that you will see a dramatic improvement in your landscape painting, with a far broader range of subjects that you feel capable of attempting.

At this point in the book I can hear one or two of you muttering "Just show me what brushes I need to use, what colours to mix and some

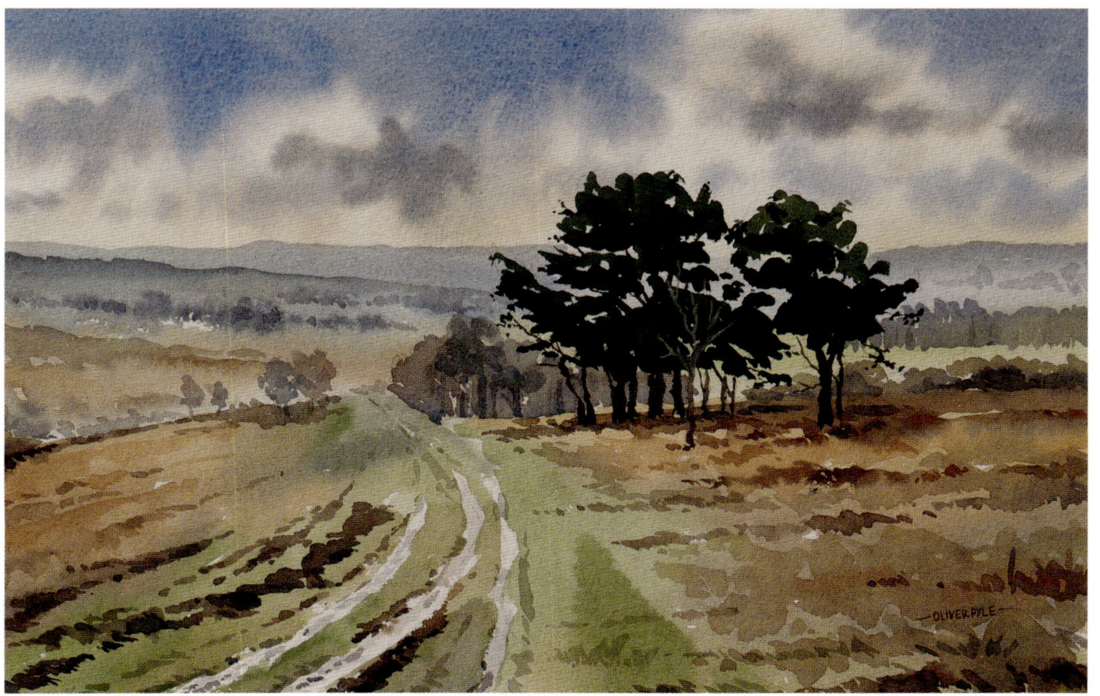

Southern Slopes, Ashdown Forest –
39cm x 29cm
An early attempt to get the better of the watercolour medium, and not a successful one. Lack of experience and practice is evident: clumsy brushstrokes, weak composition, lack of colour subtlety. Much to learn. Much to practice.

paint-along exercises so we can use your working methods and we'll be up and running in no time." Tempting as it may seem, this will not yield the results that you are hoping for, and it is why I resist this style of teaching. While I understand the thirst for immediate results in today's instant society, lasting success as a landscape painter can only come with time as you take your existing knowledge and build on that with solid principles that allow you to develop your own style and techniques. When I post paintings with tips and techniques on my social media accounts, I am regularly asked if I have a video or step-by-step guide for how to paint that specific painting. Of course, the answer is 'no.' A landscape painting is neither a set of Lego nor a steak pie – each painting does not come with its own set of instructions, nor a recipe. Teaching underlying skills and concepts that can be used in the widest set of circumstances is my preferred teaching method and understanding the importance of Colour, Contrast and Composition will help you to progress significantly with your work, far more than any follow-me guides will.

The recent proliferation of online watercolour tuition, social media or subscription-based, has provided easy access to a few of the technical skills required for landscape and watercolour painting, but unfortunately for many it has proved to be more hinderance than help. Students, unwittingly, become drawn into following their favourite tutors, many of whom offer immersive paint-along tutorials and quickly start to demonstrate some competence in their work. Their technical proficiency improves (brushstrokes, colour mixing, wash control) however most of the heavy-weight artistic decisions, the most important considerations (composition, format, colour palette, atmosphere, story-telling, focal point) have already been determined by the tutor. I have received communication from many

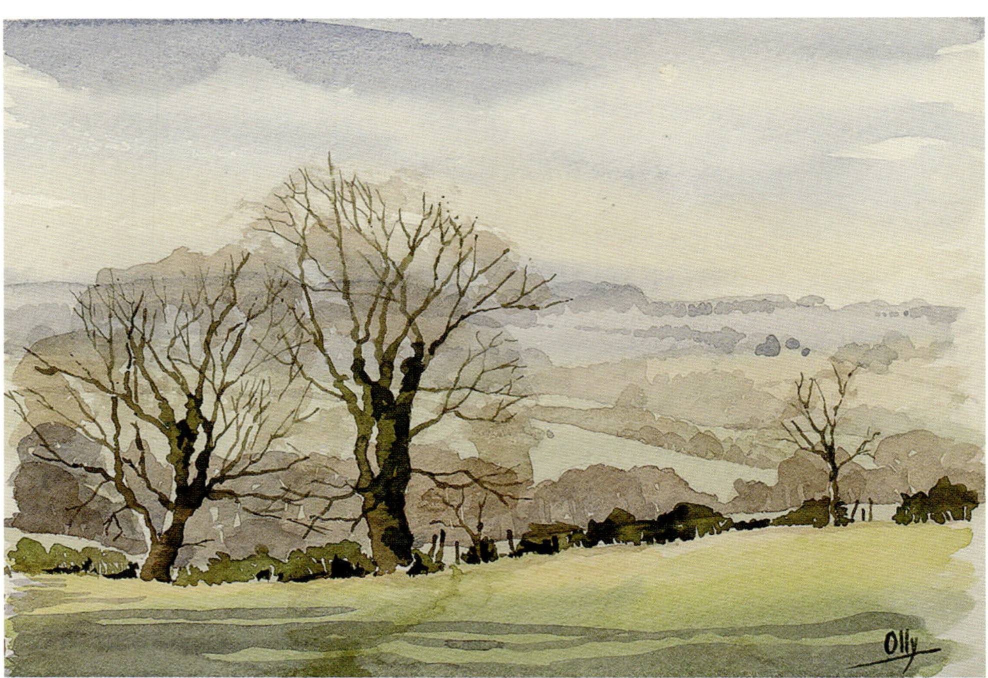

Winter Oaks near Burwash – 35cm x 25cm
One of my first attempts at painting on location, several years after I started to paint in watercolour. There is much to improve on, and the brushstrokes have a certain naivety to them, but despite that, I have a lot of fondness for this little painting; it has a sense of spontaneity and a charm that captures the moment. I remember having to make several decisions about what to include and what needed to be simplified, far more so than working from a photo or following a tutorial, and it quickly dawned on me that I was engaged in a creative hobby, more than a technical one.

beginner and intermediate painters who are unable to understand why the paintings they make under tuition seem to be so good, yet when they must confront an unfamiliar landscape on their own it feels as though they are picking up their brushes for the first time. What has happened is that the skills they have developed are as illustrators, copying the artistic capabilities of more experienced painters; to that point their development is more technical than artistic. Some argue that it is important to develop the technical skills first before becoming too concerned about the artistic side, however I contend that one cannot, indeed should not, come without the other; I see too much work and correspondence from developing artists that have lost their way to be able to recommend anything different.

Take time to understand this section carefully and you will have started to take the most significant steps to becoming a successful landscape painter, not a copyist or illustrator. Learning to paint your way, not my way, is one of the most important tips I can give you. Later on in the book I will provide you with an insight into my working methods, the structure and analysis that I use each time I paint a new work; this may help you in developing your own skills and methodologies, but for now let's take a dive into the Three Cs: Colour, Contrast and Composition.

COLOUR

The online gallery on my website details the titles that I have given to each of my paintings. A quick browse through it will reveal repeated use of the following words: warm, light, evening, dawn. Many of my paintings reflect what is known as the Golden Hour at each end of the day – the hour after sunrise and the hour before sunset, much-loved by photographers hunting dramatic and often elusive lighting conditions as the sun clings to the horizon. These are the times that I love to be in the landscape, as the sun floods coast, countryside and city with golden light, setting warm highlights against cool shadows, with subtle colour gradations and bright accents falling somewhere in-between. My approach to landscape painting differs significantly to most of my contemporaries who place tonal value – the interplay of lights and darks – at a level of greater importance than colour. Tonal contrast is an essential element of watercolour painting and we will look at this in the section on Contrast, but my experience of the landscape, my enthusiasm for painting it and my evangelical approach to sharing it is all about colour. It is for this reason that I rarely paint *contre-jour* scenes (into the light) frequently painted by watercolourists where colour is often bleached out, rendering the scene as a combination of desaturated tonal shapes. I admire such paintings and enjoy looking at them, but it is not how I usually see the landscape at the times I prefer to be in it; for my work to have any sense of integrity it is important that my work represents my feelings and engagement with the places and moments that I attempt to convey. I receive kind messages from followers and students, mentioning that when they see a new painting that I have posted, they know immediately that it is one of mine; I believe that the reason for this is the preeminence that I give to colour.

It has been said that watercolour is at its best when it doesn't shout, but whispers. Some of the thinking behind this relates to the medium's transparent nature, allowing the white paper to shine through fluid washes put down skilfully by the artist. As a result, the colours are often softer, more muted and diffused than is the case with opaque media such as oils. For many subjects, in particular British landscapes, this is a benefit that you can harness to your advantage. The cool northern light we have for most of the year renders much of what we see as subtle, muted tints and watercolour is an ideal medium for communicating a more delicate expression of colour. This is no excuse to paint washed-out landscapes where you have not used enough pigment in your washes but try to take advantage of watercolour's whispering qualities. If you want to plaster your watercolour onto the paper in dry, concentrated passages, then by

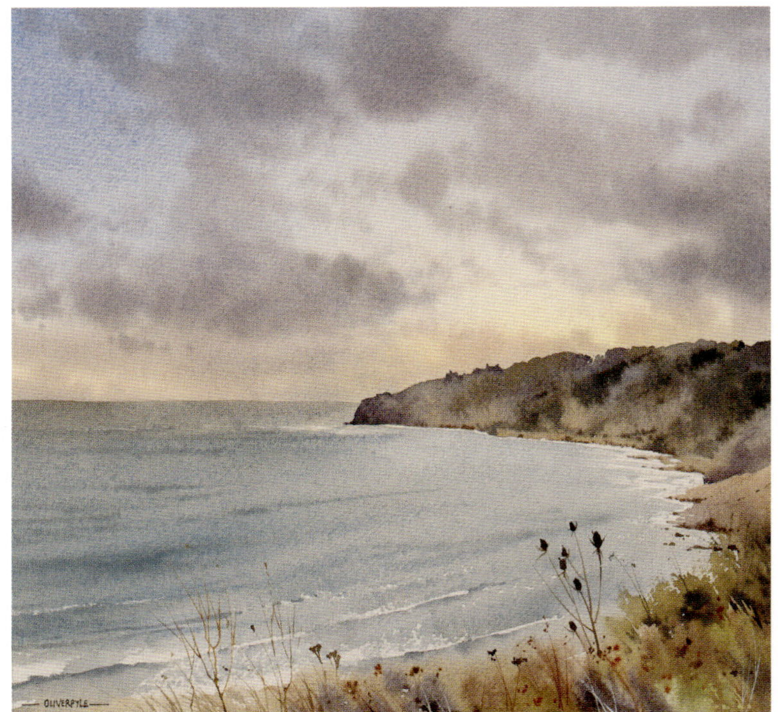

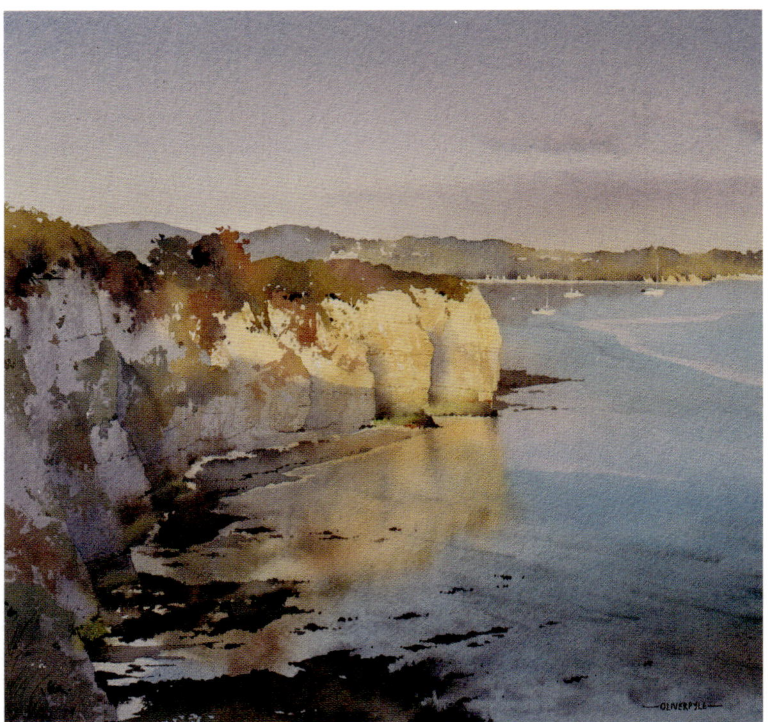

ABOVE LEFT: The Showers Passed, Durlston Bay – 30cm x 30cm
In this *contre-jour* scene, the colours in the headland, and foreground wildflowers are dark and muted.

ABOVE RIGHT: First Light at Handfast Point – 30cm x 30cm
By contrast, the strong directional light, just after dawn, floods the cliff face with warm saturated hues.

OPPOSITE: A Calm Evening at Kimmeridge – 50cm x 34cm
The hazy *contre-jour* light in this painting helps to create an atmosphere that works so well in a watercolour painting: soft, restrained colours, increasing in their tonal intensity as we move from background to foreground.

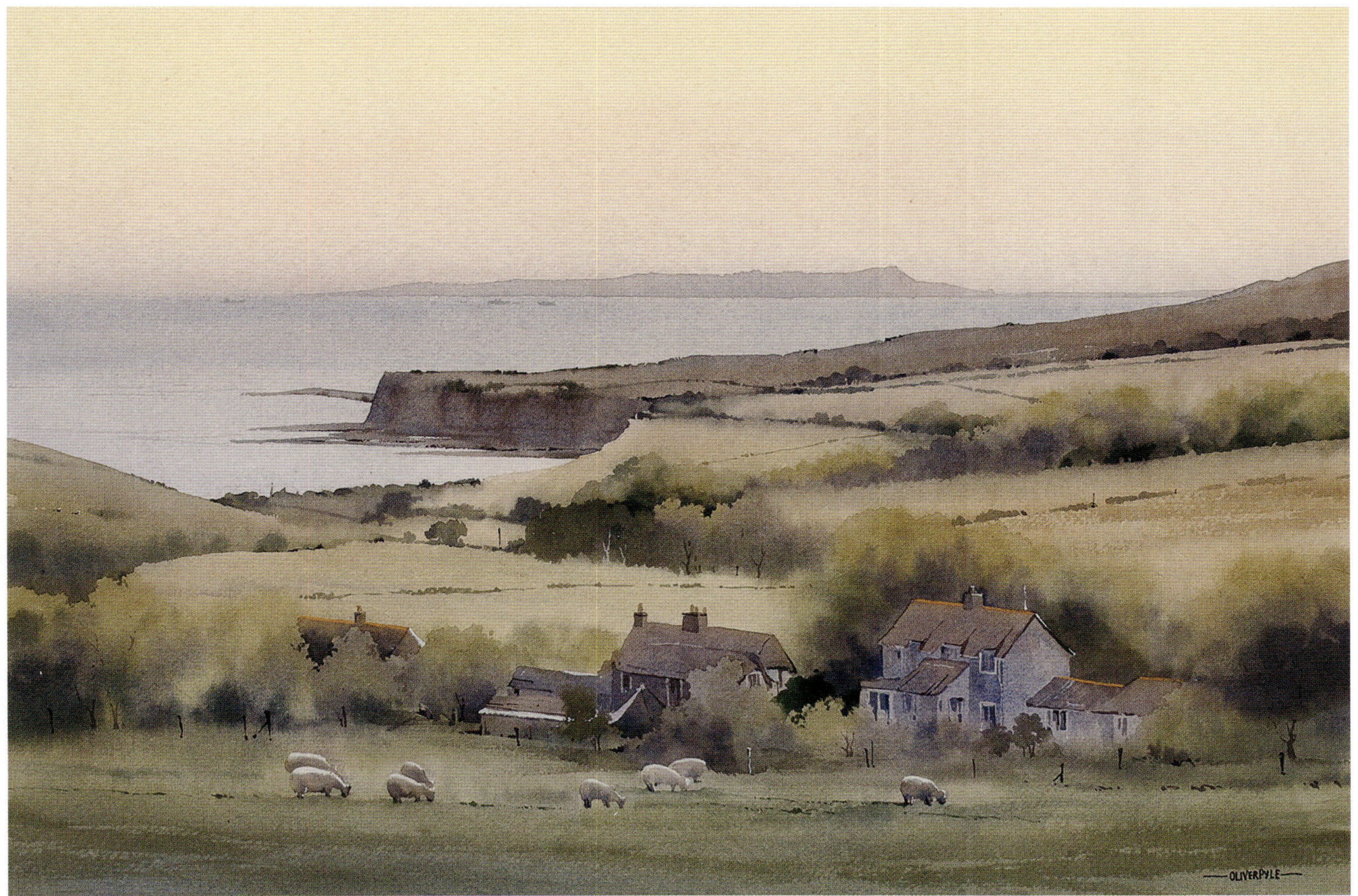

all means do so, but you will be better served by more opaque media and will not be using the medium to its best advantages – the transparency and luminosity that allow you to capture subtle, blended colour variations.

Understanding the significance of colour in the scene you are painting and how this is affected by direct and ambient light is important in communicating the sense of the place you are trying to convey. The following skills and observations will help you to improve your approach to using colour with impact and the light touch that the watercolour medium delivers so well:

• **Become familiar with your three primaries.** A landscape painter does not need to rely on an extensive palette of different pre-mixed colours. Unlike botanical art for example, the range of colours required for landscape painting is far more limited, being predominantly blue, green and a range of greys and browns. With the odd exception, almost every colour that I need can be mixed from my three primary colours – red, yellow and blue (French Ultramarine, Raw Sienna and Cadmium Red). I tend to use a warm and cool version of each primary and use them depending on the weather, season and atmosphere that I am trying to capture. Over 85 per cent of all my works are painted by mixing using just three colours. By keeping the palette limited and mixing the variety of hues that I need from the primaries, a painting hangs together with a far greater sense of unity than using individual pre-mixed colours that have little underlying correlation to each other. There is no hard and fast rule as to what those primaries should be, and every artist has an individual preference that helps to create their signature look, often being informed by the locations, times of day and lighting conditions that they prefer to paint. The trick is to find the combinations of primary colours that work best for you and practice your colour mixing on spare sheets of paper until you become familiar with the amazing variety of hues that you can create. There are no short-cuts; no one

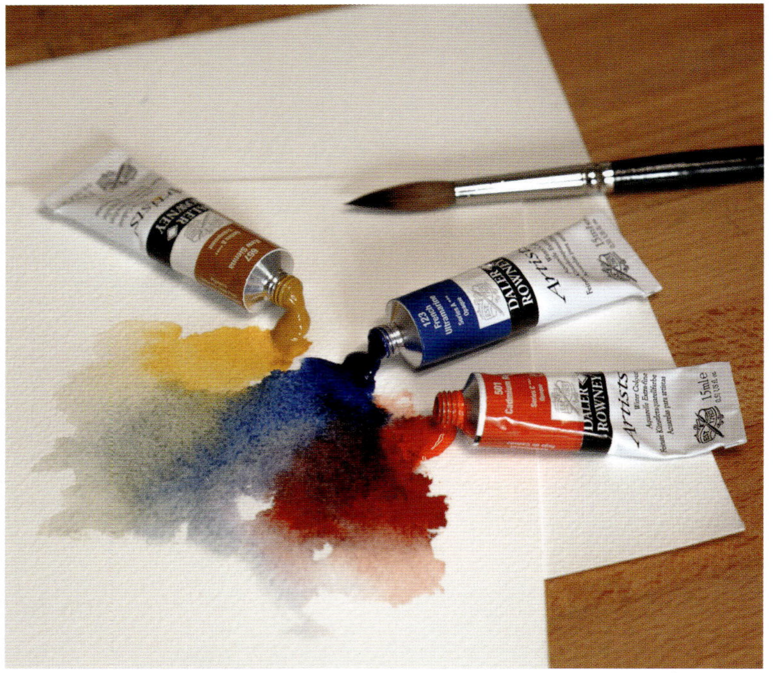

With practice, a limited palette of three primary colours is enough to mix an endless variety of different hues.

can do this for you. Students often ask me to provide a downloadable file of the colour mixing swatches that I demonstrate for them to use in their work. I resist this – the importance of observing from your own experimentation cannot be overstated and it is the most reliable way of consolidating knowledge and becoming familiar with your colour palette. It may not be the quickest, but you will learn at a deeper level. In addition to my primaries, I also like to include a few

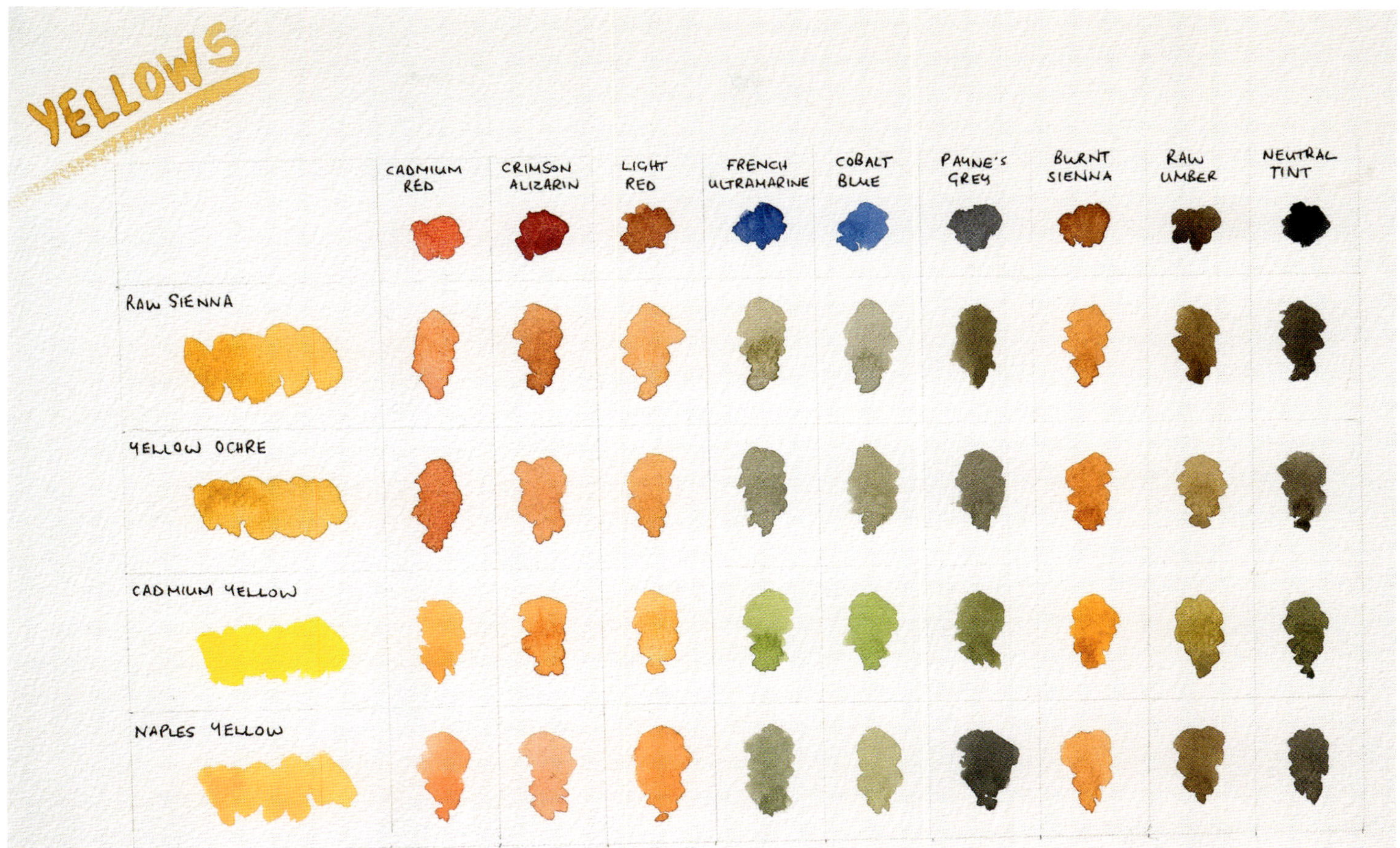

ABOVE AND OVERLEAF SPREAD: Making swatches will help you to understand the range of colour mixes that can be achieved from just a few well-chosen pigments. While these exercises are helpful for gaining familiarity with your palette, try not to use them to match every hue in your subject and painting, and aim to build up a more instinctive approach, through practice.

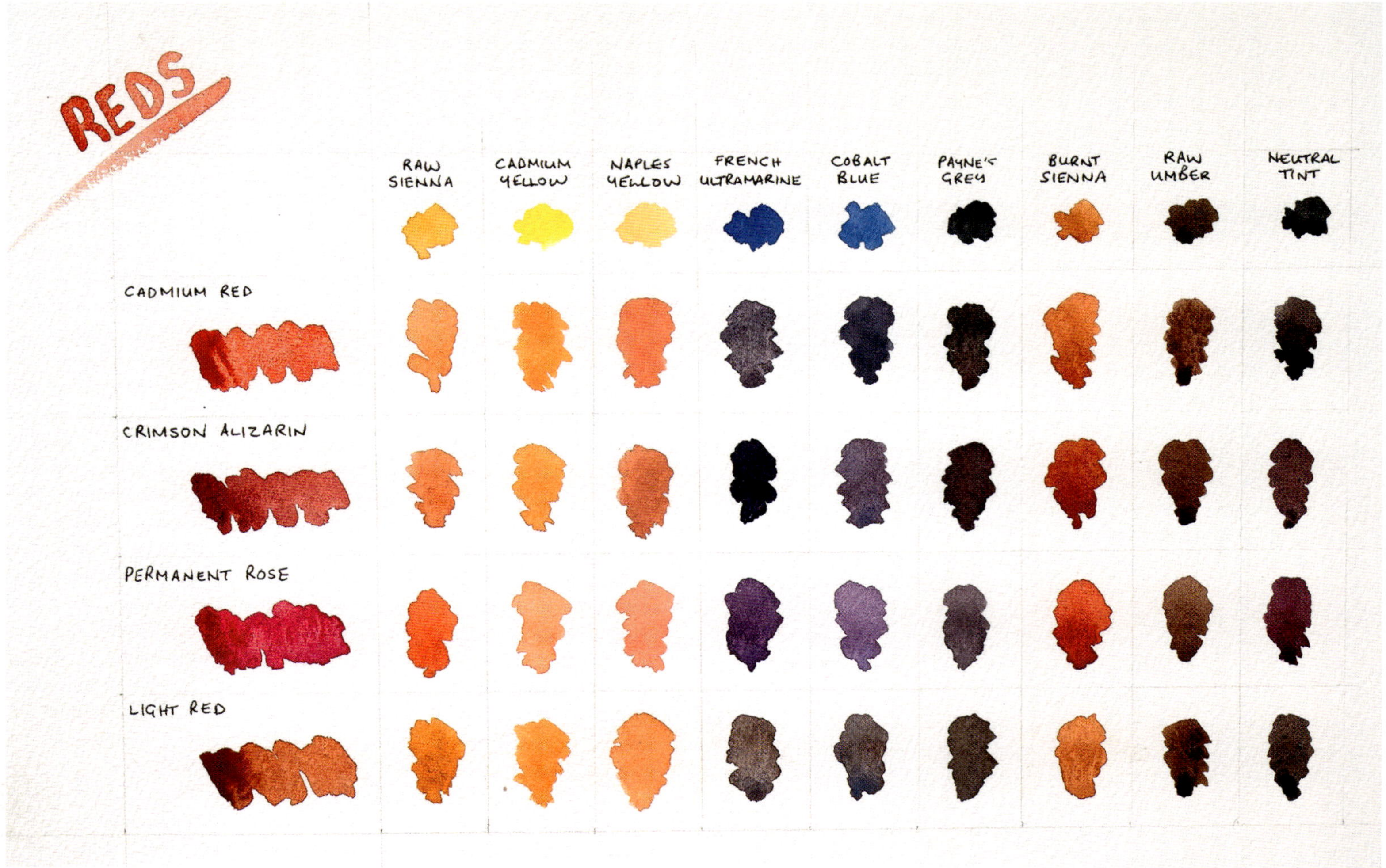
REDS
RAW SIENNA
CADMIUM YELLOW
NAPLES YELLOW
FRENCH ULTRAMARINE
COBALT BLUE
PAYNE'S GREY
BURNT SIENNA
RAW UMBER
NEUTRAL TINT
CADMIUM RED
CRIMSON ALIZARIN
PERMANENT ROSE
LIGHT RED

BLUES

	RAW SIENNA	CADMIUM YELLOW	NAPLES YELLOW	CADMIUM RED	CRIMSON ALIZARIN	LIGHT RED	BURNT SIENNA	RAW UMBER	NEUTRAL TINT
FRENCH ULTRAMARINE.									
COBALT BLUE.									
COERULEUM.									
PAYNE'S GREY.									

earth colours – siennas, umbers, ochres – and one or two local colours that fill the gaps that my primaries struggle to achieve accurately (bluebells and heather in particular). 'At Dawn on the Knoll Beach' (page 111) is a good example of the benefits of painting in just three colours (for 98 per cent of the painting). Despite there being a variety of different hues, their origin being the same three primary colours helps to promote a unified and calm appearance to the painting. If this was painted using different pigments for every subtle change in hue, the painting would have an unsettling, staccato feel to it that would spoil the atmosphere of a peaceful morning.

- **Strengthen and weaken your colours appropriately.** Try to make sure that the strength of your washes (the amount of pigment to water) is appropriate for what you are painting. Being a transparent medium, watercolour works well when background and lighter passages are rendered first, building up stronger tones of colour as you move from background to foreground, and from start to finish. Adopting this holistic approach to building up your paintings and your application of colour will produce a greater sense and unity, whereas a more fragmented approach of painting isolated areas with strong colours being deployed at an early stage can lead to confused results (the beautiful paintings of John Yardley being a notable exception to this). Before you pick up any brushes, take time to assess the scene that you are painting, making a note of where the hues are strong, catching your eye immediately, requiring a more concentrated application of paint. Work back from that to the areas of the landscape where the hues are paler, more diffused and subtle. They won't immediately catch the eye, and don't expect these areas just to be in the background, but as you take time to observe carefully you will start to notice pleasing and delicate arrangements of hues that will provide the backbone to your painting and will provide the stage for more vibrant accents. This is where my paintings start, with large initial washes, often painted wet-on-wet,

blended together to establish a combination of delicate colours, from where I can build up more concentrated and vibrant hues later in the painting. Students that are used to making studies in monochrome in order to establish a painting's tonal values (a sound idea) often find it difficult to then apply the appropriate strength of colour to those tones; it is a conundrum that I am often asked about. There is a technical solution to this, where swatches of each colour from the lightest to darkest tones are made for reference purposes, however I have never used these and don't recommend them. They tend to diminish the spontaneous approach to painting in watercolour that is so important. There's no silver bullet for this I'm afraid – it is something that comes from dedicated practice and observation of results. I can tell that I have the correct tone of a particular colour from the way the paint moves on the palette as I mix it and this has become a reliable guide for me. Of course, one of the problems that exacerbates this is that many people

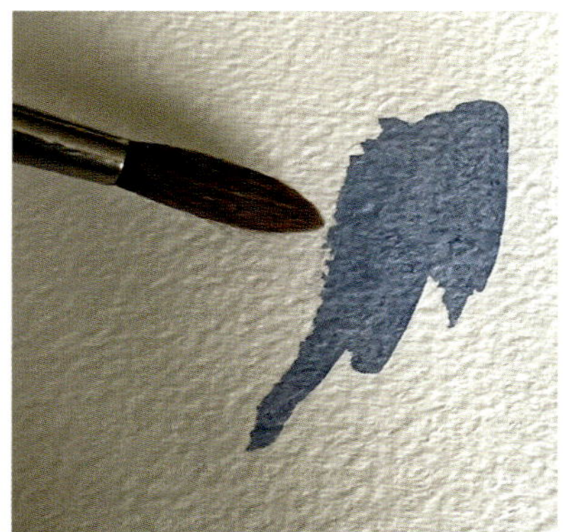

ABOVE LEFT: There is stronger tonal intensity in the paint, as it is applied wet.

ABOVE RIGHT: Once dry, it is evident that the colour is materially paler in tone.

forget to allow for the paint drying lighter, often 30 per cent, than it was when applied. Remember to factor this in, and for large areas of importance it is worth testing your mix on some spare paper and allowing it to dry if you are unsure about its strength.

- **Use subtle colour variations in your washes.** When you look at large areas in a landscape it can appear that they are all one colour: the sea is blue, the wheat field is yellow, the tree trunk is brown. While there is truth in this, such reductive analysis will result in paintings

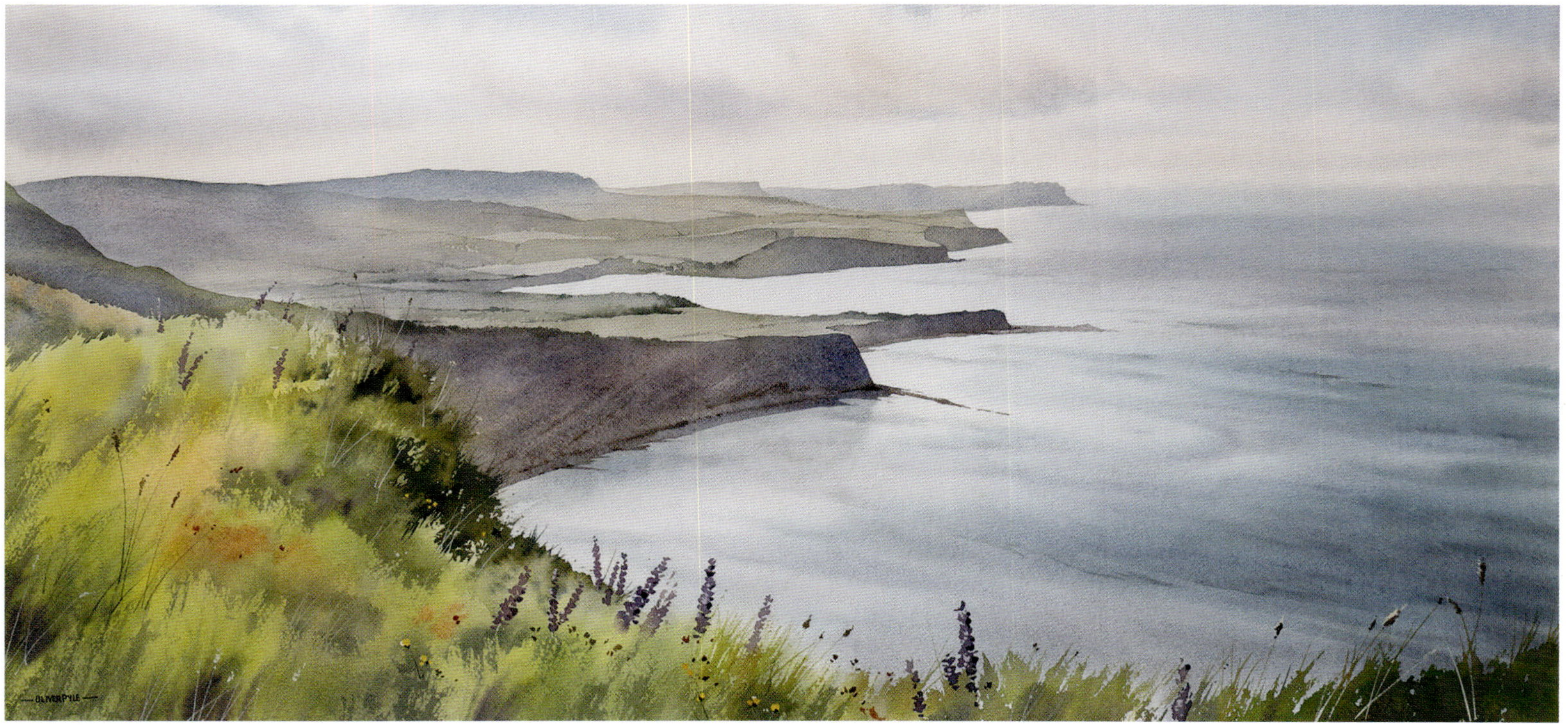

A Spring Morning on Gad Cliff – 72cm x 36cm
A significant portion of this painting is represented by the English Channel, expansive and silvery in the morning light. Despite the lack of hard edges or detail in this area of sea, it has taken a considerable amount of glazing and wet-on-wet brushstrokes to build up a surface of many different colour changes, albeit subtle and carefully placed.

that are flat and boring. I was recently sitting on the cliff top near Kimmeridge, looking across the sea towards Portland. I had been dissatisfied with how I had been rendering the middle-distance sea in my coastal paintings, feeling that those areas lacked visual interest (not detail, importantly). Observing carefully, it was clear the sea was not a uniform colour, its undulating, moving surface catching the light and reflecting a subtle combination of greys, blues and greens, all influenced by what lay under the surface. This is where our engagement with the landscape really starts to pay dividends: the level of detail and information that we can glean from photographs is simply not enough to inform our best work. By adding a little extra work, dropping in a few subtle changes in colour, I am happier with the results I can achieve. My passages of sea now have visual interest while remaining, subtle and quiet in the overall painting.

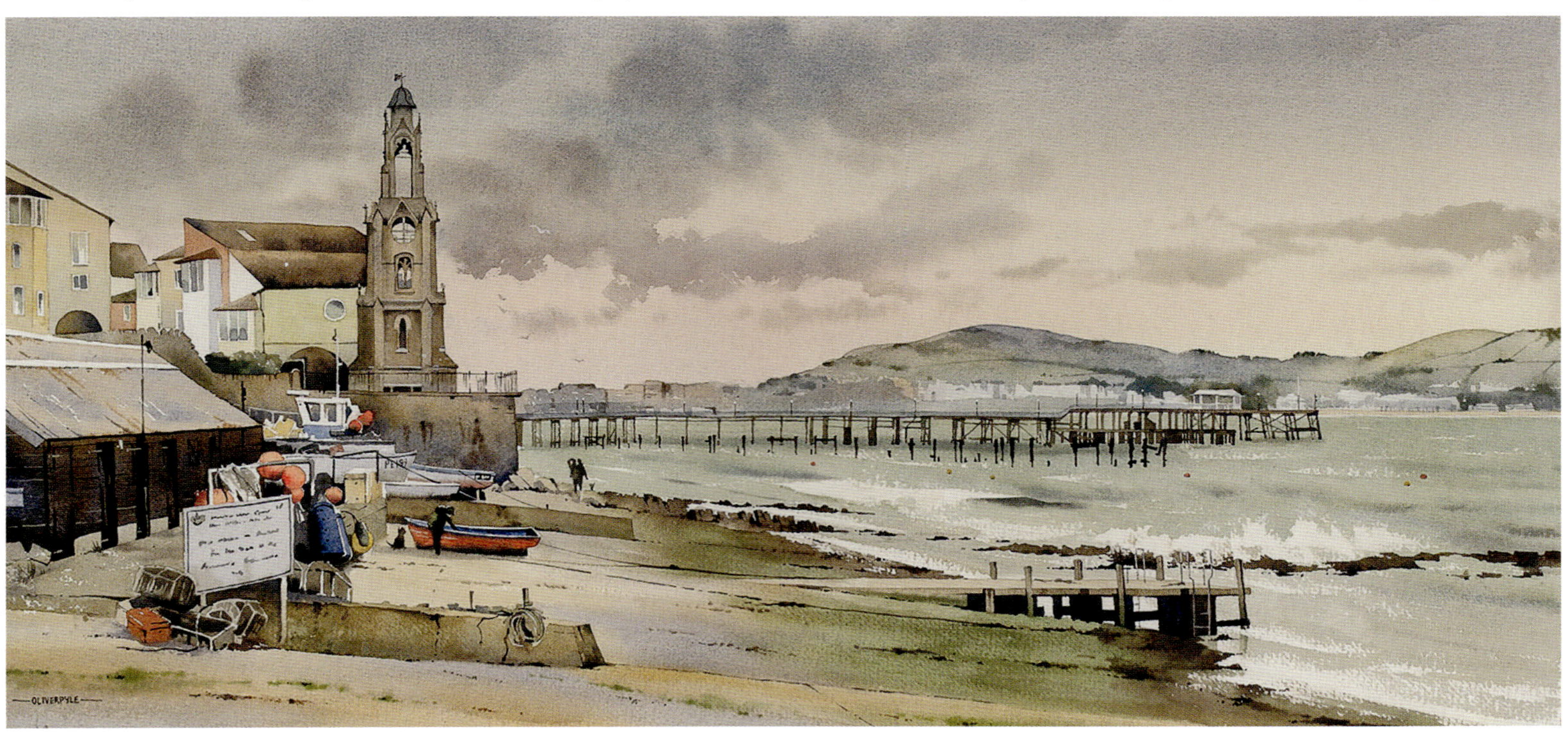

Wind and Waves, Swanage – 72cm x 36cm

In 'Wind and Waves, Swanage' the fishermen's shed on the left has a relatively new roof, and I recall that this looked uniformly pale grey, an awkward, jarring presence in the scene as it reflected what available light there was. To paint it as such would not have been wrong but would have done little to enhance the visual interest of the painting. By using a wash that includes a subtle blend of greys with some warmer areas dropped in, the result is far more satisfactory. Always try and identify opportunities where you can add some colour variation to passages that might otherwise come across as a little flat or uniform. If it helps you to make various colour mixes on your palette beforehand so that you can work quickly and dynamically while your wash is still wet, then this will buy you a little extra time to allow your pigments to blend together on the paper. Don't be fooled by the ease with which experienced painters in demonstrations appear to hit the colour mixes they need immediately, with accuracy and precision. This comes with many years of practice, often painting every day.

- **Create impact with complementary colours.** It may be that your painting's success is predicated entirely on the combination of complementary colours from opposite sides of the colour wheel. A broader discussion of colour theory is not for these pages and is easily found in many books and online tutorials. Suffice to say that from an early stage most painters are aware of the theory where the relationship between primary, secondary and tertiary colours confers benefits in the design and visual impact of a painting: the study of a bright red post box embedded in a green hedgerow for example, or the deep blue of the sea against the orange, sun-drenched cliff face on a warm summer evening. From the outset scenes and paintings like this will have an immediate and easily identifiable impact, but it is not always possible to simplify to such an extent in a more complex landscape with a

wider range of colours. In this case, the key is to look for areas within the scene where you can place objects next to each other that have complementary colours, deploying our artistic licence accordingly; in 'Wind and Waves, Swanage' I wanted to position a boat with a red hull (not originally in the scene) next to the slimy green hard-standing at the shore's edge. In a similar way, the subtle pink warmth of the sky by the clocktower works nicely in complementing the cool, pale green of the sea. Opportunities such as these may present themselves clearly when you look at a scene, or you may need to employ a little creativity to bring them about yourself. This is where your artistic sensibilities will start to sharpen: a gratuitous smattering of obvious complementary colours across your painting may look a little contrived, but the deft placing of subtle colour relationships within a scene will demonstrate the eye of a sensitive and considered artist.

- **Look for interesting colours where there may appear to be none.** I find that this discipline is extremely useful as a landscape painter in the UK. The sun isn't always shining and on a grey overcast day, especially during autumn and winter, the landscape can appear to be drained of colour. This is often the case on the Ashdown Forest, a local and extensive area of heathland that is a favourite painting location of mine. In flat light it appears to be a drab blanket of greys and browns, but by observing more carefully, I will notice plenty of subtle colour variations in the landscape and will then amplify their prominence in my paintings. Once again, this is where you can exercise your artistic flair: it is not a time to create a gaudy riot of incoherent colours on the paper, but to use a delicate touch to accentuate the colours that will help to add some impact to your work. 'Scots Pines near Chelwood Vachery' (overleaf) a location on the forest is a case in point. The thin, milky winter sunlight was doing its best to reveal what little colour was available and I decided to add

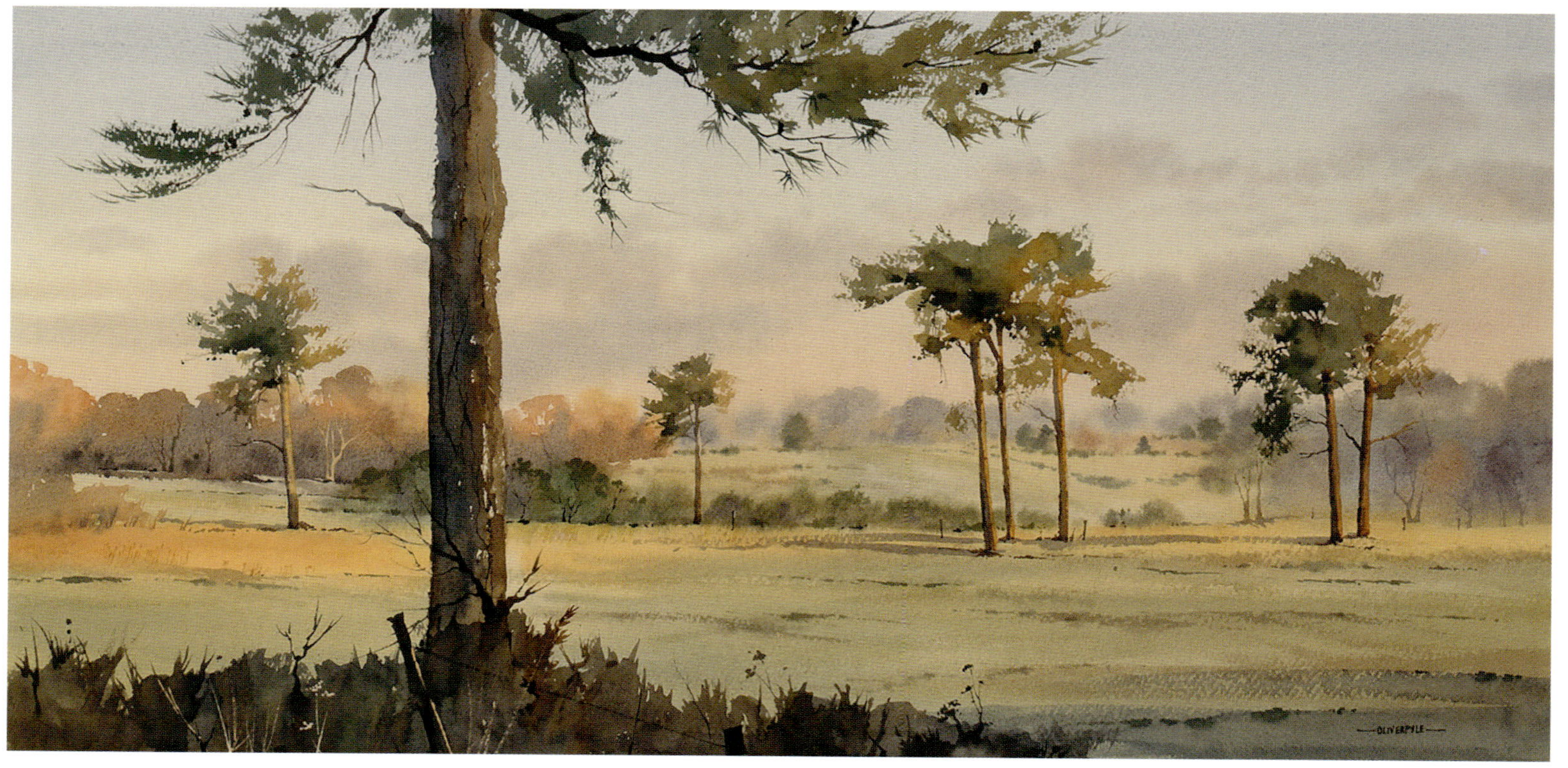

Scots Pines near Chelwood Vachery – 72cm x 36cm

more warmth to the middle-distance trees on the left and introduce some delicate yellow and pink tints to the sky, that were barely perceptible. It doesn't require much, but if you get into the habit of looking for colour then you will normally find some. When you do, just carefully dial it up a notch.

- **Try not to rely on pre-mixed greens, unless as a tinting pigment.** Your three primaries are more than adequate for mixing a wide variety of greens and doing so gives them a natural feel. Combining cool blues with your earth colours also has a similar effect: beautiful, soft greens can be achieved by combining

Prussian or Phthalo Blue with Burnt Sienna and Raw Umber. Most of my greens are built around Raw Sienna, and the blue that I have chosen to use (usually cobalt or ultramarine). I can warm these mixes up or cool them down by varying the amount of blue. The hues all have a natural feel to them, representing the landscapes that I prefer to paint. In 'The Warm Glow of Evening, Durdle Door' the bright sunlit green of the cliff face, the shaded areas on the headland and the aqua tone to the sea have all been achieved without any pre-mixed green. These have the tendency to look manufactured and lurid and seem to go against the delicate nature of watercolour. As an exception, I occasionally use Hooker's Green or Phthalo Green to add a little punch to a

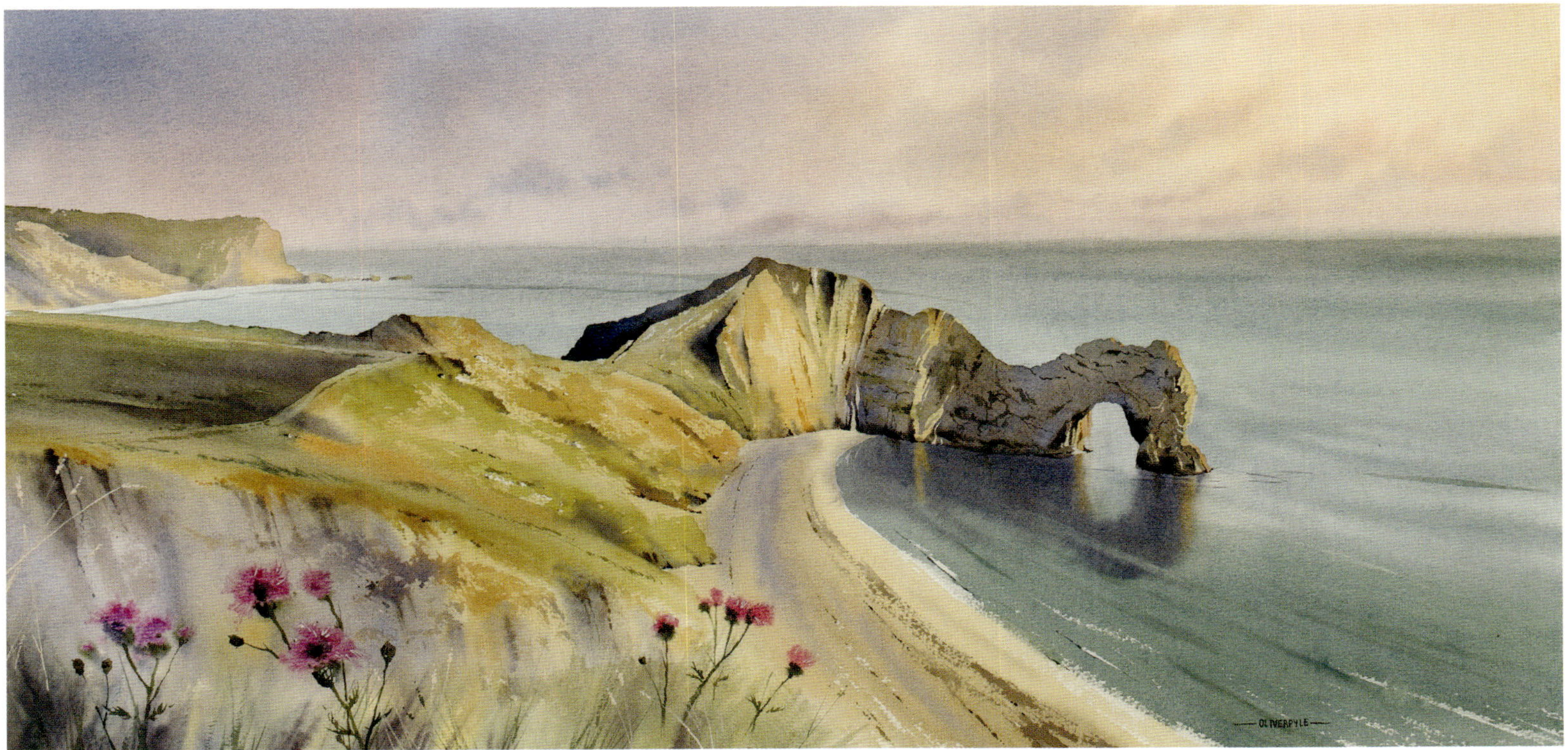

'The Warm Glow of Evening, Durdle Door' – 72cm x 36cm

mix if I need a vibrant local green – the seemingly unreal colour of some seaweed being a good example. These occurrences are rare and apart from them, try to avoid painting large areas with them straight out of the tube – they will ruin your painting.

- **Don't be afraid to introduce vivid local colours.** Despite my insistence on using your three primaries as much as possible, let me add a little extra colour to that, if you'll please excuse the pun. Having built up my painting in layers of washes, mixed from a limited palette of colours, I will often look for opportunities to inject a sharp burst of colour that catches the eye and gives the painting some zip. Despite the intricate combination of tones 'The Golden Light of Evening, London' (page 96) is nothing more than an unrelenting mosaic of warm ochres, soft blues and greys and to provide some relief, the inclusion of red on Blackfriars Bridge and the buses is vital, a key element in the overall success of the painting. In similar fashion 'Warm Glow of Evening, Durdle Door' (page 87) is an entirely different painting without the inclusion of the bright mauve thistles in the foreground. There is a suggestion of pink warmth in the evening clouds and the inclusion of a strong accent colour in a similar hue is a useful technique to bring out the warm sky colours. Look for opportunities like this to provide links to, and synergies with, other areas in the painting. It is a tried-and-tested technique used by interior designers and those with sartorial sensibilities and is a useful discipline to develop for landscape painting. May I offer a word of caution? This is not carte blanche to garnish your paintings with a scatter-gun application of your paint palette's most outlandish colours. Get it wrong, or over-use this technique and it is probable that you will have created a truly bizarre painting.

- **Understand the impact of light on colour.** As a general principle, on a clear day as the sun rises or sets you will notice a

warmth in the colours of the landscape. Areas directly under the sun's spotlight will take on orange and red tints, while its low position in the sky rakes across the landscape, throwing deep, contrasting shadows onto the scene. These are wonderful times to be in the landscape when colour saturation is at its best. As the

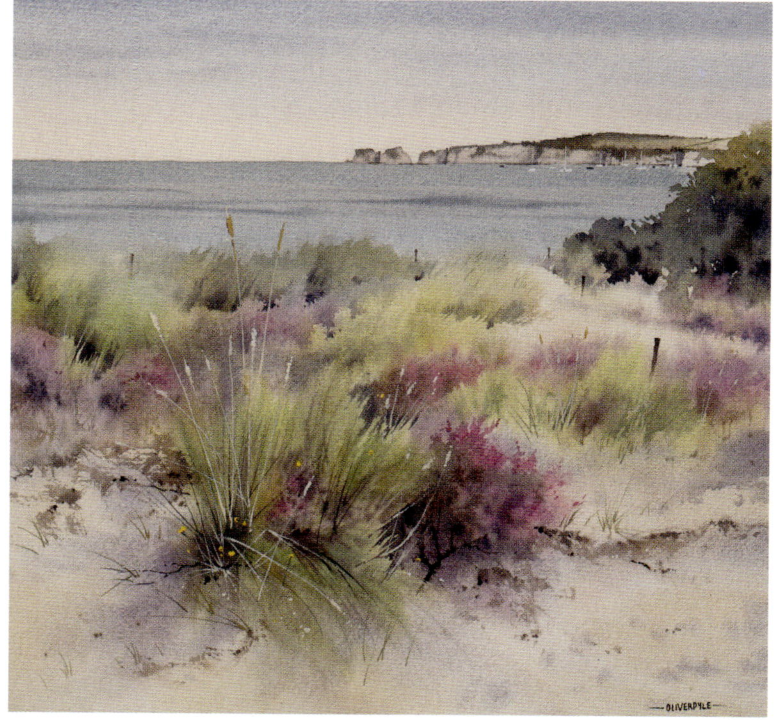

Among the Dunes, Studland Nature Reserve – 30cm x 30cm
Subtle colour variations are often more evident in overcast conditions. Use these to your advantage to bring out some of nature's own glorious colour palette.

day progresses and the sun climbs to its apex, you will notice that the colours become much cooler and shadows shorten, draining the landscape of drama, intensity and contrast. Of course, there are many times when the sun is lost in a cloudy sky and the light will become even flatter. These can still be worthwhile times to paint and are some of the best times to seek out and capture subtle colour variations. The heather's beautiful colours in the Studland nature reserve are less evident under directional light as the highlights become bleached and the shadow areas obscured. Often the range of warm, earthy tones of autumn are seen to best effect against the backdrop of a slate grey sky, without the complication of highlights and shadows. Keep your eyes peeled on overcast days; colours sometimes have an opportunity to present themselves with greater clarity – try to take advantage of these situations.

The time of day is not the only factor that affects the impact of light on landscape colours: our position relative to the light is equally significant. When we look towards the source of light our eyes are unable to manage the dynamic range between light and dark and they offer us a solution by contracting our pupils to a pin-prick. This is a compromise and it reduces the amount of light we need to register detail in many parts of the scene, and those areas and shapes are rendered as silhouettes in varying degrees of tonal strength. Consequently, we are less able to register colour and the scene assumes a quaisi-monochrome appearance. Painting scenes into the light is known as 'contre jour' meaning 'against daylight'. It is popular with watercolour painters as it simplifies the tonal map of a scene. If you are painting these types of scenes, be mindful of the effect that this has on colours and the extent to which they

October Oaks near Brook Street – 50cm x 34cm
Watery sunlight and a sky with lurking clouds are an excellent complement to the warm hues of the autumn landscape.

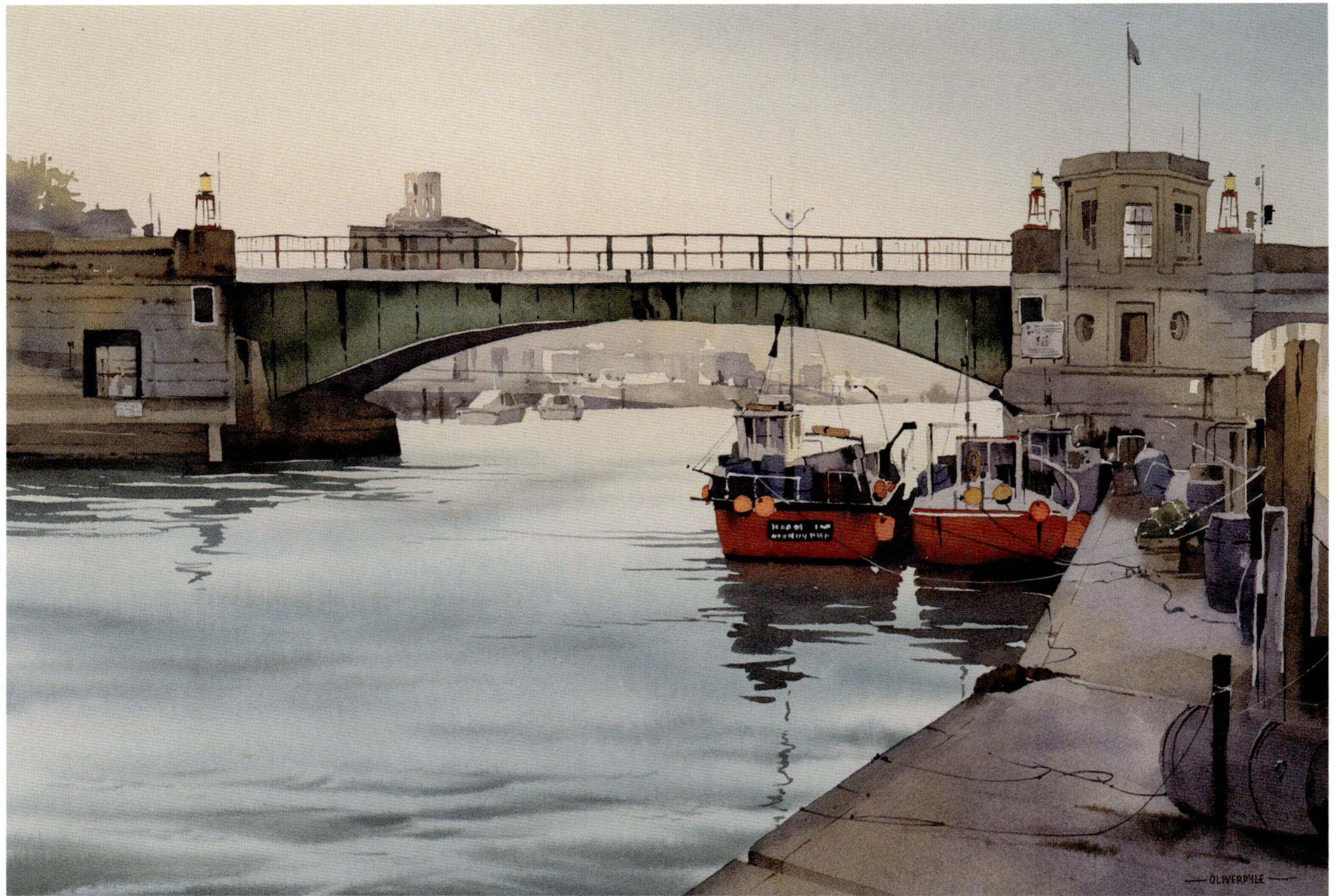

A Bright Evening, Town Bridge – 50cm x 34cm
Looking directly into the sun, the hues here have become desaturated, but register as strong tones, almost becoming silhouettes.

become desaturated. If, as I do, you place a premium on the details and colours of the landscape, then look for optimal opportunities and orientations for these to express themselves. Opportunities: dawn and dusk. Orientations: look west at dawn with the sun behind your left shoulder, or east at dusk with the sun behind your right shoulder.

Don't fall into the trap of just following current trends. Don't make desaturated *contre-jour* paintings just because others are doing so, if that's not how you see the landscape and how you want to express your feelings when you're in it. Colour is one of life's great riches and understanding how to use it to give your paintings visual impact is an important skill to develop.

FIELD TRIP – LIGHT AND COLOUR
Luminous Landscapes at Loch Lomond

'Quirky' would be to somewhat understate the décor adorning the walls of the old bar and restaurant at the Oak Tree Inn; a slightly macabre 3-d wallpaper of antlers, stuffed wildlife, forestry tools and cutlasses used by ancient clan members; old clocks and telephones – lots of them. An open fire glows, crackles, then sighs as a charred log settles in the grate, encouraging hill walkers to dry their sodden socks and boots, while enjoying the peaty richness of a good single malt whisky: a Laphroaig 10, perhaps. We are at Balmaha, on the banks of Loch Lomond in Scotland for a long weekend. With children present and our celebration of Paula's birthday requiring the most careful attention there will be little or no opportunity for sketching and painting. Worry not – in a landscape as magnificent as this, with the added charm of our Stirlingshire hospitality, it will not be difficult to revisit the memories of this place at a time more conducive for painting.

Despite the arrival of spring, the early April temperatures are struggling to make their way above freezing, with a teasing north-easterly wind

making them feel significantly lower. This will not diminish our enjoyment though: walks in the Trossachs and our exploration of the loch's wooded shoreline serve as a wonderful prelude to healthy portions of Cullen Skink and homemade pies back at the Inn. The quality of

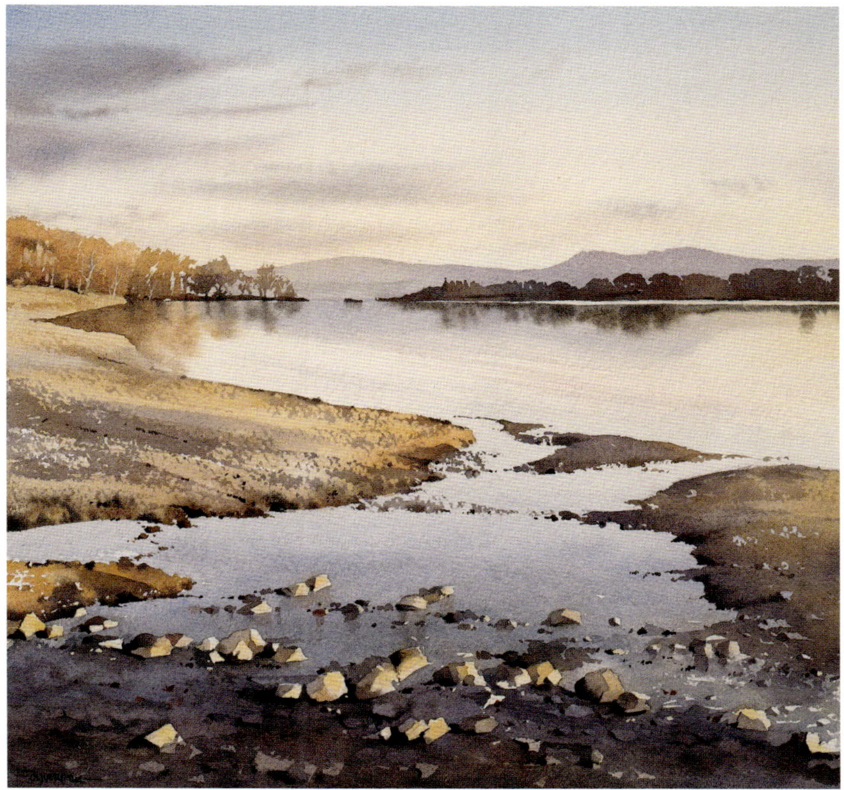

Cold and Crisp, Loch Lomond – 31cm x 33cm

the light in this cold, thin air, with little cloud to interfere, is pure. As afternoon turns to evening it appears that the landscape is being polished by the application of crystal-clear varnish: small stones sparkle on the shoreline like airport runway lights; distant wooded islands reflect a burnished sienna glow in the setting sun. I may not be able to paint these now, but the sights, the sensations, the memories, have all been dialled in to be painted in the future.

In recreating the moments at Loch Lomond and reviewing the photographs I had taken, it was clear to me that these paintings were all about the light; careful study and presentation of both colour and contrast would be essential to capture this.

There is only one way to successfully paint the light in watercolour: don't paint it. Stay with me a moment – the lightest tone in a watercolour painting will always be the white of the paper and looking at it with no contrasting darker elements it doesn't appear to be particularly bright, certainly nothing like the intensity of brightness in the sky and water at Loch Lomond in April. Any paint applied at this point, no matter how pale will make it look darker. It is the painting of dark areas that will define the luminosity and brightness of the light in our work, and this dictates a careful approach to the early stages in a painting such as 'Cold and Crisp, Loch Lomond' (page 91), often helped by making a quick tonal value study. Initial washes to describe the warm and cool hues in the sky and its reflection on the surface of the loch must be kept as pale as possible, so that the contrasting darker areas painted next to them will create the sense of shine in the scene. Understanding and carefully observing the tonal relationships along the shore and with the distant trees and island is vital. The light on the loch has been achieved by painting the darker island in

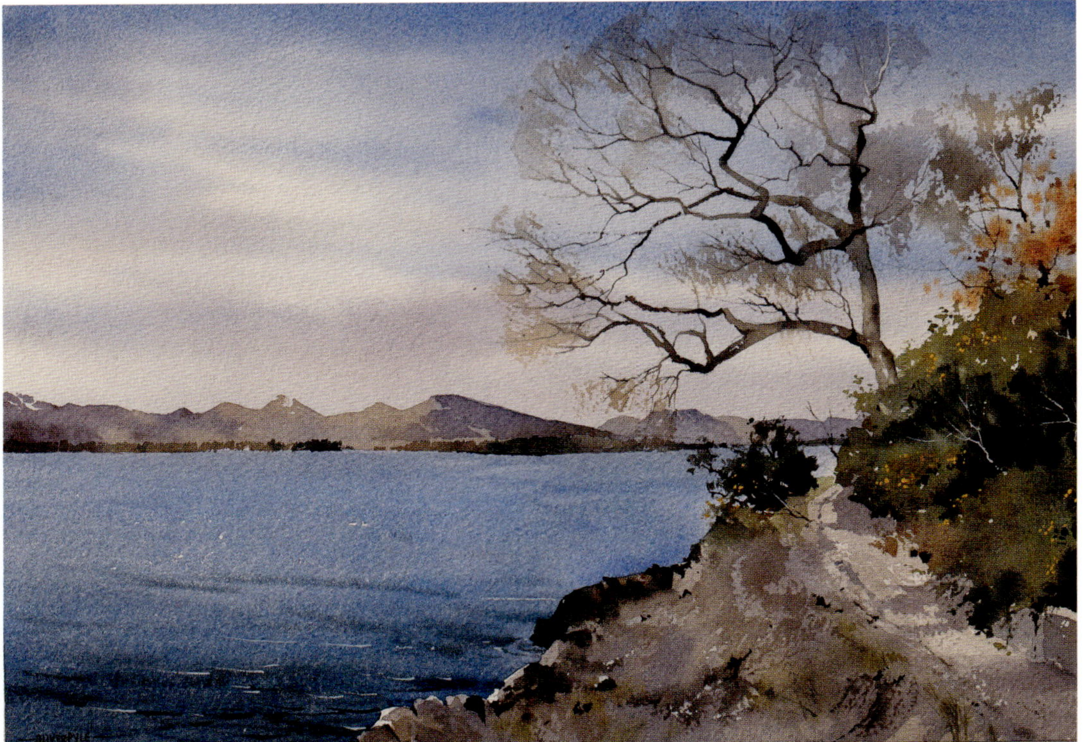

Early Spring, near Balmaha – 39cm x 29cm

the background and a significantly darker middle-distance shoreline. Then in a complete reversal, the intensity of the sun, slipping lower in the sky, is described by the brightness of the stones against the dark foreground shallows. It is the painting of the darks that enables us to create the illusion of glowing light in watercolour.

An invigorating walk along the West Highland Way from Balmaha, heading north, affords a beautiful view across the loch. The two wooded islands of Inchfad and Inchlonaig sit in front of the mountains at Edentaggart. This skeletal sessile oak, still in a state of undress and a week or so behind the gorse, made for a nice point of interest in the composition but it was the strength of colour in the sky and the deep blue of the loch that grabbed my attention. Normally, the light in the middle of the day creates less obvious, less dynamic colour combinations, but such was the clarity of the April light that contrasts seemed crisp and well defined. The deep ultramarine blue looked stunning against the vibrant yellow of the gorse and the orange leaves that had managed to cling on during winter. Considering the subject as a painting, it seemed very un-watercolour and I was unsure if it would suit the medium, but I wanted to recreate the vivid clarity of the

moment, so took the plunge. As a painter of colour, I was delighted with the result.

As dusk approached, I took a drive along the roller-coaster road between Balmaha and Millarochy, stopping in the bay to photograph the scene below that had caught my eye the day before. The fading light was lending a peaceful atmosphere to the scene and, for a change, was starting to comply with the ideas that I had for a painting. By now,

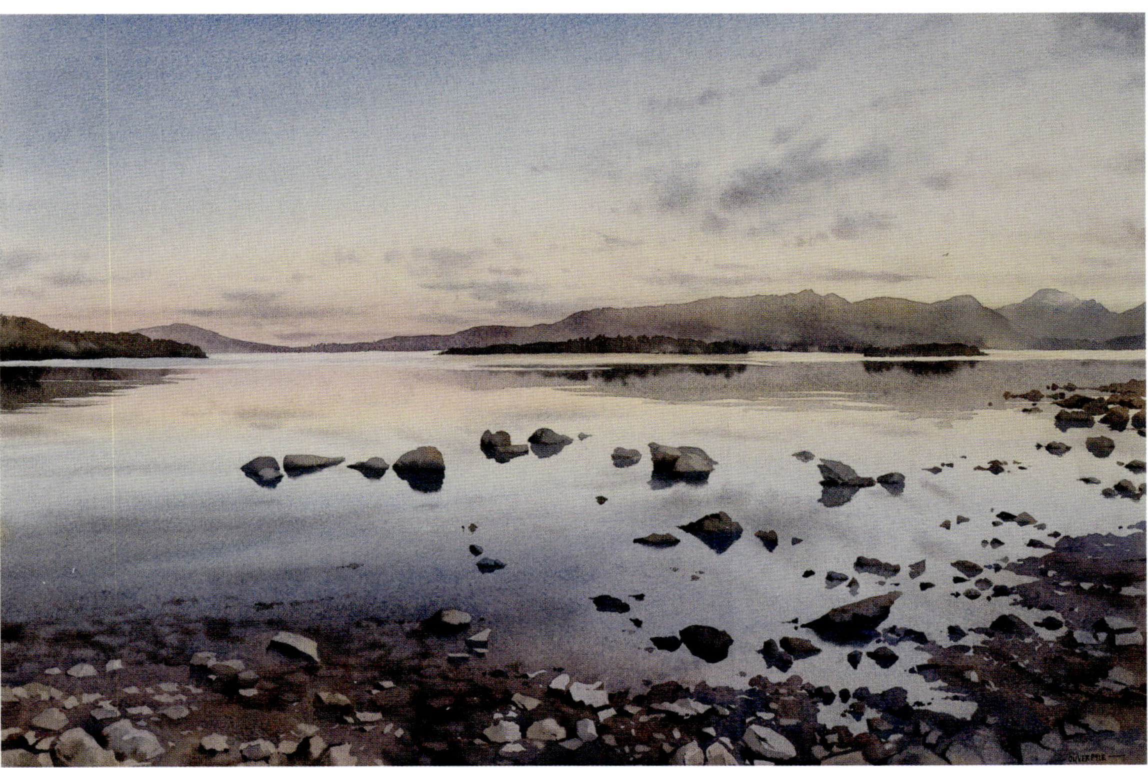

The Cold Light of Dusk, Loch Lomond – 52cm x 34cm

the cold was biting and it didn't take long for the feeling to drain from my fingers as I set up on the shore and manipulated the camera settings. Thankfully, my son Owen was on hand to help me exchange lenses and we soon had some workable images. Considering this subject as a painting, I was struck by the extent to which it is a monochrome scene: remove the soft combination of Naples Yellow and Permanent Rose at the horizon and it is little more than a tonal study in Paynes Grey. Understanding what gives a picture impact involves taking a quick step back to make some assessments as you keep the three central concepts of colour, contrast and composition in mind. This painting depicts a moment that rests on the clarity of its tonal contrasts, their counter-change at the shore, and the subtle infusion of accent colour at the horizon. With these clear ideas in mind, I knew that keeping detail to a minimum would allow the cold stillness and tranquillity of dusk to shine through, allowing the message to speak with as much clarity as possible.

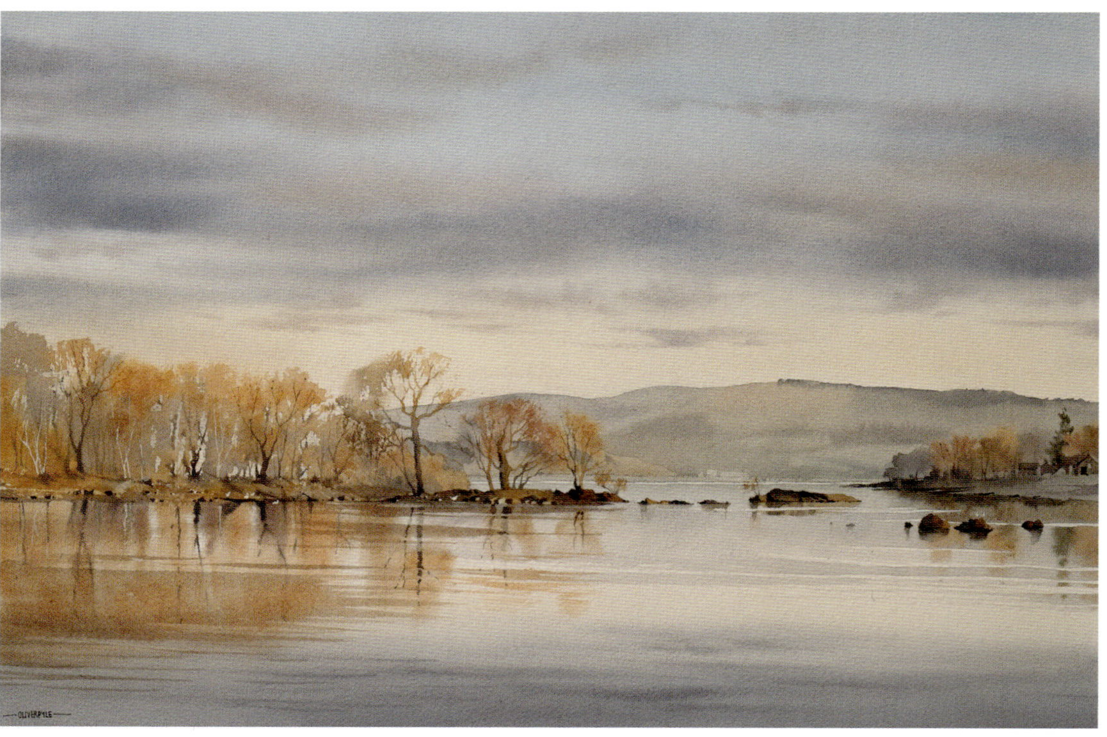

The scene for the painting 'The Quiet Loch, Balmaha' is a cropped section from the scene on page 91. Standing on the shoreline, I couldn't help sensing that the peaceful feelings pervading the evening were accentuated by zooming into the middle distance and ignoring the detail on the foreshore. It immediately translated the atmosphere from one that was more dynamic and based on strong tonal contrasts, to one that radiated calm and serenity, enhanced by the focus on a soft colour palette. Contrast is still here, but not so much tonally: it is the juxtaposition throughout the scene of warm against cool that gives this landscape impact. There are lots of colours in this painting, but with the exception of the sunlit trees on the river bank, they are subtle and the changes in hue are almost imperceptible in places. This is where watercolour really earns its living: blending soft subdued pinks into

The Quiet Loch, Balmaha – 50cm x 34cm

cool greys, sunlit ochres into shady blues, carefully mixed greens that melt into the background. This painting, perhaps more than any other, is an exemplar of the medium's capabilities, but great restraint and care is required to achieve this effect. Predominantly, it comes from a thorough understanding of how to select and control a limited palette – a reckless application of fifteen different pigments in the paint box and the effect becomes an unruly brawl that shouts rather than whispers. Prussian Blue, Burnt Sienna, Naples Yellow and Permanent Rose are all that is required and from these four colours a limitless spectrum of hues can be mixed. The simple ancestry of those mixes – just four pigments – lends the painting a unity that promotes the sense of calm.

While I would never dissuade anyone from visiting Scotland to understand how to paint light, it simply isn't possible for everyone. What you can do, with any scene, is to take a step back and consider what it is that first inspired you to paint it. If it is the light, and it often is in landscape painting, then ask yourself how your use of colour and contrast can be best combined for optimal effect. Study the colours, explore the contrasts.

CONTRAST

Go to any decent restaurant and you will notice that their dishes often combine contrasts: flavours that are sweet and sour, spicy and cooling. Textures that are soft and crisp. The symphonies of Gustav Mahler – particular favourites of mine – benefit from the clever use of extreme contrast between quiet passages, and towering orchestral *crescendi*. Good novels, plays and films involve heroes and villains. It is no different with Fine Art and if you are finding that your paintings are lacking impact, then I would hazard a guess that they are contrast deficient. Try to keep some of these ideas in mind when you approach your next subject:

- **Introduce strong tonal contrast.** Much like Mahler's music, the clever placing of tones (darks and lights) within your composition will help to create drama and strong visual interest. In particular, and if possible, aim to arrange the tones in your painting such that the strongest contrast between dark and light is found at your centre of interest or focal point. It is where the eye is ultimately drawn to. In 'The Golden Light of Evening, London' (page 96) the strong evening sunlight is creating powerful, golden highlights on the buildings that are, in turn, casting deep shadows across other parts of the scene. The stark contrast between the white structure on Blackfriars Bridge, just behind the bus, and the dark shadow next to it helps to direct attention to St Paul's Cathedral (as if it needed it!) Understanding these contrasts and using them to define wide areas, shapes and smaller textures in a landscape is an important skill to learn. Before you start to paint it often helps to make a tonal sketch in monochrome. Without the distraction of identifying which colour to use you can resolve where your contrasting lights, darks and mid-tones should be placed and combined to help enhance your composition. On a heavily overcast day, where there is a lack of strong cast shadows, tonal contrast is less evident and it can be more difficult to reveal the shape and form of subjects within your painting.

- **Combine verticals with horizontals.** If your subject has strong vertical elements (office buildings, boat masts, telegraph poles, pine trees) they can be used successfully as the primary motif of a painting and amplifying their presence within a composition can work very well. I don't know why, but this never seems to be quite the same for a painting with strong horizontal elements; they are a more frequent presence in the landscape and rarely seem to command the same impact. Perhaps it is a vertical's ability to link us to the sky that has some subliminal appeal. Unless you are making either horizontals or verticals the defining feature of

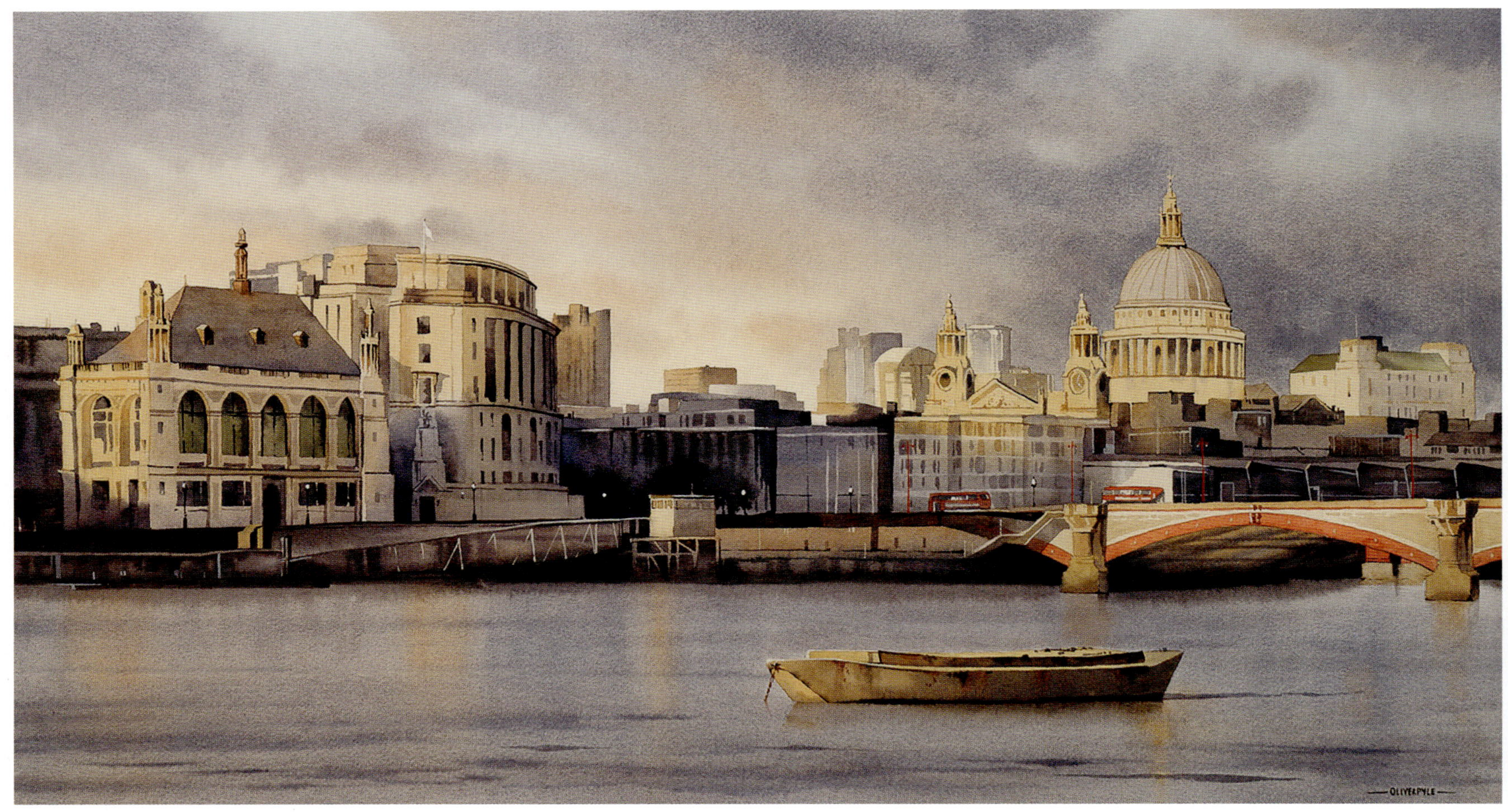

The Golden Light of Evening, London – 72cm x 42cm

your painting, it is a good idea to present a contrast between the two. The strong horizontals of the pier and jetties in 'Wind and Waves, Swanage' (page 84) are well balanced by the contrasting vertical of the Wellington Clock Tower. This principle has a wider application too – look for opportunities to contrast straight and angular lines with curved shapes for example.

- **Balance busy detailed areas with quieter, supporting passages.** The importance of this cannot be overstated, and I find that students at my workshops often struggle with this. As a painter that enjoys exploring the landscape's details it is essential to find a way of managing this in my paintings. In a scene that includes a significant amount of detail it is important that you allow the detail room to breathe. Normally there will be most detail at your painting's centre of interest, enhanced by stronger tonal contrasts, and to ensure that your painting doesn't look cluttered and confusing you will need to play down the detail in other supporting areas. This is a fine balancing act however; if the reduction in detail is too abrupt then it appears that you have used two entirely different styles to capture the scene and there will be a lack of rhythm to the painting. Learning how to phase the detail out across your work so that busy and quiet passages sit comfortably together requires experience and judgement that come with practice. In my painting of London on the opposite page, there is a proliferation of architectural detail that defines the subject. To give this centre stage and not confuse the eye it was important to play down the reflections in the River Thames and ensure that there were no

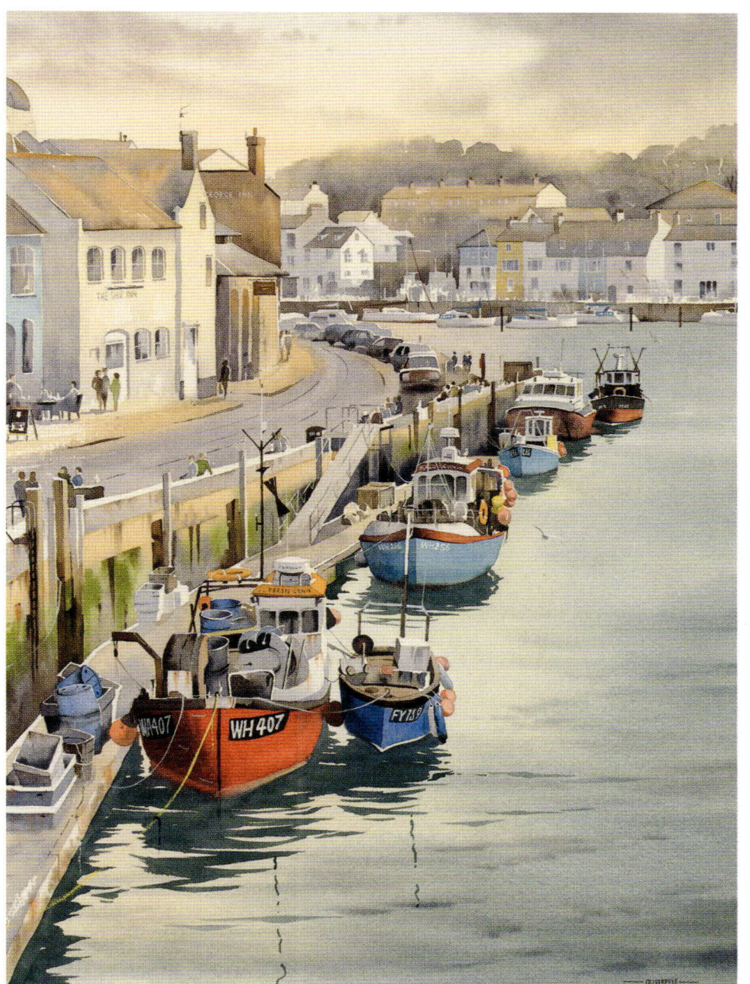

RIGHT: **The Old Harbour from Town Bridge** – 52cm x 72cm
The large empty space of the sea and the quiet treatment of the harbour-side buildings ensures that the fishing boats command the centre of attention, preventing a complex scene becoming a riot of conflicting details.

distracting hard-edged clouds in the sky. Large empty areas that lack detail can be rather intimidating but knowing when they need to be included in a scene helps you to create a contrast with busy, detailed passages, affording them greater prominence in the composition.

- **Identify areas of warm and cool colour.** We explored the importance of understanding the effects of chromatic perspective

on a scene in the first section of the book. Typically, to create a sense of depth in the landscape we use cooler colours in the background and warmer colours in the foreground, evident in 'Evening Light on Cleeve Hill'. Of course, subjects are not always so simple and with strong directional light it is inevitable that you will find areas in the painting that are lit or in shade. These contrasts help greatly to not only present a sense of recession from

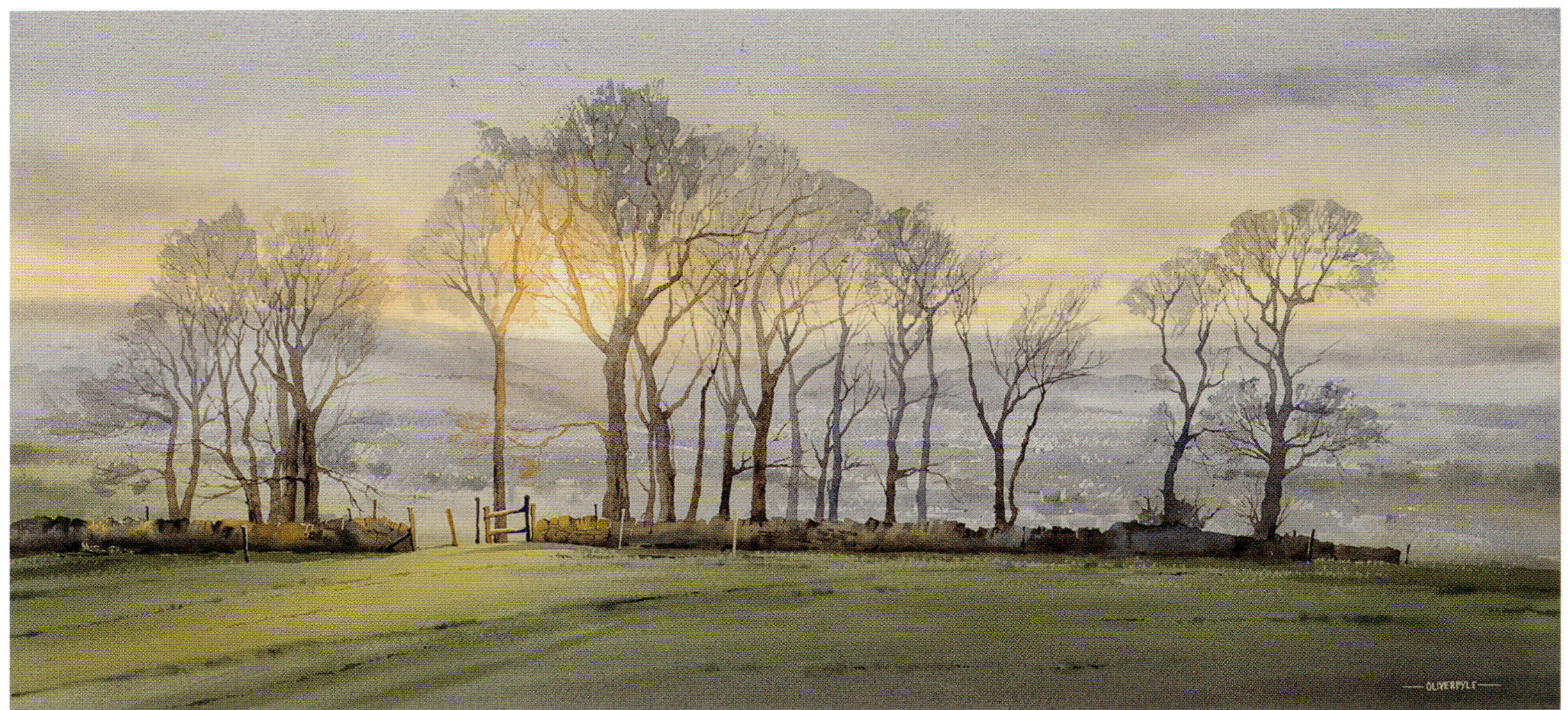

Evening Light on Cleeve Hill – 72cm x 34cm

front to back in a scene, but they also help to establish form, defining shapes and structures closer to the viewer.

This is the case in the London painting (page 96) where cool and warm sit next to each other on the same plane, but also from front to back. This is where it can become a little tricky and with complex subjects the placement of warm and cool contrasts needs careful consideration and mapping, or it could make your composition more difficult to read. Always keep in mind that the colour temperature transition from front to back may sometimes be inverted. I find this often in painting coastal scenery in Purbeck, where the cool foreground shade plays a supporting role to the glowing warmth of more distant headlands, catching the rising or setting sun, as you can see in 'Coastal Highlights near Kimmeridge'. Here is not the place to explore this in greater depth, but I would

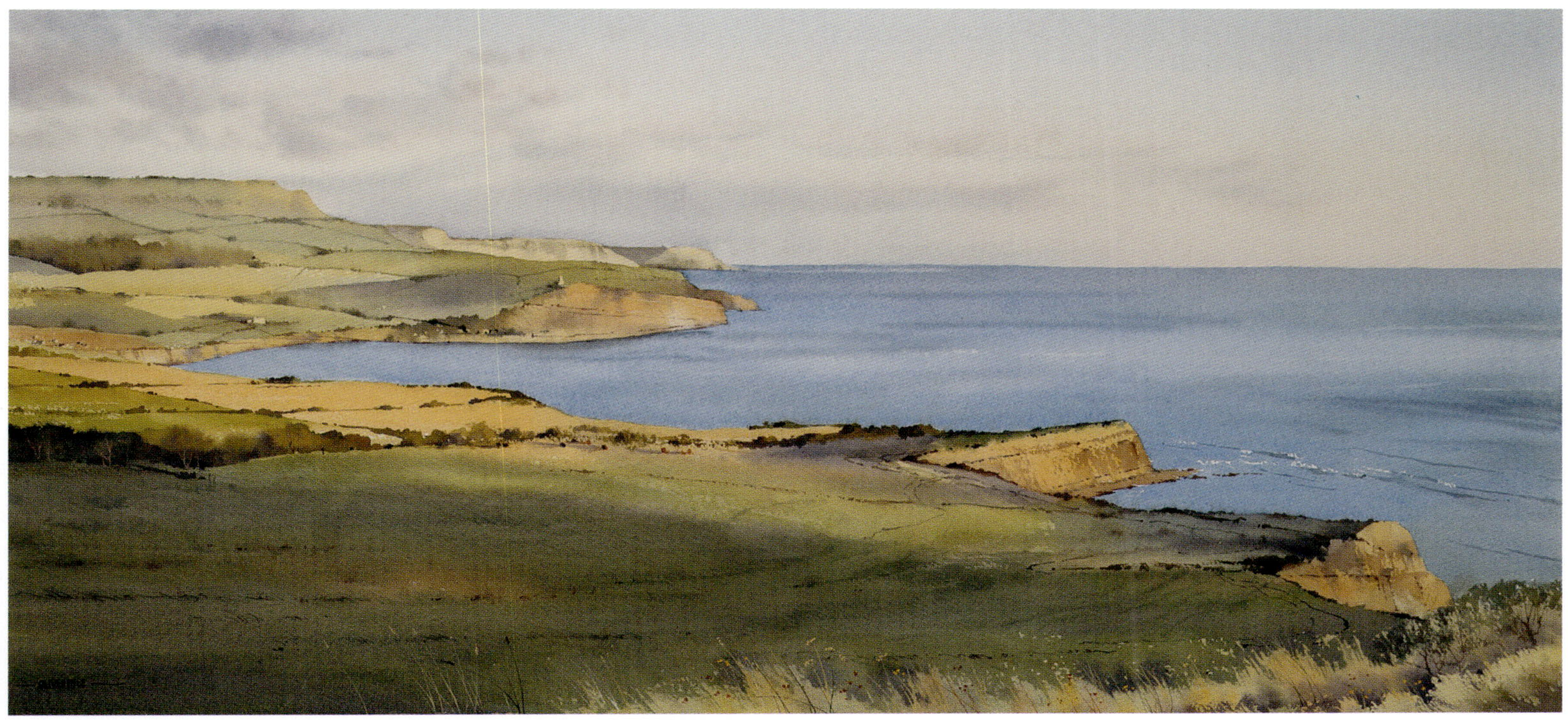

Coastal Highlights near Kimmeridge – 72cm x 36cm

recommend getting hold of a copy of 'Architect of Light' by American watercolourist Thomas W. Schaller for an excellent and thorough presentation of these ideas.

- **Contrast soft wet–on–wet areas with sharply defined wet–on–dry edges.** Painting successful and compelling watercolours requires great skill in managing the edges of shapes and passages within your painting. Using a wet-on-wet technique allows you to develop areas of soft blended colour without strongly defined edges. I use this technique widely in my skies, and for

establishing areas of warm and cool colour in the middle distance and foreground. Painting wet-on-wet enables you to paint one element next to another without crisp definition. These soft areas contrast beautifully with the strongly defined edges that you can achieve when you paint wet-on-dry. In 'Scots Pines near Chelwood Vachery' (page 86) the middle-distance trees are painted wet-on-wet, the colours running together, albeit in a controlled fashion, to create soft outlines. The contrast with the hard edges of the pines' trunks is striking and gives the painting a strong visual impact. Had the background been painted with hard

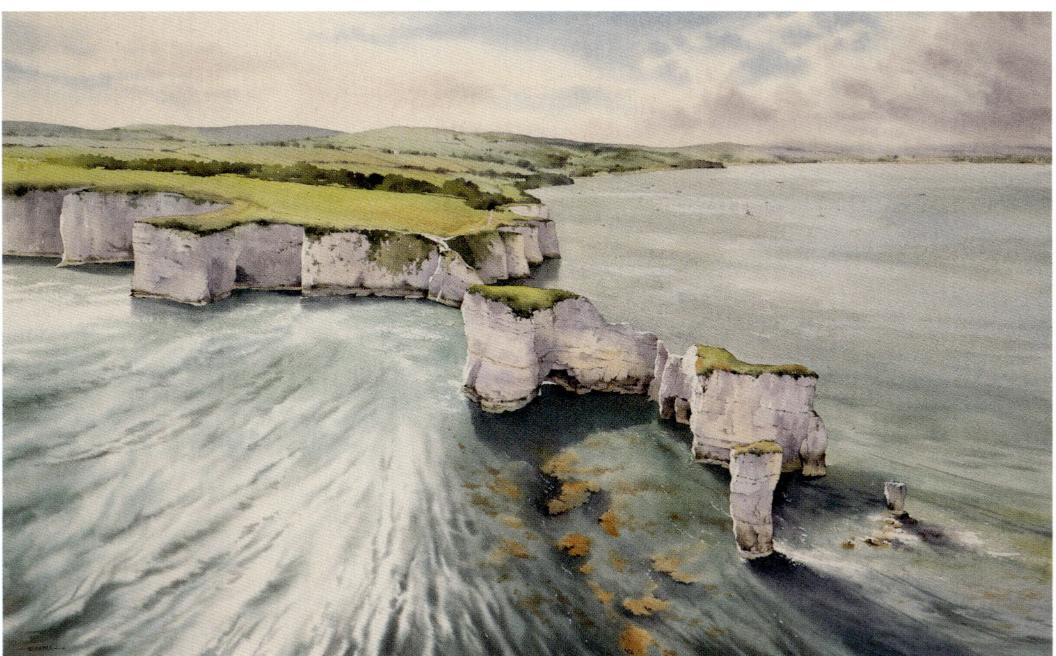

The Seagull's View, Old Harry Rocks
103cm x 65cm
This view, captured by my friend Peter Goulding's drone, already has plenty of drama but a combination of hard and soft edges helps to dial this up a notch or two. I wanted the crisp definition of the rocks' outlines to create an impact and this would have been less effective if the light catching the sea's ripples on the left had been painted with hard edges. Painting them using a wet-on-wet technique has helped to give them a sense of movement and fluidity. The distant trees, hedges and areas of woodland have also been painted as soft-edged which allows them to melt into the background. A treatment of lost-and-found edges on the orange Japanese wireweed (*sargassum muticum*) gives it just enough prominence without it dominating the scene.

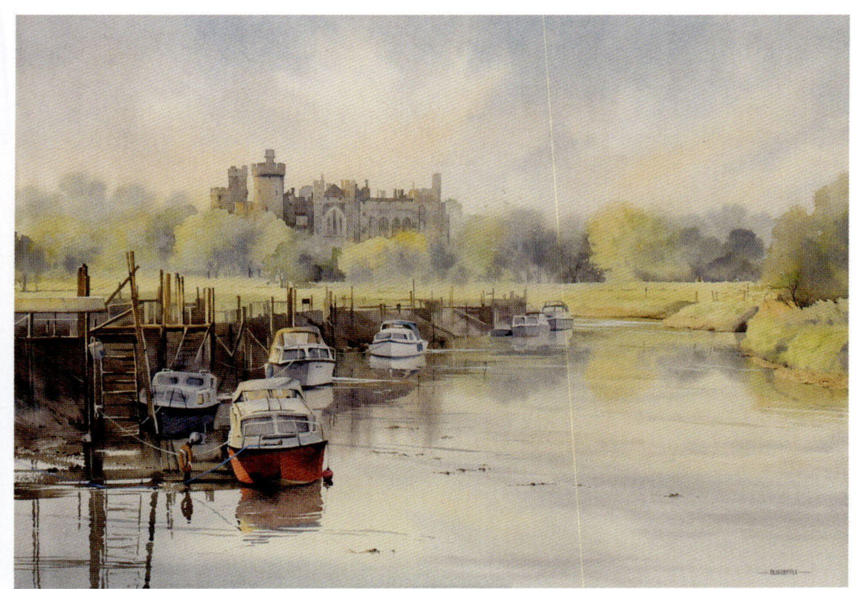

Reflections of Summer, Arundel – 72cm x 52cm
This scene had a high degree of complexity and detail: boats, mooring posts, jetties, trees, the castle, reflections. By taking decisions before starting the painting on where to keep crisp edges for detail and soft edges for supporting areas, I have been able to simplify the scene and give prominence to the focal point.

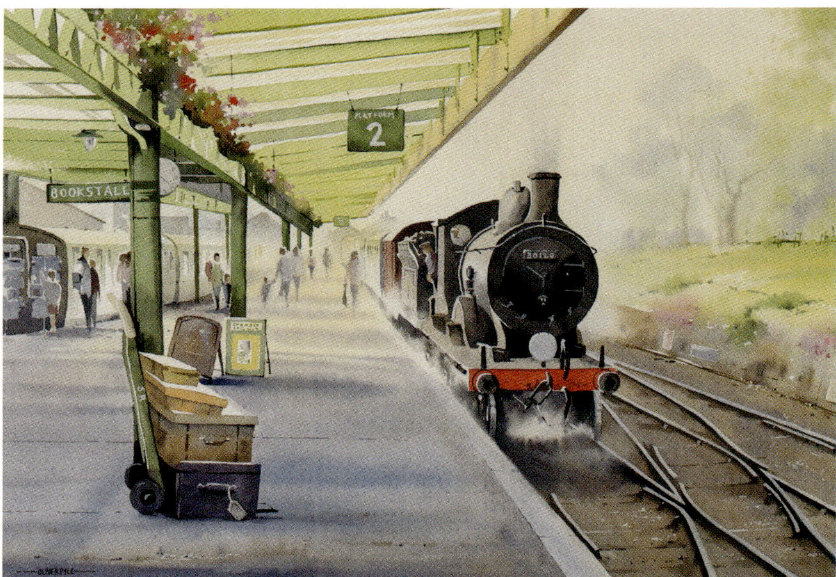

No. 30120 Letting off Steam at Swanage – 50cm x 34cm
Using soft edges is a good way to create a feeling of haze in a painting. Here, the soft edges to passengers, platform edge and part of the train help to describe the accumulation of steam under the station canopy, while partially obscuring the background trees. It makes for a nice contrast with the crisp rails and canopy structure.

edges, then this dynamic would have been lost and the painting would have assumed a more cluttered and staccato appearance.

• **Explore the contrast of ideas within the painting.** The contrast need not be purely visual, it can be ideological and conceptual too. In 'The Golden Light of Evening, London' (page 96) there are some interesting contrasts to note. Modes of transport, old and new, are very much in competition; the shiny new Routemaster bus makes an interesting counterpoint to the old Thames barge, now resigned to be a rusting spectator in the most glamorous of surroundings. Then there is the River Thames itself, fluctuating and fluid, in stark contrast to St Paul's Cathedral, an immutable presence and London's reliable sentinel for generations. There are a few exceptions, but I tend to prefer painting landscapes without

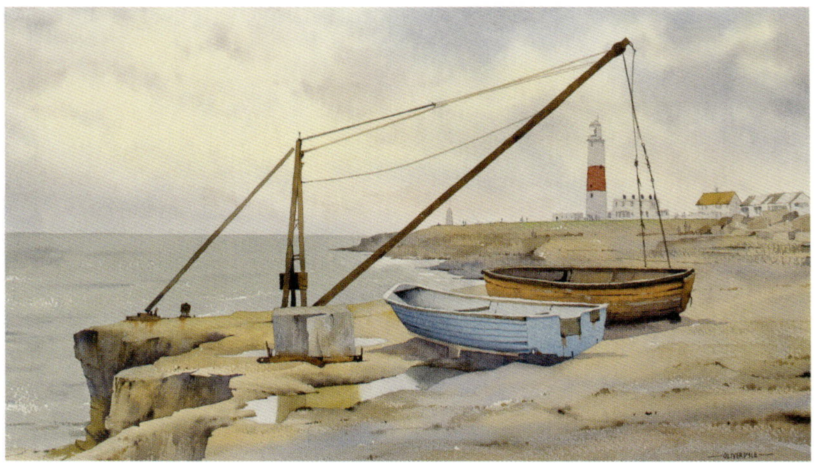

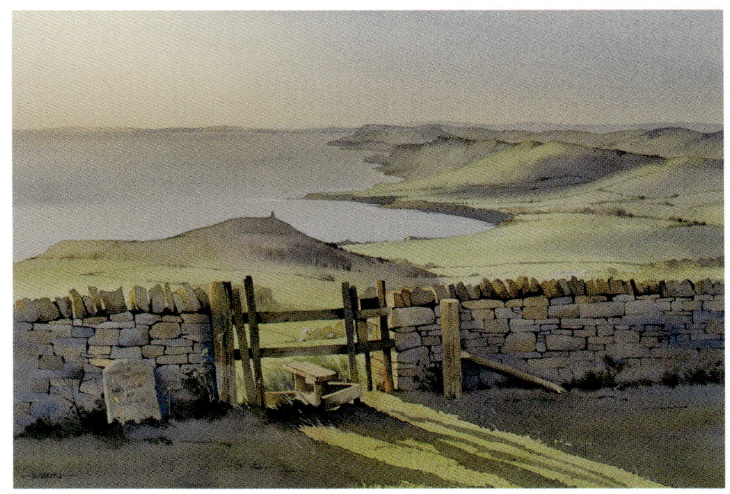

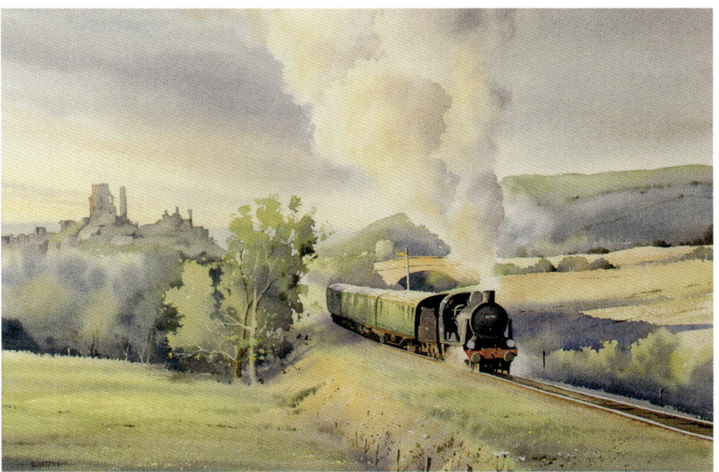

ABOVE LEFT: After the Rain, Portland Bill – 50cm x 34cm
The resolute presence of the Portland stone makes a pleasing contrast to the rusting decay of the old quarry crane. The lighthouse stands as a reminder that while we have attempted to control nature, it takes very little for it to gain the upper hand.

ABOVE RIGHT: Over the Stile and On To Kimmeridge – 50cm x 34cm
Look for opportunities and subjects that demonstrate human engagement with the landscape – you will find it everywhere. This dry-stone wall, recently rebuilt, repurposes local stone and creates a wonderfully biodiverse home for small creatures and insects; we are not always as destructive and out-of-step with nature as some people might suggest. The effect of the late afternoon sun is created by the careful placement of warm and cool colours, the strong tonal contrasts at the stile helping to describe the sun's low position in the sky.

RIGHT: No. 31806 Heads the Last Service to Swanage – 50cm x 34cm
The presence of Corfe Castle's ruins and the Swanage Railway branch line are prominent features here, but it is still unmistakably a landscape painting. Habitation, conflict and transport have played influential roles in shaping our landscapes. Finding ways to convey that is an essential aspect of landscape art.

the inclusion of people. I'm not being misanthropic, but I prefer to explore the transient, but sometimes lasting, impact of our influence on the landscape: quarries, fences, stiles, villages, dry-stone walls, copiced trees, bridges, railways. The human footprint within a natural countryside context offers pleasing contrasts – always look for opportunities to explore these.

Try to notice contrast in all aspects of life, and the extent to which it improves almost everything. If your artwork displays clear contrasts then it is far more likely to have an impact than a bland piece, offering little variety.

COMPOSITION

My relationship with composition is an uneasy one: it can be the most important element in a painting one day, and almost irrelevant the next.

Let's deal with its importance first, as understanding these principles will have a positive impact on the quality of your work. As we explored earlier, the reason we must even think about composition is simply that the process of imposing a boundary or frame around the landscape removes it from its wider context, giving the selected elements an unnatural emphasis. These then need to be organised so that our normal ways of looking are able to comprehend them; 'reading a painting' as it is sometimes described. Without an unrestrained view to help us read what is in front of us, we rely on a number of compositional manoeuvres to provide a pleasing viewing experience.

Typically, if the elements in your painting are incoherently arranged and unable to convey a pleasing aesthetic message, then no amount of beautiful colour or dramatic contrast will be able to redeem it. The accepted understanding of composition refers to the placement

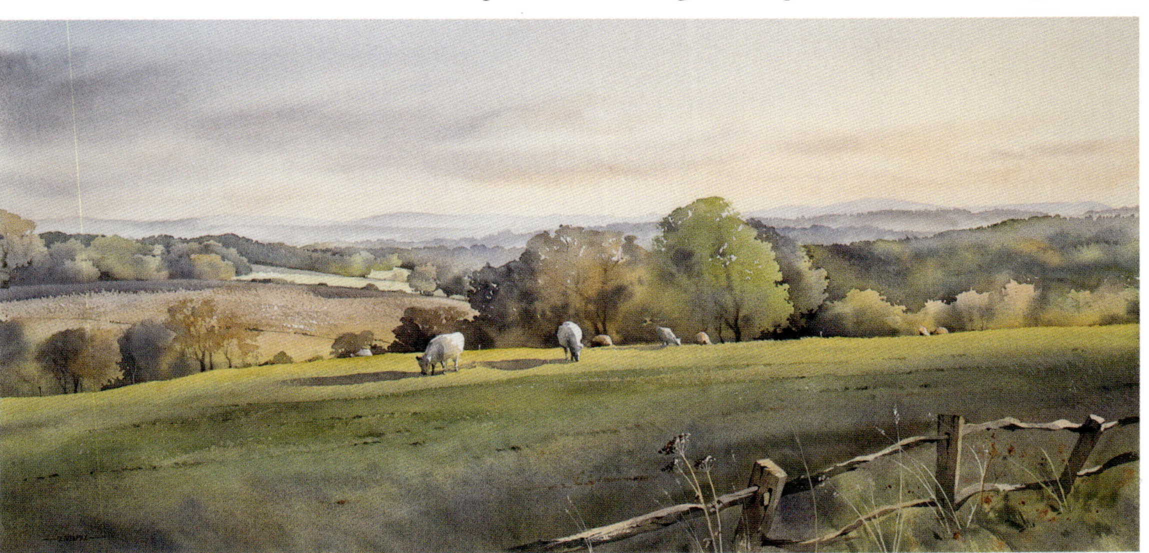

Long Views and Lasting Memories, Turners Hill – 72cm x 36cm
In my preliminary sketch for this painting, I had looked at a composition with no fence, and fence on the left. The fence created the feeling of observing the scene from the roadside vantage point, but on the left-hand side it tended to close off the view, leading the eye to the right of the scene. Wanting to encourage the eye through the valley and to the long view beyond, the fence was far better placed in the right-hand corner.

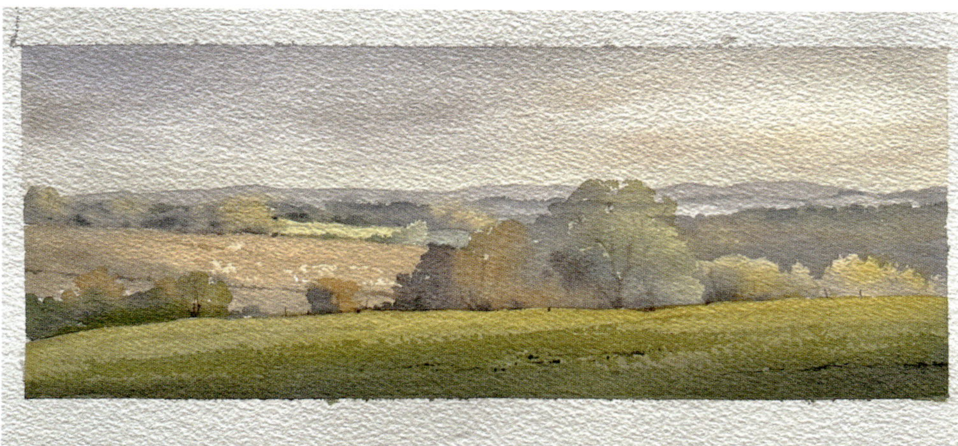

Sketch 1 No fence, no cattle.

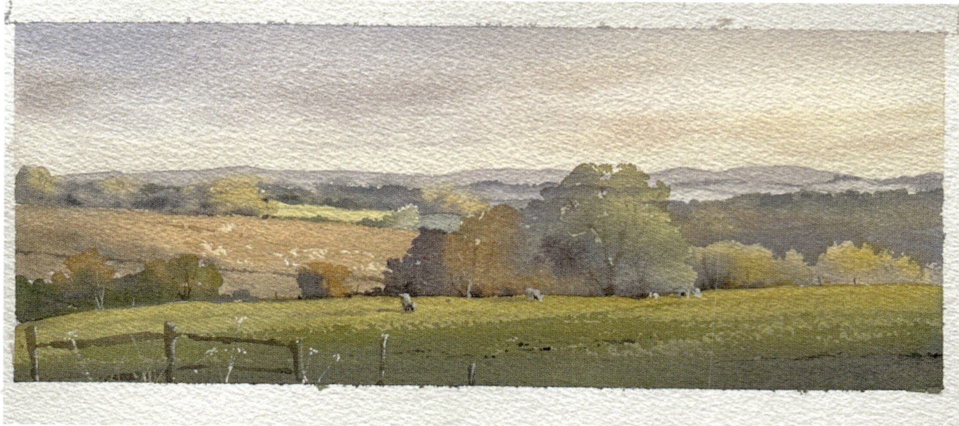

Sketch 2 Fence suggested on the left.

and arrangement of components within the painting, normally in such a way that is pleasing to the eye. Without wading too deep into the somewhat murky philosophical waters of aesthetics, there are a number of arrangements, patterns and aspects, often occurring in nature that we find instinctively agreeable. Noticing these and incorporating them in our work will result in landscape paintings that have impact.

There is a definite skill, a natural eye perhaps, for spotting a subject that lends itself to a strong composition, and occasionally you will find subjects that require little or no embellishment at all to improve what you see in front of you. At other times there may be significant edits and enhancements required to help the scene appear more interesting and dynamic. Next time you paint, think about the points below and try to incorporate some of them into your work, particularly at the development stage:

- **Identify your focal point.** It may seem axiomatic, but it is important to restate that viewing a landscape directly is not the same as looking at a painting of the same landscape. We looked at this in some depth in the first section of the book, accepting the challenge of landscape painting. Outdoors, the breadth of a countryside vista becomes very appealing: unconstrained by the boundaries of a piece of paper, the eye is free to sweep from left to right (or up and down). Without these boundaries, or spatial constraint as I refer to it, the need for a focal point becomes unimportant, and the seemingly infinite spatial grandeur of the landscape takes on great significance. Within the confines of the painting, the sweeping vista – while often an important aspect of the landscape – is unable to deliver same impact; nature is going to beat you, every time. With the painting's boundaries defining our field of vision it becomes a more satisfying experience if the eye is able to settle on a focal point, since we have needed to edit what we are presenting to the viewer – the message and elements that we have chosen to communicate. Finding a focal point and understanding it in relation to the wider view is important in presenting a centre of interest and a strong composition. We want the eye to be able to move around the painted scene, but ultimately it needs to come to rest somewhere, ideally not on the painting that hangs next to it in the gallery! Often, the focal point readily announces itself: a specimen tree, a boat moored next to the riverbank, a dramatic tonal contrast on the side of a building. In these circumstances your job as the editor becomes more straightforward. When an obvious focal is not apparent, then you should ask questions about the scene and what it is that has attracted you to it and

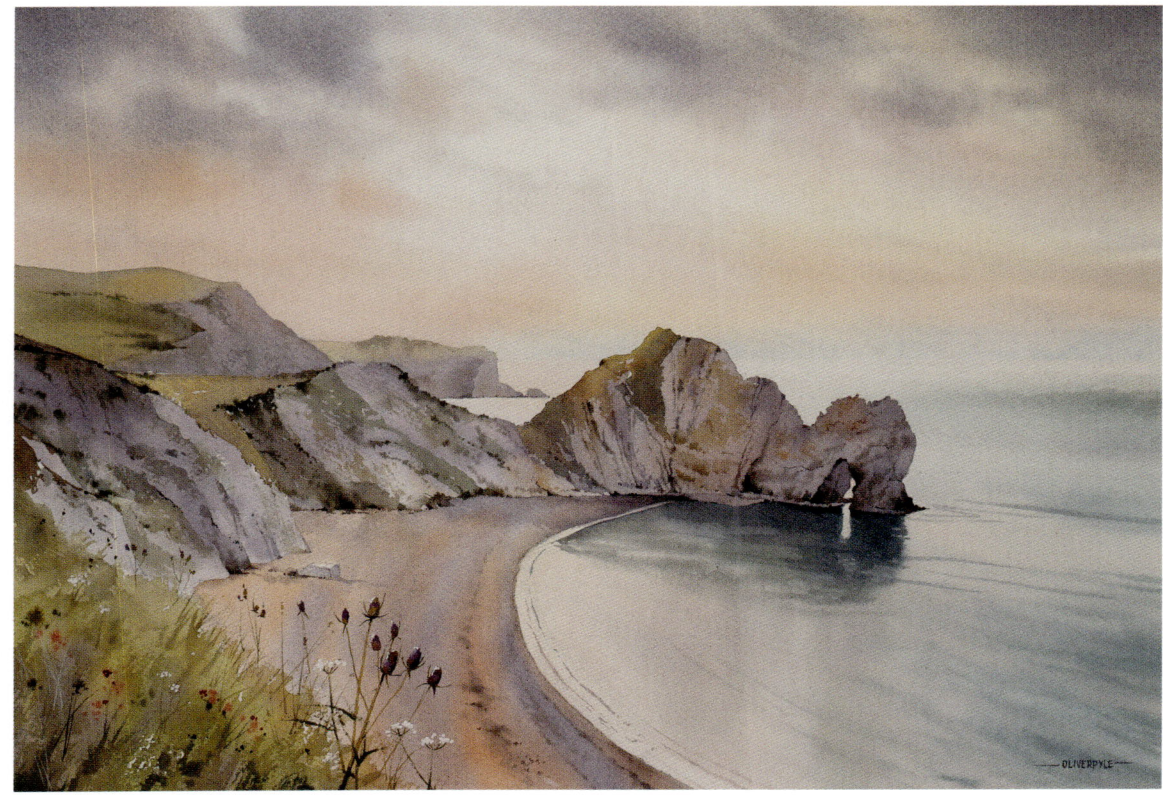

Wildflowers, Durdle Door –
50cm x 34cm
There is a strong focal point in this painting – the arch in Durdle Door and it's reflection in the sea. Its tonal contrasts are strong, the sweep of the bay and the direction of the gentle waves all take your eye in that direction, helping to emphasise its prominence.

motivated you to paint it. You may not need a focal point, or you may have (controversially) more than one. The key is not to force the issue, but I will expand on this point a little later in the section.

- **Placing your focal point.** In aesthetics there is a well-established concept, naturally occurring in nature and based on the geometric principle of the Golden Ratio. Often referred to as the Rule of Thirds (although thirds is not entirely accurate in a mathematical

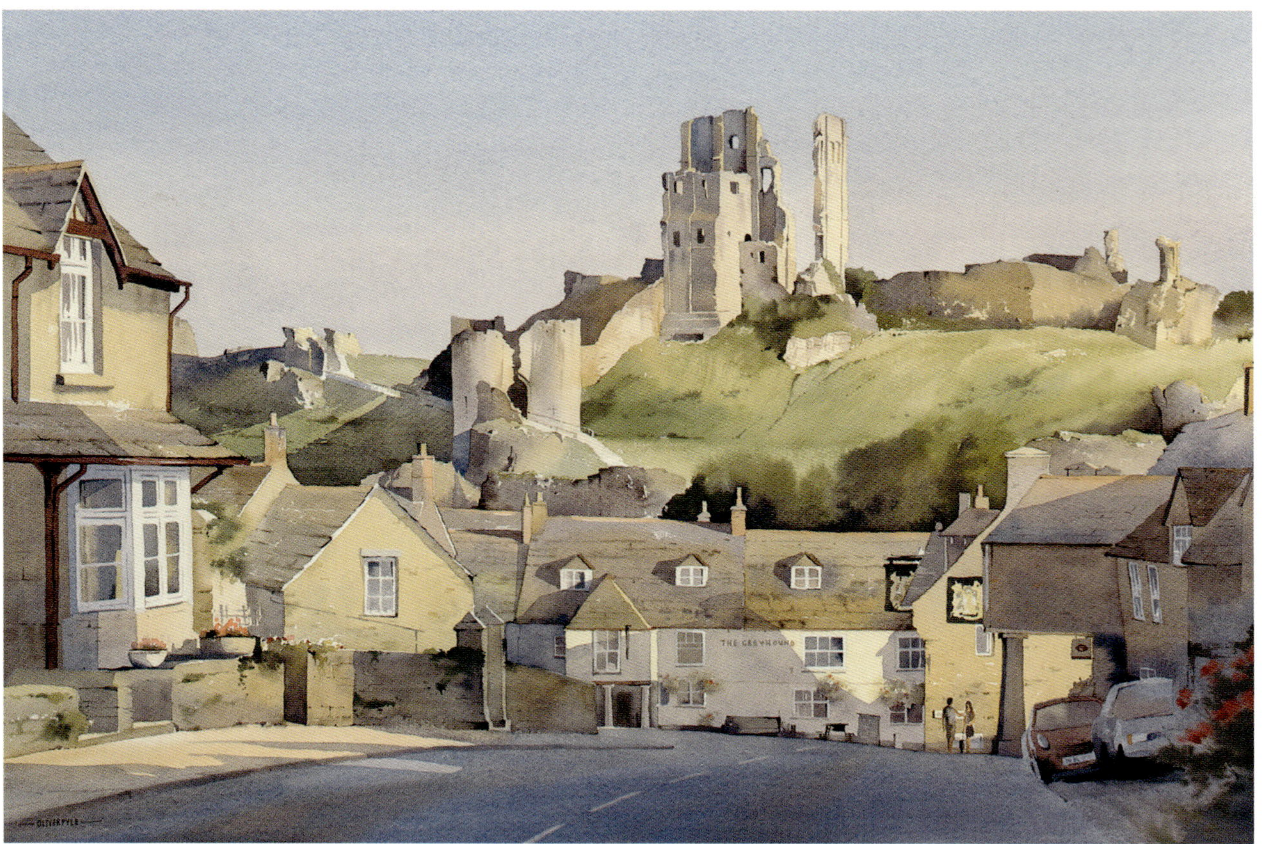

A Beautiful Start to the Day, Corfe Castle – 72cm x 52cm
The dominating presence of Corfe Castle is a natural focal point however detail and interest in the village make an equally important contribution to the scene. The establishment and placement of a focal point becomes less important, secondary to the need to create a balance of shapes and details throughout the scene; notice the nice combination of rectangles and triangles, helping to give a rhythm to the painting.

sense) or appearing as the Fibonacci Spiral, it suggests the most auspicious location for your painting's focal point. Divide your paper vertically and horizontally into 'thirds' and place your focal point on any of the lines' intersections and according to orthodox teaching, you have the perfect composition. Well, so the theory goes, but it is only a rule and of course rules are there to be broken so don't be too concerned by following this slavishly when perhaps a more obvious arrangement of the elements presents itself. Often in complex scenes where a combination of many elements combines to create an overall impact, trying to comply with the Rule of Thirds can lead to a contrived composition that makes little sense of the subject. As a general guide though, it is hard to go wrong if you follow this principle, especially in scenes that are less complex.

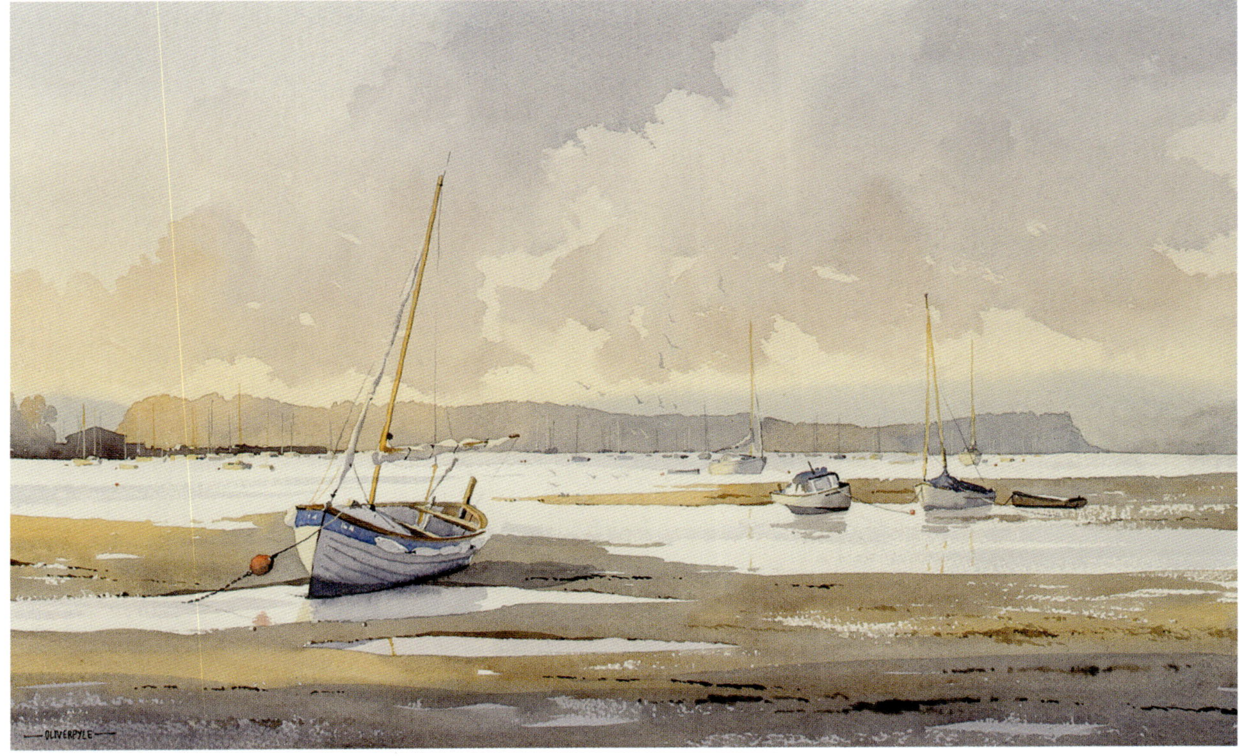

Gathering Clouds, Poole Harbour – 50cm x 34cm
In a relatively empty scene such as this, the establishment and placement of a focal point is important to anchor the eye and create visual interest. Placement of the main boat using the traditional Rule of Thirds method works well, the inward leaning mast ensuring that the eye moves into the scene.

- **Where do you want your horizon?** If your scene includes a visible horizon – often unavoidable in landscape painting – then where you place it will determine where you attribute importance and will communicate how you tend to see the landscape. Was it the drama in the sky that attracted you to the scene? If so, use a low horizon that allows the sky to dominate. Or were you drawn to an arrangement of wildflowers next to the meadow path? A high horizon will direct the viewer toward the foreground where your initial inspiration lay. A horizon that splits the painting into two equal halves rarely works. It presents two equal-sized areas that will try to compete for attention, failing to provide the viewer with clear directions. Identify what is most important and what message you want to communicate to the viewer and place your horizon accordingly.

- **Are the components in the painting nicely balanced?** Take a look at the landscape in front of you, and look for strong shapes, areas of detail, dominant colours, and vivid contrasts. How do they contribute to, or distract from, a sense of balance in the painting? For instance, are all the dark elements on one side of the composition, leaving the other side feeling too light? A dominant church spire to one side may require a distant tree on the other to address the scene's imbalance. A heavy sky full of dark clouds in the top left of the painting may require a counterbalance in the bottom right area. Don't limit yourself to the information that you have in the scene, but feel free to introduce elements if you feel that they will help you to promote a greater sense of balance to the painting.

- **Ensure that your painting's margins are free from distraction.** A sound composition will allow the eye to move through the painting and rest on the focal point. Placing vivid colours, strong contrasts, or extraneous detail toward the edge of the painting will not help to

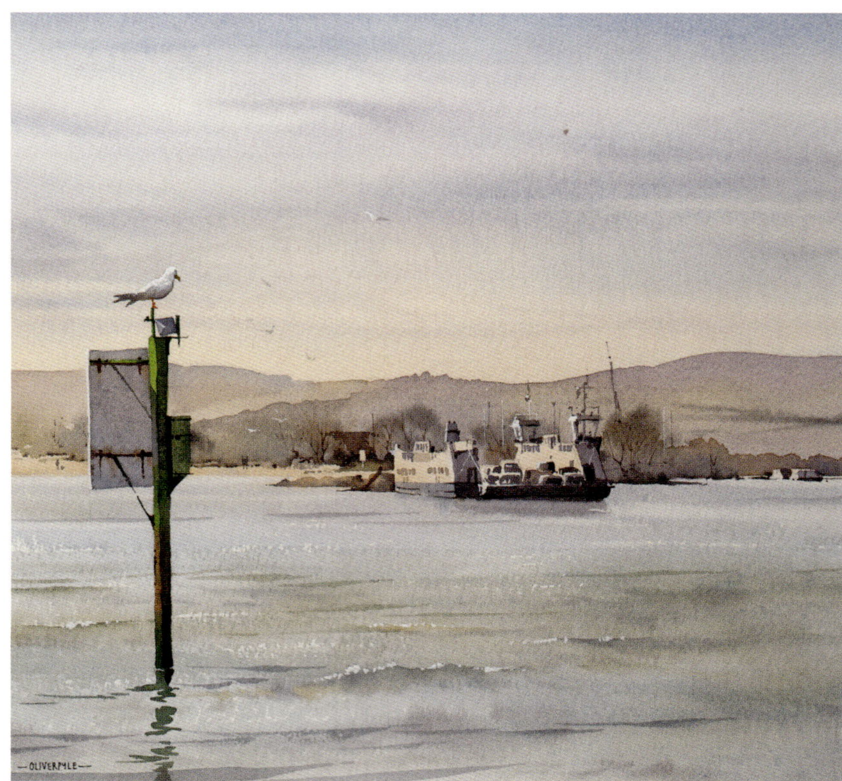

First Crossing of the Day – 30cm x 30cm
In this view of the quirky chain ferry, viewed from Sandbanks and arriving on the Studland side of Poole Harbour's entrance, the 6-knot speed limit post is just out of the picture to the left. Without it, the sketch I made felt rather empty and unbalanced, with everything on a middle-distant plane. I decided to move it into view by a couple of yards and with the seagull atop it adds a perfect balance to the scene.

promote this. A good rule of thumb is to try and envisage a 1-inch border inside the painting that should be kept free from anything out of place or jarring that might distract the eye. It is a principle observed by professional photographers and is well worth heeding.

- **Identify the optimal format.** Landscape format has earned its name for good reason – the rectangle with greater width than height is ideally suited to landscape work. It allows for a broad field of view and plenty of scope for the placement of traditional landscape components as focal points (trees, gates, boats, buildings etc.). I am particularly fond of a panoramic format, a stretched version of 'landscape' that has a 2:1 ratio. It works very well for coastal subjects, with their sweeping curved beaches, cliffs and headlands. It is a useful format too for city skylines. By using a landscape format and especially a panoramic format you are encouraging your viewer to participate a little more in the side-to-side sweep of the eye, as if you are in the landscape yourself. Consequently, the importance of focal points has more significance in these formats. Use a panoramic format to emphasise horizontal elements in a painting (depending on your view point): horizon, lines in a ploughed field, ripples on water, shorelines, promontories, hedgerows. A portrait format (greater height than width) can also be ideal for landscapes that have a strong foreground element, allowing the painter to commit a proportionally large amount of the paper to it. This can work particularly well as a way of encouraging your viewer to feel that they are being drawn into the painting, down a woodland path, along an empty beach or through a street. Portrait format is often a natural choice for paintings where the centre of interest is a strong vertical: church spire, boat mast, city building, prominent tree. Square landscape

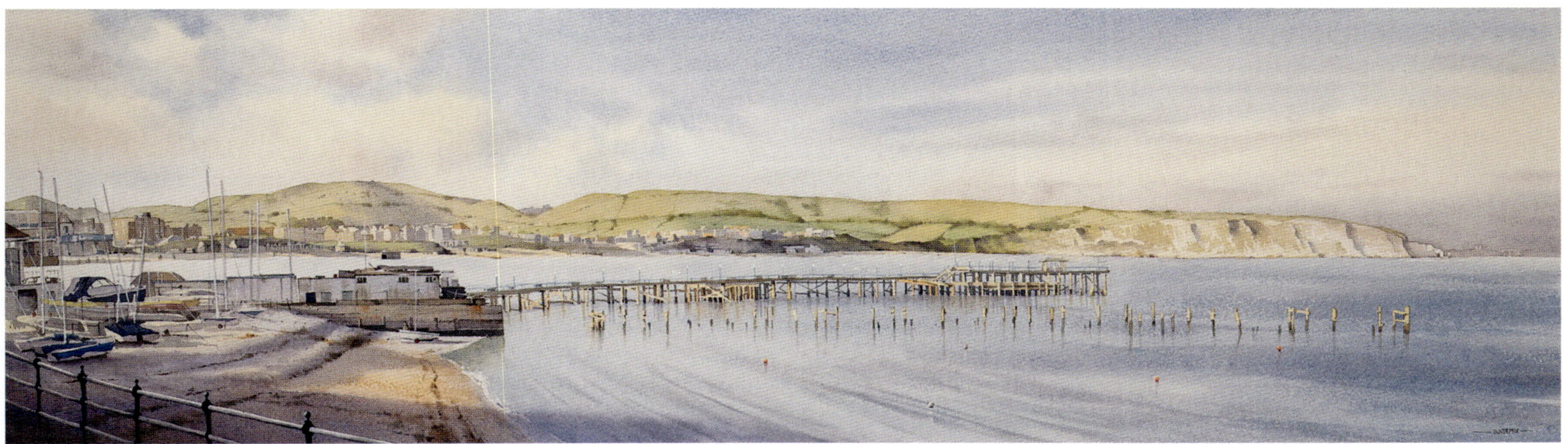

Calm Evening, Swanage Bay – 103cm x 30cm
The panoramic 'letterbox' format is perfect for accentuating the strong horizontals of the old pier, new pier and Ballard Down.

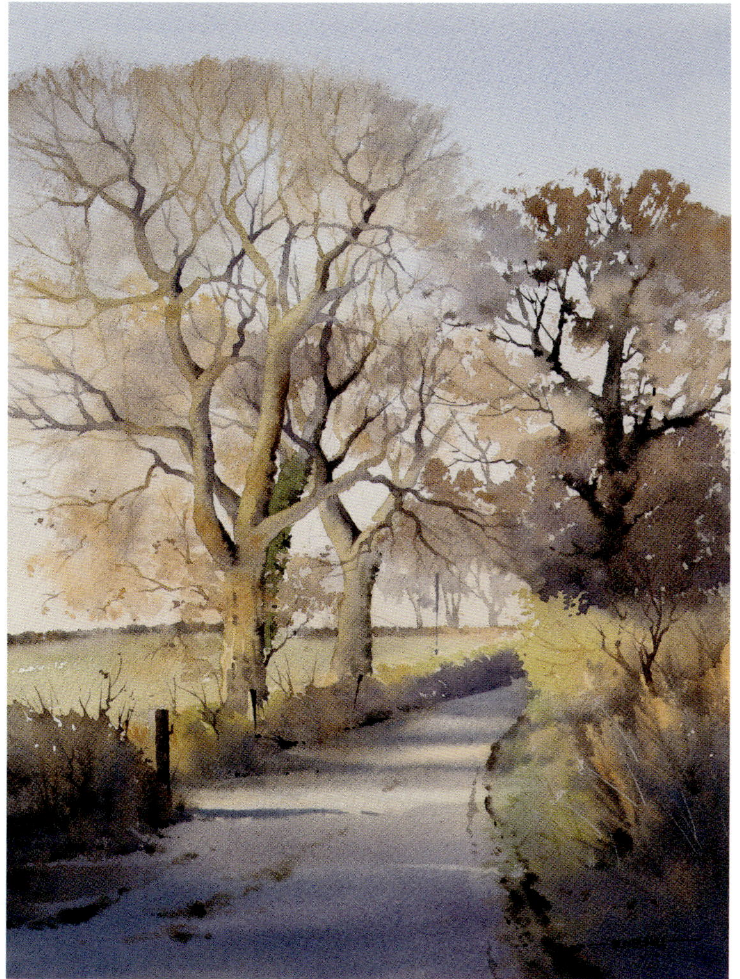

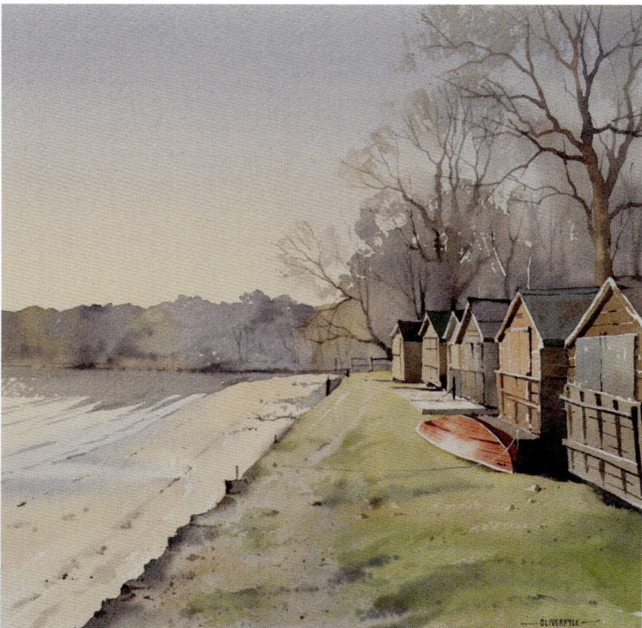

LEFT: November Colours in the Lane – 29cm x 39cm
The portrait format works well for this scene, close to home in Cuckfield, inviting you to walk up the lane, kicking your boots through the fallen leaves. The strong verticals of the tree trunks and fenceposts reinforce this idea.

ABOVE: Winter Morning, South Beach, Studland – 30cm x 30cm
This scene posed a compositional conundrum: the central horizon line and its coincidence with the strong diagonals of the edge of the retaining wall and the beach huts was rather inconvenient. In a square format, these issues take on far less significance; because there is no dominant dimension (height and width are equal) to the paper, the eye is not trying to sweep from left to right or up and down – it just takes in the scene and is satisfied.

paintings, beloved by greetings card manufacturers, have a contemporary feel and are less reliant on traditional compositional rules. The format has the effect of restricting the field of vision, while allowing the eye to wander anywhere it wants to inside the frame. There is less propensity for the side-to-side, up-and-down movement encouraged by the more traditional formats. If you want to paint a scene but can't resolve where your focal point should be, try making a quick sketch in square format – you might be surprised at the extent to which this helps.

- **Create a 'path' for the viewer with leading lines.** Be kind and help your viewer. You want to guide their eye around your painting and towards your carefully selected and positioned focal point and there are many useful elements you can use to achieve this. It can be obvious: a line of fence posts (we'll come back to these,) a winding footpath or the crop rows in a farmer's field. It can also be quite subtle; in the painting 'At Dawn on the Knoll Beach' you might notice a Z-shape that starts on the right, travels through the foreground rocks and then diagonally up the beach, where it then heads back out to sea on the horizon from right to left. It is important to avoid a common mistake when using objects or

landscape patterns as sight lines; a dry-stone wall that stretches across the width of the scene will block the viewing transition from one part of the painting to another. Always allow strategically placed gaps and breaks to prevent this from happening, as blocking a line of sight is a sure-fire way to kill a good composition.

- **Simplify – leave out unnecessary detail/objects.** The mind is always more engaged when it must configure elements that are abstract or unknown. While there would be a tremendous amount of technical skill involved in painting every house in a distant village it would not be a satisfying aesthetic experience for the viewer. If everything is stated clearly and defined, the eye moves swiftly on, content that all

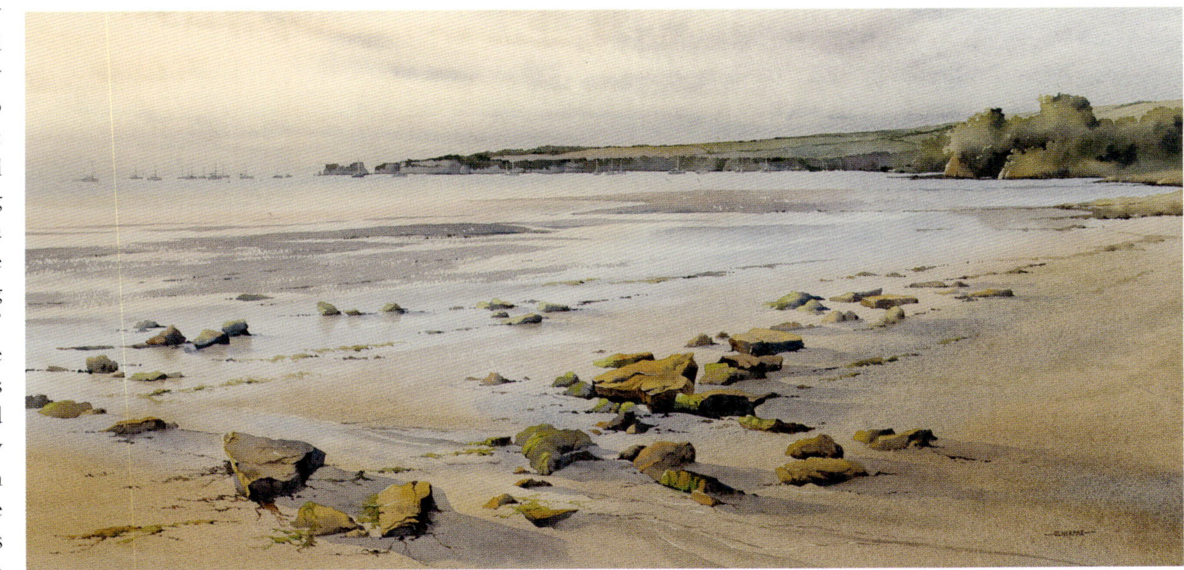

At Dawn on the Knoll Beach – 72cm x 36cm

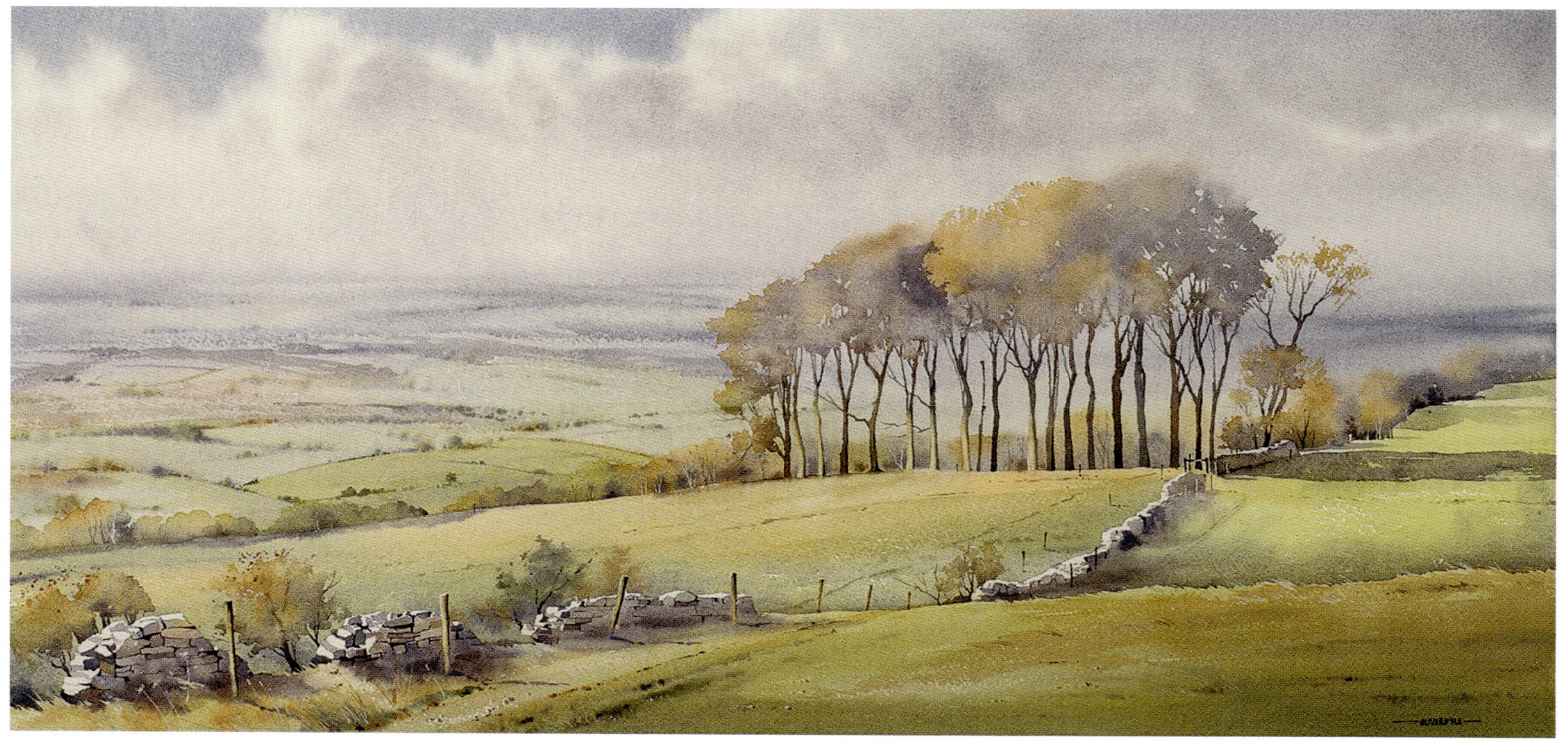

Views of Cheltenham from Cleeve Hill – 72cm x 36cm
This broken old dry-stone wall does a wonderful job of leading the eye across the landscape to the spinney of beech trees. Its disappearance and re-emergence beneath the brow of the hill prevents it from being too dominating and creating a partition through the painting.

is in order. Instead, if the houses are simply suggested the viewers will use their judgement and imagination to visualise what the artist is trying to convey, and consequently they are more engaged with the painting as the eye lingers for longer, helping the mind to interpret the visual clues on the paper. In 'The Three Sisters' the view through the trees includes the large town of Cheltenham in the distance. It has been rendered with the simplest of broken brushstrokes and minimal marks that hint at an urban conglomeration of buildings and rooftops, a far more satisfactory approach than a laboured rendering of each building, supporting and providing context to the main subject of the trees, instead of competing with it. This idea of simplifying extends further than just employing a looser style of painting to suggest detail. Sometimes larger objects in their entirety may need to be left out. If they don't contribute anything positive to the scene and distract from a compelling composition, leave them out or move them elsewhere in the scene. Knowing what to include and what to exclude, and the simplification of passages within the painting are essential in supporting a good composition. Of course, you will employ your own common sense; a painting of the River Thames, looking downstream from London Bridge, might look a little odd if you decide to remove Tower Bridge as a distracting component in your composition!

- **Use odd numbers.** Even numbers suggest completion and order. They help our minds to feel settled and we conclude that there is nothing more to see and discover. Odd numbers create a slight sense of tension and unease — what

could be missing? The eye looks again, the mind imagines where it might be, and the experience for the viewer becomes one of deeper engagement with the work. In an estuary scene, three boats as opposed to two or four will always look better. Don't paint four Scots Pine trees, isolated on the heathland — paint

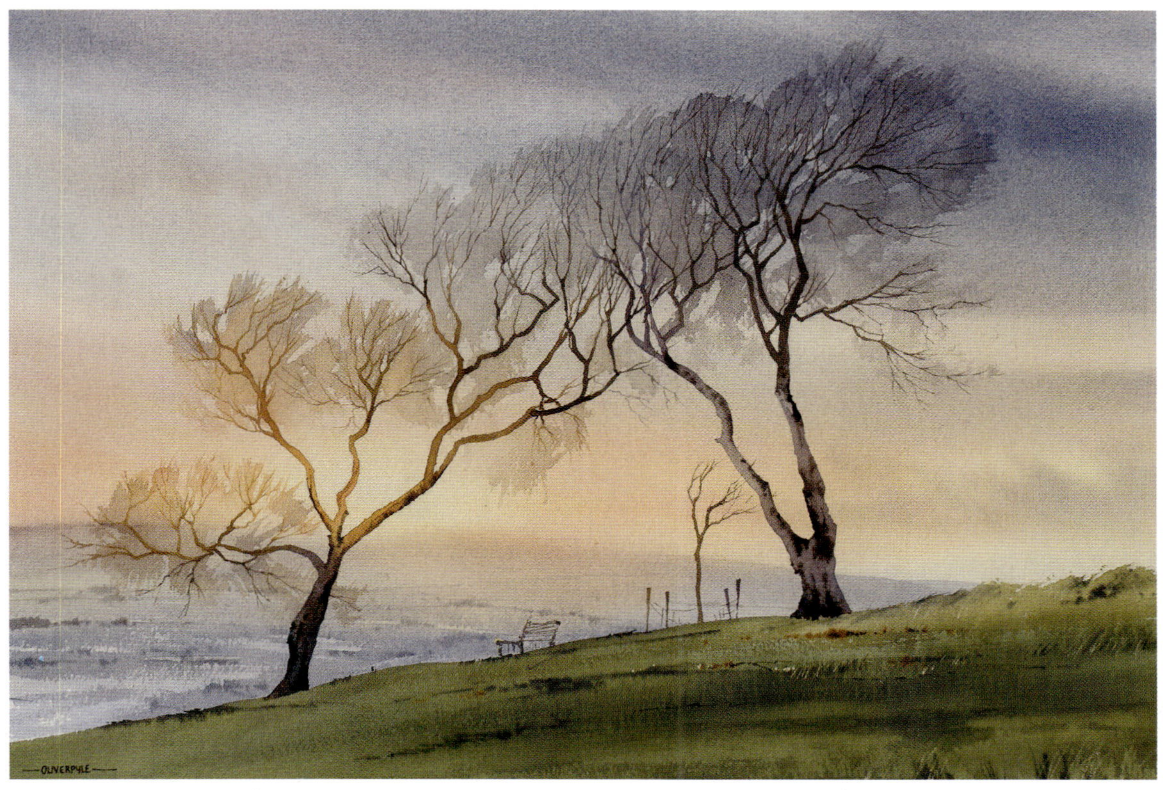

The Three Sisters – 50cm x 34cm

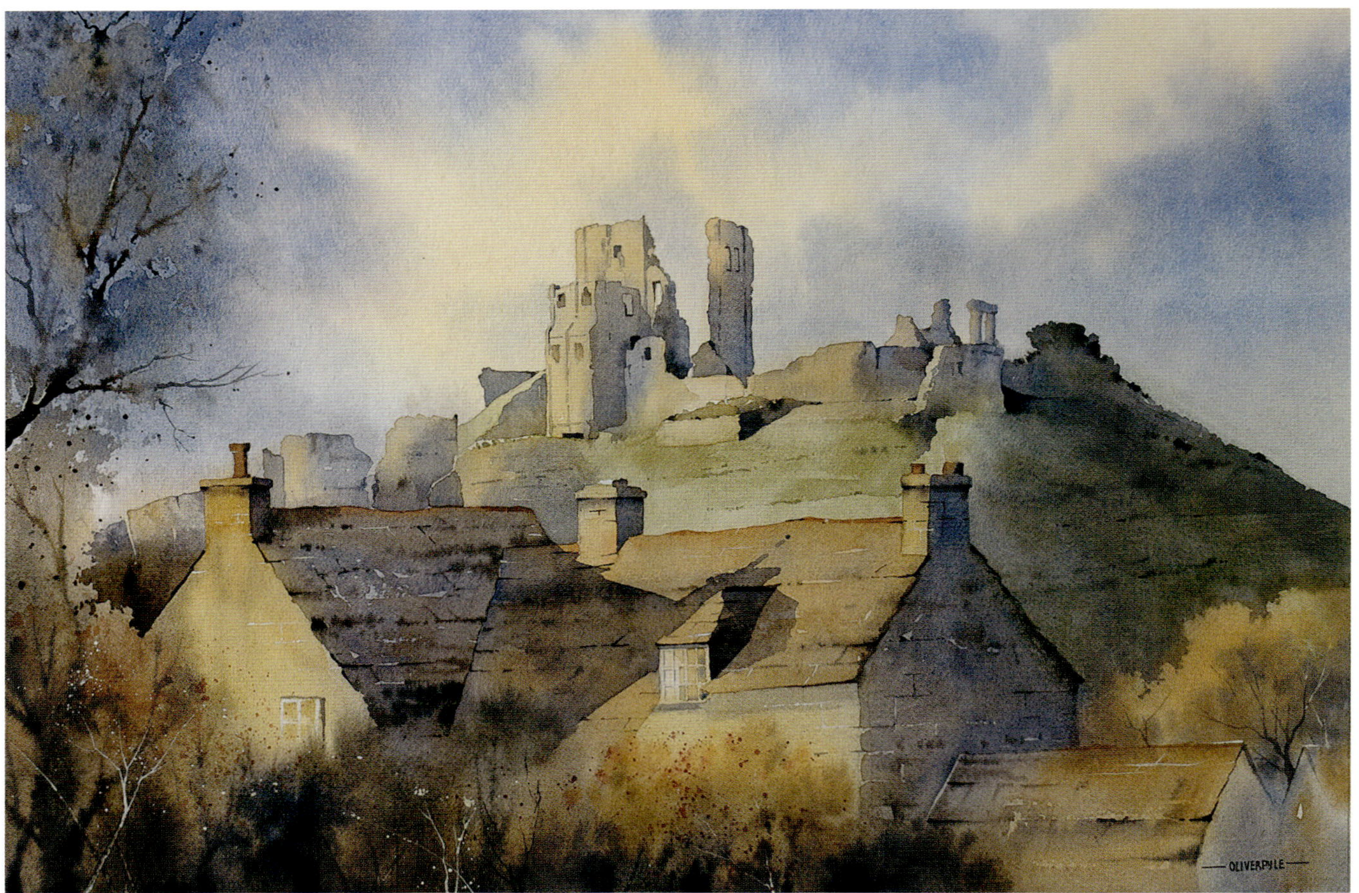

Across the Rooftops, Corfe Castle – 50cm x 34cm
There was no need to detail every tile on the roof. The simple suggestion of a few here and there gives the viewer all the clues they need to conclude that they are looking at a tiled roof.

three or five. In a busy harbour scene of more than five boats, then this consideration becomes less relevant, but where there is a small number of strongly defined, similar elements, opt for an odd number.

- **Look for dominant shapes.** It is surprising how often we can find repeated shapes in the landscape if we take the time to observe carefully. When we do, it can greatly help a composition if we enhance these and even introduce further examples. Imagine a small harbour-side village if you will. You can see the triangular spire of the parish church and two triangular conifer trees in the background. Small sailing boats are moored in the estuary, sails furled. If you paint them with their sails unfurled, you have immediately introduced additional triangles. Think about varying the height of the masts and their position relative to the church spire so their apices become the points of an imaginary triangle. Repeated shapes in the landscape create a sense of rhythm that makes for a pleasing composition. A nice design element to a composition is to play off two different repeating shapes against each other, as was the case in 'A Beautiful Start to the Day, Corfe Castle' (page 106). Occasionally you will find that nature offers you a happy coincidence of repeating shapes. In the painting 'Clouds of Heather' there is a shape in the cloud that is repeated in both the foliage of the Scots Pine and a clump of foreground heather. It's subtle, but there was enough similarity in the scene for me to play with this and enhance the effect slightly.

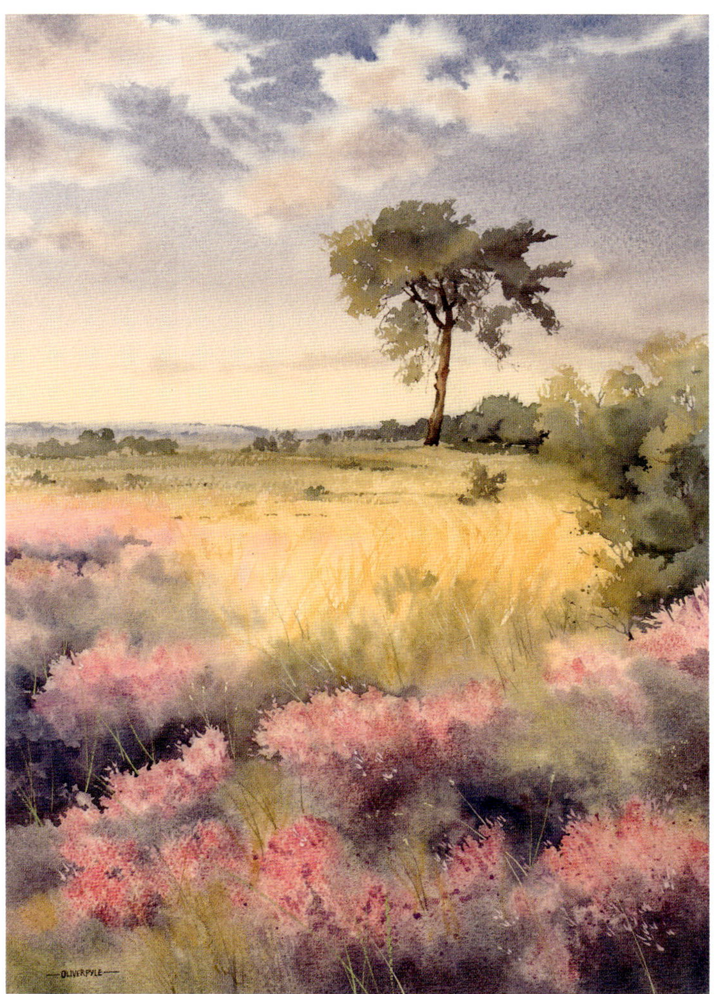

Clouds of Heather – 34cm x 50cm

- **Avoid uniformity and repetition…** and repetition and uniformity. In much the same way that odd numbers are more aesthetically helpful than even numbers, a lack of uniformity across a painting is highly desirable. Let's return to our fence posts; in reality they will be evenly spaced and sunk to the same height. To paint them like this will probably spoil your painting. Leave a couple out, make one taller and another shorter, vary their spacing and paint some at a jaunty angle – it will look so much better. In 'Scots Pines near Chelwood Vachery' (page 86) the spacing of the pines in the middle distance has been carefully planned, improving on what was in front of me by considering their proximity to each other and the larger foreground trunk. It is subtle, but if I painted it to include the regular spacing I observed in the original scene you would notice the difference, and the overall painting would not have the same impact. It also pays to avoid coincidence; the top of a line of trees coinciding with the top of a distant hill just looks terrible. Bring them beneath the brow of the hill or extend them above and it will be a vast improvement. Lack of uniformity is important when creating areas of texture in a painting: tree bark, stones on the beach, foreground grass, distant woodlands. It is easy to settle into repeatable brushstrokes that start to form a regular pattern and before you know it the field you were hoping would look natural has started to resemble a design for wallpaper. Being able to rely on a variable and random approach to your brushstrokes enables you to render these passages with a lack of uniformity that encourages a loose, yet realistic feel to your work. Practising the free and random movement of your brush will help significantly to reduce the appearance of regularity in your work; remember, the landscape is an irregular and disorganised place. One of the reasons why I prefer standing up to paint is that it allows me to paint with my arm as opposed to my wrist, allowing broader movements on a larger piece of paper. Give this a try, it is an excellent way of helping to minimise uniformity in your brushstrokes.

- **The importance of connectivity.** In many landscapes there are passages and components that stand apart and can seem isolated. This is rarely a good look as there is far more pleasure in viewing a unified whole. To avoid this, we can introduce elements that help to connect one part of a painting to another – ripples on a river, cloud patterns, fence posts, shadows, a suggested line of rough grass. We can also close up gaps or link areas together by placing elements

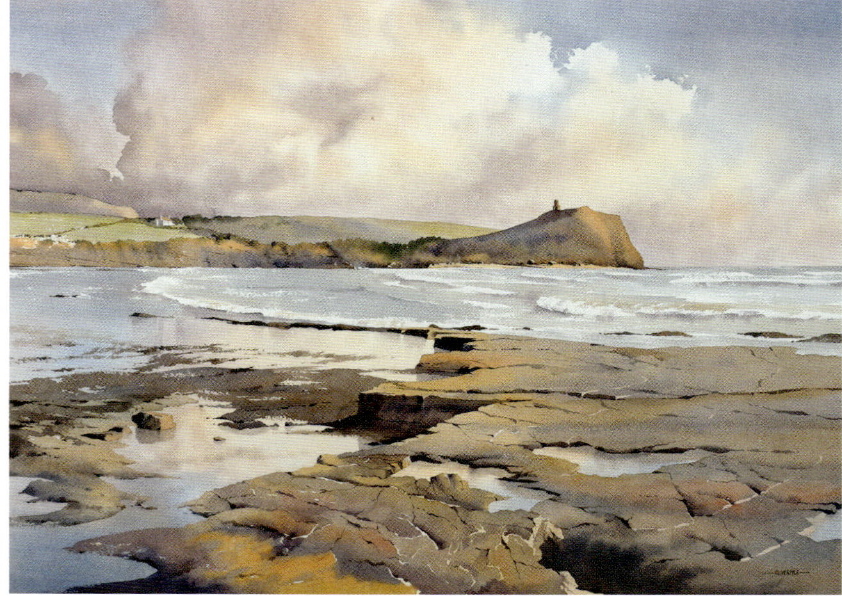

Light on the Ledges, Kimmeridge Bay – 70cm x 51cm
The separation of background and foreground at Kimmeridge can present a problem, with the sea acting as a barrier between the two. The dark extremity of the rock ledge helps to close the gap a little, but the inclusion of the wave breaking behind it, sweeping around the bay helps to connect front to back.

between them: trees, hedges, boats, rocks, seaweed. 'Wind and Waves, Swanage' (page 84) presented me with a small compositional problem; the main elements of the painting are all very well connected, apart from the foreground jetty that looked rather incidental, even isolated. To close the gap between this and the fishing tackle and boats on the left I introduced a couple of ropes and cables between the two, and a few strategically positioned strands of seaweed. When deploying this tactic to improve your composition it is essential that you observe the previous point – carefully position them so that the elements or spaces are all different, and you don't introduce any unwelcome uniformity.

Try to take time before you launch into a painting to ensure that you have a strong composition, or you will often struggle to present a compelling finished piece. It helps greatly to make several small thumbnail sketches to resolve any potential problems. This allows you to play around with elements that you might want to exclude, or indeed introduce to improve the composition. The sketch that works best should then act as your map to help you produce a strong composition.

Our ability to design paintings that are dynamic and have visual interest flows from a solid understanding of Colour, Contrast and Composition and an awareness of how you can manipulate these to achieve the effects you want; think of them as controls that you can tweak if you need to. The following four paintings are all examples of how I have used these controls to design paintings that capture my feelings of the moment and the place, and produce paintings that have impact.

At the start of this section on composition I mentioned that sometimes these considerations are almost an irrelevance. Why would I say that

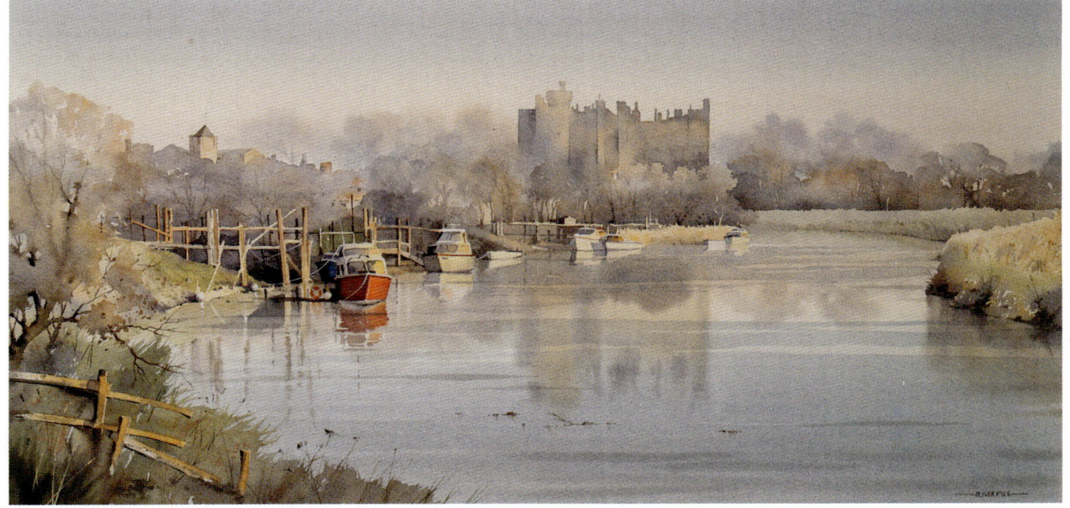

Calm and Frosty, River Arun – 72cm x 36cm
I created this image from various different photos and sketches and of course my knowledge of a place that I know well. To enhance the feeling of a frosty winter's morning with the sunlight just breaking through I used a combination of warm and cool colours, but keeping the temperature variation between them close; dramatic differences would have suggested harsher lighting. Keeping detail to a minimum on the castle and background trees creates an illusion of mist starting to lift from the riverside and reducing the size of the tree on the left opened up the scene, permitting a clearer view of the red boat and the sunlight catching the jetty and riverbank. I decided to dial up the warmth of light catching the boats, especially the red hull – this sharp accent colour in an otherwise subdued colour palette really does lift the painting.

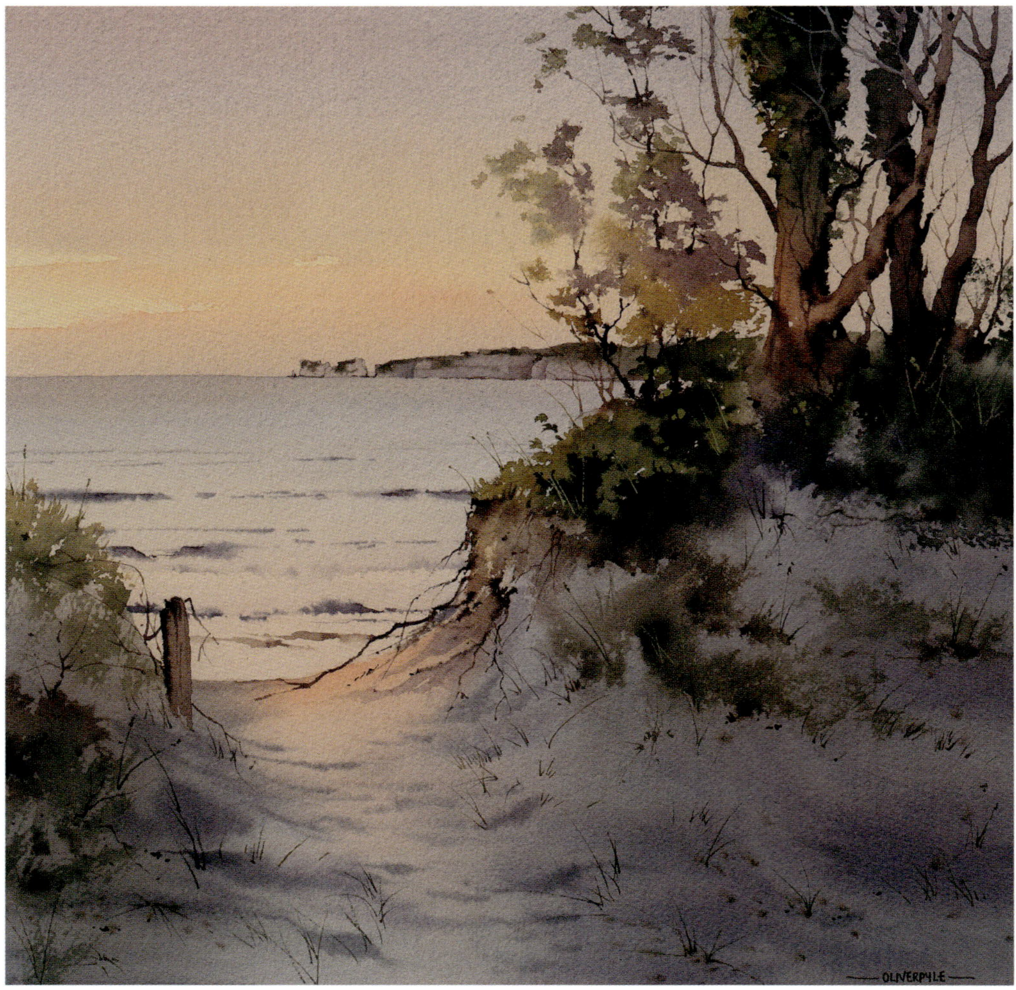

having been at pains to explain and demonstrate the benefits of a sound composition? Recently, I have become increasingly engaged by the idea that my motivation for painting a subject is often founded on an immediate impression of it and exploring what are the best ways of conveying that. My gaze doesn't always sweep the landscape, establishing context, but will fix directly on the impact of a specific element, or elements: a grand old oak tree doffing its cap to the evening sun, a neglected telephone box choked by the encroaching landscape, the endless emptiness of the ocean, shining like liquid metal in the evening sun. In painting these situations, I feel that there

First Light on Middle Beach – 30cm x 30cm
The explosive sunrise half an hour earlier had mellowed as the sun slipped behind a thin layer of cloud. The ensuing pastel hues were beautiful and there was just the slightest hint of sun catching the edge of the sand dune where the path led down to the beach. By increasing the reflected sunlight in that area, introducing some warmth on the foliage and tree trunk on top of the dune, then darkening the foreground shadow, the painting encourages the viewer to move down the path towards the light.
The glow in the sky was important but there was more cloud detail that I felt was distracting. I settled on a higher horizon and left out much of the detail in the sky, with just a suggestion on the left where the sun was breaking through. Being alone on Studland beach at dawn exudes tranquillity; this painting captures that moment.

Peaceful Reflections, Old Harry Rocks –
52cm x 52cm
I find fault with most of my paintings; there are
things that didn't quite work out as intended, or
I wish I had painted differently. This painting is
an exception, I wouldn't change anything about
it. I had made a quick sketch (overleaf) forty-five
minutes earlier, just as the sun was coming up on
a bitterly cold April morning and returned to the
scene as the light was becoming warmer, picking
out highlights on the chalk stacks and the grassy
cliff top. There is a lot of colour here: a warm
sienna glow to sky and chalk; an array of warm and
cool greens; orange scrub clinging to the cliff face;
different blues in sky and sea. There is always a
danger in situations like these to go overboard with
the colour, but I was conscious that the peaceful
cliff top feeling and calming views could only be
captured with the utmost care and restraint on the
palette: cobalt blue, light red, permanent rose, raw
sienna, gamboge hue. 'Watercolour is best when
it whispers, not shouts' I kept reminding myself.
The distant land (Bournemouth) would be nothing
more than the faintest suggestion, clouds and the
surface of the sea would be free of hard edges,
while a few would be permitted in the tufts of cliff
top grass. To achieve the feeling of delicate, early-
morning light, every area I painted would include
regular and soft transitions of colour, almost
imperceptible in places. It worked; every time I look
at this I am immediately back on the headland,
feeling the cold breeze, watching the morning sun
creep across the cliff face.

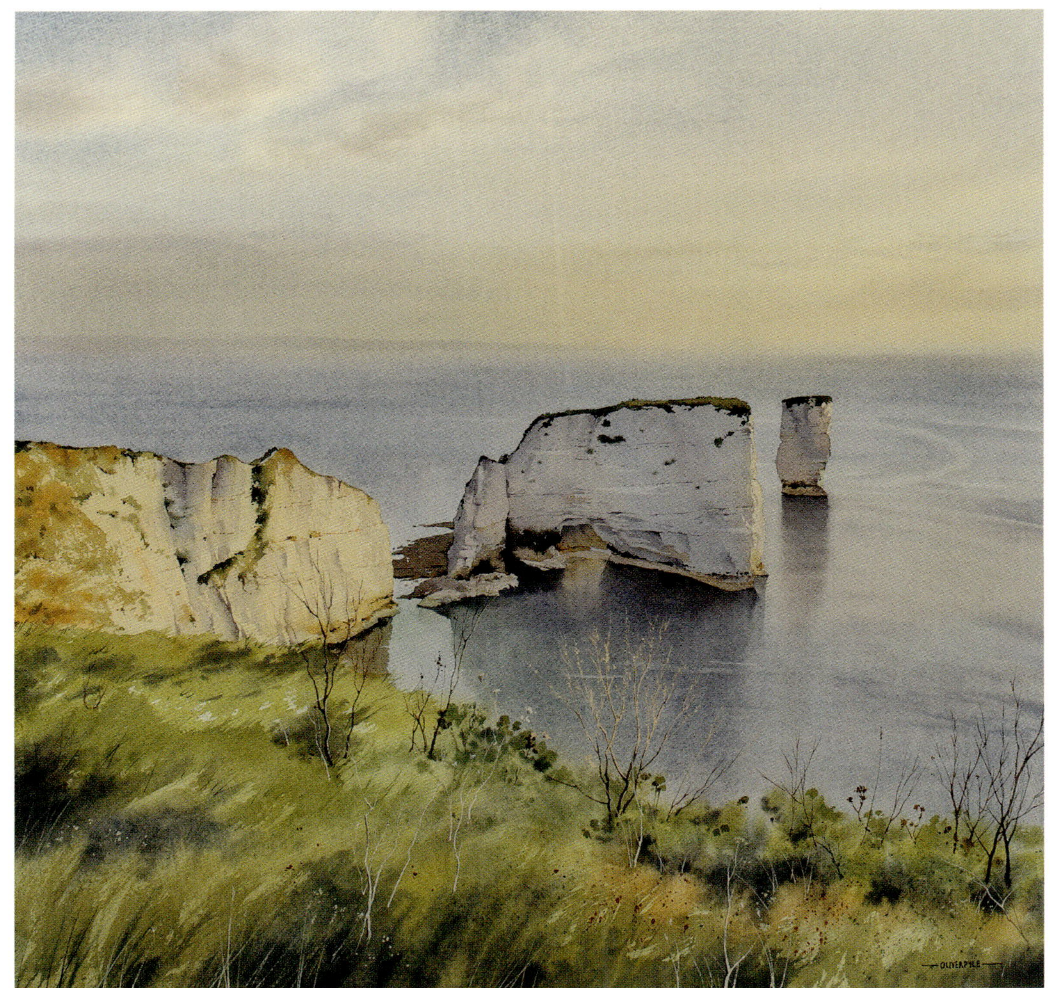

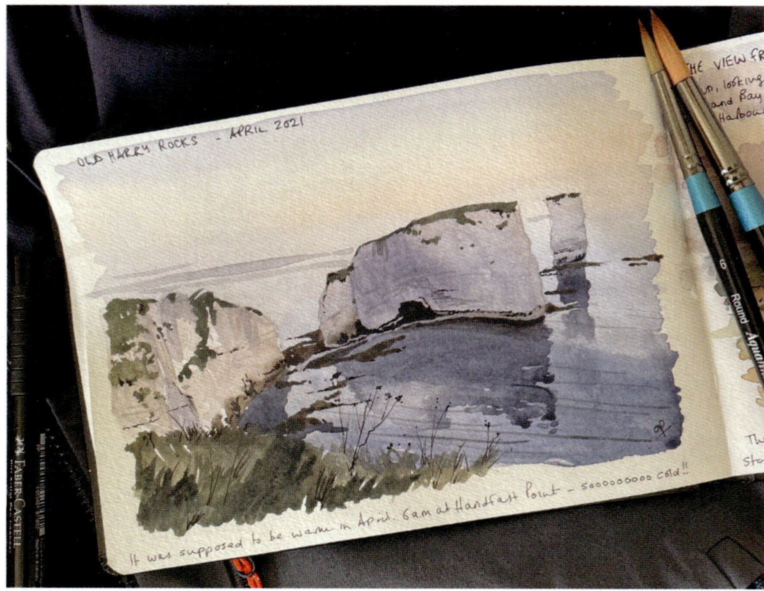

ABOVE: A dawn sketch at Old Harry Rocks

RIGHT: There is a Light That Never Goes Out – 29cm x 39cm
For several months I walked past this old, disused phone box, just outside Balcombe train station in Sussex, its last caller a distant memory, as faded as its peeling paintwork. Although there is no cause for carelessness or complacency on our part, nature is largely undaunted by our interference in the landscape and the moment we retreat a little, it insists on regaining control; brambles and ivy usurping the place of telephone directories and late-night callers. Despite this natural changing-of-the-guard, it seemed to me that all the elements were getting on rather well together. Years of neglect had not taken their toll, surprisingly, on the light bulb which cast a warm, approving glow inside. It was not a typical painting subject for me, and a challenging exercise in the placement of warm and cool colour hues, and an excellent workout for improving brush control skills.

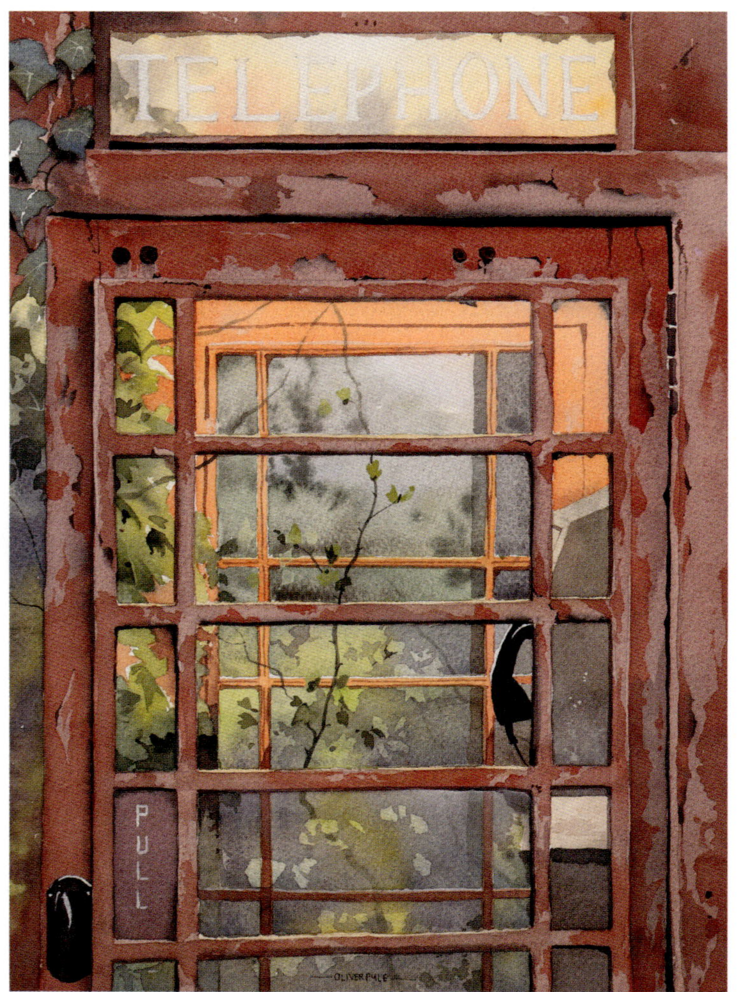

is perhaps a greater honesty to be found in presenting them in the way that I saw them, without the imposition of any (or as little as possible) technical thinking. In the following field trip to Dancing Ledge, you will notice all manner of compositional irregularities: absent focal points, multiple focal points, dodgy horizons, imbalanced scenes. I will walk you through some of these, and why it was important to present these subjects as I initially saw them, with as little editing and embellishment as possible.

I apologise readily for presenting you with this composition confusion, however I feel that it serves an important creative purpose. Much of today's teaching about landscape painting is prescriptive, with a tendency to adopt a rules-based approach that can lead to complacent and formulaic work. Allowing a little tension to creep into our understanding of how to look at the landscape and record its impact is a good thing that will keep us on our creative toes. Hopefully it will lead to an abundance of interpretations, subjects and styles with new perspectives and challenging compositions.

FIELD TRIP 5 – COMPOSITION

Composition Confusion at Dancing Ledge

It would be logical to conclude that the coastal footpaths in Dorset lead to the sea or run adjacent to it. Your conclusion would be correct; these well-trodden ways traverse headlands, cross beaches, climb to cliff tops, descend into valleys, cut through dry-stone walls, skip over stiles, wind through grassy meadows, and all the time sounds and smells of the sea are inescapable. The salty air of the English Channel and the stunning vistas of bays, rocks and promontories are reason enough to walk and learn these paths, yet for me, they offer an immediate route to a more profound and evocative destination: my childhood and adolescent years.

In August 1982, one month before my tenth birthday, the Pyle family took the first of many holidays in Swanage, Dorset, returning almost every year following. From the top of the street where we were staying, we found the Priest's Way, an ancient track used in medieval times by the local priest, visiting his flock of worshippers, split between the town of Swanage and the nearby village of Worth Matravers. It was different to the landscapes I had witnessed at home in Sussex, an enclosed, heavily wooded county. Instead, here was a new place, a land of dry-stone walls, sheep everywhere, dew-drenched meadows, teasels, piles of old, quarried Purbeck stone and magnificent views of the coast. One of my first memories was walking to Dancing Ledge, a disused quarry on the coast, easily reached from Priest's Way, followed by a steep walk down to the sea.

As years passed and other parts of the Purbeck coast path became familiar, different locations became favourites and Dancing Ledge was forgotten and brushed aside. The spectacular ledges at Kimmeridge, the dramatic arrangement of Old Harry Rocks, the jeopardy of being blown to smithereens by stepping on an unexploded shell on the Ministry of Defence's artillery ranges at Lulworth – these all had more to offer. Dancing Ledge had become a rather dull waltz by comparison.

Returning to Purbeck in recent years with sketchpad in hand, my focus had remained on the more dramatic sambas and tangos at Kimmeridge and Studland until one evening, while camping near Corfe Castle, I remembered Dancing Ledge and recalled the impact and enjoyment that it had offered decades earlier; I wanted to revisit that. There was to be no sketching this time, just a simple observation of the place and a sensory impression of the moment to be experienced and committed to memory (and my little book for jotting field notes). A small, unkept track from the village of Langton Matravers led to the carpark used by walkers; this hadn't changed, its surface still pockmarked by pot-holes, challenging the most robust of car suspension systems. The evening was warm and calm; the sky, bright and cloudless. Residual particles of the day's activity formed a hazy curtain, draped over the horizon. It evoked distant memories of the place and I resolved to make several paintings when I returned home that would do nothing more than record my immediate impressions and feelings.

Shortly after leaving the carpark, the path made its way past an old farmyard, albeit still a working one, including the historic Spyway Barn. There was a rather pleasing neglected feel to the scene: old gates testing their hinges, crumbling stonework, abandoned agricultural equipment, peeling paint, unkempt grass, rust, rambling wildflowers. It was difficult to identify a focal point for the painting, but this was of little concern to me. Received wisdom suggests that the eye needs to come to rest somewhere within the scene, however in this instance, the painting was not so much about the buildings, but the space beyond. As I approached the barn, I was impressed by the empty glow of the evening sky, pulling me forward, knowing that just past the farmyard would be a view of the coast behind the hedge on the right of the picture. Detail has been distributed evenly across the foreground and buildings, where the tonal range has been kept deliberately narrow to promote a glow on the horizon. As much as there was interest to be found in the farmyard, my immediate impression was the anticipation of what lay beyond; it is a painting of expectation.

I remember this scene well from years earlier: walking round the side of the barn to a view across the meadows, a pastoral patchwork stitched together by dry-stone walls, with the calm sea beyond. The evening countryside smelled sweet, invigorated by the dew that was starting to creep in. A small sailboat made its way back towards Swanage. Later, I made a

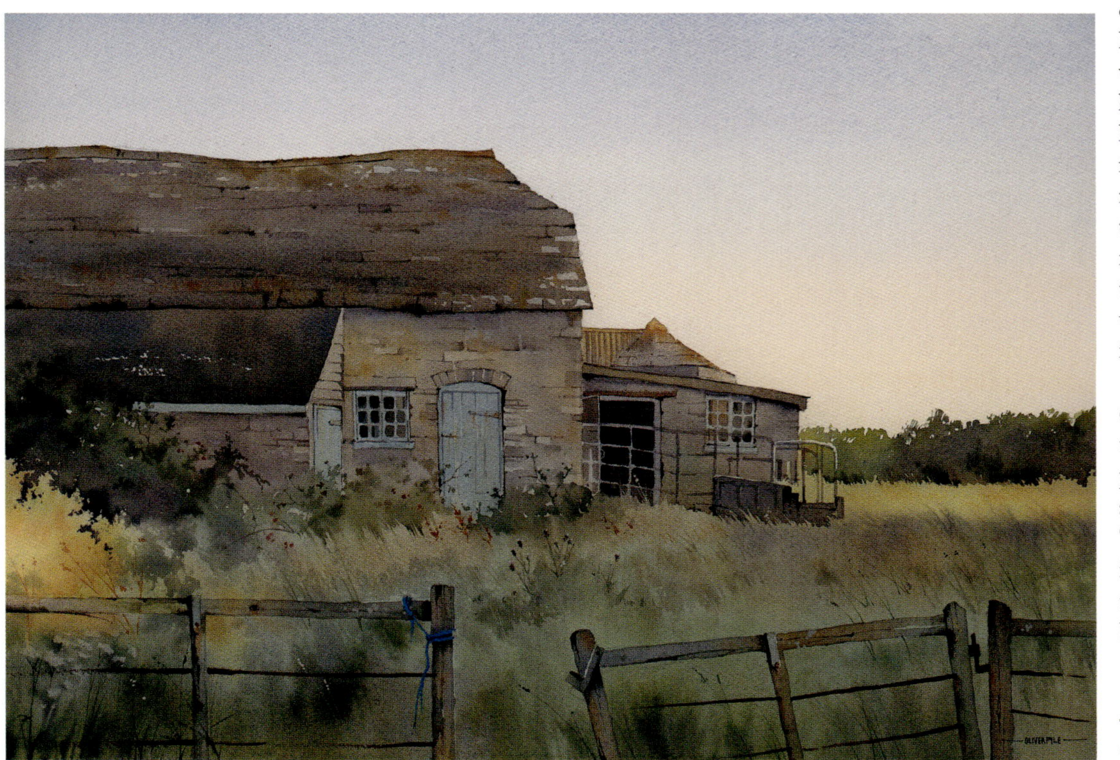

The Forgotten Farmyard, Spyway Barn –
50cm x 34cm

couple of thumbnail sketches of the scene, with a higher and lower horizon line as any good student of composition would; I was unsatisfied with both. Neither of these technically 'correct' compositions helped to capture my impression of the moment, with the meadows falling away towards the sea, the distant gate inviting us to take the steep slope down to Dancing Ledge below, and the sky slipping seamlessly into the calm English Channel. The horizon here is worryingly close to the centre of the painting and with the open space taking the eye directly through the centre of the painting, compositional shortcomings are easy to see. It was a quick, simple painting and I was not concerned by these technicalities. Ludwig van Beethoven's *Symphony No. 6* is a beautiful piece of thematic music, describing a day in the countryside. Its first movement is entitled

Erwachen heiterer Empfindungen bei der Ankunft auf dem Land or *Awakening of Cheerful Feelings on Arrival in the Country*. It is how I feel about this scene and my task as a painter was to simply act as a conduit, allowing those feelings to be transferred to the viewer. Landscape painting rarely benefits from over-thinking; studious analysis can have its place but always make sure that you explore and understand the relationship between aesthetics and experience and where the priorities should lie.

Passing through the gate, the gentle amble across the meadows became a steep path down to the coast. Dancing Ledge is the name of the rock platform to be found underneath the old quarry, last worked in Victorian times and used as a mooring point for boats, transporting the quarried Portland Freestone for grand building projects in London

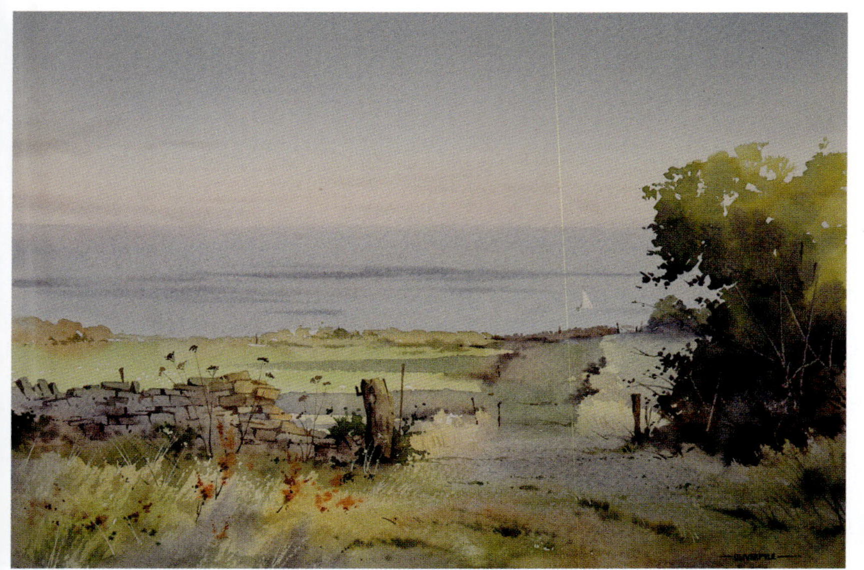

Across The Meadows to Dancing Ledge – 35cm x 25cm

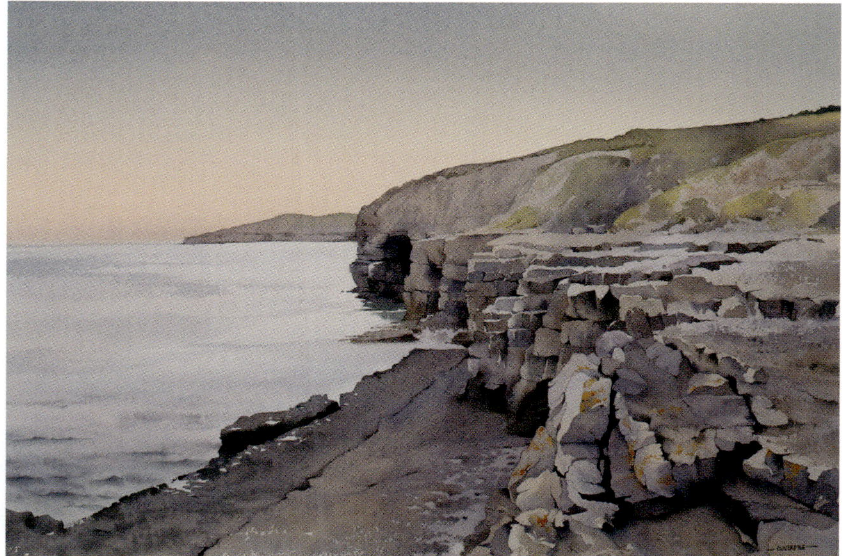

The Old Cliff Quarry, Dancing Ledge – 50cm x 34cm

and beyond. The sun was edging lower, lending a peachy glow to the horizon, an important colour note in an increasingly monochrome landscape. We were there alone and there was a cool silence, only punctuated now and then by the calls of guillemots and cormorants and the sea gently lapping the ledges. The strong diagonal of the ledge is a helpful compositional tool to lead the eye into the scene, but it abandons us in the centre of the picture. Not ideal. Like the farmyard,

there is no real focal point here; it is tempting to think of the dark inlet in the middle distance as the centre of interest, but an equally plausible case could be made for the quarried area in the foreground, defined by dark cracks and crevasses. Does it have two focal points? Can it have two focal points? Does it need any focal points? My priorities with this painting were firstly to convey a sense of the place, in particular the deep scars in the landscape and the quarried remains: disorderly layers

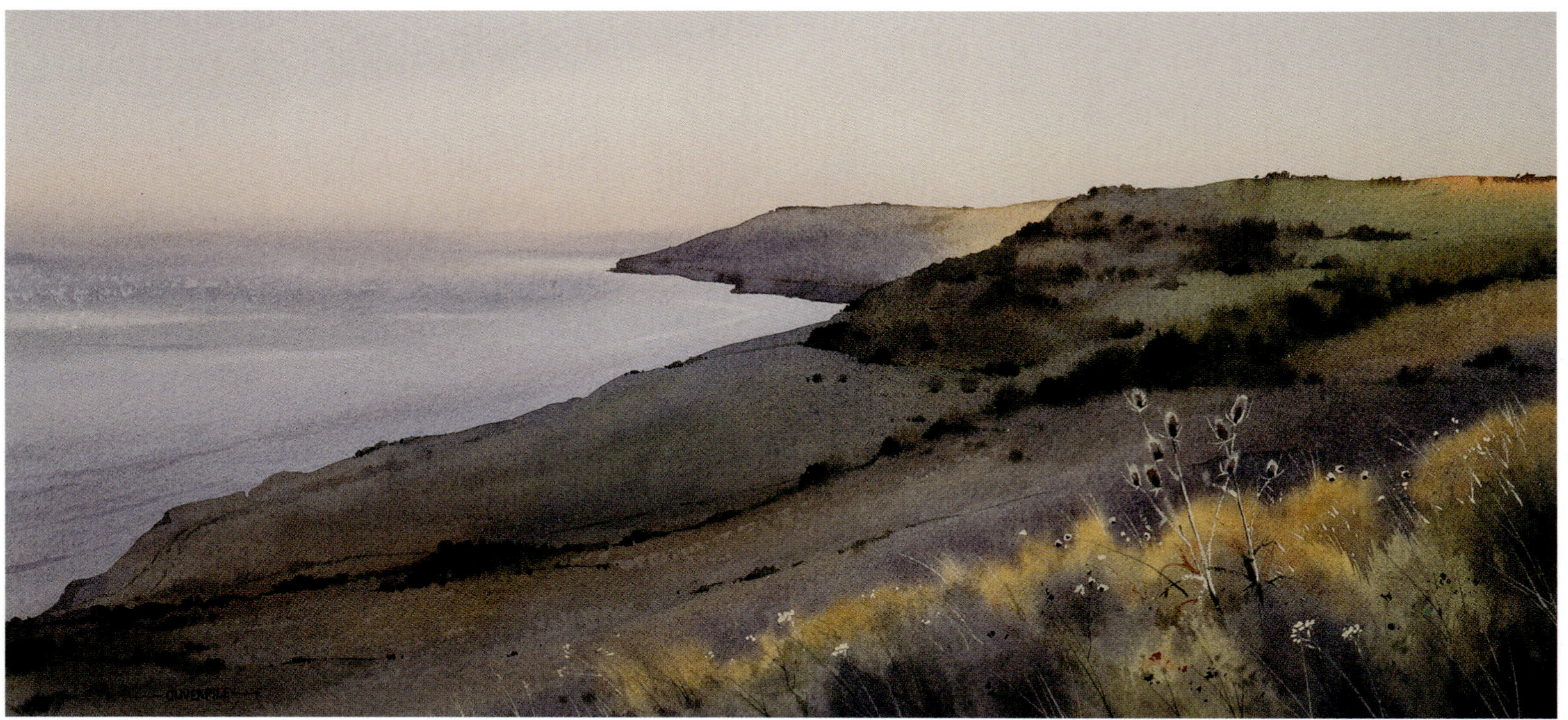

Teasels and Thistles, Dancing Ledge – 35cm x 17cm

of limestone Lego. Then, and perhaps more importantly, I needed to capture the unique, irreplaceable feeling of looking along the coastline: solid rock to one side, fluid sea to the other; everything to the right, nothing to the left. It is the thing of nightmares for those with delicate compositional sensibilities; almost everything sits on one side of the painting, full of form and detail, while the other is open and empty. However, this pronounced sense of imbalance is representative of coastal vistas and a studied approach to compositional compliance makes little sense of places and moments like this. This is a painting of scarring, but ultimately one of space, stillness and solitude.

Back up the path to the gate. Legs burning, lungs doing much the same. We sat on a sward, just as the sun had slipped away, its afterglow catching the tops of the headlands, illuminating a spray of thistles and teasels that had also caught the interest of a pair of speckled wood butterflies. The scene presents a composition even more unbalanced than 'The Old Cliff Quarry' painting. The orthodox tutor would sternly comment on the extent to which the strong tonal contrast of the coastline leads the eye along the headland toward the horizon, slipping out of the left-hand side of the painting. Excellent – this is precisely what I hoped it would do! It is how I remembered the moment and how I wanted to paint it. The allure of the coast lies not only in the richness of its flora and fauna but mostly in the ostensible infinity of the sea and the open views across it. J. Meade Faulkner wrote in his classic novel, *Moonfleet*, 'while behind all is spread as a curtain the eternal sea, ever the same and ever changing' and there cannot be another statement to represent my feelings of this moment with greater elegance and precision. Looking out to the vague horizon – nothing more than a delicate change in hue and tone – the eye is unrestrained, being allowed to continue and escape. Compositional tricks to keep our focus in the frame would not convey my feelings at this lovely spot on the Dorset coast and the allure of the sea.

My return to Dancing Ledge had been everything I had wished for, and more. The inspiration to record my experience here was easily found and by presenting these four scenes in as unstudied a way as possible, I hope to have been able to pass that experience on to you. Painting the landscape in an instinctive way, trusting your immediate impressions of a place is liberating, but I would suggest that it is better suited to a more experienced painter. It will not always work and for those that are new to landscape painting, by no means should you discard the collective wisdom of centuries of artistic thinking, far more erudite than my own, that has helped us to create compelling art through careful attention to composition. Nail that down first, but then start to consider the extent to which this approach might help to promote some freedom and creativity in your artistic expression.

ESTABLISHING A STRUCTURE

A quick browse through my email inbox will show you that I hear regularly from students at varying stages of skill and development, struggling to translate the techniques that they have learned in tutorials to painting their own scenes. Invariably, these emails may be summarised as 'I know what I want to paint, but I just don't know where to start' or 'my results seem to bear no resemblance to the scene in front of me and what I was hoping to express in my painting.' In this section I invite you to take a look at the structure and strategies that I use in my paintings, hoping they will provide you with a framework for approaching your own work with confidence.

It is clear to me that this problem of standing stymied in front of our own subjects is largely a result of approaching what we are doing without a structure or analytical approach. On many occasions in the past I would shy away from certain subjects (complex scenes and dominating foregrounds for example) that I didn't consider to be 'watercolour-ready' and it became apparent that my approach to painting was insufficiently resilient and poorly developed, so I took some time to think through what I was doing and how I could become a more versatile, complete painter, able to adapt to any subject. Such an analytical approach seems to be the antithesis of the expressive approach required for painting the landscape in watercolour: surely the confident, free flowing hand of the experienced painter cannot be reduced to such dry analysis and methodical procedure. Well, take a look at the structure I have designed and used for some years now; far from compromising my creativity it has given me the freedom in my work to express what I want to say about the landscape with spontaneity, with an ability to tackle both simple and complex scenes. Somewhat prosaically it is called the Four Ds: Decisions, Development, Definition and Detail. In this section I will show you how I use this methodology, looking at each stage, each 'D', in two paintings of varying complexity.

In teaching this method, I have created a Landscape Painting Checklist that may act as a useful prompt as you approach each new subject. It combines what we considered as the Three Cs (colour, contrast, composition) and the ideas that I will demonstrate for the Four Ds. It may seem onerous, but after a while much of this thought process becomes instinctive, as you become experienced at assessing the scene in front of you. There is no need to use

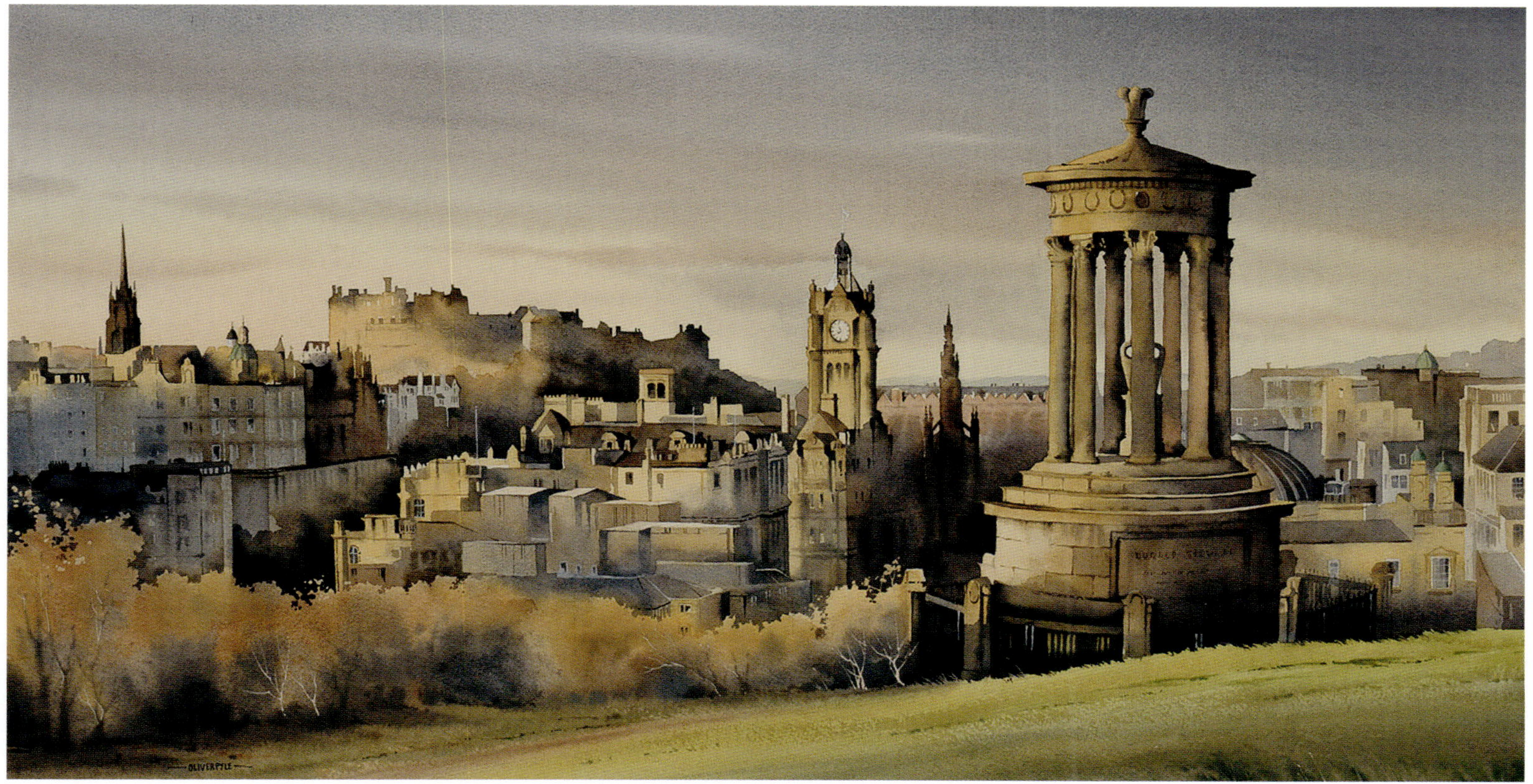

The Golden Glow of Morning, Edinburgh – 72cm x 45cm

it rigidly as a tick list to be completed for each painting and often some of the points to consider may not be applicable; it is designed to introduce an analytical way of thinking that provides you with a process for developing your own work. Care has been taken in designing and promoting this strategy to ensure that it only provides a structure around which your own feelings, ways of looking at the landscape and preferred technical methods can develop and thrive; think of it as the frame of a tent that I'm lending you to support your own fly sheet.

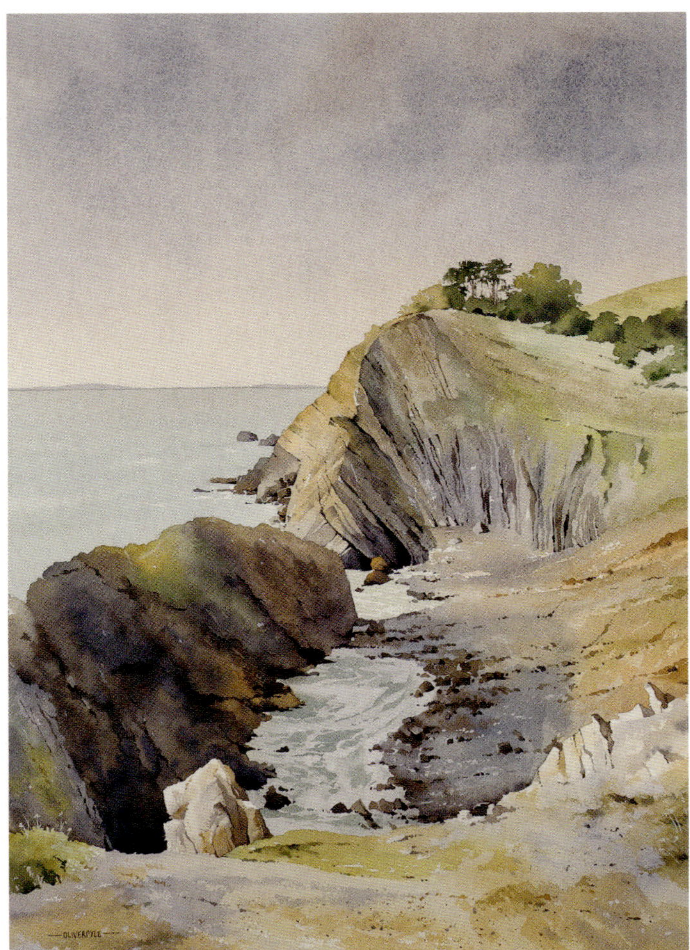

Stair Hole near Lulworth – 34cm x 50cm

LANDSCAPE PAINTING CHECKLIST

STAGE 1 – Creative Planning

Motivation

- What is the initial inspiration that initially attracted me to paint the scene and how can I best present this?
- What are my feelings and emotions as I view the scene?
- Is there a story that I can convey to the viewer?

Composition

- What format will work best for the scene: landscape/portrait/panorama/square?
- Is there a clear focal point or centre of interest, or is the scene describing a wider view?
- Are the elements in the picture helping to emphasise the focal point or are they a hindrance? Do they contribute positively to the composition?
- Should any elements or details be added or removed to improve the composition?
- Does that help, or do I need to make some thumbnail sketches to resolve this?
- Is the composition well balanced – tones, textures, shapes, busy/quiet passages etc.?
- What needs to be simplified and where does detail need to be preserved?

Lighting

- Which direction is the light coming from?
- Does ambient and reflected light have an impact on the scene?

- Are the shadows strong or weak, long or short, flat or multi-coloured?
- Do I need to introduce some stronger directional light?
- If so, is the lighting consistent with the locality/seasons?

Colours

- Does colour play an important role in the painting?
- Is there an opportunity to carefully enhance muted colours?
- Are Complimentary Colours a feature? Can they be used to add impact – overall, or in specific areas of the painting?
- Using a limited palette, what colours will I require?
- Have I identified where cool and warm colours should be used?

Tones

- What is the darkest aspect of the scene?
- What is the lightest?
- What are the tonal values in between?
- Can I introduce strong tonal contrasts, and what is their impact on the focal point?
- Will a monochrome sketch of tonal values help to inform the final painting?

STAGE 2 – Preparation

- At this stage it usually helps to transfer your thoughts, and your chosen thumbnail sketch into a larger sketch, introducing colour.
- What size of painting do I want to paint?
- What weight and surface of paper should I use? Is the painting about detail, or is a looser, impressionistic style required?

- Will I need any special kit – e.g. masking fluid?
- How complex will the washes be, especially the sky? Will I need to stretch my paper and work with large wet washes?

STAGE 3 – Painting

- How am I going to construct the painting, in terms of wash sequences?
- Will I be using lost/found techniques?
- Which passages will be painted wet-into-wet?
- Will I be using dry-brushing to suggest texture and detail?
- Which light areas do I need to preserve?
- Where do I need soft edges to avoid overlapping lines?
- Where are the potential pitfalls likely to occur (run-backs, mud etc.)?

Take some time to familiarise yourself with the ideas in the Landscape Painting Checklist. One of the best ways of doing this is to find a few of your paintings that may not have worked so well (we all have plenty!), and apply some of the ideas in the checklist to see if there are techniques and passages that could be improved upon.

Decisions

Let's start by taking a look at the first step in painting a scene – the first of my Four Ds' – Decisions. In many respects, this is the most important of the four stages and is where the 'art' happens. What do I mean by that? The landscape artist's responsibility is to select, edit and present their own view of a scene and their experience of being there. It should be more than simply a visual record, an illustration, of a place. This involves understanding where your inspiration and motivation for painting the scene lies and the decisions you make to present that. Much of this appears to be subconscious and I know many artists that will say

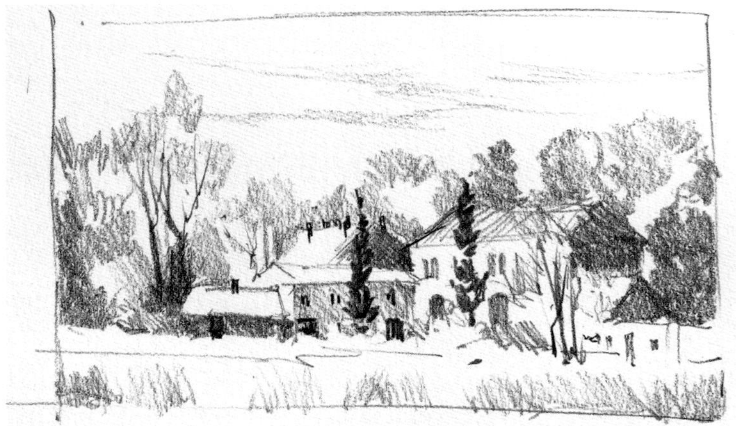

In this commission of an elegant but dilapidated grand house in Poland, a subject and area that I had no familiarity with, sketching ideas out beforehand was critical to resolve ideas and gain a stronger understanding of the project. One possible composition...

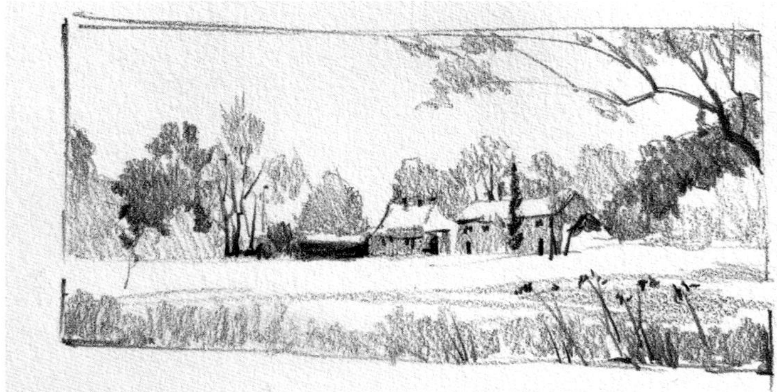

...and another.

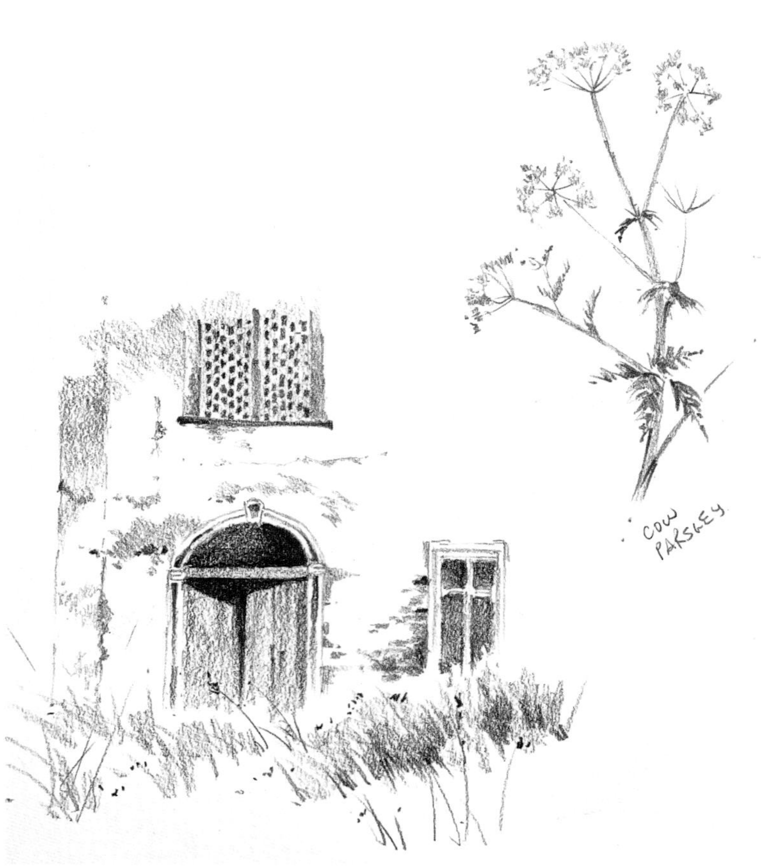

Sketches like this are a good way of helping you feel your way into an unfamiliar subject.

'you're over-thinking it; you see a scene and you paint it.' There is some truth to that, but I know that these thoughts will be there and have been developed over their careers. The difference here is that I'm revealing the hidden wiring that is present in the minds of most landscape painters, in order to help you to think like an artist.

During the Decisions stage, the importance of making small thumbnail sketches is critical, not only resolving a number of considerations that I outlined in the checklist, but it helps you to feel your way around the subject before launching into a painting, unprepared. Should you do this every time you paint? Do I do this every time I paint? No, not necessarily. When I sketch and paint quickly outdoors, I am making an immediate response to the subject and I find this to be an important reference if I then decide to develop these sketches into large, more considered studio paintings; at that point I may need to resolve some ideas with a few quick thumbnail sketches. Also, there will be times when we happily stumble upon 'watercolour-ready' scenes that require little or no editing and we are able to just dive in. As a general principle, though, you will find a rapid improvement in your paintings if you take

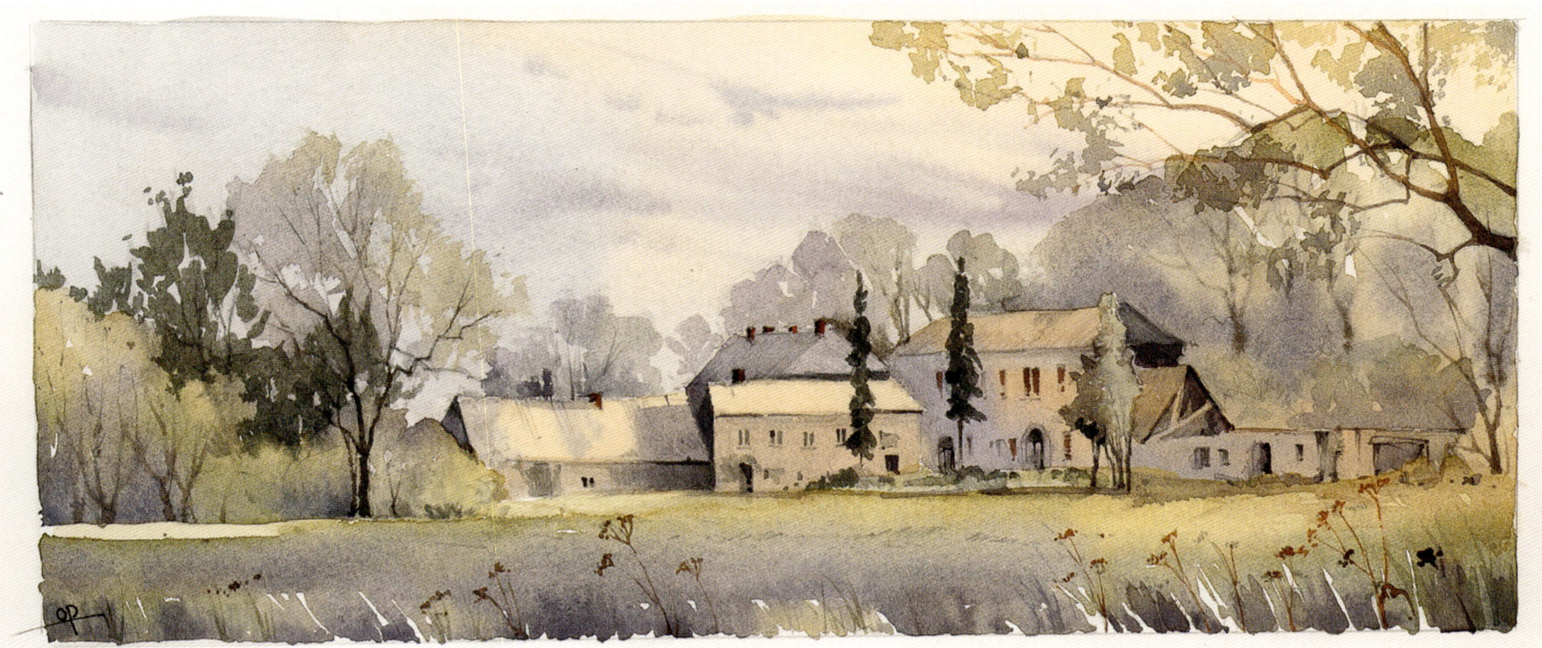

Making a small-scale watercolour sketch is a helpful way to make decisions on colour and atmosphere.

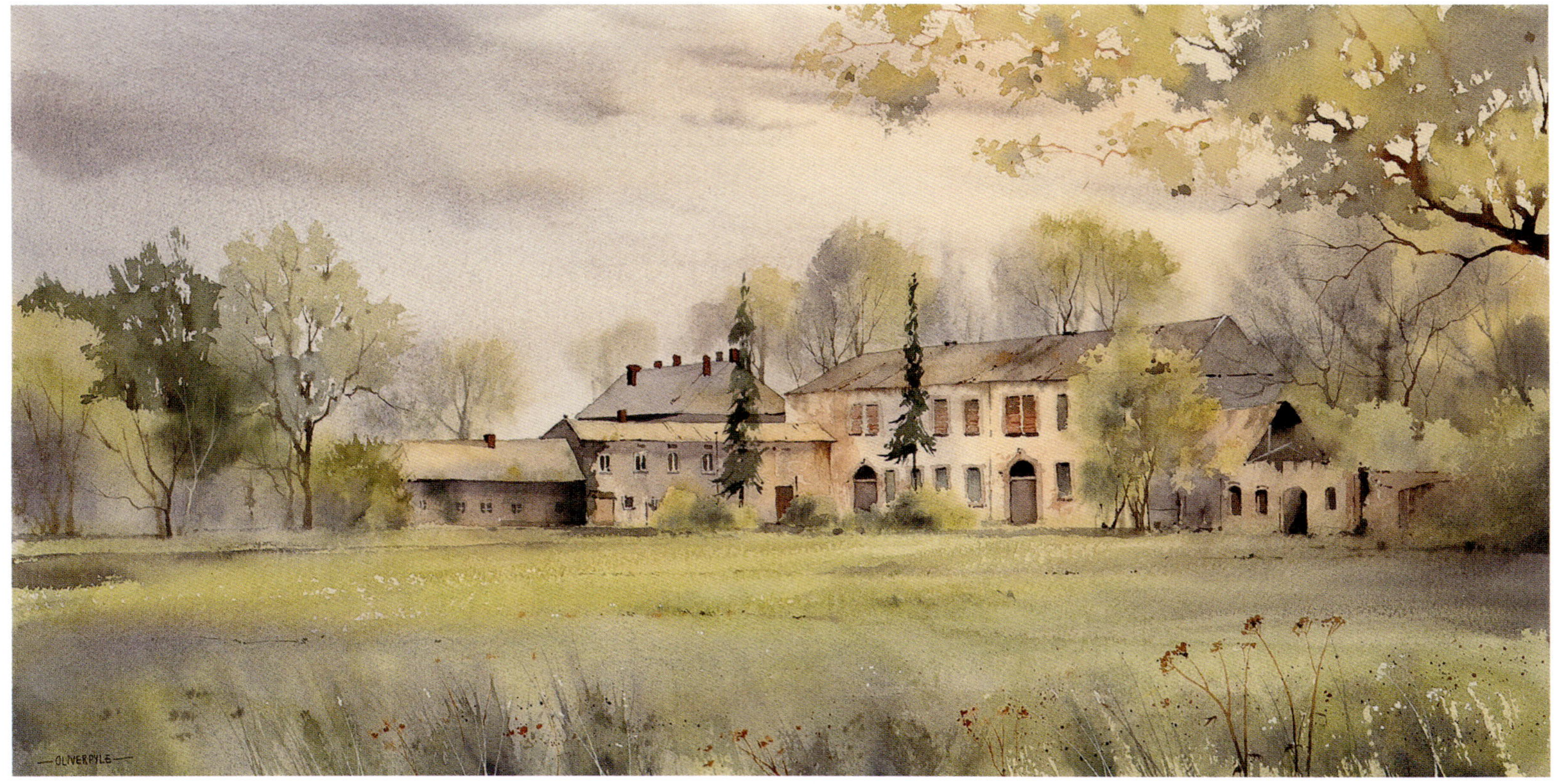

The finished painting – a direct result of the preparatory work undertaken at the Decisions stage.

the time to sketch your ideas out beforehand; remember, we are not just making a perfunctory record of what we see, but as artists our role is to emphasise and embellish, reduce and retract, and some thought needs to be given to how this may be best achieved.

Having assessed and analysed our subject we are ready to start our painting. My preference is to sketch out the scene in pencil, with as loose an outline as possible. My concern is to simply establish the components in the right place in the composition as a guide for painting, more than anything else. Of course, some subjects require careful draughtsmanship – recognisable buildings, arrangements with strong linear perspective, iconic coastlines, boats. For the most part though, my scenes comprise elements that require very little drawing: fields, trees, beaches, sea, riverbanks, hedges. These are best rendered directly with paint and brush, allowing the medium to make up its own mind.

Development

With the scene drawn, my aim in the Development Stage is to cover as much of the paper with initial washes without over-working any specific area of the painting. This allows me to establish passages of underpainting for texture, initiate the relationship between areas of warm and cool colour and to preserve areas of unpainted paper for highlights. At this stage, I am often working using a wet-on-wet technique into areas of the paper that I have pre-wet with clear water. I prefer to stretch my paper and concentrate on individual zones in the painting, wetting each area as required – sky, sea, fields, background, foreground – as opposed to wetting the whole sheet and dropping the paint in across the entire scene. I have developed this way of working as I prefer painting larger sized paintings (half sheet to full sheet and occasionally beyond) and it enables me to control the development of the washes and avoid potential technical problems with timing across a larger space. At this stage, my focus is on

Initial washes for sea and sky in the Development Stage build the foundation for the rest of the painting (see image on page 83 for the finished painting).

colour development more than tonal work. I will be using large brushes and generally avoiding the addition of concentrated, darker tones.

There is little merit in me continuing to describe this process in words here, and the two step-by-step examples further on will provide a more eloquent explanation.

Definition

At this stage of a painting, it can be easy to lose sight of where the painting is going and there can be a propensity to make hasty conclusions abouts its ultimate chance of success. When we paint the landscape in watercolour it is essential that we keep in mind the direction that we

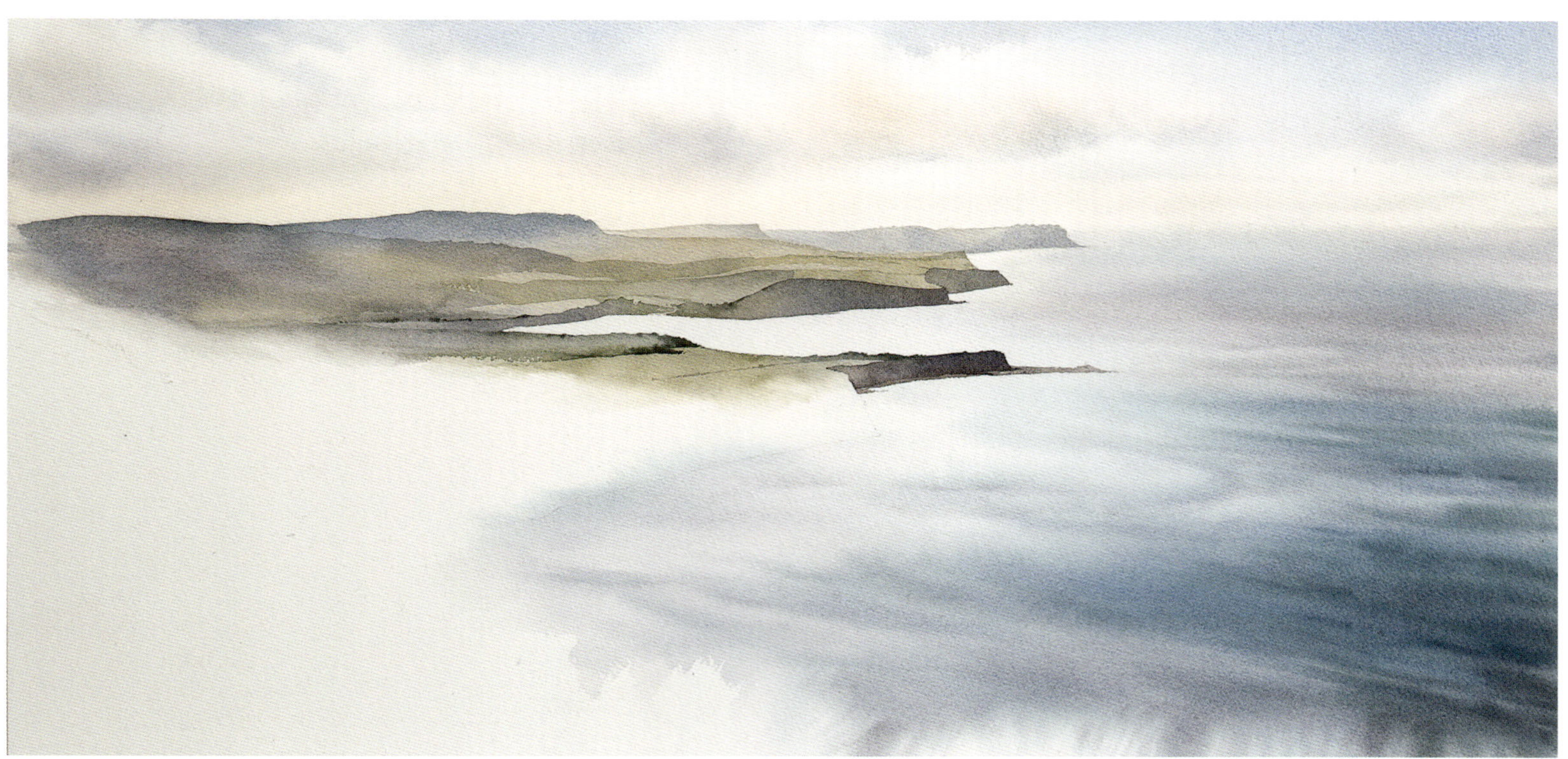

As the Definition Stage progresses, washes become more localised as shapes and areas of the painting progress.

want the work to go, always looking forward to realising our initial vision of the completed painting, remaining locked on to our original inspiration. This is why making an initial sketch is so important, be it a quick thumbnail sketch in pencil, a quick study to establish colours or a tonal map that allows us to evaluate the relationship between darks, lights, shapes and edges. The initial considerations in my Painting Checklist that may have seemed like cursory thoughts, now take on a weighty importance; without these reference points it is easy to become confused and disheartened with the process, with the ostensible mess and chaotic shapes we have created in the Development and Definition stages.

As you will see from the following demonstration examples, we are now at a stage in the painting where we start to define a number of elements:

Shapes

The most useful tool in defining the shapes in our composition is tone; the relationship between light and dark areas and the mid-tones in between enables us to describe the form of components in the painting: buildings, boats, beaches, trees. Connecting elements of similar tonal value to each other helps to create a sense of unity and rhythm to a painting as opposed to a tangle of isolated shapes; this becomes increasingly important as we start to paint complex scenes that require significant simplification. I recommend you check out the work of American watercolourist Andy Evansen: Andy teaches this idea superbly, having designed a methodology where he creates simple monochrome studies of his subjects to map out the tonal values, translating this information in stages into his finished painting.

Edges

With much of the paper covered by the initial washes that were made in the Development Stage, we can further describe and define the shapes in the painting through revealing or hiding their edges, something that we refer to as 'lost-and-found'. Managing edges and their interaction is one of the most

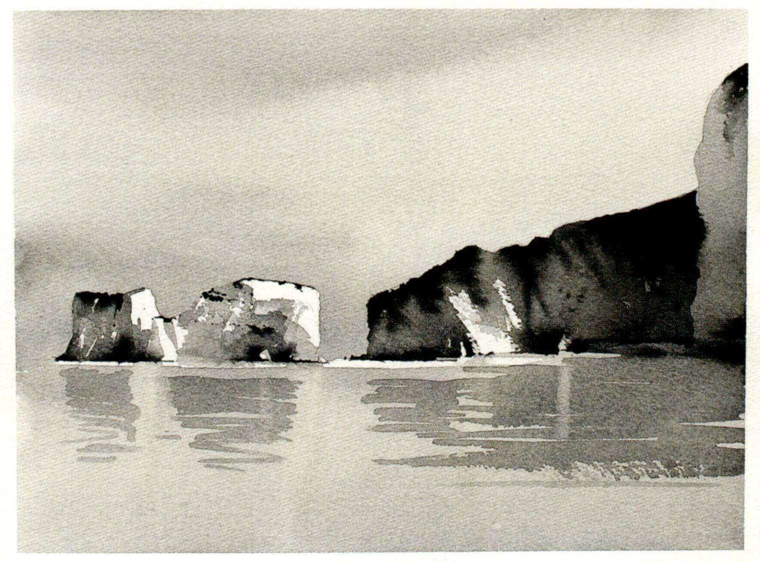

This tonal study of Old Harry Rocks is vital in resolving the tonal relationship between neighbouring shapes, particularly those that don't comply with our expectations of reality – i.e. white chalk cliffs painted dark grey.

important aspects in creating successful watercolour paintings. The crisp edge of an old, sunlit barn is defined by the dark cloud behind it: emphasise and 'find' this edge. The shadow on the side of the building melts softly into the trees beside it, similar in tonal value: understate and 'lose' this edge. Once again, time spent at the Decision stage enables you to identify how and where to deploy this edge-management technique across the painting.

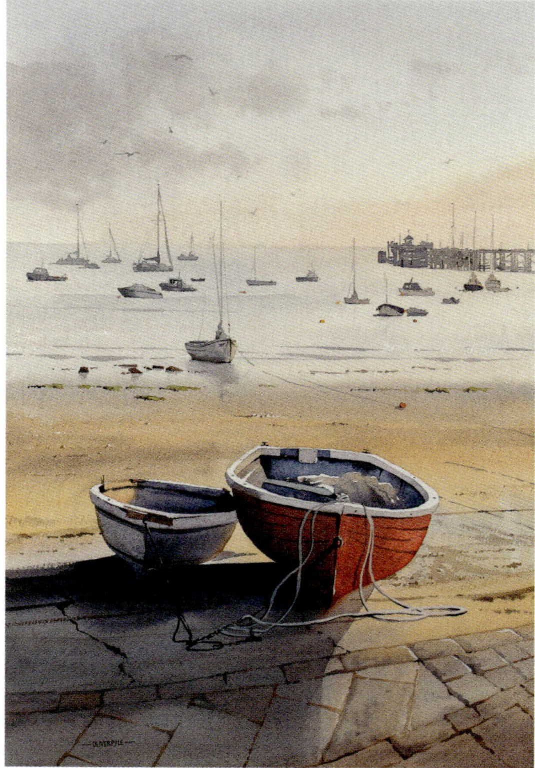

Swanage Serenity – 34cm x 50cm
Note how preserving the crisp found edge on the lefthand side of the red boat defines the brightness of the backlit beach. No such treatment is required to define where the boats' hulls meet the ground and their shadows beneath – they all merge together, based on the proximity of their tonal values. The placement of lost-and-found edges is a pleasing contrast and it helps to add emphasis to the right areas in a painting.

Colours

In the Development stage, the initial washes help me to establish the colours that I am using and where they need to be. Although there are exceptions to this, my focus up to this point has been to keep cooler hues of blue, grey and purple in distant areas of a painting, while warmer mixes of yellows, greens and browns become predominant in the foreground areas. Having these washes in place not only acts as a helpful map, but it enables me to place additional washes and glazes on top, avoiding the white of the paper from showing through where additional washes may not always meet each other, but also where gaps in the wash are deliberately left to allow some of the underpainting to show

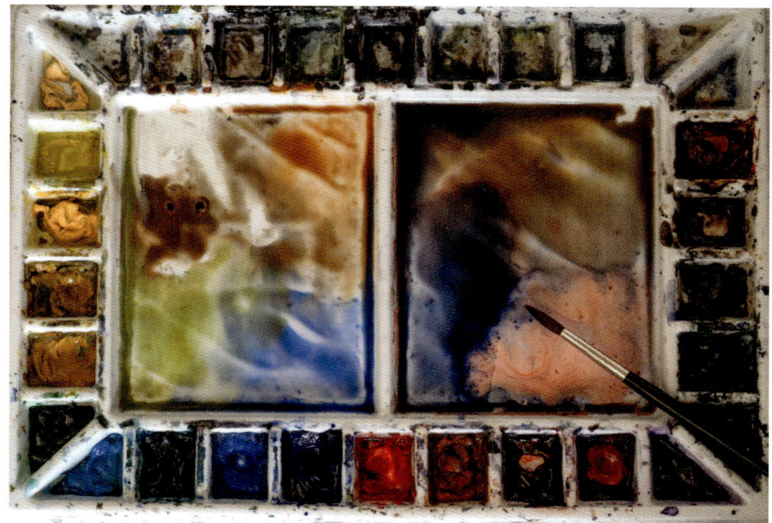

Never be afraid to allow your mixes to merge together on the palette – there will always be room for the resulting collaborations somewhere in your painting, often to make subtle variations to your washes.

through. This helps to promote a sense of unity to a painting and makes the management of edges simpler, avoiding the uneasy feeling that many independent and unrelated shapes can lead to.

Working with a limited palette of colours, I allow these to run together in my mixing areas and on the paper, knowing that the combinations are ones I am familiar with and will deliver tried and tested results. Without a limited palette, the painter is required to find precise, matching pigments, keeping these organised in bewildering arrays of palettes and mixing wells. In most landscapes the colour range is limited, yet highly varied: subtle changes in the greens of a field, a finely nuanced combination of greys and browns for rocky ledges on the shore, endless threads of blue, green and grey, twisting together as the river flows past. As I start to define each area of the painting, I ensure that my brush is continually being loaded with paint, often before it needs it, with a subtly different mix. Not only does this create visual interest in the painting by breaking up the

November Light near Kimmeridge –
72cm x 36cm
The success of painting a scene like this on a full sheet is to maintain visual interest by varying the colour hues in each wash. By working with a limited palette of primary colours, this becomes manageable by simply adjusting each colour mix with a small amount of each primary colour – a touch of blue to cool it down, a touch of red to warm it up, for example. Can you image the impossible task that would confront you if each small modification required an entirely new pigment – would Chromium Green Oxide give you a warmer green than Undersea Green? Or was it Terre Verte? Paint manufacturers offering more than 200 pigments may not be as helpful as they purport to be. They are certainly helpful at lightening your wallet though!

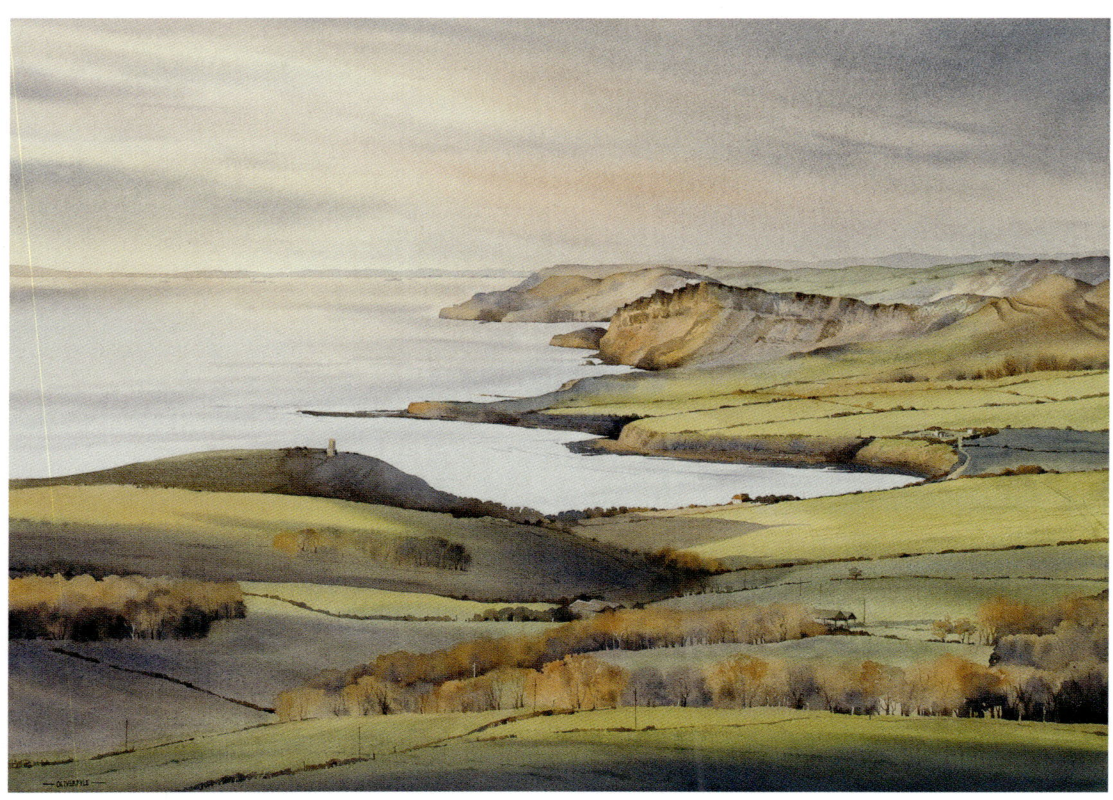

monotony of unrealistic slabs of uniform colour, but it reflects what we observe in the landscape itself; visual uniformity rarely exists in nature, so inviting this into our work is a sure-fire way of producing dull, artificial-looking paintings.

It is important at this stage to continue bringing all the areas of the painting forward instead of concentrating time and focus on a specific area, which might lead to over-working parts of the painting that cannot be subsequently corrected. With the transparent nature of watercolour, every mark and shape that you put down will have a consequence later in the painting. Keep in mind the overall vision and the direction in which you are taking the painting – it won't have arrived there yet, but your role at this stage is to guide it forward, putting the building blocks in place, defining shapes and giving the painting structure.

As I define the shapes and areas within the painting, I am keeping my eye on the final stage – Detail. I like to use a technique that I refer to as 'Painting in Threes', essentially making three separate visits to a wash while it is still workable (i.e. between wet and damp). In painting a copse of middle distance trees I will paint an initial variegated wash, allowing the colours to blend together (first visit). As this wash starts to dry and tighten up, I will drop in some darker tones, often of the same colours, to help define the form of different trees (second visit). Just before the wash has dried, but while it is slightly damp I can then suggest a few trunks and branches with an even more concentrated mix of pigments (third visit). This works for almost any area of the painting in the Definition Stage and allows you to start describing form and detail without spelling it out word-by-word, the soft, hazy edges to the darker marks you have made simply preparing the way for final details.

By now the painting should be starting to assume the appearance of a finished piece with most, if not all, of the paper covered and the shapes, tones and colours defined.

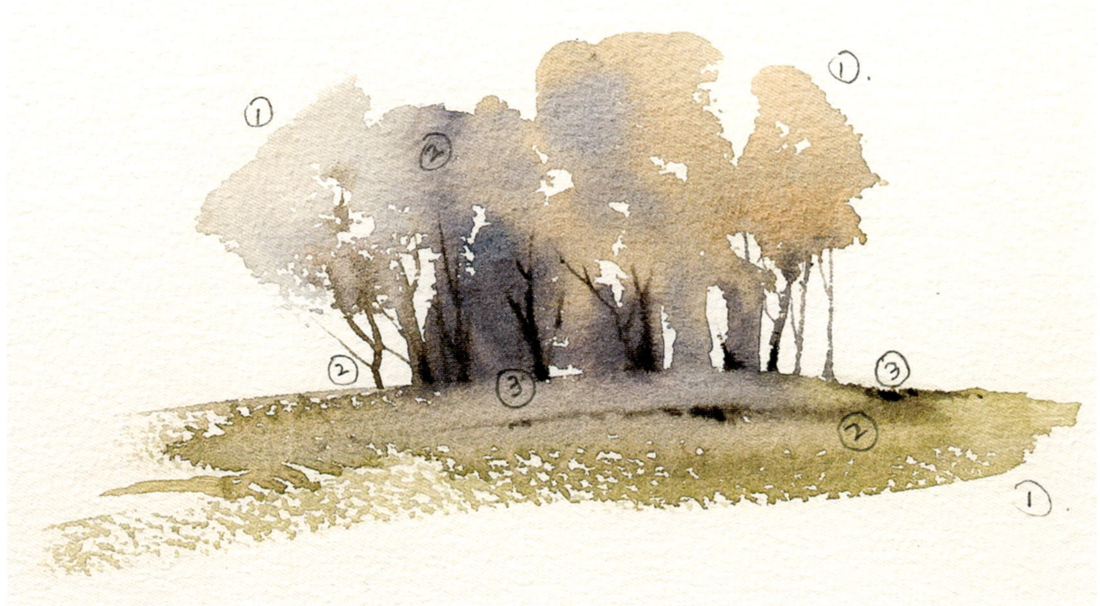

In this example of Painting in Threes, the 1 represents the first wash, painted in the palest tone, 2 represents darker toned hues added as the first wash starts to dry. The number 3 denotes small marks of concentrated paint, applied just before the paper dries.

Detail

It seems that 'detail' is often a dirty word in the world of watercolour. Fussy, overworked paintings, their meanings and atmospheric impact smothered by the injudicious application of detail could be the reason why. Much teaching over recent years has focussed on keeping detail to an absolute minimum, allowing larger shapes and tonal contrasts to tell the story. After all, we are told, paintings are to be viewed across a room, from a distance of at least 3 metres at the very least where detail has a minimal role to play, its only contribution being to add a sense of confusion to the painting's message. I can understand why this thinking has evolved and I have seen many paintings, my own included, that have been ruined by a lack of care and restraint when applying details. Are we to avoid detail in our paintings then? Absolutely not! I have observed customers at my gallery in Swanage viewing paintings on display and the vast majority enjoy looking at them in close proximity and I regularly hear the comment 'I love the detail on the…' Furthermore, detailed paintings sell in greater numbers than abstract works.

Now that could just be the way it is at our gallery, but other gallery owners I know have confirmed similar results.

So, let's not discard detail but find a way of using it to give our paintings visual interest and impact. The importance of working through the Development and Definition stages, without overworking any specific area cannot be overstated. It enables us to apply detail in the right places – it is rarely required across the entire painting. Once again, this is where our earlier investment of thinking carefully – sketching if required – at the Decisions

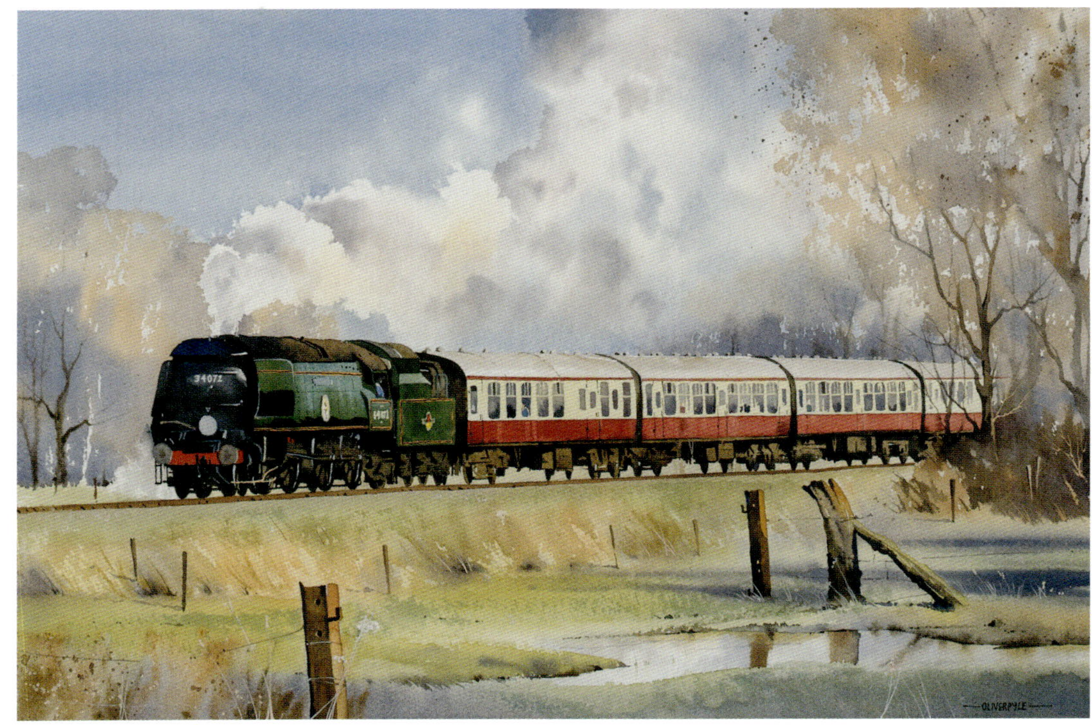

No. 34072, '257 Squadron' Steams Through Purbeck – 50cm x 34cm
I find subjects such as this thoroughly enjoyable to paint. The challenge of accurate drawing and the importance of attention to detail has always appealed to me. The key is to allocate the detail to the areas of the painting where it is most required.

stage, starts to pay dividends. With the painting close to completion, the temptation is to think that finishing off the details is an easy home-run. This could not be further from the truth. Details applied carelessly or in an area of the painting where they should be absent have the capacity to ruin its balance. There are some useful principles that will help to guide us through this exciting, yet potentially hazardous stage of the painting:

- To start with, apply your detail around the painting's focal point. Detail adds crispness and sharpness to the shapes that we have developed in the previous stages of the painting, giving them prominence. Since we want our viewers' gaze to rest on the painting's centre of interest, this is where our we want to concentrate our firepower.

- Don't confuse the eye. I won't delve into the philosophical rationale for this, but when we look at areas of light and shade, our eyes are naturally drawn to the light; detailed areas of shade rarely read well in a painting and persuade us to concentrate our focus on areas where our eye doesn't naturally settle. Work those details into the lit areas of your painting. The same principle applies to the background. We looked at the reasons behind this when considering the idea of aerial perspective in an earlier chapter. We see very little detail in distant areas, so don't put it there. Placing detailed objects in front of areas with little to no detail gives them greater impact and there will be less chance of confusing the eye since the object is not competing for attention with its equally detailed surroundings.

- Be instinctive with your application of details. Having drawn attention to the focal point by enhancing detail, it is a good time to walk away from the painting before you fall under the hypnotic trance of your fine rigger brush, whispering in your ear that every corner of the painting needs a little more attention; it is a difficult

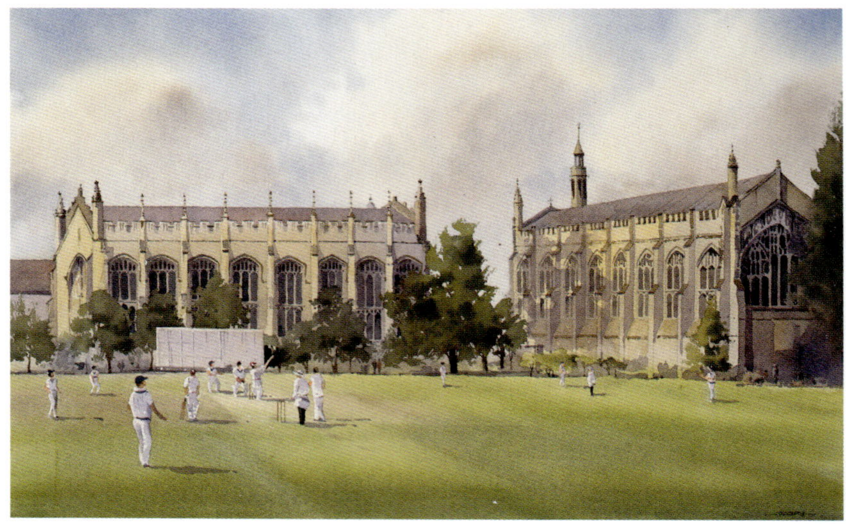

In this commission, I played down the detail on the chapel window, given its proximity to the edge of the painting and its potential to distract from the cricket. The client pointed out, quite rightly, that the window was an iconic feature and memory for the alumni of Cheltenham College, and requested that I add more detail to this. With ample detail elsewhere in the scene to balance this out, it works well.

temptation to resist. Put the kettle on, take the dog for a walk, watch a few overs of cricket, but don't go anywhere near your painting. One of the benefits of painting on location is that this temptation is less prevalent; the lack of comfort and changing conditions often dictate a faster working pace and this leads to a more immediate approach to your subject. There is little time for fiddling around with your rigger brush, compared to the comforts of the home or studio. If you have become a slave to your rigger, then get outdoors with the sketchbook. If you develop your sketches into a painting, spend more time looking at the sketch than your subject, or photographs of it and as you gain experience your instinct will tell you where to place what should be the finishing touches to the painting: some foreground wildflowers, stones on the pathway, ripples on the river, fence posts (always fence posts!) The key here is to suggest detail in areas where of course there is more, allowing the viewer to fill in the rest of the details, invoking their imagination. An indication of one or two simply suggested winter trees will tell us that the abstract shape in the middle distance is an area of woodland. There is no need to paint every tree, our imagination enables us to make that connection.

- Ensure that the level of detail across the painting is coherent. If you are painting a scene that involves a highly detailed subject then you will need to gradually phase out the detail in areas that support the focal point; an abrupt transition from highly detailed to no detail

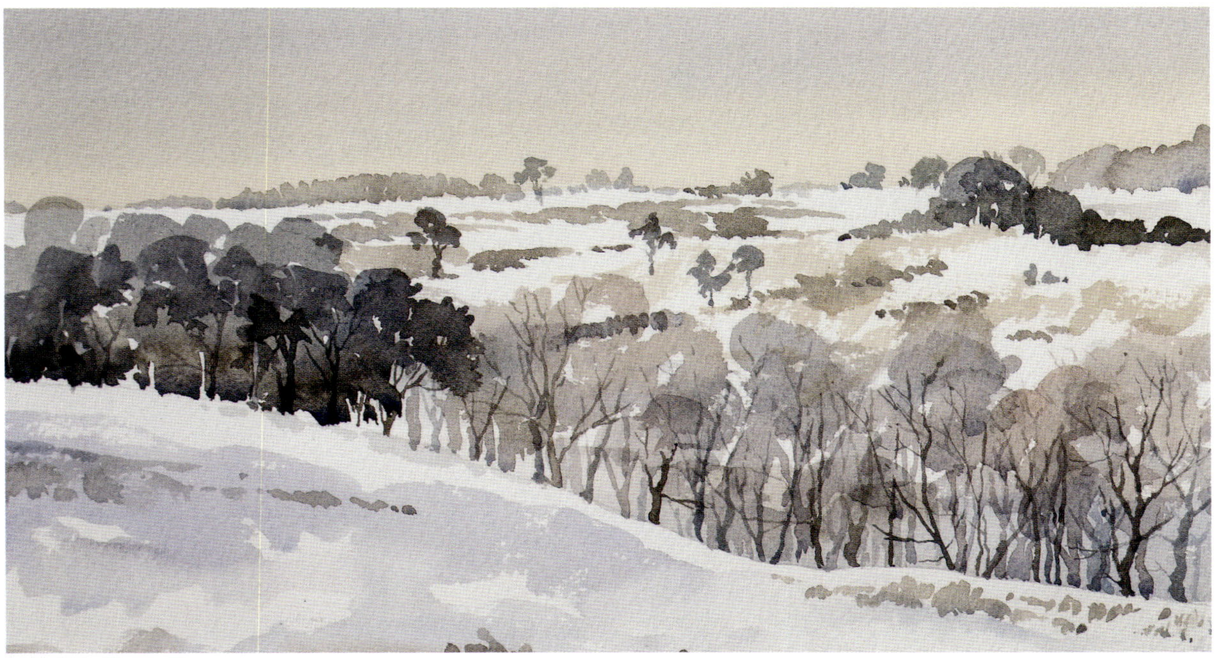

A very early painting of mine, where my appreciation of detail placement was somewhat immature. The unnecessary detail crammed into these middle distance trees only creates a busy mess that overwhelms the eye.

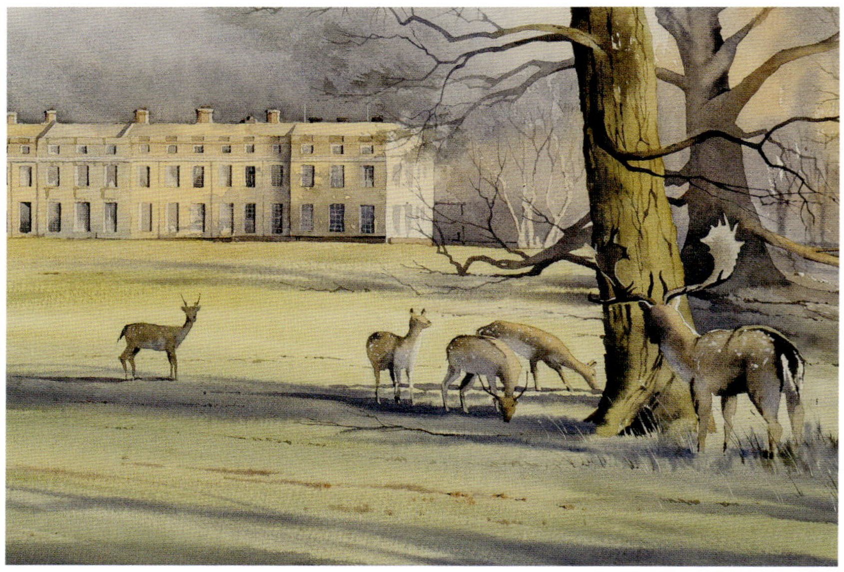

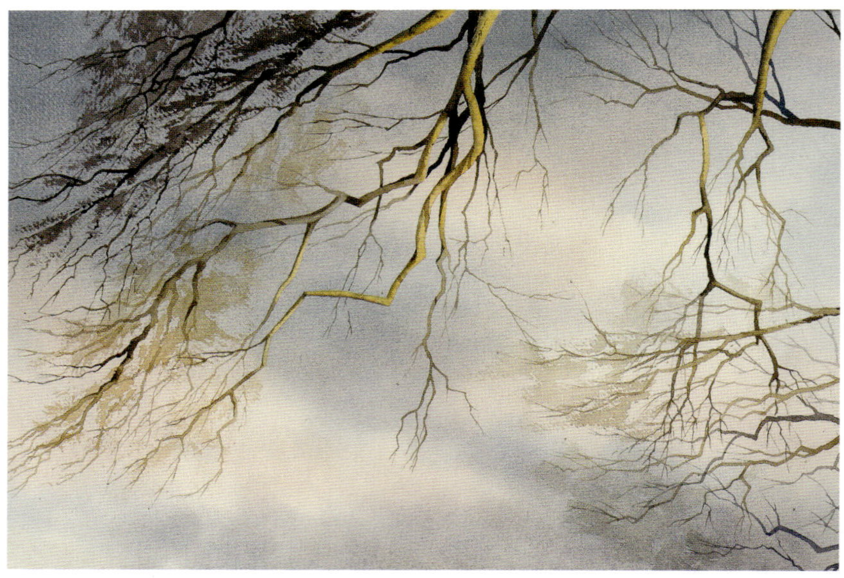

Look at the distant trees, sitting behind the foreground tree and deer, detailed elements in the painting. They have been rendered with a looser technique and a subtle approach, with detail kept to a minimum.

In the same painting, a high level of detail was committed to the branches of the main tree. Painting detail successfully is reliant upon calculated and judicious placement.

will not read well and the finished painting will appear to have been painted with two different styles. In a painting that does not include a detailed focal point – a broad vista for example – it becomes much easier to leave larger passages of work with very little detail.

- Detail is not always dark. I often see students adding details to their paintings, all painted in concentrated Paynes Grey or Neutral Tint, creating a quasi pen-and-wash appearance to their work. Dark marks certainly add crispness to a painting,

and pen-and-wash is a wonderful technique to use, but in most circumstances the details we need to add require more subtlety than that. Use a range of tones, mixed from your limited palette to give your work a more nuanced, sophisticated finish.

- Don't be afraid of using titanium white to pick out highlight details. I have always been a proponent of using the white of the paper as the lightest tone in a watercolour painting, however there are times when a carefully applied mark to suggest highlight detail in titanium white provides greater control and definition than can be achieved by leaving unpainted paper or using masking fluid. Try not to concern yourselves with whether this is right or wrong – a consideration that should have nothing to do with art – but whether it contributes positively to your work and allows you to paint with confidence and achieve the results you want. John Singer Sargent, J.M.W. Turner and Rowland Hilder had no qualms in using this technique, so I think I'm on reasonably safe ground in suggesting it here. The key is to keep it to the absolute minimum and just for the finest of details: sunlit cow parsley mixed from titanium white and yellow ochre works wonders to break up the dark mass of a hedgerow in the shade.

By looking at the different stages of the following paintings you will be able to see how this process, the Four Ds, has enabled me to approach two entirely different subjects, each with their own challenges and specific considerations, with the confidence that I will achieve consistent results. Don't fall into the trap of thinking that watercolour's fluidity, it's proclivity to create dynamic, immediate impressions of the subjects that inspire us, are the result of a paint-first-think-later approach. The surfeit of watercolour timelapse paintings on social media platforms is misleading and unhelpful as they try to persuade you otherwise; I can assure you that the most experienced of hands, moving with speed and purpose between palette and paper, are controlled by carefully considered thoughts and planned outcomes.

If you feel that this structure will help you to achieve consistent results in your paintings then go with it, but remember it's only my way of doing so – it is not the 'right' way to paint, if ever such a thing existed. Equally, explore your own thoughts, analyse how you view scenes and make decisions before and during the painting, developing your own methodology that you can rely upon. The two following paintings will help to demonstrate how this structure works in practice:

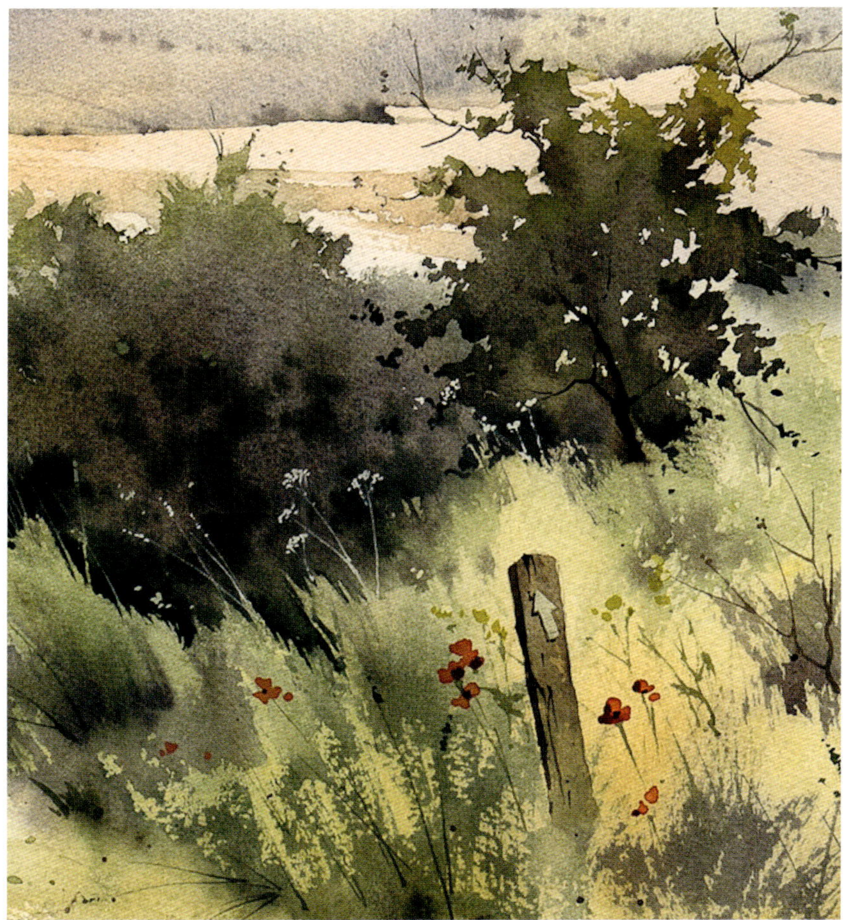

A small amount of opaque colour, such as Titanium White can really help to add small highlight detail against areas of darker surroundings.

A WARM EVENING, BOSHAM

This is a complex scene that I painted in the studio, having spent a warm evening in the beautiful village of Bosham, on the edge of Chichester Harbour. It required some careful thought and a few thumbnail sketches to test some ideas before I went anywhere near my paints and brushes. I recall my years as an amateur painter and how this would have been a process that I always tried to avoid, desperate to get started with the painting. Consequently, I would finish the painting and wonder why it was such a poor imitation of the scene that had inspired me. Lesson: you cannot expect to make quality paintings in watercolour by trying to avoid the planning stage. I know many accomplished painters that do not paint complicated

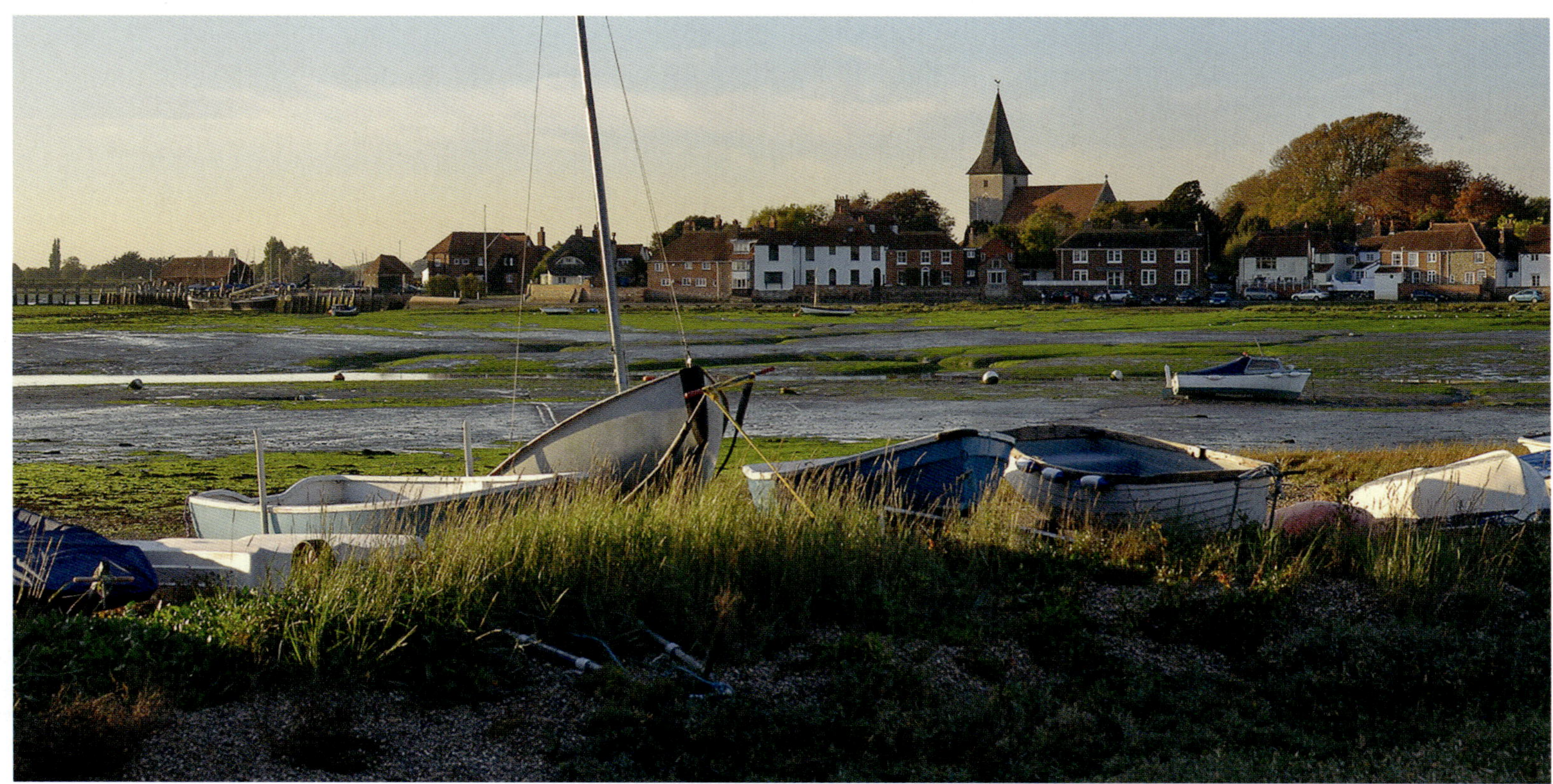

subjects and I wonder if a reason for that is an unwillingness to engage in the preparatory thinking required to execute such paintings; they certainly have the painting skills to achieve it. But I get that; there is something liberating in jumping right in and making an instinctive response to what has inspired you. Don't think that complex scenes are out of reach though or too difficult; they just require a different, more considered approach and there is much satisfaction in accepting the challenge and succeeding. Using a strategic approach to your work is a tremendous help for subjects like this and consider the extent to which the Four Ds approach could help you to tackle subjects that might be outside of your comfort zone.

Decisions

At the Decisions stage these are the points that I considered:

Format. My original photograph had included the top of the boat mast, but this created a scene that was half sky, half land and didn't make for a satisfying composition. A panoramic 2:1 format resolved this issue, giving more emphasis to the line of boats and the harbour mud flats. A simple crop of the photo (shown here) in Lightroom allowed me to play around with the optimal configuration.

Composition. I was concerned that the boats in the foreground were creating a 'them-and-us' situation: boats at the front, buildings at the back with little connection in between. By removing a couple of small dinghies on the left-hand side, it helped to open up the scene and promote connection between front and back. To build on this, I accentuated the prominence of the two boats on the mud flats which then take the eye towards the church. The boat trolley in the grass was distracting and so I left this out. Excluding the small, upturned boats on the extreme left also helped to simplify the scene.

Contrast. I was initially concerned about the mast leaving the top edge of the painting, but the more I looked at the scene, the more it seemed to be dominated by strong horizontals: the line of boats, the harbour side, the small rivulet running across the mudflats. The painting needed a dominant vertical to add some interest, and by running it out of the scene it became more prominent. It also helped to echo the church spire, leaving a pleasing contrast between verticals and horizontals.

Colour. These evening colours are ones that I am always drawn to, but I felt that the strong dynamic range between lights and darks, in particular the heavy shadows, was just hiding some of the colour subtlety. I reduced the dynamic range, creating a more mellow appearance to the scene, especially in the foreground where the interplay between the light on the boats and the shaded grass was creating a rather busy, staccato feel that diminished the sense of evening calm. A decision was made on the colour palette: French Ultramarine, Cadmium Red and Raw Sienna would do all the heavy lifting, making up 90 per cent of the painting, with the addition of a little Light Red, Gamboge Hue, Burnt Umber and Cerulean.

Equipment. Using broken brushstrokes to suggest detail in several areas of the painting – distant trees, foreground grass, marine plants on the mudflats – I decided to use a rough texture paper. I could see that some glazes would be required to achieve the look that I wanted in the middle distance and foreground areas and chose Arches 140lb that allows extensive glazing while resisting the disturbance of previous washes.

Edge management. Often in evening scenes with strong directional light, there will be many instances where light and dark shapes sit next to each other. I needed to decide at this point how best to manage that: I considered masking fluid, but not being a big fan of using it, I could see that a combination of washes would enable me to achieve what I wanted. Before starting to paint, this is one of the areas where time spent plotting ahead pays dividends later. Try to visualise the sequence of washes that you need to make in order to describe edges that you want to be prominent, and where other edges can be lost, allowing them to merge into adjacent shapes and washes. As I work through this example, you will see how this thinking plays out in practice.

Drawing. Having clarified my thinking and taken the necessary decisions, I drew the main components of the scene in pencil. I like to include this in the Decisions stage as it helps me to consolidate my thoughts and commit them to the paper. Even in a complex scene like this, my drawing is restrained and acts more as a guide than anything else, ensuring that buildings are accurate, boats are correctly positioned and shaped and that the relationships between key elements of the painting are established and in proportion. In doing so, I often notice

other smaller compositional elements or details that could be improved or tweaked and this is a good time to do so before your fire up your paint palette.

Development

At the Development stage, I started building up the painting in loose washes, often painted wet-on-wet, to cover as much of the paper as possible in preparation for shapes to be defined and detail applied as the painting moved towards a conclusion. This starts by wetting the whole paper, painting the sky and establishing warm and cool colour in areas that will be defined by darker edges, painted wet-on-dry. For adjacent shapes and areas, with clearly defined edges I work on the principle that wherever possible it is best to *define an edge, just once, with the application of the darkest tone,* a principle that will repeatedly help you to manage your edges and wash sequences. Consequently, I was unconcerned that the colour applied to the boats and buildings were soft and outside of their drawn boundaries at this point.

Once this initial wet-on-wet phase had dried completely, I looked for areas that could be described by broken brushstrokes — foreground grass, texture on the mudflats. I knew that these would then be glazed over

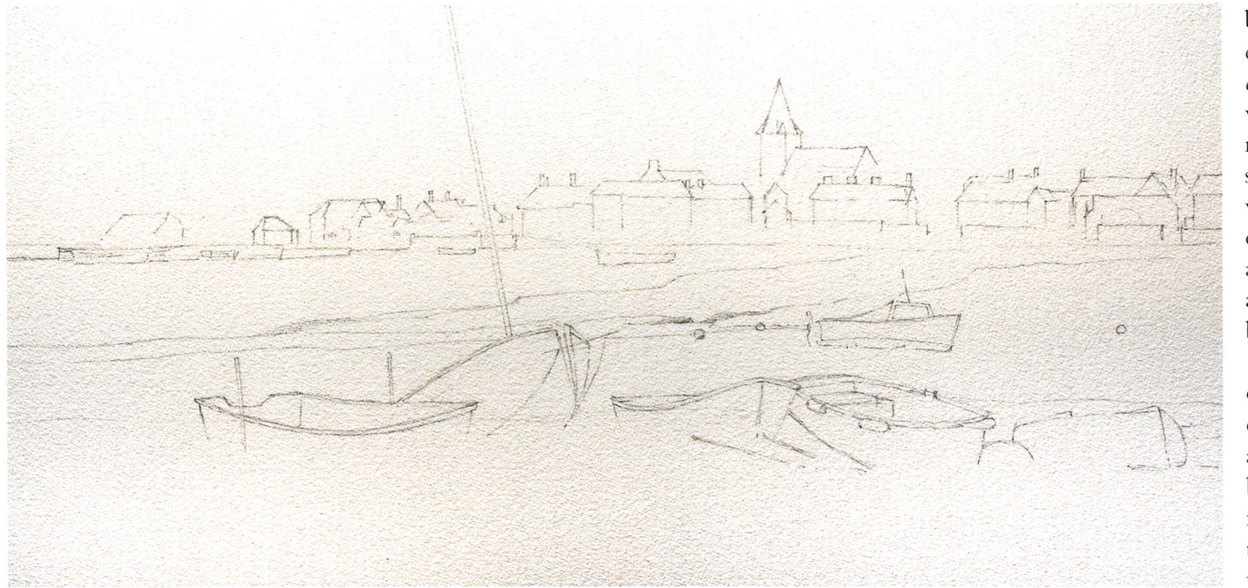

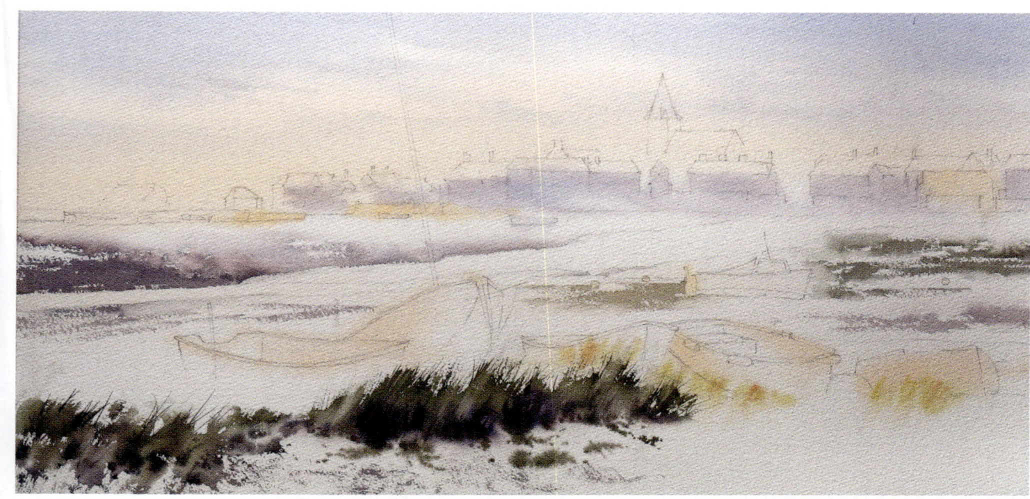

the bottom of the paper, continually dropping in darker tones to build up shadows and using a small brush to suggest clumps of grass, stones and general harbour detritus.

The Development stage was complete: the paper had been covered, warm and cool colour temperatures were established, lighter and darker tones were beginning to come together. I had created a backdrop against which shapes could now be defined within the context of the overall painting. Working in this way helps me to judge colour – balance, temperature, intensity – and tonal values, by seeing all parts of the painting progressing instead of becoming side-tracked by just working in an isolated area; there would be plenty of time for that in the Definition stage.

which would help to knock back their alarming conspicuity. I like to put these areas in at this point for three reasons: it helps to suggest shape and form; the unpainted paper is at its most resistant to wet paint, making the broken edges easier to achieve; by glazing over them carefully, the effect is softened ever so slightly which lends a lovely natural feel to the textured areas. I then added a few more broken areas in bright green, near the harbour wall.

With everything completely dry I glazed over this area carefully with a very wet wash, combining a soft grey shadow colour with some warmer brown hues using a large soft mop brush. Care was taken to paint around the boats, allowing the darker tone to now add a crisp definition to their edges. I allowed this to dry and then painted another glaze from the bottom of the boats (which I had pre-wet with clear water) to

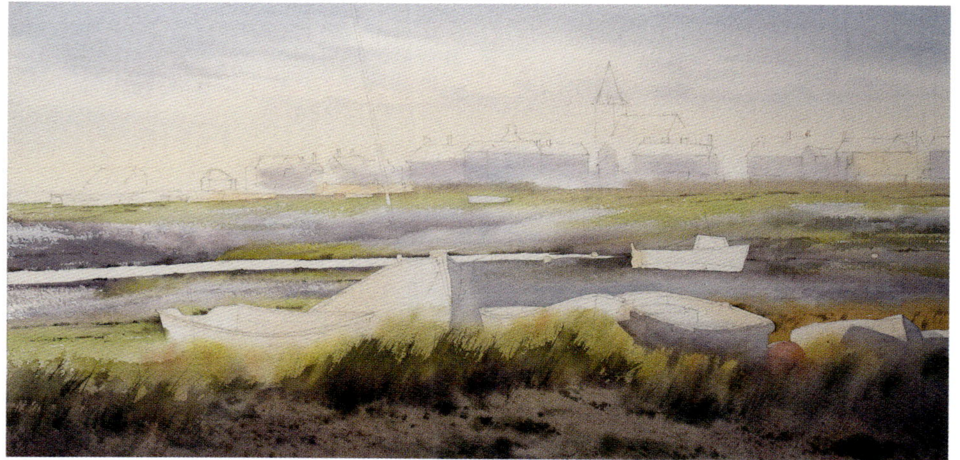

Definition

With a combination of washes, painted wet-on-dry, I worked my way around the painting building up shapes and defining edges, bringing all areas of the painting to a point where it started to assume the look of a finished painting. As I defined the shapes, I allowed some of them to merge into each other, losing the edge between them, particularly where the adjacent shapes were a similar tone. You can see this between some of the buildings and background trees and where shadow areas on the boats meet the foreground grass. Not every edge needed to be defined and by allowing some of them to merge together, the painting has a more natural feel to it. I continued to build up the definition with increasingly darker washes: sides of buildings, shadows on boat hulls, undulations to the mud flats. Working this way helps to build up the form of shapes in the scene, starting to suggest a three-dimensional aspect.

At this stage of the painting I was mindful of the areas where I wanted to present most of the detail and started suggesting some of this while these washes were still damp, by dropping in darker tones: the bottom of the middle distance boat, for example. It was important to maintain a broad view of the painting while I worked; I have a tendency to jump ahead and start having fun with my rigger brush, working detail into an area of the painting that I sometimes regret later on. When you get to this stage of a painting, you should be happy with the balance of the colours and tones and just be left with the feeling that it's missing something. Walk away from the painting and do something different for a while, so you are not used to looking at it – when you return your eye will often see a few things that need a little adjustment and now is the time to make those.

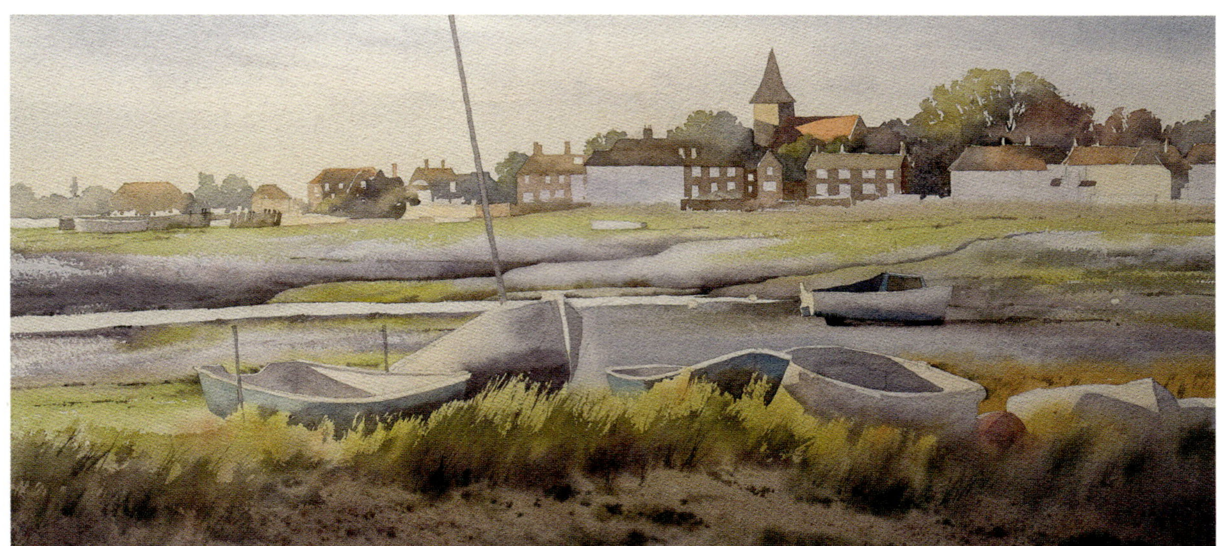

Detail

To finish the painting I started to apply details to the cluster of boats in the foreground, being the closest and most prominent objects. Using a rigger brush and a combination of different dark mixes to add subtlety to the finish, I picked out ropes, rigging, clinker, seeded grass, fenders and gunwales. With this area complete, I was able to assess the other areas of the scene that should include detail. I was tempted to severely restrict the detail in the village, however it wasn't a hot summer evening where dust and haze from the day had reduced the definition and detail in the background. There was a cool crispness in the air, so some detail was important to help describe its clarity. Carefully suggesting windows, parked cars, mooring buoys, staithes and distant masts with simple marks created the effect I was looking for.

To finish off, a few small details on the mud flats, foreground stones and grasses, gave the painting a lovely clarity and the judicious application of a few fine details in titanium white provided a little sparkle to the finished work.

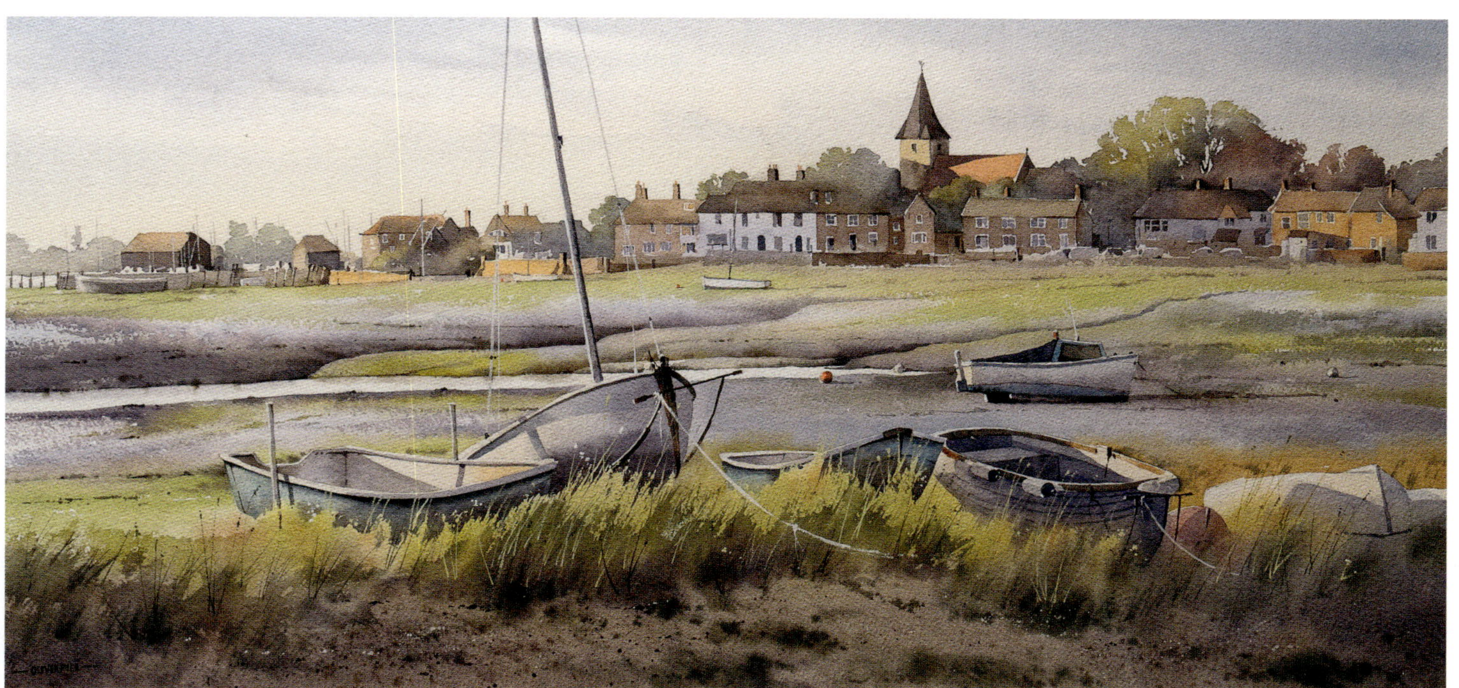

THE OLD FLINT BARN, NEAR FIRLE

This painting captures a moment that I mentioned previously in the first of our Field Trips, in the Introduction – a pleasant walk at Firle Beacon on the South Downs in Sussex. On my route back, I walked past this lovely flint barn, so characteristic of old agricultural architecture in this part of the county. Not having time to sketch on location, I took a quick reference photograph and decided to make a painting at a later date. My aim was to capture the sense of a warm summer breeze and the barn's

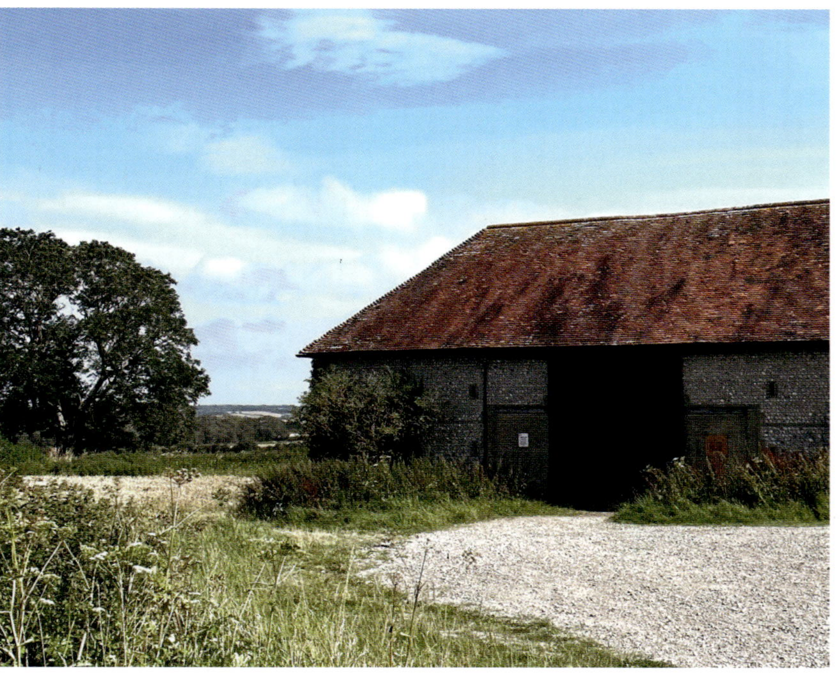

position in the landscape. The photo itself had a rather static feel to it and didn't recreate my feeling at the time, so it was just as important to revisit my memories of the day as it was to refer to the photograph.

To achieve the painting I had in my mind's eye, some work would be needed to arrive at a composition I was happy with and would help to tell the story of the afternoon's walk. In particular, I remember noticing a footpath that disappeared round the side of the barn and although there wasn't an opportunity to explore it on this occasion, I was intrigued where it would lead to. As we've looked at previously, photographs tend to compress front-to-back distance and here the space is lost, so the path isn't evident. I could recall it though and wanted to include it as a feature of the painting, using some artistic licence to help improve the composition of the scene.

The scene itself is relatively simple, however a number of issues presented themselves which needed to be resolved before starting the painting. This is where time spent at the Decisions stage is invaluable.

Decisions

1. Composition

I was uncomfortable with the composition of the scene and realised that it could be improved in several ways. Firstly, the eye tended to leave the bottom righthand corner of the image where the stone track led away from the barn. By making something more of the hidden footpath that I had recalled, there was an opportunity to take the viewer round the side of the barn and through the field to the Downs beyond. I was happy with that as a concept and decided to open a gap in the hedgerow, introducing a signpost and a couple of fence posts to act as a focal point. Secondly, I wanted to add some emphasis to the Downs and decided to make them more prominent, introducing a gentle curve to the ridge, so redolent of this part of the Sussex landscape.

I made a quick thumbnail sketch of the scene that incorporated my ideas. Simple sketches like these really help to visualise the changes

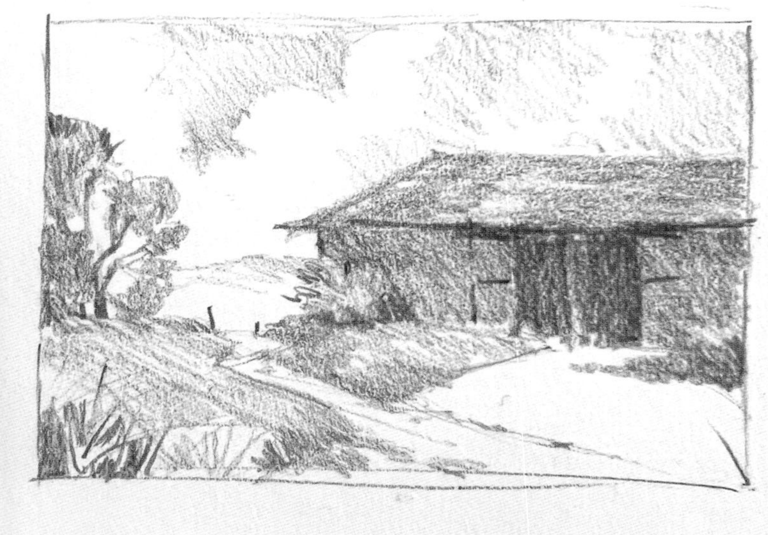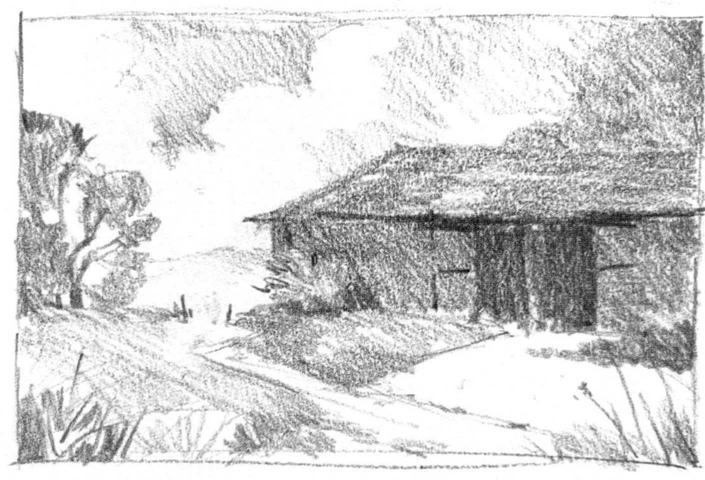

that you want to make, and they act as an essential reference point once you come to paint. You can see where I have opened the middle distance, creating a centre of interest and to add further emphasis to this I introduced a different design element to the sky: a hard-edged break in the clouds just above the focal point. I still wasn't sure that the large area of the track leaving the righthand side of the scene had been dealt with satisfactorily.

I darkened the cloud shadow on the right to push the eye more towards the light area of sky and decided to close off the edge of the painting with a suggestion of foreground grass and wildflowers (in the second image, above right). It occurred to me that by including some figures in the gateway it would help to promote the story and the focal point even more. There is always a trade-off when including people or animals in a painting – it immediately becomes about them, and on reflection I felt that this would perhaps distract from what initially attracted me to the scene: the barn sitting in the landscape with the Downs beyond. With a few deft flicks of the eraser, they were gone. I couldn't help thinking that the size of the barn in the photograph was perhaps a little too dominant and so I decided to reduce it in size, but on completion of the sketch I decided that it should be a little smaller still, which would help to give greater prominence to the landscape around it.

2. Size & Format

The majority of my gallery work is half-sheet size or larger (55cm x 38cm) however I enjoy painting smaller works for simple subjects like this and it allows me to employ a more direct approach to painting, with less need for extensive glazing and wet-on-wet work that I might use for larger, more complex scenes. It allows me to work on a watercolour block without the need for stretching the paper and for this rural scene of trees, rough ground and old masonry, Arches 140lb Rough would be perfect to allow me to suggest these textures with broken brushstrokes.

3. Colour and Tone

Although the barn is a lovely building, it represented a rather dark block in the reference photo, with the black doors dominating the scene. I made the decision to lighten the wall slightly, and the doors significantly. The darker cloud shadow on the right would help to bring the tonal values into a narrower range, which I felt would give a more harmonious feel to the painting. I also wanted to show some cracks and gaps in the doors' woodwork to break up the solid mass of colour and give the barn a more rugged appearance. There was plenty of interesting colour in the old roof tiles and I wanted to dial this up a little, introducing some green moss in places which is a nice colour complement to the red tiles. Overall, I wanted the colour to be a little softer than the photograph, where the light is a touch too harsh.

4. Equipment

A limited palette of three primary colours – French Ultramarine, Yellow Ochre and Light Red – was sufficient for 85% of the painting, with the addition of Burnt Sienna, Gamboge Hue and Cadmium Red lending some assistance in places. Titanium While helped to pick out some heads of cow parsley here and there. A size 6 mop, 10 and 6 round sables and a No. 1 rigger brush covered all eventualities.

Development

With the important decisions made, the next stage was the painting's Development. This started with the transfer of thoughts and decisions onto paper – a light pencil sketch to ensure that elements in the painting were correctly placed in relation to each other and the overall composition. In general, I try to include as little drawing as possible, certainly for simple subjects such as this, preferring to allow the brush to define fields, trees, clouds and other irregular shapes; it helps to promote a looser, more natural feel to a landscape painting than the filling in of pre-drawn shapes. Here, a simple outline of the main shapes in 2B pencil was all that was needed to get started.

With the scene drawn, my aim in the Development stage was to cover as much of the paper as possible with initial washes, without over-

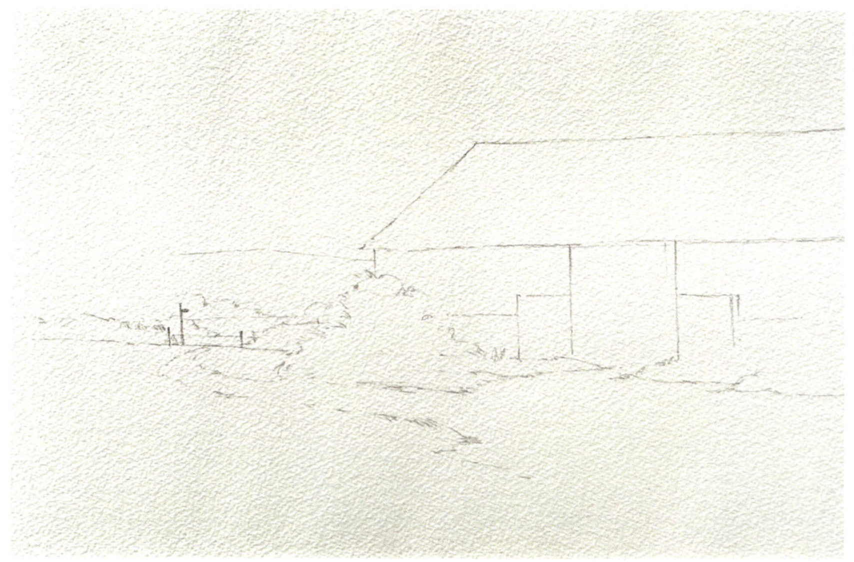

working any specific area of the painting. This allowed me to establish passages of underpainting for texture, initiating the relationship between areas of warm and cool colour and preserving areas of unpainted paper for highlights. At this stage, I am often working using a wet-on-wet technique into areas of the paper that I have pre-wet with clear water, however for a smaller sized painting like this, it's easier to add each wash individually. For this painting, my focus was on colour development more than tonal work. I wanted to use large brushes to establish colour and avoid the addition of concentrated, darker tones at this stage.

The sky is often the starting point, and it enables me to strike the right note to establish the atmosphere of the painting. Colours mixed, the sky was painted using a soft mop brush, with a focus on combining some hard-edged clouds with those that were soft, using clear water and a blending technique. Reference to my small sketch reminded me to keep a crisp break in the clouds just above the focal point below. I was happy to bring the sky wash down over the barn roof – this helped to add texture once the roof wash was painted. Broken washes were then added to describe areas of grass and wildflowers growing by the track and in front of the barn, using an energetic dry-brush technique to produce random, hit-and-miss results. As mentioned in the Bosham painting, I like to do this at an early stage while the paper is at its most resistant to the washes, which helps to make this technique simpler. Note how the direction of my brushstrokes changed from horizontal to vertical, closer to the foreground in anticipation of the grasses that would be in that area. When this was completely dry, the distant Downs were added, painting a glaze over the areas of grass, changing colours from cool distant hues to warmer ones in the foreground as the wash was brought down the paper. Just before it had dried completely, some distant hedges and trees were suggested on the Downs, with some trees dropped in just behind the signpost, ensuring that their edges were soft, helping to create an illusion of depth in the painting. You will see that as the glaze nears the barn and the Downs disappear behind the tree which is yet to be painted, I softened the edges with a

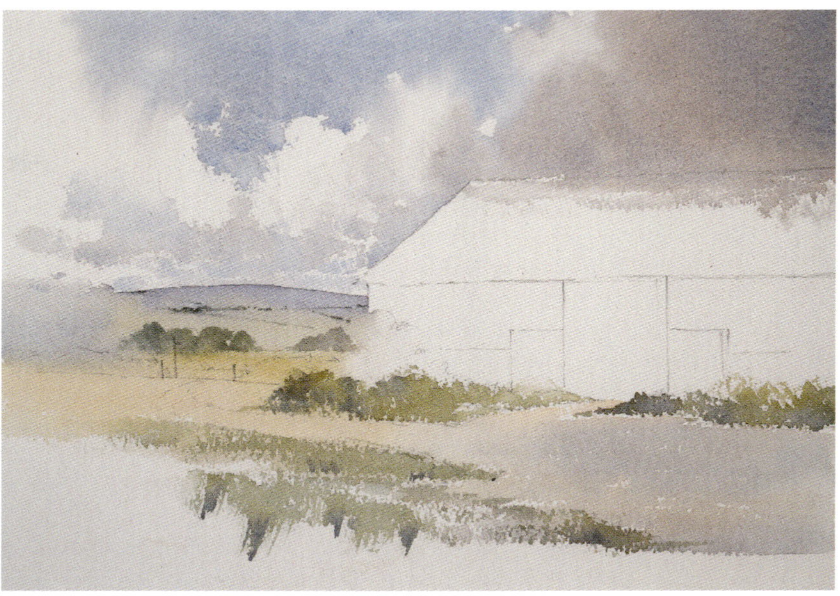

damp brush, allowing me to then paint over the top without overlapping hard edges, once the glaze had dried.

At this stage of the painting, I was happy that the atmosphere had been established and that the main washes were in place, helping to add some depth to the scene. It was the perfect base from which to move on, defining different elements in the painting.

Definition

Once you have started a painting, it can be easy to lose sight of where it is all going to end up and as I mentioned previously, there can be a risk of making hasty conclusions about its ultimate chance of success; shapes look strange and areas of the painting that will later seem to settle down, instead take on an artificial prominence. This is why making the initial thumbnail sketch is so important as it acts as a map, allowing me to continually evaluate the relationship between darks, lights, shapes and edges, plotting the sequence of each wash carefully.

When I start to define the different elements in a painting, I tend to work from back to front as this helps to create depth and recession throughout the painting. In watercolour, we usually paint from light to dark and with distant elements usually paler than closer ones, this seems to be a logical way to work.

The tree and hedge were painted with the large sable brush, allowing broken washes to suggest leaves and while this was still damp some branches were added with the rigger brush. The barn was then painted with fluid washes, continually varying the colour subtly to add visual interest. Before this dried, some darker tones and accent colours were dropped in to suggest texture: broken tiles, moss, flints in the wall. Note how the small tree at the edge of the barn has been allowed to run into the stonework, creating a lost edge, while the dark shadow at its base creates a found edge, defining the top of the area of grass and scrub in front of it, using a negative painting technique.

Now was not the time to add in the details. If I could bring as much of the painting further forward as possible it would help to ensure that areas of the painting that shouldn't become overworked wouldn't receive too much attention. The foreground needed to be added and this was done using broken washes of stronger-toned paint with the large mop brush. Areas of unpainted paper were left to add some sparkle and suggest detail – grass seed-heads, stones, wildflowers. Dark tones were dropped in to add depth and form to the areas of grass, with a few individual blades picked out with the rigger brush, while everything was still damp and workable. The barn doors were added, allowing some of the previous wash to show through.

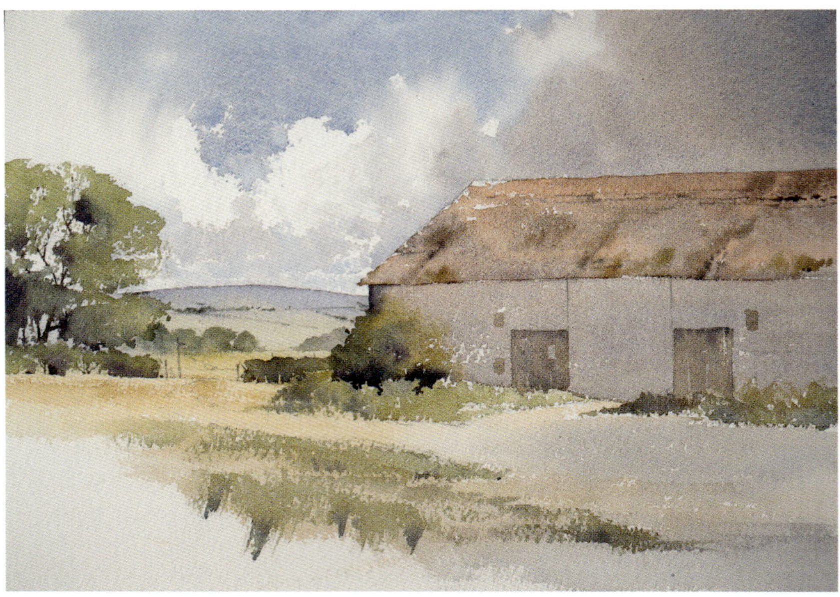

With all the paper covered, all the elements defined, it was now starting to assume the look of a finished painting. At this point it is good to walk away, take a short break and then assess any areas that may need to be fine-tuned. I prefer to do it at this point before applying the final details; once they are done, the painting should be finished. So, looking at the painting, I felt that a light cloud shadow in the top left corner would finish the sky nicely, so this was added, blending the edges with a damp brush. A few small dry-brush marks on the track helped to suggest some detail without being too explicit.

Everything had now been defined and the painting was holding together nicely, ready to be finished off with some fine details.

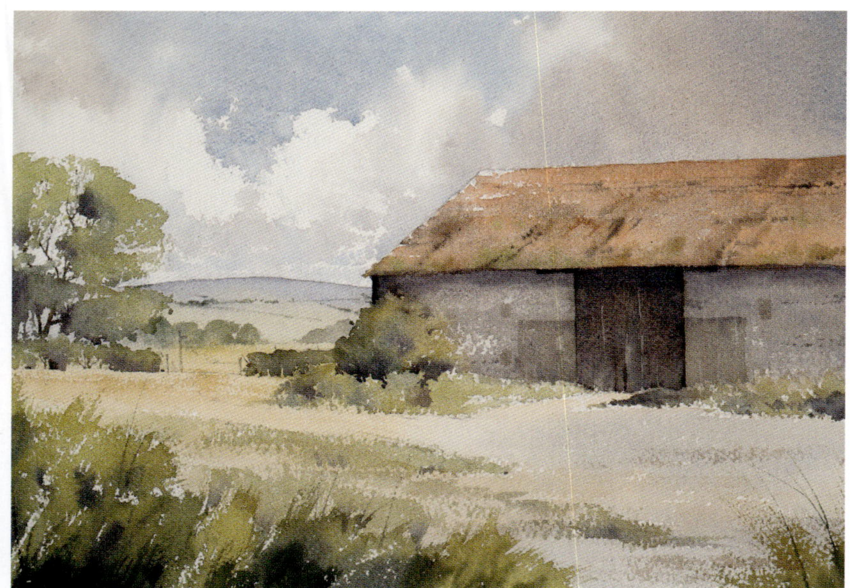

too. The key to success here was just to indicate a few elements and allow the viewer to complete the rest; painting a few roof tiles is always better than painting each one, as are the flints in the barn wall and the foreground grasses and wildflowers. Some detail was applied to the barn doors and some shadows placed next to unpainted areas on the track to describe stones. Small areas of shadow on the grass and scrub helped to add form and some marks of burnt sienna added a little zip of colour to the foreground.

Knowing when to stop and not overwork the painting comes with experience as you learn to exercise your judgement. Almost always it is a case of 'less is more' and please refer to the finished painting below to see how these details helped bring it to life.

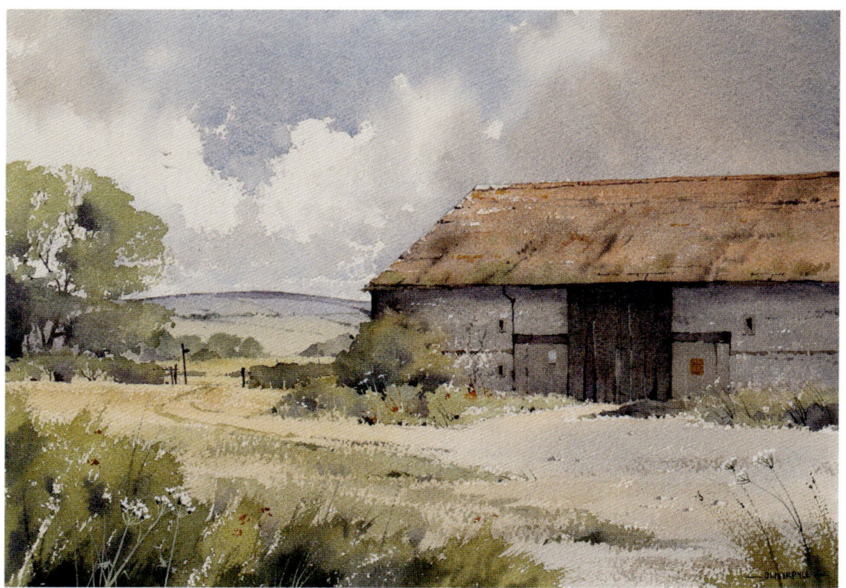

Details

In the grand scheme of things, fine details represent a small percentage of a painting. It is easy to think that, with the painting having progressed well to this point, it's a homerun to finish the painting successfully. Beware – there is significant potential for the painting to be ruined by the careless or over-zealous application of fine details!

Always start with the focal point and then stop to assess if any further details need to be added. I painted the signpost and the fence posts and suggested two red kites – magnificent birds that had been gliding and swirling on the thermals above us for much of the walk. That worked well, but other areas of the scene required a little detail

The four Ds structure has helped me to develop a successful strategy for designing paintings and making the process simpler. Whether I am painting a complex, detailed scene, or a simpler landscape such as this, it is a structure that yields repeatable results for me. Painting is an intuitive and individual creative endeavour, and it may be that this methodology doesn't sit comfortably with your way of working – that's perfectly understandable. However, if you are looking for some structure to your work and how to design paintings that represent your vision of your favourite landscapes, then why don't you give this a try?

FINAL THOUGHTS

The art of landscape painting is a paradox: simple, yet complex. All we are doing is creating an image of a place and its elements, reflected at a moment in time. If there is honesty to our work, we are simply communicating our vision, feelings and experiences through our artwork, and watercolour is a wonderful medium for doing so. It is a difficult medium to control, let alone master, and as landscape painters our requirement to translate our experience of a three-dimensional, unconstrained place onto a two-dimensional piece of paper, limited by its four sides, poses a great deal of complexity in how we approach our observation, interpret the landscape, and develop our skills.

Understanding and overcoming these complexities is important if we are to progress and develop as successful landscape painters and my hope is that this book provides some useful signposts along the way. Ultimately, it is nothing more than a collection of thoughts and observations that has developed over the years, but nevertheless, they have informed my work and enabled me to not only earn a living, but derive tremendous enjoyment and fulfilment by combining two separate passions: being outdoors and creating artwork. As your technique and experience grows my happiest thought is that this book will be left on your shelf for increasingly longer periods, being dusted off just once in a while, as your start to rely on, and learn from, your own experiences. Your ambition must always be to paint your way, not my way and if these pages help to give you a nudge closer to that outcome, then they will have certainly been worth writing.

Most of all, embrace the simplicity of landscape painting and the enjoyment that comes from observing our surroundings, understanding our influence on them, and sharing our experiences of witnessing that through the art we create.

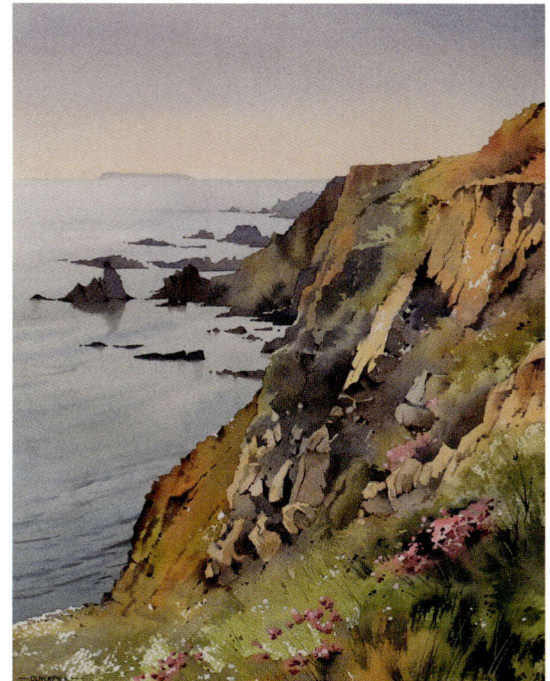

Sea Thrift at Hartland Point – 29cm x 39cm

Section 5
MAXIMISING YOUR POTENTIAL

For many, landscape painting will remain a wonderful and fulfilling hobby, without taking on a commercial dimension, not through lack of ability or ambition, but often as a result of life and career choices. I know many wonderful artists that have other full-time jobs and established careers, and just because they are not professional artists it does not diminish the quality of their work. For others, opportunities may have presented themselves, such that they are able to take their art from being a hobby to a full-time career. Although one assumes that such a move is indicative of the quality of their work, it doesn't always follow that a professional artist produces work of higher quality (subjective though that assessment

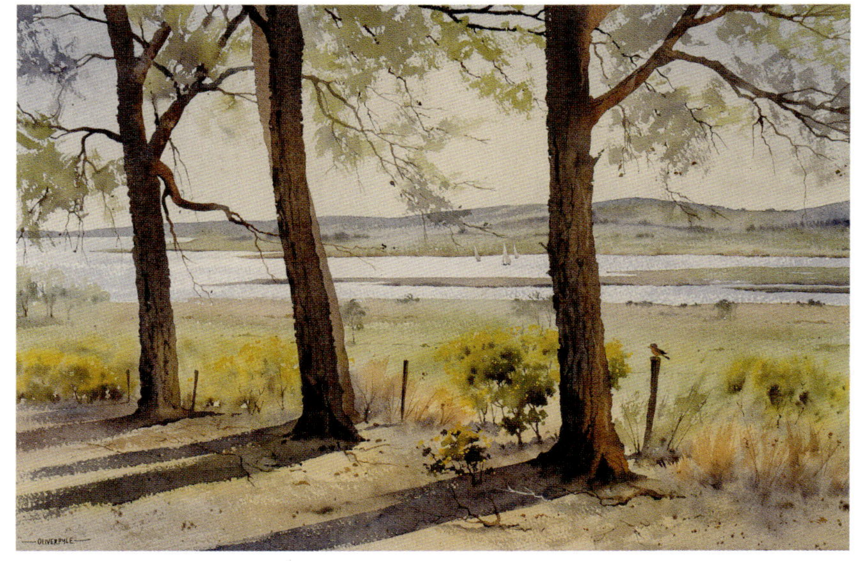

Spring Sunlight, Arne Nature Reserve – 50cm x 34cm
A favourite place of mine, to walk, sit, paint, relax, Arne Nature Reserve, managed by the Royal Society for the Protection of Birds, is a wonderful heathland landscape on the banks of Poole Harbour. I love this view, looking out from the shade of the Scots Pines across the shimmering water of Middlebere Lake, and it's always nice when a little Dartford Warbler decides to put in an appearance.

is) than the talented amateur. What sets the two apart is a conscious decision to make the transition from amateur painter to full-time artist. The term 'professional' is not just an imprimatur of skill and quality, but it describes an artist whose work is their primary source of income. This section isn't supposed to read like the motivational pages of a self-help book, instead I will take you through the pros and cons of making this transition, giving you a few tips for success, informed by my own experience and a wider observation of the visual arts industry. In particular, we'll take a look at the influence of the internet and the help and hinderance of social media in getting your art career started. I am fully aware that with no formal art training, some of the comments here may be out-of-step with orthodox art-world thinking and practice. I make no apologies for that; my own experience is valid, insofar as it has been coloured by mistakes and successes in the practice of full-time commercial art. My aim is to share that experience with you.

If you have arrived at a stage with your painting and find yourself at a junction in your life where becoming a full-time artist might be a serious career option, then I hope you find this section helpful with your deliberations and decision making.

BREAKING DOWN THE MYTHS

Over the years, I have become aware of several ideas that may not have a solid grounding in reality and are not entirely helpful when considering art as a career choice. It's important that we get these out of the way before we look at the steps you may need to take to succeed as a professional artist.

Myth One – 'It must be easy doing what you love as your career'
I started painting landscapes in my late teens and for the next twenty years or so it became a wonderful hobby, something that would often be a relaxing activity and a way of connecting with the landscape and expressing my experiences of it. Having been a full-time artist for over twelve years now, the hobbyist element has disappeared. Painting has become a necessity in order to earn a living, not just something that allows me to relax and escape from the rigours of daily life. This is not a bad thing, and painting more regularly for galleries, commissions and demonstrations is no less enjoyable: it is different and it is not easy. I have been fortunate to enjoy other hobbies (cooking, cricket, photography) and so I now have to approach my painting with an entirely different attitude: it is still just as enjoyable, but it is also work. If you are considering becoming a full-time artist, relying on the income, then it's important that you are realistic about this. There will be times when you don't want to paint, but will need to grind through it and you may not be ready to introduce that dynamic to something that you love doing. Be aware of this. When I encounter these feelings, I remind myself that I'm still painting the landscape and I love doing that. It is work, but it's really not that bad; it certainly beats an awkward quarterly meeting with your boss, knowing that you have not achieved your sales targets.

Myth Two – 'The self taught artist has more appeal than the formally trained'
Or vice versa. Having never taken an art class nor any formal tuition, it is quite evident that I am a self-taught artist, learning from my own experience and from a few books over the years. Many see this as a selling point that gives them a level of authenticity and appeal that is not available to those that have been formally trained. I know a number of classically trained artists and from speaking with them, they also consider themselves to be self-taught, and in many respects they are quite right. The evolution of scope and quality in an artist's work over time is not a function of a university degree or art college education – helpful though that will have been – but the constant dedication to their craft, learning

from their successes and failures. So, whether you feel there is some benefit from building your identity around either your formal training or lack thereof, it really is a non-issue as far as I'm concerned.

Myth Three – 'Just paint what you want – if it's good enough, people will buy it'

This may indeed be true, when you have become an established painter with an international reputation and a solid base of loyal collectors. However, there is a huge gulf to be bridged between such an enviable status and the start of your artistic career, where every sale counts. To be successful in a professional sense (and I am measuring that success in terms of the ability to rely on your art-related income) you will need to balance the necessity of painting what inspires you with the importance of adopting a commercial approach to your work. I have built my business around the sale of original paintings and Fine Art prints through six established galleries in England and online. For this to be successful it is essential that I paint subjects that are in demand with the customers of those specific galleries. For example, having exhibited my work for years at the Cove Gallery in Weymouth, I know that there are certain subjects that will sell quickly, while others are likely to remain on the gallery wall for longer. It would be unhelpful to me commercially if I insisted on continually painting the less popular work – 'because that's what I want to paint, and not doing so is compromising my artistic integrity' – and it would not encourage a long-term relationship with the owners, Paul and Geraldine (pleasant and patient though they are), who need to ensure that their gallery is commercially viable. Starting off as a professional artist, you will have identified your target customers and the sales channels to reach them, so make sure that the work you produce is likely to be in their purchasing sweet-spots. I have many wonderful subjects waiting to be painted from moments and memories, past and present but I cannot be confident of their success commercially

(given the location of my galleries) so I have to focus my efforts on the commercial home-runs unless I want to subject my family to an existence of eating stale bread and watery soup. 'What a shame that you can't paint what you want' I hear you say. Maybe, but don't forget that the subjects I do paint are still the ones that inspire me and feature the landscapes and moments that I love. We simply can't paint everything we want, and when there is a commercial dimension, then sensible choices need to be made and priorities need to be established; it's all highly un-artistic!

Myth Four – 'Art should never be about the money'

In many ways this is true. If your primary motivation and inspiration for being an artist is financial, then you will soon be found out. If, however, your work is of a sufficient standard to attract collectors, to command places on commercial gallery walls or receive the backing of established art companies (such as art equipment manufacturers or educational content providers) then considering opportunities to become professional and earn income from your work may be a sensible thing to do. Once you have made this transition and become reliant on that income your outlook will need to shift from one that is all about your art, to one that requires commercial considerations; a professional artist is in a luxurious position when they can produce work without needing to think about its possible commercial success. The notion that artistic endeavour stands above the grubby world of commercialism is not one to be found in history; many of our most celebrated artists sought the connections and patrons that would enable them to earn a living from their work and went through dark periods of self-doubt and introspection during moments of commercial and creative stagnation. Focussing on the commercial aspects should not compromise the integrity of your work. The key is to be inspired first and to ensure that this inspiration drives everything that you do. You will then need to assess your customer base and analyse the optimal sales channels for your work. It is effort taken here that will provide you with the freedom to paint what inspires you; in the next section I will give you some pointers on how to achieve this.

Myth Five – 'You are the best judge of your work'

Take a look at this painting of Ashdown Forest in Sussex, that I painted in 2011: the familiar clump of Scots pines on the Southern Slopes, stunted in their growth by exposure to the prevailing winds, made for a nice composition in the hazy afternoon light of early autumn. The expectation exceeded the execution and after I had finished the painting there were a number of elements that I was unhappy with.

I was preparing for my first solo exhibition, a two-month display at the visitor centre on the Ashdown Forest, a lovely, old, half-timber barn conversion, where I could display (and hopefully sell) thirty paintings. I had compiled a collection of scenes of The Forest, but as I discussed them with my framer, I realised I only had twenty-nine. It took me a little while to persuade myself that this painting should be included to complete the thirty. The painting annoyed me: I knew where the problems were and I didn't want others to see them. Inevitably, it was the first painting to sell, in what ended up being a successful exhibition and the final push for me to 'turn pro'.

To this day it remains one of the most important lessons that I have learned and it's never far from my mind. When we paint a scene we become inextricably linked with the process of painting it; we have our

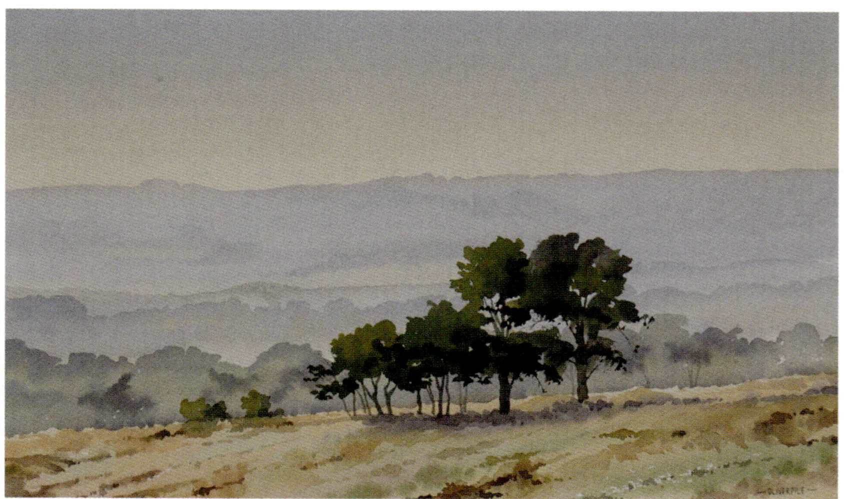

Scots Pines on the Southern Slopes – 39cm x 29cm
The first to sell…

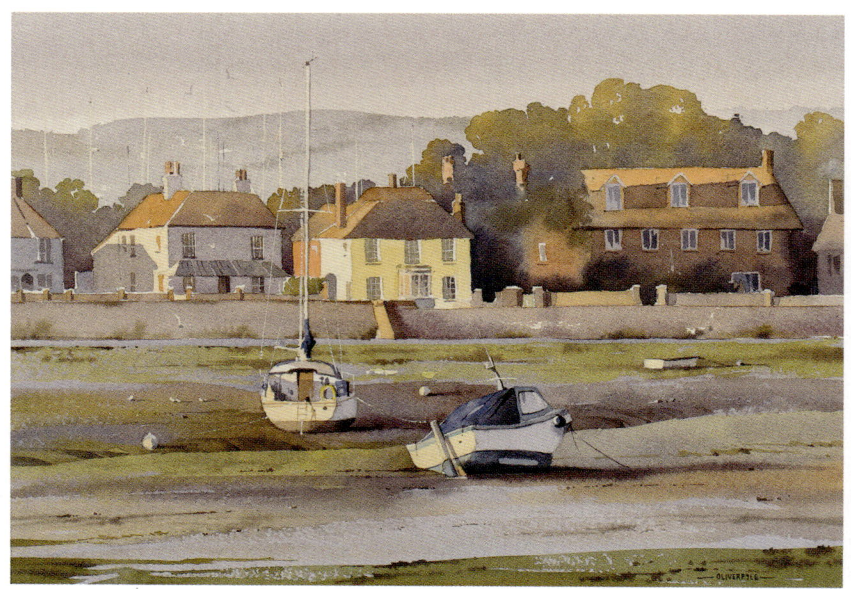

A Summer Evening at Bosham – 39cm x 29cm

preconceptions of what we want it to look like and how we should achieve that, technically. The capricious nature of watercolour is such that we are not always able to say precisely what we want and we get caught up appraising our own work based upon individual brushstrokes and passages that didn't quite work out as intended. With reference to this painting, I knew where the technical problems were, but the viewer didn't. Without being party to the painting process and my own perceived shortcomings, they viewed the painting as it should be viewed – a simple expression of the Southern Slopes and it struck a chord with them.

Listen to your customers and collectors and interact closely with any galleries that are considering representing you. It provides you with invaluable feedback to help you position and develop your work.

TESTING THE MARKET

The first significant step you should take in becoming a professional artist is to assess the public's reaction to your work. The currency for this is neither the warm comments of friends and family, nor the number of 'likes' on your social media posts – neither of these will pay the bills – but the cold, hard cash that comes from selling your work. Establishing a presence on a social media platform may be a helpful starting point but be aware that many social media subscribers and followers are not art purchasers, but predominantly other amateur artists. There are various available routes to explore as your art business progresses, but these must all be founded on the credibility of your artwork. With the scope of the internet and the freedom with which Instagram accounts, YouTube channels, Patreon and Skillshare platforms can be established, it is disappointing to see that some who are hoping to make a career from their art are bypassing this foundation – the quality of their artwork, evidenced by its commercial viability. Before you start thinking about becoming the

next in a long line of inexperienced online art tutors, test the market and explore the public's willingness to regularly pay for your work.

Other than a number of occasional commissions undertaken, generally for friends, family and colleagues, the first opportunity I had to test the market was the solo exhibition I previously mentioned at the visitor centre on the Ashdown Forest in 2012. Work is required to find suitable venues and I was fortunate to have an extended period at the centre, a popular resource and retail location for visitors to Ashdown. Being an area that I have a strong connection to and love to paint, it was a good starting point. We agreed a simple arrangement whereby

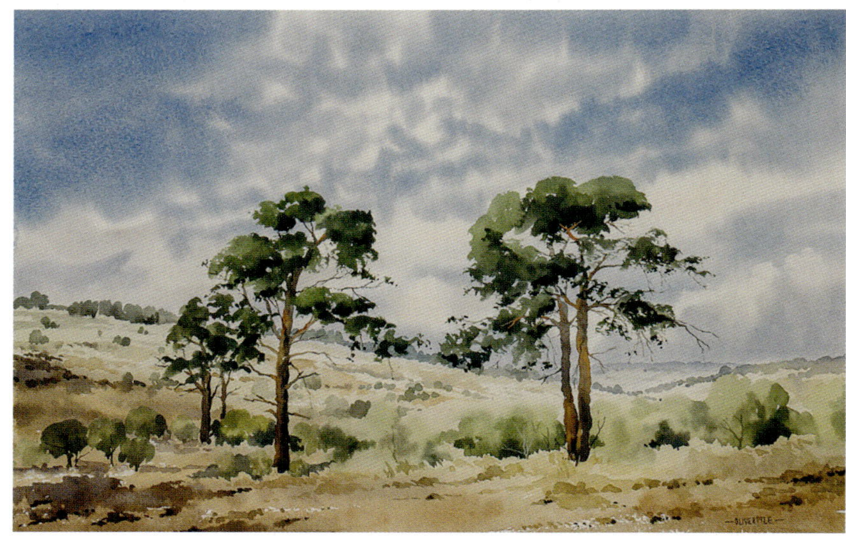

Scots Pines at Wren's Warren – 50cm x 34cm
My work has progressed significantly from my first exhibition, yet this painting and the one overleaf that I sold will always represent an important signpost to future pathways and directions.

The exhibition was successful for both the centre and I. It became clear that there was a market for my work and that the pricing I had envisaged and would need to rely on to earn a living, was not an obstacle to progress. Demand for work – tick. Pricing level – tick.

If your first attempt at engaging with the public's wallets falls flat, but you still believe in the commercial potential of your work, then review what worked and what didn't, but don't give up. Success in any business venture requires persistence and a dogged determination to achieve your ambition.

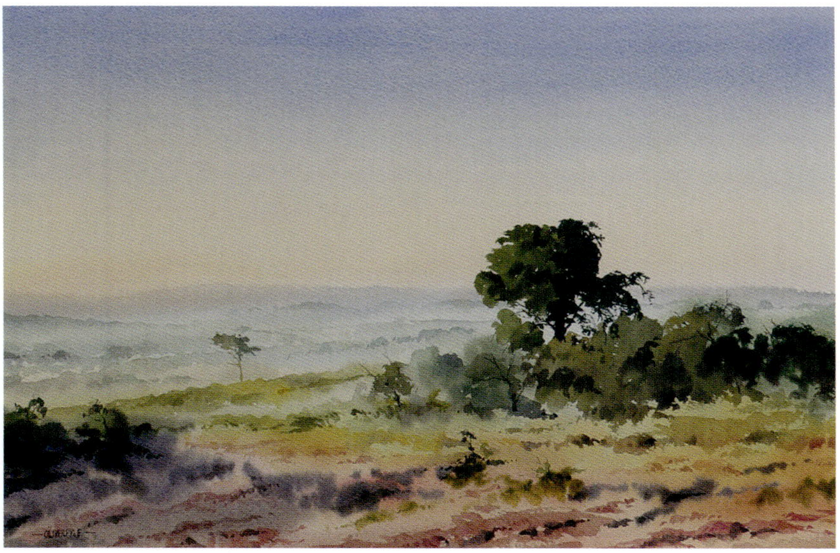

Summer Evening at Gill's Lap – 50cm x 34cm

there was no rental costs for the exhibition space, just a commission split on whatever sold during the exhibition. Look for opportunities like this where there is not a substantial upfront cost. Keep it simple. These venues and opportunities rarely come knocking on your door – you will need to do the hard yards to create these opportunities yourself and they come in all different shapes and sizes: the walls of a local restaurant, an art society exhibition, regional and national competitions, village art weeks. Do your research, create openings for yourself, then provide your very best work (don't keep this for yourself!) that will be appropriate for the venue and potential customer base that will view your work. Make sure to involve yourself with any promotional initiatives that the venue organises – the paying public are always keen to meet the artist.

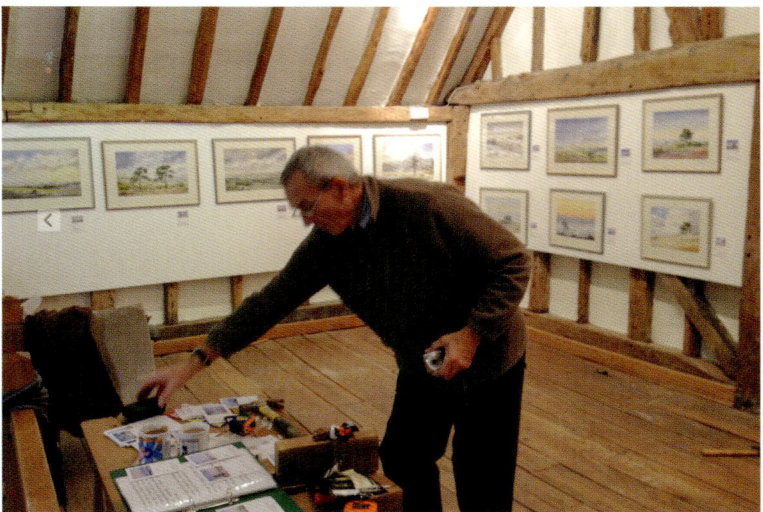

Dad helping me to hang paintings for my first exhibition. From my earliest childhood memories, he would always enjoy seeing a new drawing I had done, and his enthusiasm for my work was a tremendous support. A mathematician by trade, but a far more skilled draughtsman than he would ever have claimed, I remember with much fondness the small drawings and witty illustrations in my birthday cards, all made with the left hand. A wonderfully kind man, always interested in others and generous with his time, I miss him every day.

PRICING YOUR WORK

Finding the correct level to price your work is important, but it is an imprecise science. It may sound as though I'm stating the obvious when I say that your primary concern should be to set prices at a level that will maximise your sales, however I have seen many occasions where this is not always the case; artists sometimes price their work as if it is a vanity project – 'my paintings are worth far more than that!' Well, your paintings are only worth what someone is prepared to pay for them; be realistic about that. Being a gallery owner, it helps to see the other side of the equation, advising new artists on finding a pricing structure for their work that results in regular sales; this is always based on optimising the turnover of their work. That may sound a little mercenary, but selling your artwork is a commercial activity (that you will depend upon if you are thinking of becoming a full-time artist) and a commercial gallery is in the business of selling paintings, it's not just a place for hanging pretty pictures on walls. My advice in considering a starting price for your work is as follows:

1) Look at the prices of other artists selling similar work to you, through similar channels. Do this over a period of time to see if the work sells regularly, or if the same pieces are there year–in, year-out.

2) Make a calculation of the prices that you need to command in order to make a living, based on your projections of anticipated sales. Factor in the time spent and the cost of materials used in order to have a starting level of costs on which to base your calculations. If you will be selling your work through a third-party (gallery or online platform) then factor in the external costs that will need to be deducted from the sales price: sales commission and shipping costs.

3) Under-pricing your work is not good, but it is better than over-pricing. You can always increase your prices as demand dictates, but existing purchasers and collectors of your work will not thank

you for reducing the value and cachet of the art they have bought, should you need to reduce your prices.

4) Think of a sale as more than the sum of money you will receive. When a painting sells, it will hang on someone's wall and others will see it; your sold paintings become your best advertisements. Furthermore, each sale creates a new opportunity: a space on the gallery wall for you to fill with another piece. This is why setting a realistic price to encourage sales, as opposed to massaging your ego, is so important.

5) Research your potential customer base. Understanding your sales channel and those that frequent it with their open wallets will help you calibrate your pricing. Will they be hanging your work as a statement piece on the walls of their gracious and spacious Tuscan villa, or will the painting be a memento of a long weekend, taking pride of place above the kitchen table, next to the calendar on which the kids' dental appointments have been scribbled? A word of caution though: if you intend your work to be available through multiple channels and locations, don't fall into the trap of setting pricing for your most wealthy clients – you will dramatically reduce the size of your potential customer base.

6) Price your work in a way that will not compromise your consistency as your business develops. If you are in the happy position of having more than one sales outlet for your work, you will need to ensure that the pricing is consistent across all. This is particularly important for work that is sold commission-free, often through an artist's own website; keep your own prices the same as those of the gallery. Flexing your prices significantly to take advantage of gallery locations, sales opportunities, or customer demographics will become unmanageable in the long term and create confusion for your customers.

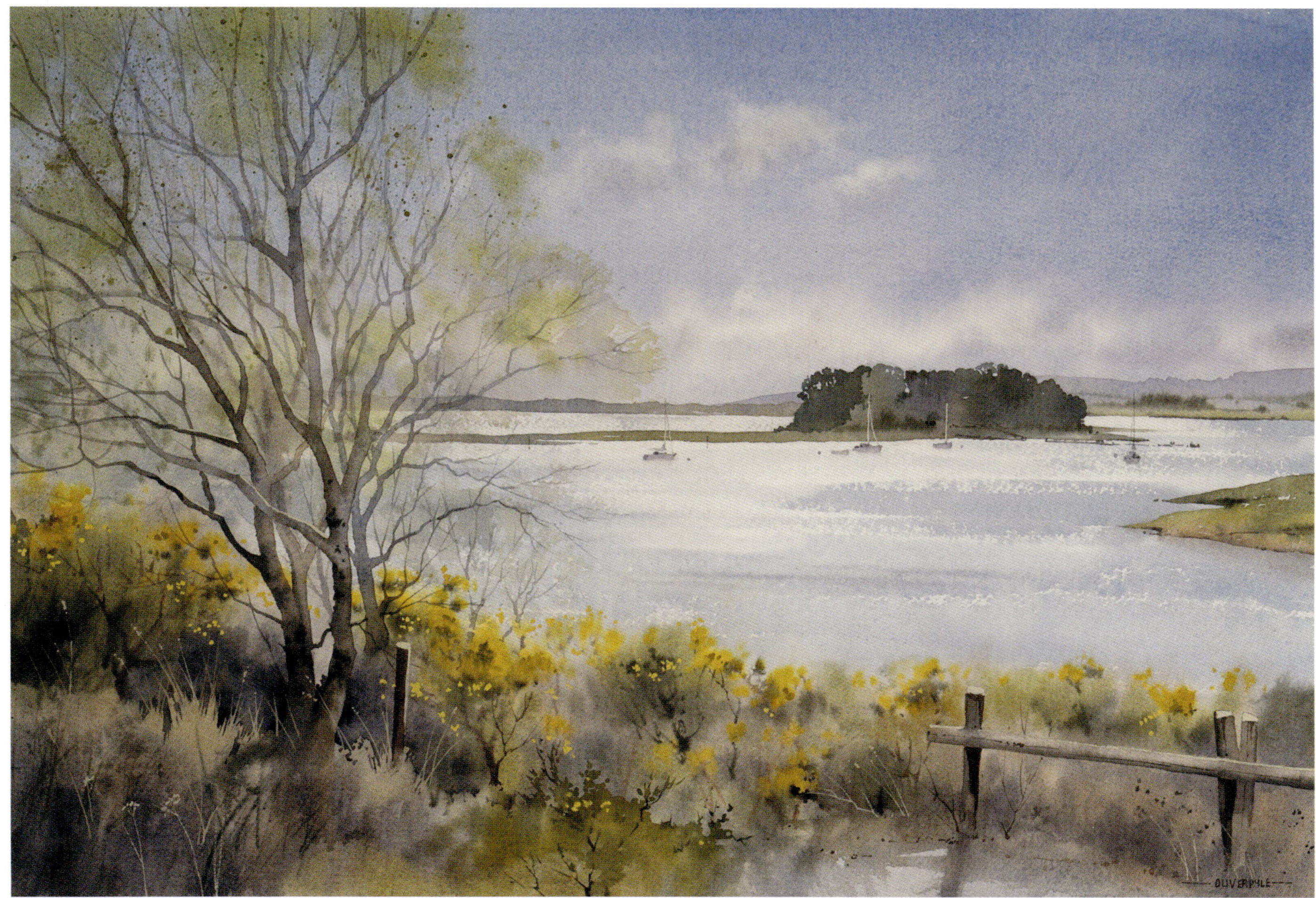

Spring Views from Shipstal Hill, Arne – 50cm x 34cm

ESTABLISH AN IDENTITY

You have found opportunities to test the market and settled on a level of pricing that is encouraging sales of your work. The path to further success lies ahead and despite it being straight and obvious, it is a long and challenging one that many artists struggle to navigate. The increased popularity of social media platforms is a contributor to this; it is easy to look at the weight of followers, subscribers and 'likes' enjoyed by some of our favourite, well-established artists and conclude that their style and subjects represent a path to success. There may be some truth in this, but that is their path, not yours. Visual art is a world of creativity and individualism, not duplication and conformity.

There was a moment after my first exhibition when I had secured representation with a high street gallery and felt that there might be a short cut to wider success. I had noticed that landscape painters with a looser, more abstract style seemed to be the ones that were popular and successful at the time; now was the time to switch things up and follow this stylistic zeitgeist, I thought. This was the only time in my career that I had stopped to think about the nebulous artistic concept of 'style' and the resulting work was an abject failure, caught between trying to emulate the work and style of others, while still painting with the instinct that helped me create work that had been selling well up to that point. All that resulted was a confused mess of inauthentic expression. It was, and will be, the last time I stop to think about my painting style. I reverted to what had previously worked well and stuck to it. Over the years I have become known as the Englishman that paints representative, peaceful landscapes in watercolour, using an unusual combination of loose technique and crisp detail. My work is predominantly based on colour, not tone, and I focus on detail rather than larger shapes. These are both a departure from current art-world trends, but it's how I view the landscape and therefore informs how I paint it. It works for me and it is what defines my artistic identity.

I hear regularly from people saying that when they see a new painting of mine, they know immediately that it is my work without needing to search for any signatures or credits. This is commercial gold dust, but it can only be found through persistence and a dedicated resolve to paint your way, not someone else's.

Take great care in establishing an identity to your work. You will achieve this through a consistent approach, concentrating on the subjects that inspire you. Never be afraid of becoming a specialist; find a niche and concentrate your focus on developing it. It will always yield more sustainable results than the artist that tries their hand at every new trend that presents itself. Those that follow and purchase your work and the potential galleries that might represent you in future, will be engaged by the integrity and authenticity of your work, not your ability to replicate the work of others or your embodiment of the old adage 'Jack of all trades, master of none'.

Understanding what and why you paint will help you to nurture an identity that will help tremendously as you seek new outlets and sales channels for your work, saving you wasted time in approaching venues, galleries and opportunities that are simply not appropriate for your work. These points may help you to develop your identity. Although this is a book on landscape painting, the principles hold for any genre:

- Only paint subjects that inspire you.
- Develop a firm grasp on just a few places/subjects rather than a light touch on many.
- Pay little attention to 'style' – it is generally a term used by others to comment on, and categorise your work; just allow it to develop naturally. It is not something that is easily defined but is the result of how **you** look at the landscape, how **you** feel about the landscape and the techniques **you** prefer using to communicate this.
- Be an artistic solipsist: keep a laser-like focus on your own work, not the work of others.

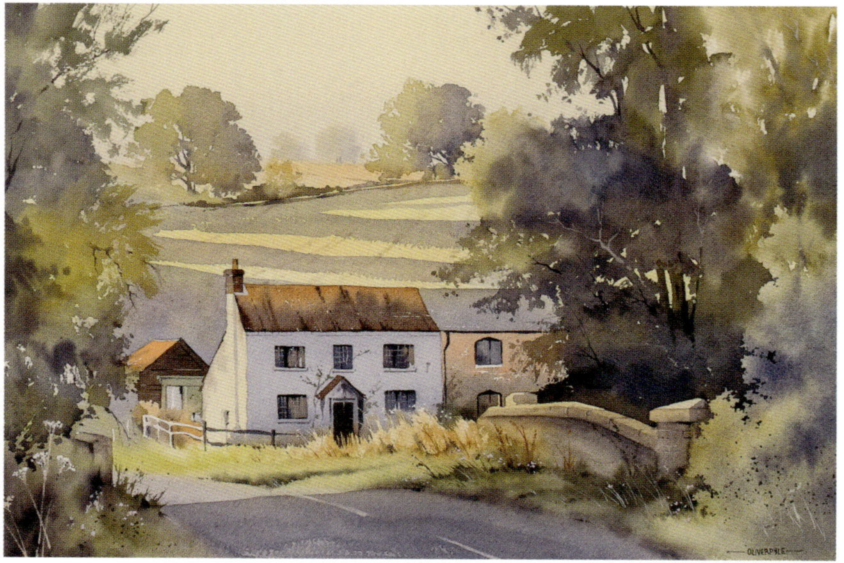

The Old Wharf Cottages – 50cm x 34cm

- Do not paint for social media 'likes'. Landscape painting should be an insight into our world, an individual interpretation where the artist communicates their inspiration of moments and places. It is not a tool for harvesting the approbation of the public.

WORKING WITH GALLERIES

It is unlikely that you will be able to achieve sufficient traction early on in your career by only selling your work through your own channels – website, social media platforms, or your own studio gallery (should you be fortunate enough to have one). You will probably need to find a gallery, or galleries, to represent and sell your work, whether physical or online. In doing so, there will be a realisation that a substantial portion of your sales price (sometimes 50 per cent) will be retained by a gallery as commission. Having dealt with your feelings of mild outrage, you will assess the extent to which this is something that you ought to investigate. To help you, consider the following benefits that your retained gallery commission will pay for:

- Direct access to a large art-focussed customer base.
- The ability to build relationships with collectors of your work.
- A source of introduced commissions.
- Dedicated staff to sell your work.
- Promotion of you and your work through the gallery and online.
- An endorsement of quality.
- A location for the public to physically see your framed original work. It always has greater impact than an online or printed image, no matter the quality of the digital file.

Finding galleries to represent you is no easy task. You may have been fortunate enough to receive an invitation to exhibit from a gallery, but it is most likely that you will need to profile galleries that are appropriate for your work and make approaches to them. This can be soul-destroying work and you will need a thick skin to deal with the frequent, inevitable unenthusiastic responses; keep going and don't take it as an indicator that your work is unattractive. Success in establishing a relationship with a gallery often comes from a disciplined and targeted approach. Asking the following questions will help you to profile and target the galleries where you are most likely to have a positive result:

- Is the gallery a logical fit for the subjects that I like to paint? For landscape painting, this is often a geographical consideration.

- Does my style of work complement the existing work at the gallery?
- Does the gallery offer to display my work all year, or will it just be displayed for periodic exhibitions and how does this fit in with my work and output?
- Is my preference to exhibit in galleries that prefer mixed exhibitions (multiple artists) or solo exhibitions?
- Is the work taken on a sale-or-return basis or purchased by the gallery up-front?
- Does the gallery have a solid social media presence and a proactive approach to the representation of its artists' work?
- Looking at the work currently represented by the gallery, am I being realistic in appraising the quality of my work, or will I be punching well above my weight?

- Will my work be delivered framed to the gallery, or does the gallery offer this service?
- Is it easy, logistically, to deliver my work?

RIGHT AND OVERLEAF SPREAD:
An excerpt of a presentation of work that I made to The Cove Gallery in Weymouth. Time taken presenting your work with a professional approach will help you to stand out among the many applications that galleries receive.

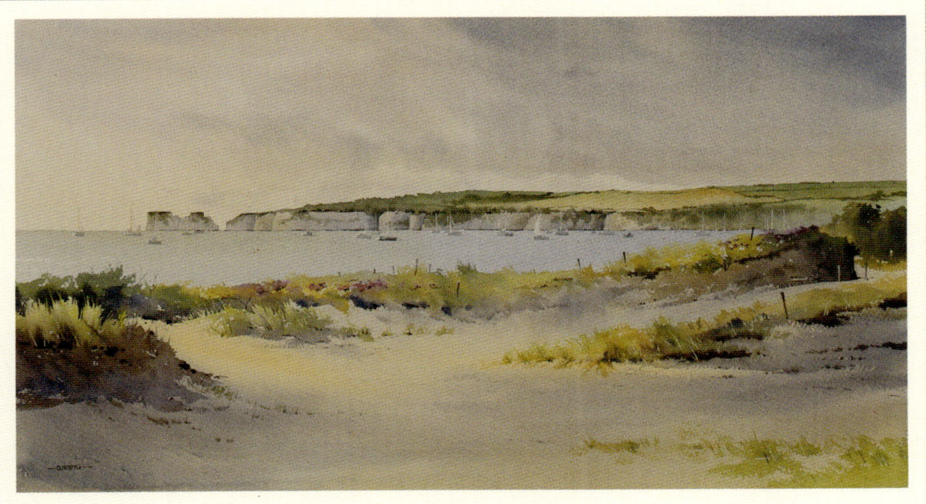

The Coast

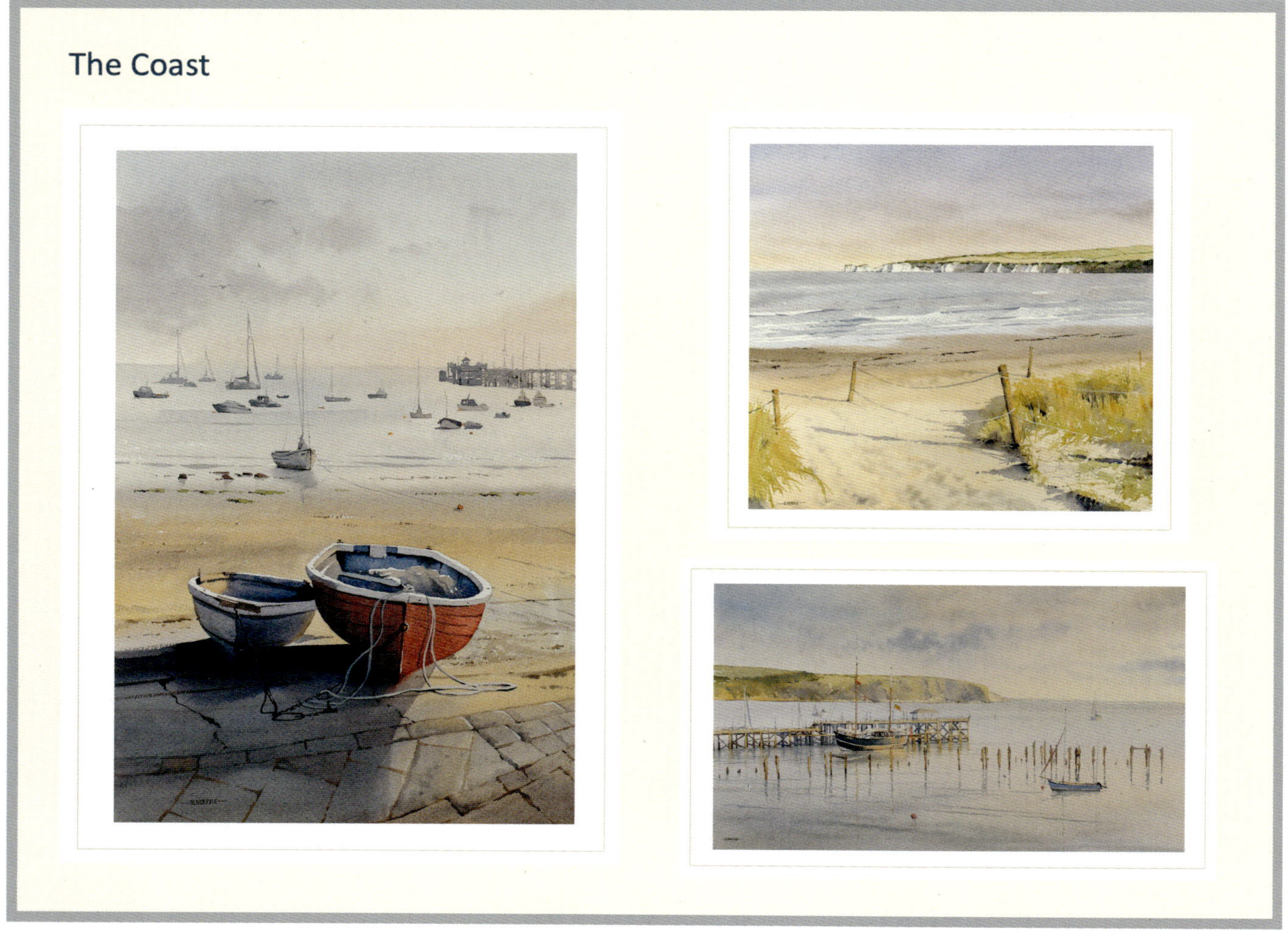

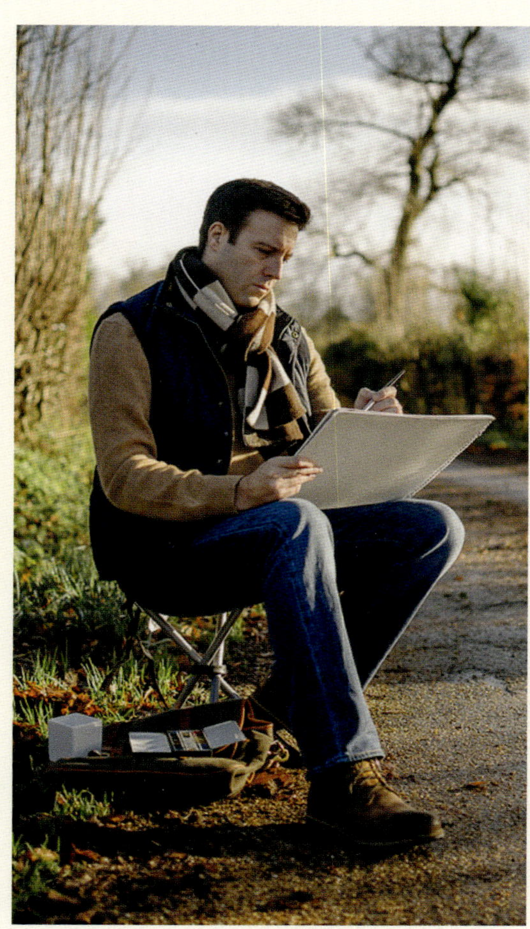

The Artist

Oliver has established himself as a successful landscape artist working exclusively in watercolour. Based in Sussex and entirely self-taught, his work is to be found in collections across the country and internationally, selling through UK galleries and online. Oliver's art is much in demand and features as part of the UK's most well established and prestigious Fine Art greetings card publisher, Medici Cards. Under the brand the company has created The Oliver Pyle Collection. Oliver teaches watercolour and painting techniques through workshops and demonstrations and is a regular contributor of articles to industry and local publications.

Through Oliver's work we explore the impact of light, the weather, and the seasons and how these combine to achieve paintings that are evocative and atmospheric; "As a landscape artist my inspiration comes from being outdoors where light, smells, sounds, and textures all combine to deliver an outstanding sensory experience - let's call it 'atmosphere' if you like. My aim is never to simply describe or illustrate a scene, rather to create a painting that provides an experience of the place. Watercolour is the perfect medium for capturing the vicissitudes of the British climate and allows me to make a spontaneous response to the delicate Northern light that is with us for much of the year. "

The Opportunity

With Oliver's work becoming increasingly sought after, and to maximise opportunities following the launch of the Medici Card range, he is seeking further strategic partnerships with established Fine Art galleries in the South of England.

Every gallery has different requirements. however Oliver is equally happy providing local scenes (which works very well with Mulberry Tree Gallery in Dorset,) or more generic scenes and cityscapes, which is successful with The Ashdown Gallery in Sussex. At this stage Oliver is open to exploring solo-exhibitions but would be equally pleased to work with the gallery to provide paintings for seasonal/periodic exhibitions, acting as a regular gallery contributor throughout the year.

The following pages contain a small collection of recent paintings, some of which are to be found in The Oliver Pyle Collection for Medici Cards

Having targeted the galleries you would like to represent you, your approach to them will need to be carefully considered. Galleries receive many approaches from artists interested in exhibiting their work and these are often poorly presented, unspecific, sometimes presumptuous, lazily composed, and showing work that is clearly a poor fit considering the gallery's existing collection of work. You only have one opportunity to make an impression so make sure that you take some time to ensure that it is a good one. Make a crisp presentation that highlights your best and most relevant work and then send it to the gallery with a covering email. Don't arrive unannounced at galleries with portfolios of your work – gallery owners do not appreciate this and like to take time to consider how new work will fit in with their existing range of artists. It will most likely lead to a 'no thank you.' If you feel that this is the best way of demonstrating your work, then at least contact the gallery beforehand.

Having sent your email to the gallery, be prepared for a negative response – many galleries are limited in terms of the new work they are able to take. It is probable that you will need to keep trying and knocking on other doors. These opportunities rarely fall into your lap and finding the

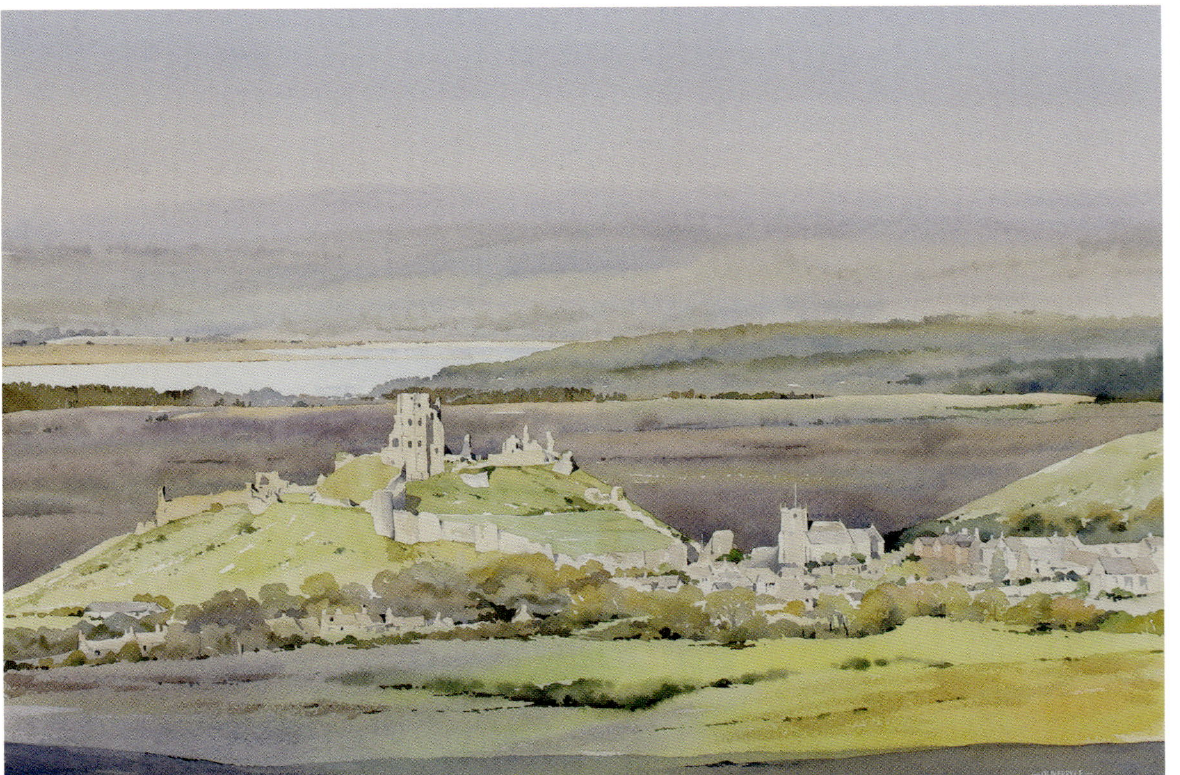

Corfe Castle and Beyond –
72cm x 54cm
I love this view from the beer garden of The Scott Arms in Kingston, and it made the perfect subject for my first full-sheet painting. It was one of five that I delivered to the Mulberry Tree Gallery in Swanage as my first consignment for an independent high street gallery. Four sold in the first week – I was up and running!

right representation requires persistence. After my first solo exhibition, I targeted galleries in Purbeck to represent my work, being an area that I knew well and loved to paint. I approached five galleries in the area before I was accepted by the Mulberry Tree Gallery, which I have since gone on to own. I am now represented by 6 galleries in the UK, but the approaches I have made to galleries over time exceeds fifty. Keep knocking.

Art Galleries – Physical or Online?

With the scope and reach of the internet, many artists are asking whether physical galleries have a future with online galleries likely to offer a broader and more direct route to finding buyers of their work. Opinion differs on this, however for the art that I produce – location-specific, representational landscapes – the sales that I achieve through

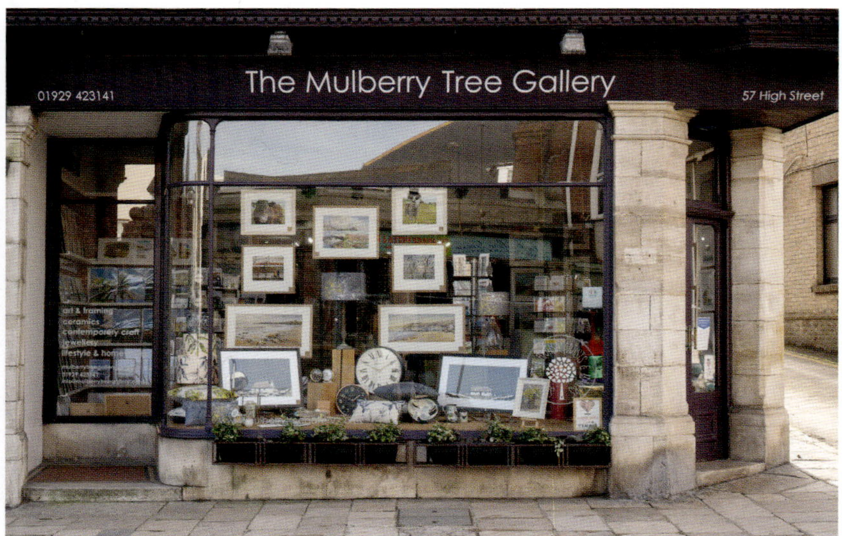

The Mulberry Tree Gallery, Swanage Dorset
This lovely old gallery on the High Street has been an integral part of my work's commercial journey, progressing from a contributing artist to co-owner with my colleague Steve. It has something for everyone, from greetings cards to large oil paintings and attractive ceramics. The work we display is focussed on the iconic Purbeck land and seascapes, that I have always loved to paint, and its flora and fauna; it's what our customers want to see and buy. Know your customers.

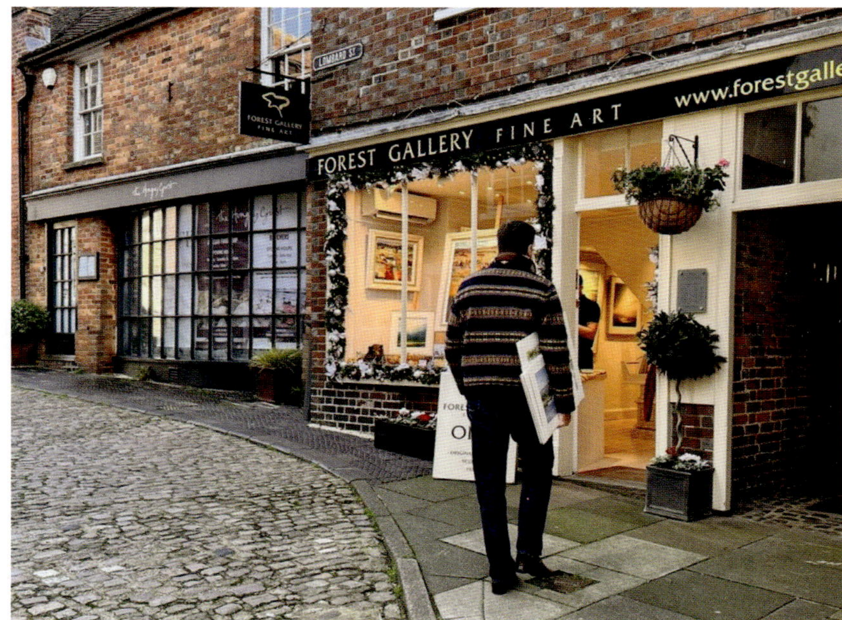

Forest Gallery Fine Art in the historic town of Petworth has been a great support over the years, and a reliable outlet for many of my Sussex scenes. Here, I'm dropping off a new consignment for framing – it's always nice to catch up with Ashley and Cristina.

physical galleries exceeds those that I sell online by approximately ten to one. I notice this too with the Mulberry Tree Gallery. Despite having an active social media presence, promoting our location and artists, the overwhelming majority of our work is sold physically in the gallery. My take on this is that art buyers in general, and those buying landscape paintings in particular, make unplanned purchases; something catches the eye on a weekend trip to Petworth, or a week's holiday in Swanage. I'm unaware of many purchasers of landscape art that sit down at the computer and Google different options to fill a space on the living room wall. It does happen of course, but my experience is that purchasers still like to see the art they are buying hanging on a gallery wall.

A good place to start might be with some of the self-curated online shops ('galleries' is perhaps too strong a term) such a Etsy. These can be a useful way to establish an online sales presence but tend to work best with work priced under £250 (a sensible starting price in any case for watercolour paintings).

WORKING WITH SOCIAL MEDIA

Many good resources exist that cover this subject and there's no need to replicate their contents here. The only addition I have to make is to remind you of my comments in the section Establish An Identity and the need to be authentic. Having taken care to create and position your work, nurturing your identity, your social media presence should simply be an extension of that. It is your shop window, so use it carefully to display your work and promote yourself.

Unfortunately the internet is awash with disingenuous timelines (for the visual arts sector, predominantly on Instagram) where the artist's own identity and work is obscured, sometimes invisible. A substantial number of artists that are hoping to make a transition from beginner to full-time believe that there is a short-cut to success, achieved by copying the work and style of established artists with large social media followings. They pay to attend their workshops, even purchase their work, pose for selfies with their admired 'elite' artist and then proceed to cram their timelines with their own poor imitations of the artist's work. In a year or so, another artist will be in-Vogue and the same process is repeated. And repeated. This problem only tends to exist in the watercolour community and some responsibility for this falls at the door of the promoters (often not the artists themselves) of 'global superstar painters' or 'international watercolour masters' – spurious designations indeed.

You can spot these timelines a mile off. Do not be tempted to go down this route. It is not a short cut to success but ultimately a dead-end that will not help you to develop a sustainable and credible career. The following tips may help you:

- Keep your identity foremost. Be authentic.
- Curate and develop your social media presence as your work develops naturally. Genuine followers will appreciate your integrity and consistency.
- Engage with your followers. If they have taken time to contact you, take some time to respond. Of course, as your presence grows it is simply not possible to answer every comment, but don't then switch from all to nothing; continue to communicate in a way that is manageable for you.
- Be nice. You won't make many friends and followers by becoming known for your acerbic replies and sardonic comments.
- Make your engagements original, regular, interesting, but primarily focussed on your work. Continual posts describing 'the journey', scattered with regular inspirational quotations are often an indication that your paintings themselves do not command the presence you would want them to.

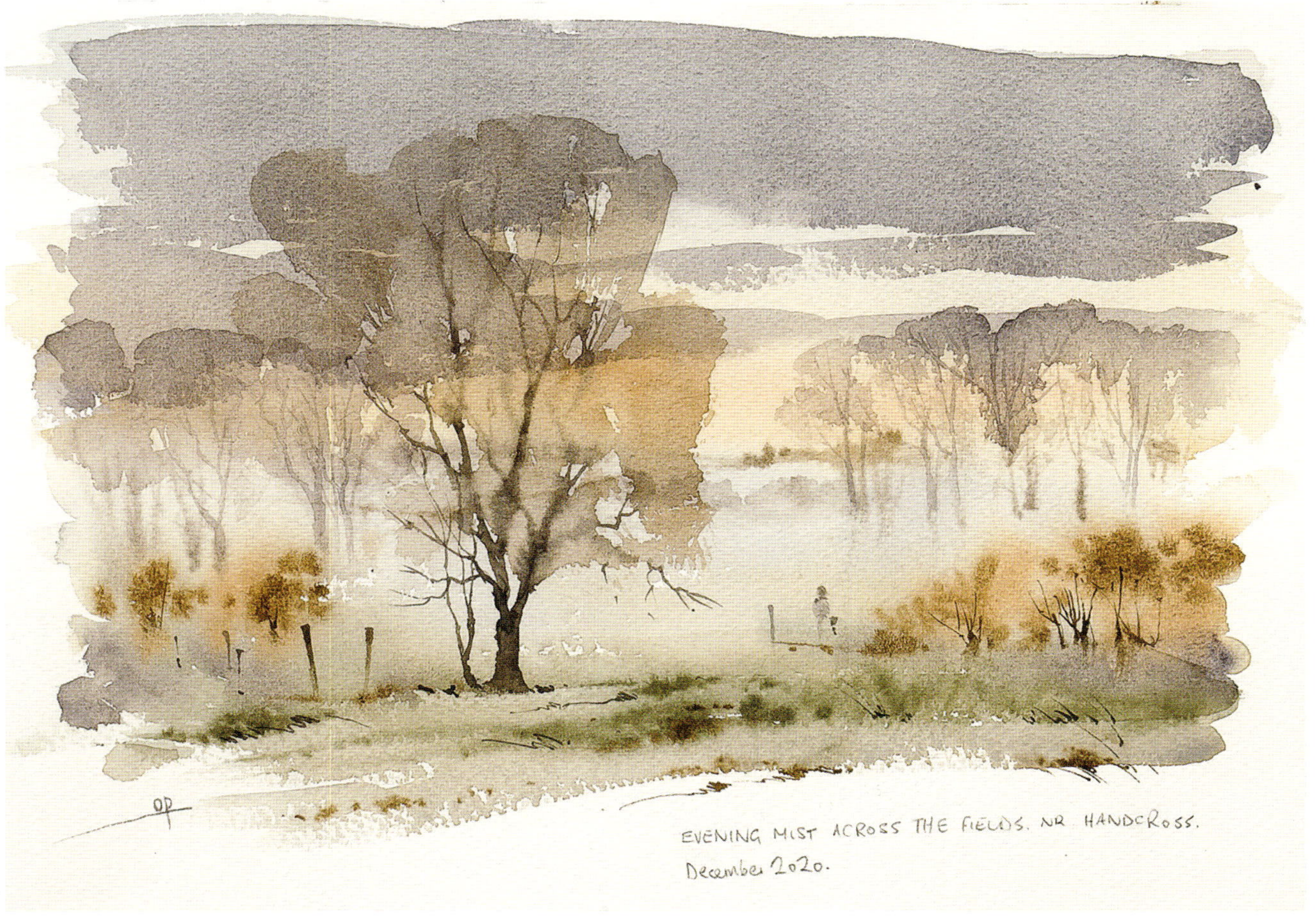

A simple sketch that I made quickly from memory, on return from driving my kids to the dentist! There's always time to record a fleeting observation, and its nice to share impromptu moments like this with followers on social media.

EXPANDING YOUR BUSINESS

As a landscape painter, a wide range of different opportunities is available as your business expands. You have achieved a foothold by establishing a relationship with a recognised gallery and from that point it becomes a little easier to find additional galleries. Build these relationships carefully without over-extending yourself. You need to be able to manage your workflow and output and it is important to take time consolidating a position with your new gallery(s) so that your work becomes familiar with their customer base.

Since making landscape painting my career, I have tried to introduce a new initiative each year. This has provided me with diversified income that has been important in mitigating the commercial risk of relying on painting sales from one gallery, or from a specific opportunity becoming no longer available. Here are some ideas to consider as your business grows:

- Write articles for artistic magazines and other suitable publications.
- Issue Limited Edition or Fine Art prints of your work.
- Seek licencing opportunities for your paintings, such as greetings cards and calendars.
- Write a blog or create a forum to engage with your followers and customers.
- Be available to take commissions.
- Establish a partnership with an art supplies manufacturer to endorse their products (but only do so if they are the products that you use and believe in).
- Illustration contracts can be a good way of not only earning income, but helping to grow exposure to your work.

There are other opportunities, but I suggest these with a cautionary note:

- Offer painting demonstrations to art groups and societies.
- Provide painting workshops.

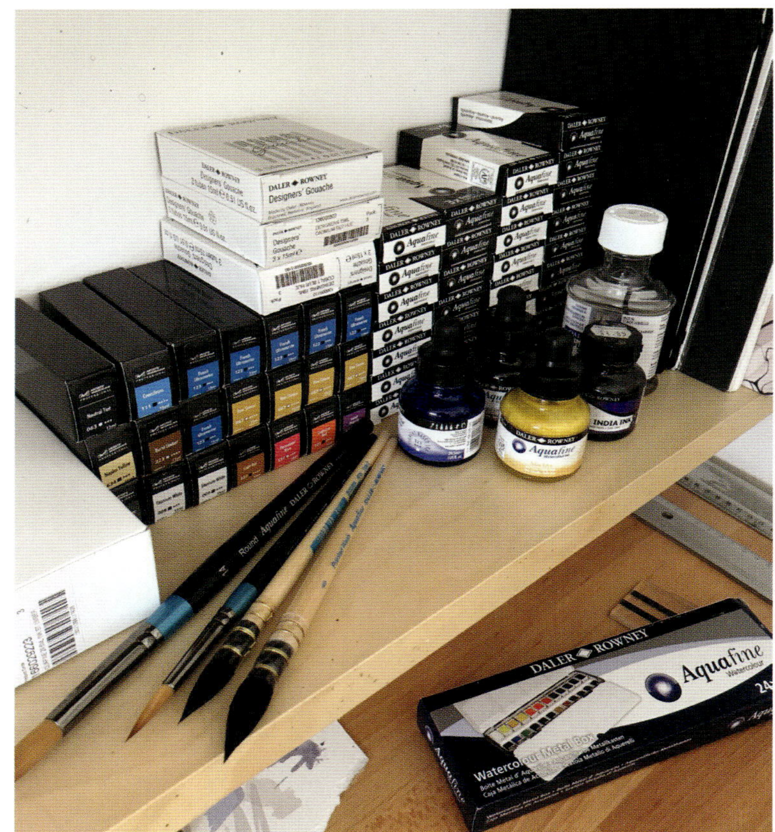

Daler Rowney equipment. From day one I have used the paint, paper and brushes from this wonderful British company. I know what it is able to deliver – consistent results primarily – and it never lets me down. Becoming an ambassador for the company's products was a logical fit and I'm grateful for their support and collaboration over the years.

- Create tutorial content for online platforms – streaming and downloadable – and also DVD.
- Write books.

Cautionary note – only consider these four options once you have established a level of credibility with your work. Before the self-promotion of the internet existed, there was a quality and experience threshold to be reached before you would be provided with a platform to teach others your skills. An established book publisher, a television channel, video production company or art materials manufacturer would only approach those with the skills and established presence in the industry to sell the products that they were backing financially. This worked well and ensured that, for the most part, those teaching others were established, proven artists with work that was recognisable and of a high quality; years of experience coloured their content with knowledge, wisdom and excellent advice.

With the availability of the internet, it is now possible to promote our own work without having to negotiate the quality barrier, and many do. On a monthly basis I see new artists springing up, having only been painting for a short time, looking to find credibility and acceptance in the industry by becoming online 'teachers'. This is not just confined to YouTube, but some offer paid for content through platforms such as Skillshare and Patreon too. The reality is that there is very little experience to be taught and I would advise any artist considering the four opportunities above not to think about them as options until they have years of experience, together with the quality stamp from an established gallery, art materials company or publisher. Amateur painters and hobbyists learning how to paint should not have to thrash their way through a thicket of inexperienced teaching, often paying for it, before they settle on helpful instruction.

RIGHT: Writing articles for well distributed publications can be a useful way to increase the visibility of your work.

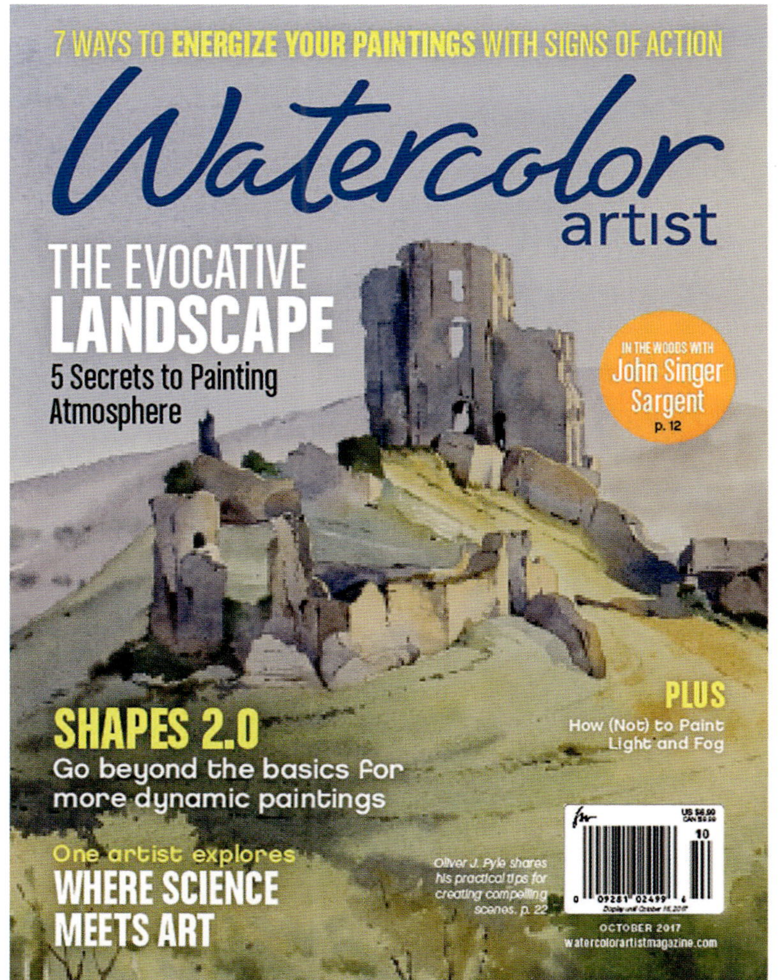

SOME GENERAL BUSINESS ADVICE

When you choose to pursue your dream, turning your art from hobby to career, please consider a few important points.

- You will become self-employed. The upside is easy to identify: you will be your own boss, you will decide the direction of your career, your working hours will be flexible and determined by you, your work will be doing something you love. However, not everyone that makes this transition is aware of the potential downside.

- Your work days, weekends and holidays will blend into one; there is often little distinction between them.

- You will no longer receive a regular pay cheque – income arrives sporadically and there will be times when you have to confront an impending mismatch between income and expenditure. Some people are unable to operate well without the comfort and structure that a monthly salary affords. Art is a creative endeavour; financial-linked anxiety and stress are dangerous predators that will easily devour your creative mindset.

- In the early years, it is likely that you will need to become multi-skilled. I now perform the following roles each month, in varying degrees of course: painter, social-media manager, secretary, bookkeeper, banker, camera man, film editor, production director, author, online shop assistant, warehouse worker, IT manager, advertising executive and research assistant. I have always been a firm believer in the importance of learning new skills and enjoy this side of self-employment. It is not for everyone however and please don't be under any illusion that

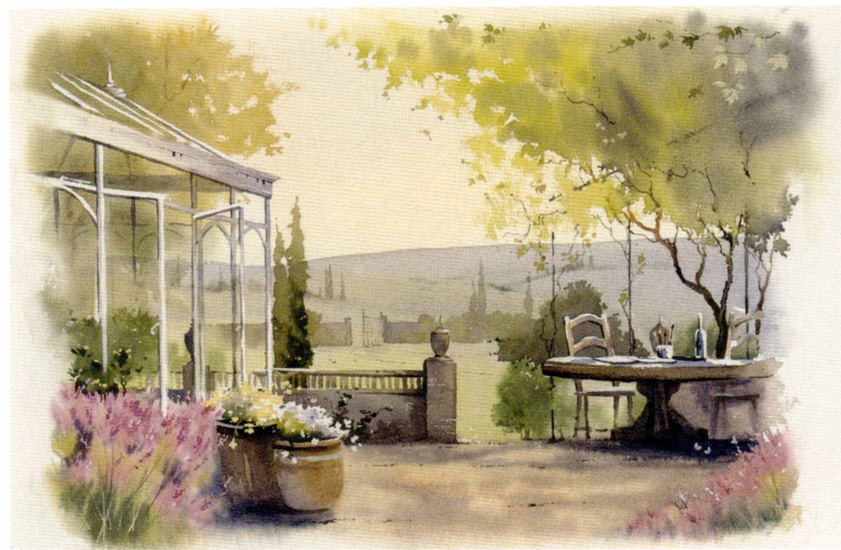

ABOVE AND OPPOSITE: Surprise illustrative work for the gaming app industry. It was a pleasure working with Lykke Studios on this fun project.

as you start your art career it will just be painting and sketching from 9.00 am to 5.00 pm.

To be successful in launching your career as an artist, I have several recommendations that have helped me over the years:

- Embrace new opportunities no matter how daunting they may seem initially.

- Think strategically. Don't rush into something that may not be a good fit with the brand and identity that you are projecting, even

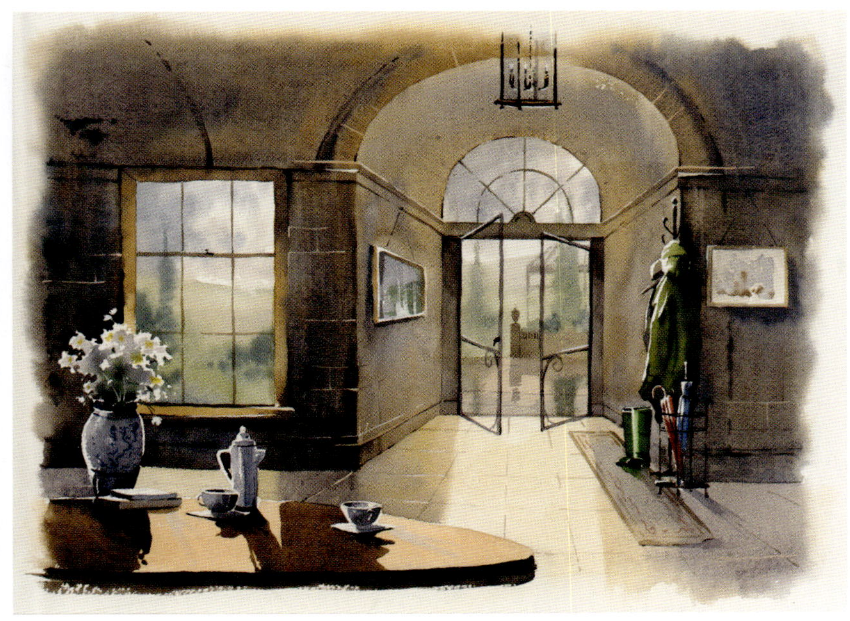

an artist can be a lonely existence; even if the colleagues you had from your previous job may have been annoying at times, they were a sounding board and the workplace was somewhere you could play around with ideas between each other. It is important to be in touch regularly with those whose opinions you value and take an interest in your work and development.

- Ensure that every interaction that your existing/potential customers have with you and your business is positive. Arranging a refund for a damaged print requires just as much thought and attention to detail as you put into your work or the enthusiastic replies to the flowing complements you receive on your social media page. It's no good spelling your name right when you sign your paintings if your website is then strewn with careless mistakes.

- Treat returning customers like gold dust. Repeat business means that your work has created a favourable impression, and the customer wants more. It is not easy to continually find new customers, but if your existing ones are happy then you are giving your business a fighting chance.

- Be versatile. I once received an email from a couple of Scandinavian chaps, based in Thailand, requesting some illustrative work for an app-based game. My thought process developed from 'probable scam' to 'I'll check it out' to 'this is way outside my normal line of work' to 'this looks like an interesting project – I'm in!' It gave me eighteen months of work, that can still be seen in the Tint app by Lykke Studios on Apple Arcade. Don't turn your nose up at projects and work that you feel is beneath you or unusual – they may turn out to be engaging and worthwhile. Yes, your artistic integrity is important, but so is your ability to pay the bills.

if the commercial rationale seems strong – it may preclude you from broader opportunities in the future.

- Make a business plan, no matter how simple it may be. It is important to set yourself some targets and then identify the steps required to achieve them. Keep updating and refreshing the plan as you progress and new horizons come into view – it should not be a static document.

- Make contacts with those that are in a similar situation to you, not just in the creative art business, but in other industries too. Being

- Make sure you enjoy what you are doing. When you feel your interest waning and the fun disappearing from what you are doing, accept it and then find ways to spark your motivation again; anything can be achieved if your enjoyment of a project and the motivation to do it are high.

Little remains to be said. Whether you are continuing to improve your landscape painting to find greater enjoyment from a wonderful hobby, looking for opportunities to add a commercial element to your work, or seeking to expand your art business, may I wish you all the very best and much success with your endeavours. Keep painting!

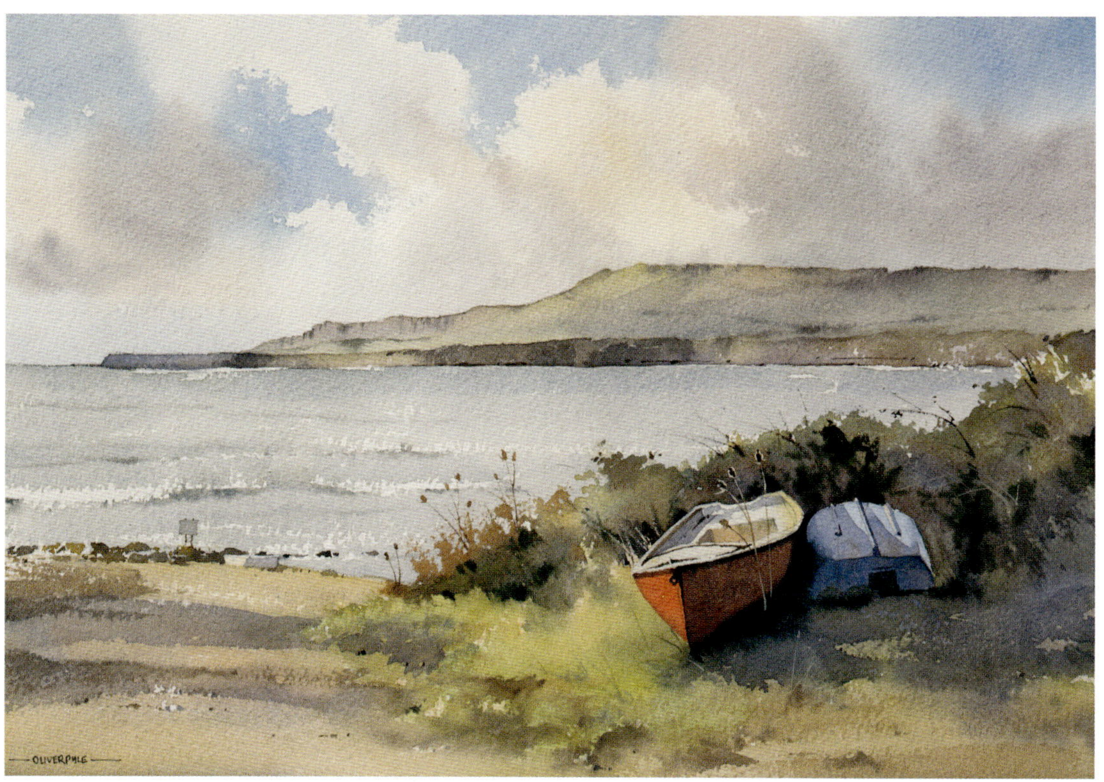

Sunny Intervals, Kimmeridge Bay – 39cm x 29cm

A GALLERY OF PAINTINGS AND SKETCHES

I have included a few paintings and sketches in this section, not because I consider them to be my best work technically, but because they represent the values that I have always considered to be foundational in my work, and are outcomes that have made an impact on me at different stages of my career.

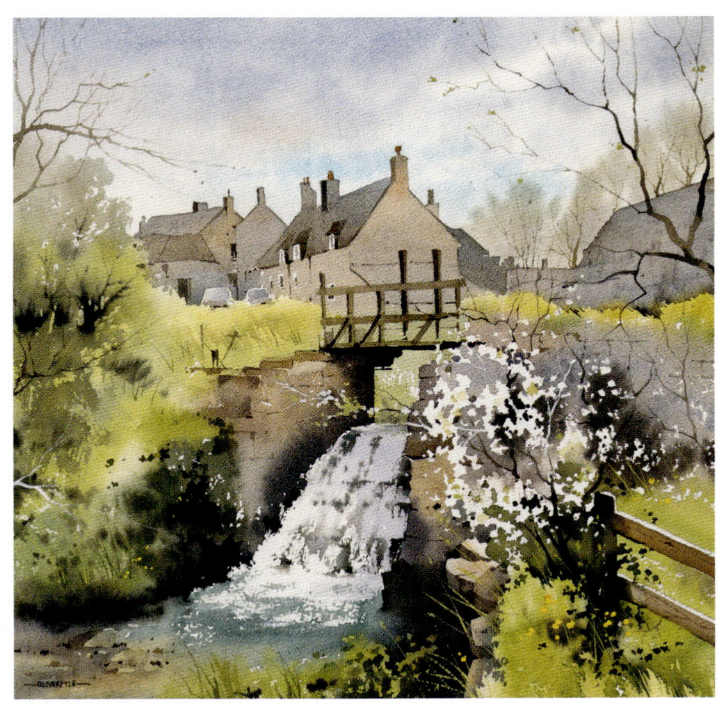

The Old Water Mill, Corfe Castle – 30cm x 30cm
Look for inspiration in the less obvious places. Just out of view to the right, is the magnificent ruin of Corfe Castle. It is a subject that I've painted many times, but if we are alert to our surroundings we will notice inspiration and subjects that might be easily overlooked. I often stop at the bridge to watch this lovely waterfall bubble past the old mill and under the road; it is a subject just as worthy as the castle itself.

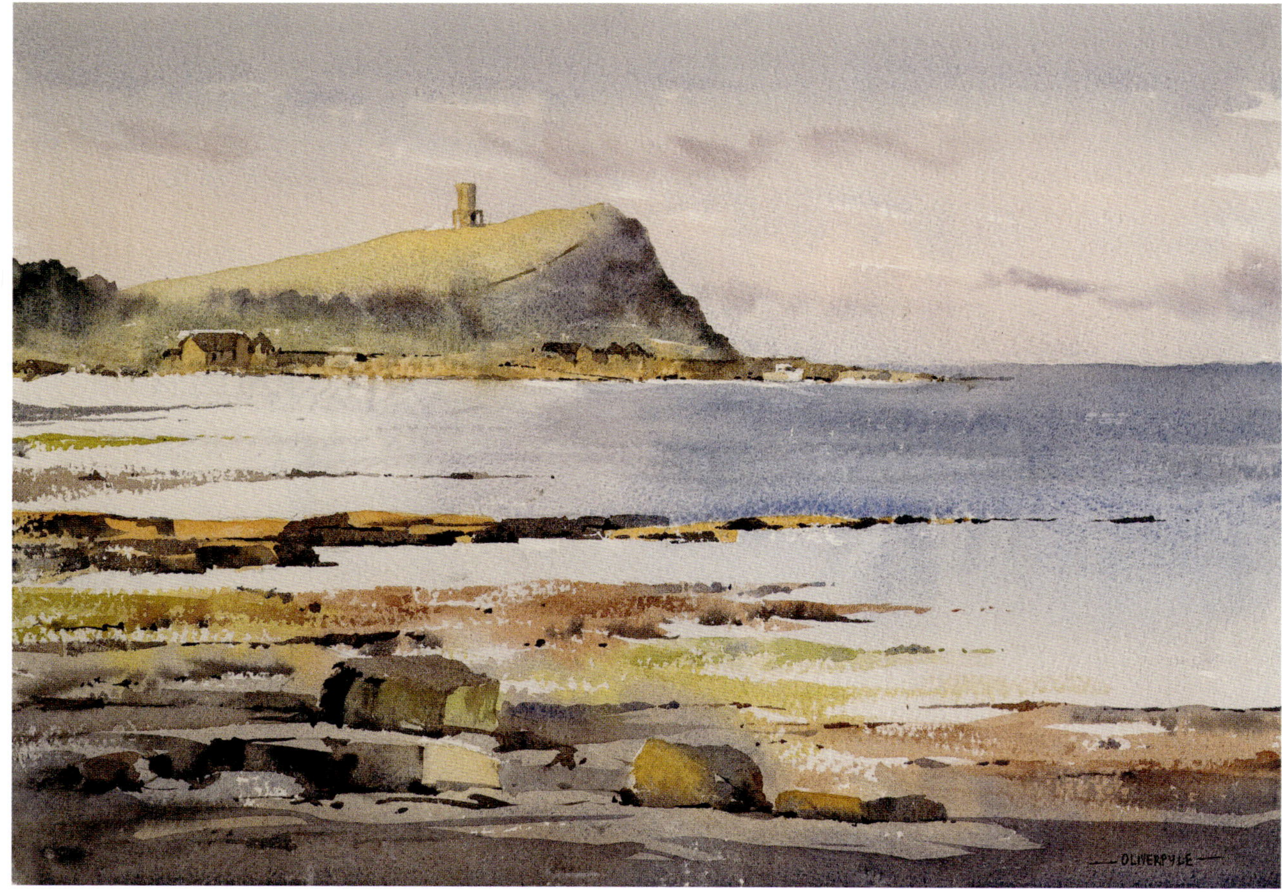

Light and Ledges at Kimmeridge Bay – 36cm x 26cm
Paint on location; it is unavoidable for the serious landscape painter. Familiarity with your subject will always trump the more remote experience of painting places we have never been to. Kimmeridge is a favourite haunt of mine, and I loved painting this scene for one of my YouTube films on a cold and crisp spring morning.

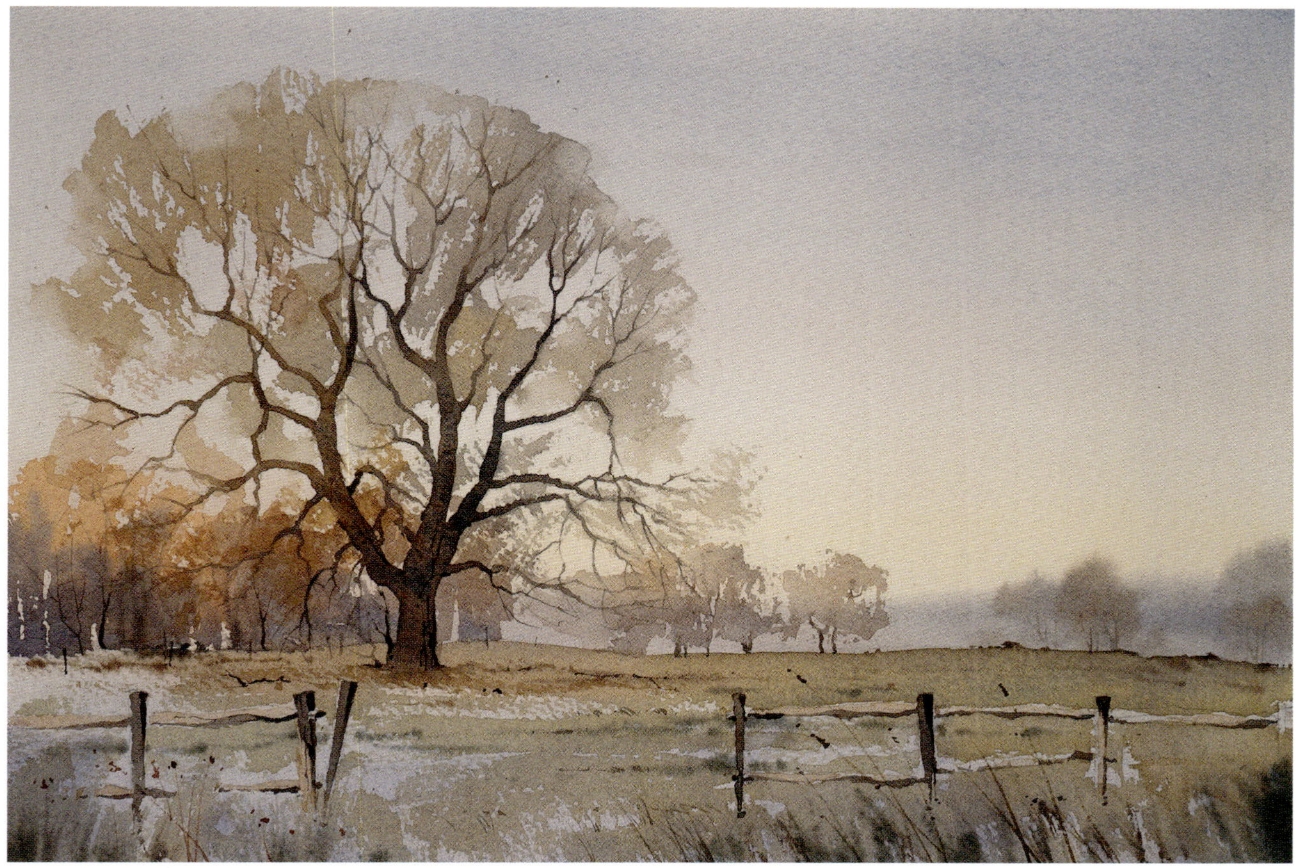

Winter Oak – 33cm x 23cm
Share your expertise and experience. One of my father's greatest attributes was his willingness to share his time and knowledge with others. It is a good thing to do and I find it rewarding; I wish I had more time to commit to this, but the commerce of painting often dictates otherwise. This is a favourite oak tree, close to home and I enjoyed sharing this demonstration for a recent YouTube Christmas special.

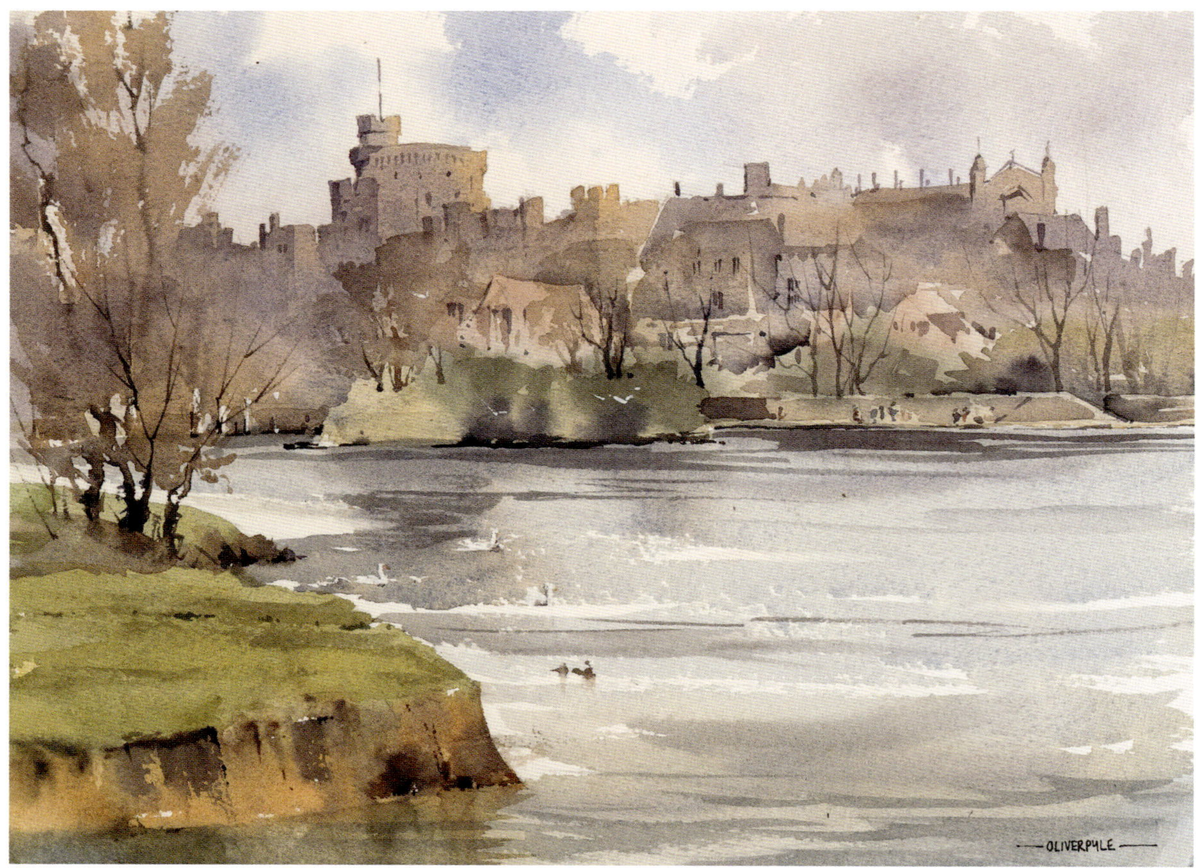

Early Spring, Windsor Castle – 30cm x 23cm
Keep going, even when you're up against it. I filmed this painting of Windsor Castle for a Patreon tutorial, and remember the coldness of the April morning biting at my fingers (and my son Thom's as he filmed). The light seemed to be changing every couple of minutes and it was difficult to achieve continuity for the purposes of filming and painting. We kept at it, and were pleased with the end results.

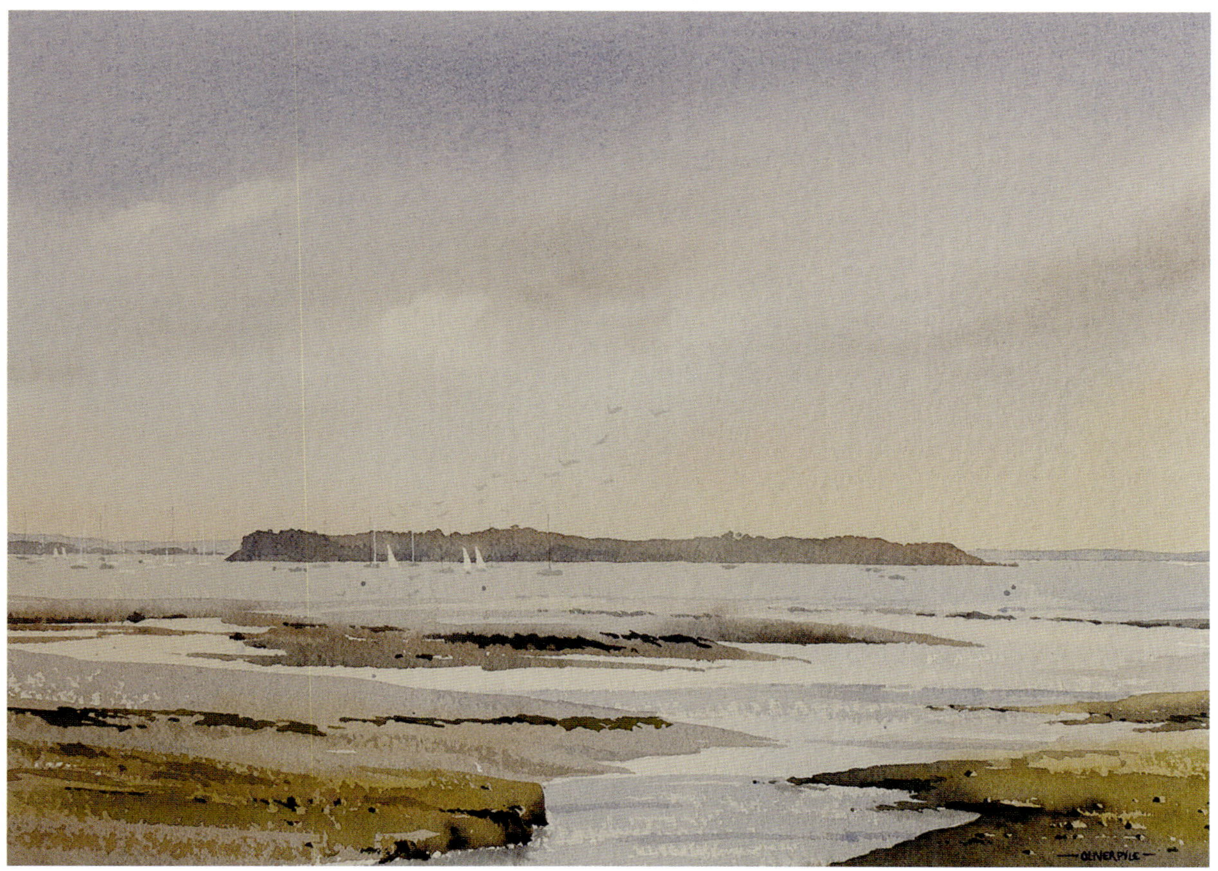

Low Tide, Poole Harbour – 39cm x 29cm
Enjoy your painting, but strive to improve. I love this view across the mudflats towards Brownsea Island and this painting, made some years back, marked an important point for me: for the first time, I had painted with a clarity and looseness to my washes that I had not achieved before (and have failed to achieve since on more than one occasion).

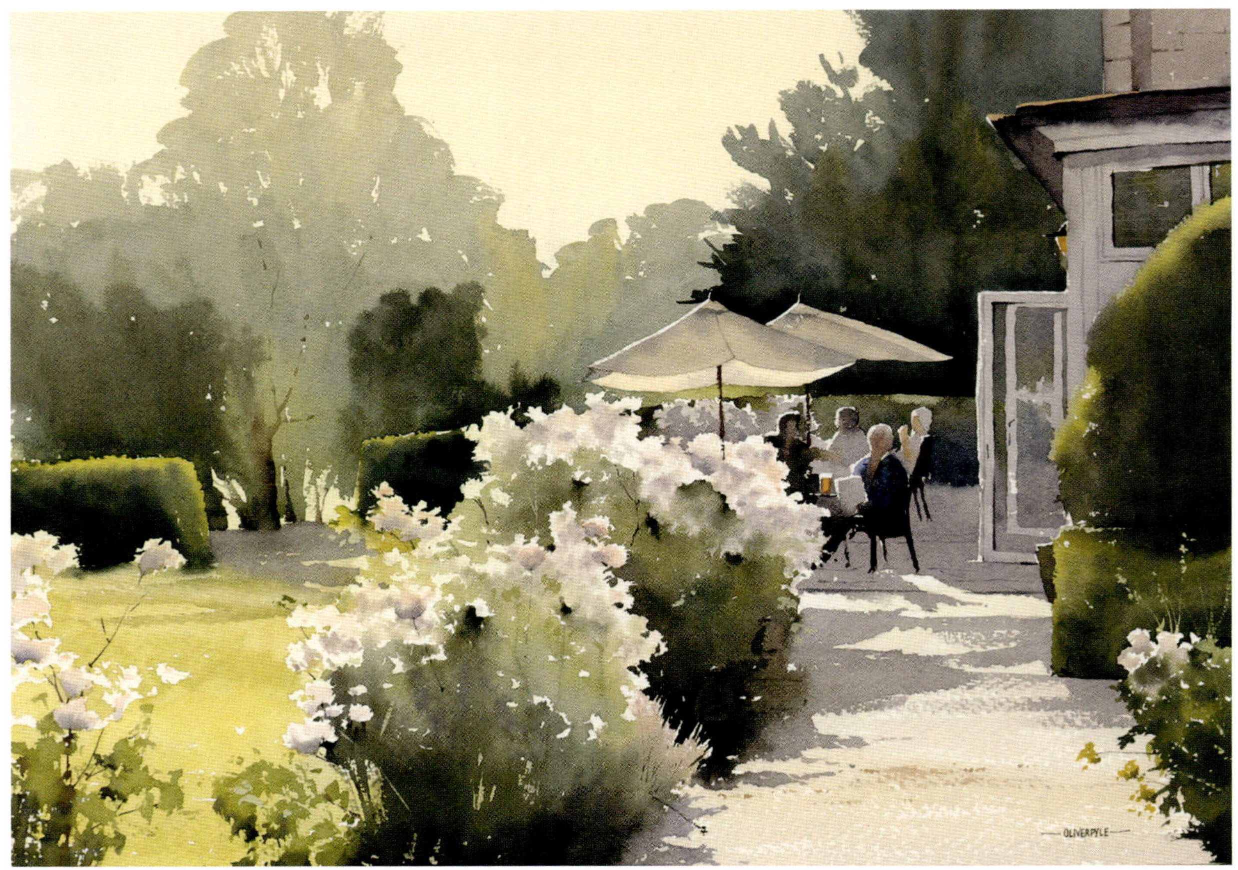

The Summer Menu, Ockenden Manor – 50cm x 34cm

Develop your 'Landscape looking', – the skill of seeing scenes and subjects in the landscape will present you with a never-ending source of ideas to paint. Wandering through my village of Cuckfield, I thought I'd take a look at the gardens and terrace at Ockenden Manor as the summer evening sun was going down. I don't normally paint *contre-jour* scenes, but the backlit roses against the dark trees and hedges were impossible to resist.

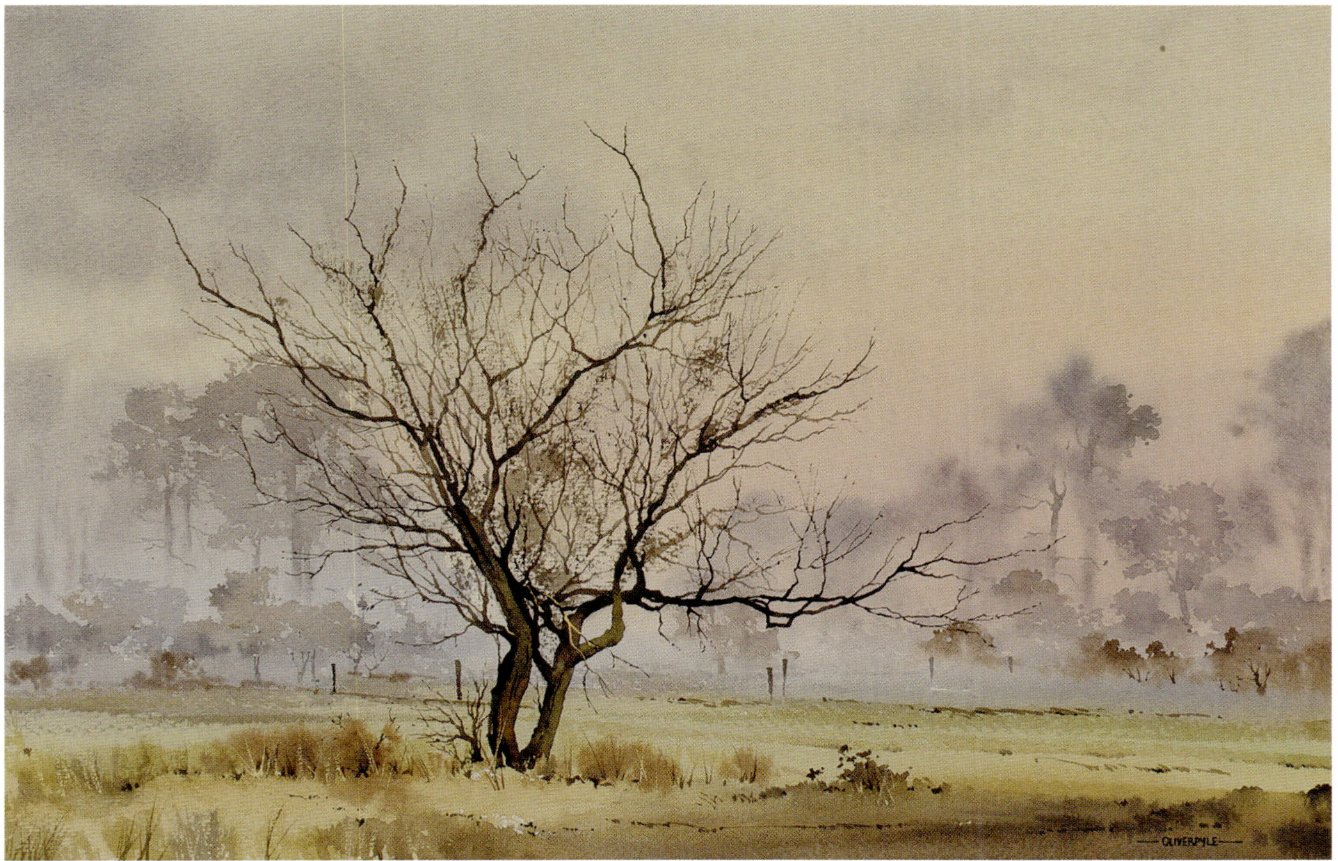

The Winter Hawthorn – 50cm x 34cm
Create, don't copy. Use your imagination to help improve the scenes and compositions that you are working on. I took this shot on Ashdown Forest in thick fog, completely obscuring the background. I wanted to include some context though, so imagined the fog starting to lift and added some distant pines with a combination of broken brushstrokes and wet-on-wet shapes, warming up the colours in the sky. Never be afraid to imagine – painting is a creative endeavour.

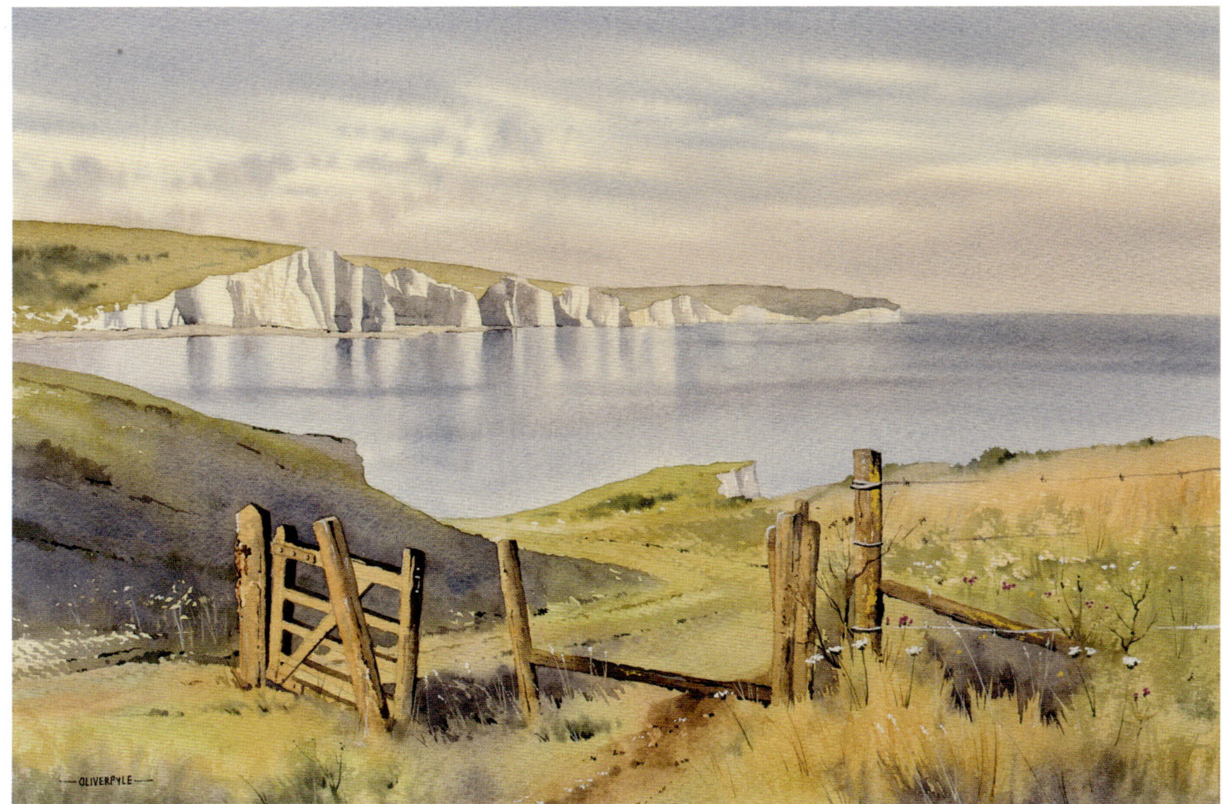

Evening Tranquility, Hope Gap – 50cm x 34cm

Play to your strengths. This scene ticks all the boxes for me: late evening sunlight, coastal spleandour, family memories, wildflowers and, most importantly, fence posts! Don't worry if you find the same scenes or elements appearing regularly in you work – repetition can be an excellent way to learn. Your paintings will be so much better when you paint the subjects that inspire you. If you don't enjoy painting red awnings on Parisian cafés, or car lights in rain-soaked streets, then don't paint them; just because other established artists have been inspired by similar scenes and made beautiful paintings and successful careers from them, doesn't mean you should. Again, create, don't copy.

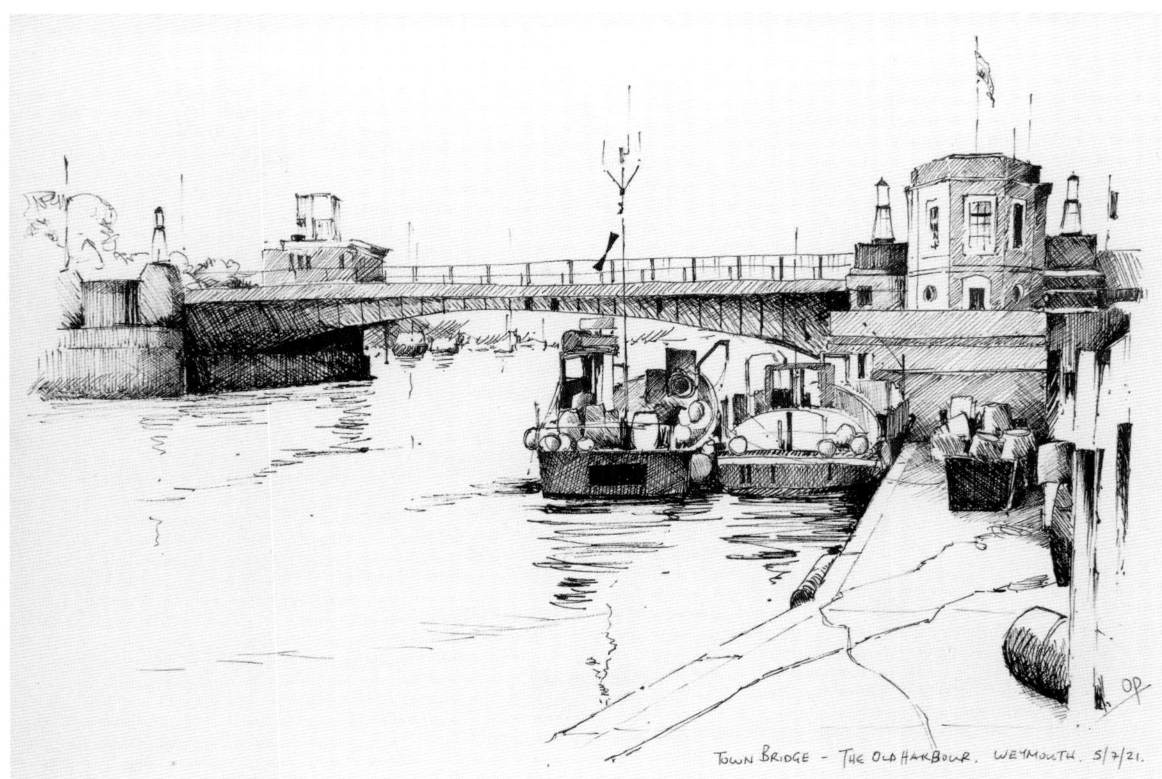

Pen and ink drawing of Town Bridge, Weymouth – 30cm x 23cm

Learn to draw. I correspond with many who are learning how to paint the landscape, and blame for disappointing results is quickly attributed to painting skills, inadequate equipment, lack of teaching and other innocent parties, when the finger of blame should be pointed at poor drawing skills. Even if you favour an abstract style of painting, you cannot hide behind an inability to draw; our most celebrated abstract painters – Picasso being a great example – were exceptional draughtsmen. To be able to paint the landscape well, especially in the watercolour medium, you cannot bypass the importance of drawing – observing carefully and recording accurately. I had almost forgotten the enjoyment of drawing for drawing's sake, and I resisted the urge to add some quick washes to this. It was great fun to do and gave me a renewed enthusiasm for good old-fashioned drawing.

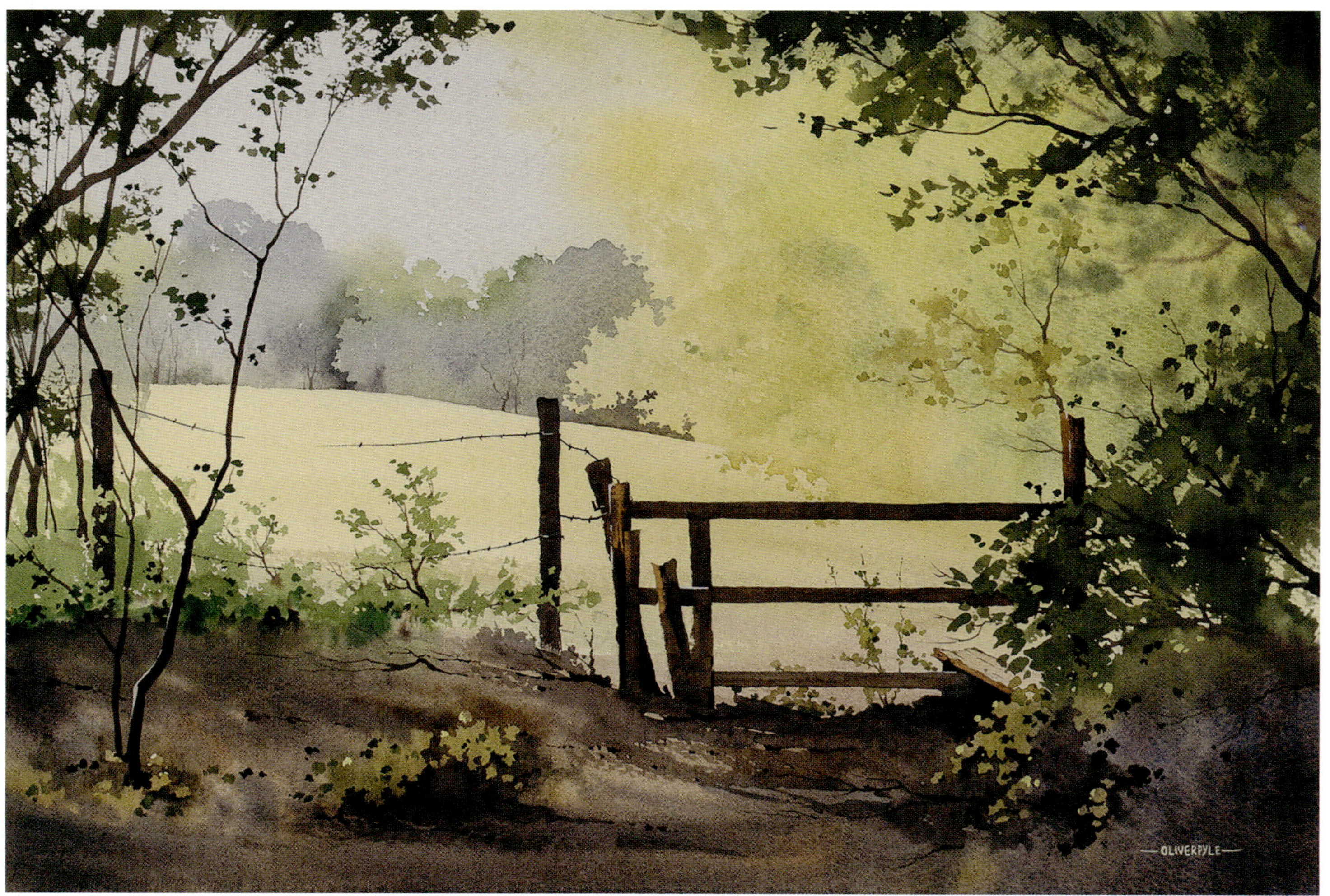
OLIVERPYLE

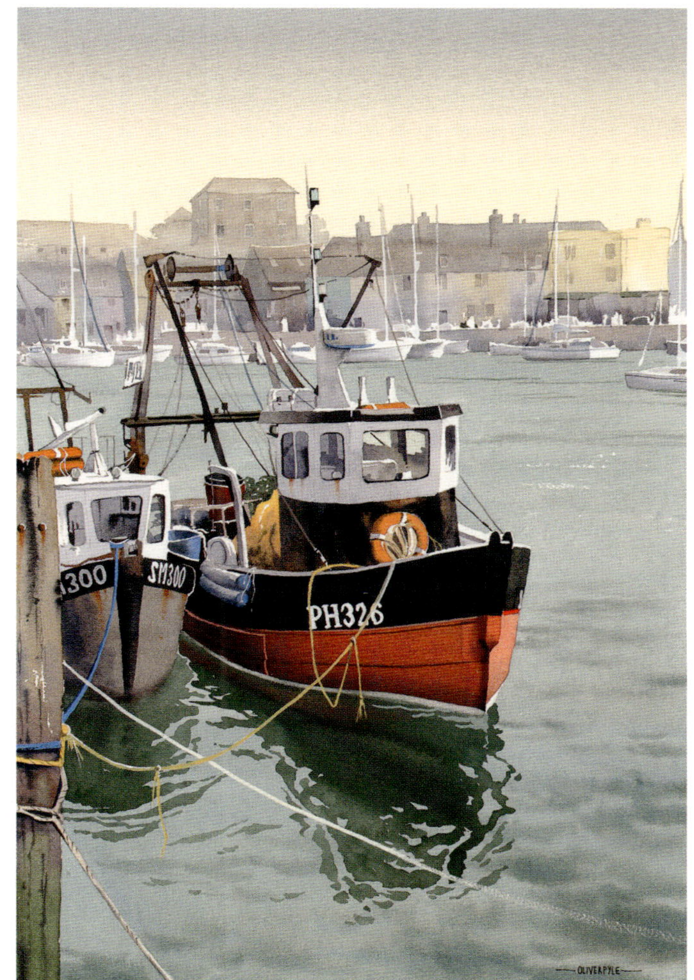

OPPOSITE: Woodland Shade – 50cm x 34cm
Confront your fears. For years I avoided scenes that included significant dark passages.
I would never paint them well, poor technique resulting in disappointing muddy areas.
It limited my ability to respond to inspiring scenes and so I sought out opportunities to
practice this. I remember feeling particularly pleased with this painting – the shady areas
painted with oodles of dark wet pigment, allowed different hues to run together, which I
then left well alone as everything dried. Identify your nemeses, and take them down one
at a time.

RIGHT: Finished for the Day – 34cm x 50cm
Don't be afraid to be different. I love bright colour and I love painting detail – two aspects
that are often treated as second-class citizens in the watercolour world. This painting
of the Old Harbour in Weymouth enabled me to indulge my guilty pleasures, quite
unashamedly. Don't be afraid to do the same – paint for you and your customers, not the
applause of the establishment or your peers.

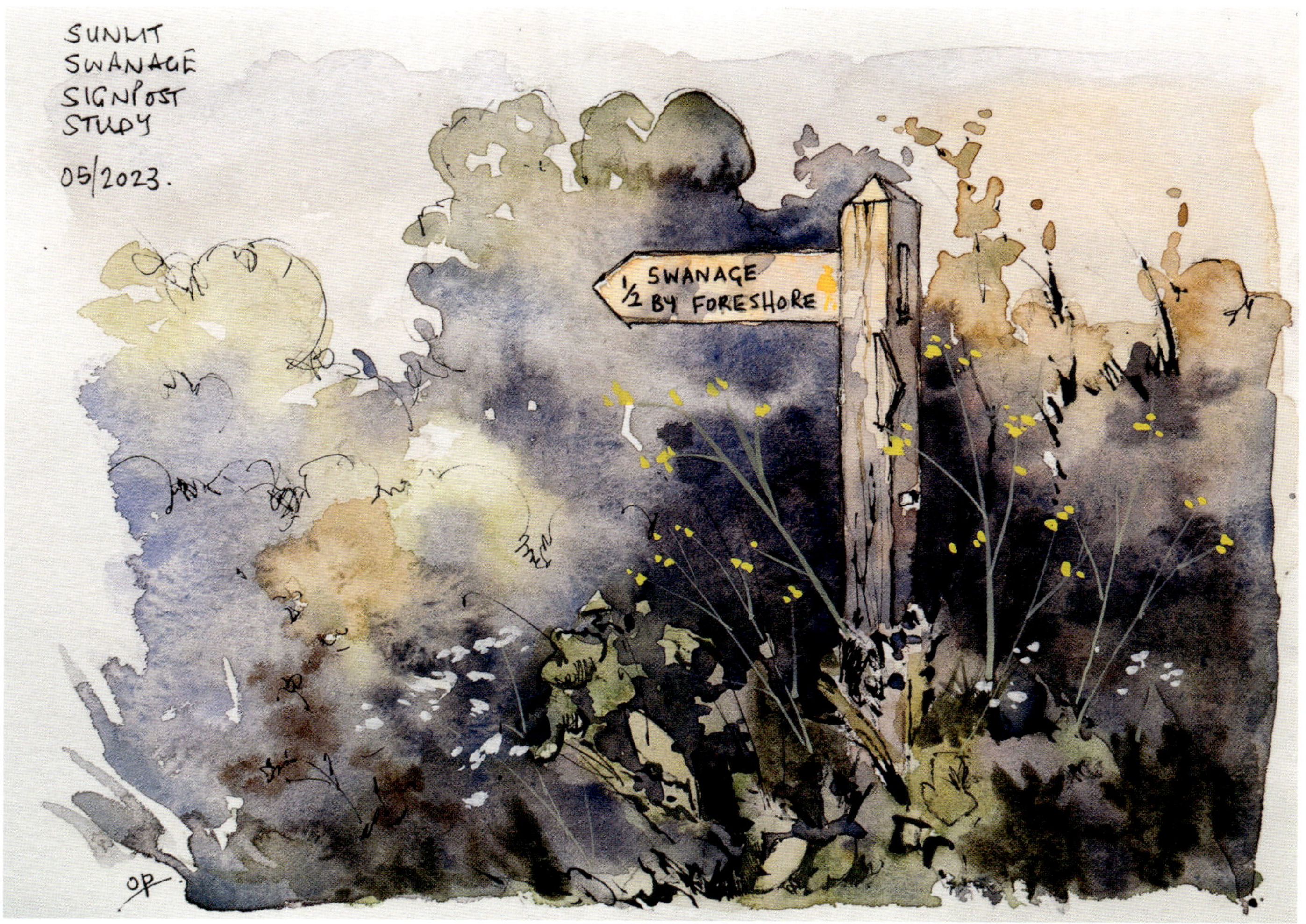
SUNLIT
SWANAGE
SIGNPOST
STUDY

05/2023.

½ SWANAGE
BY FORESHORE

OPPOSITE: Sunlit Swanage Signpost Study – 20cm x 14cm
Always be sketching. I noticed this signpost catching the sunlight as I returned
from Swanage Downs along the coast path – it made for a wonderful sketch.
Being able to sketch, to quickly turn fleeting moments, places and details,
into images is the engine room of landscape painting. It is where we sharpen
our observation skills and deepen our emotional connection to the landscape.
The very best landscape painters were consummate sketchers, never to be
found without a sketchpad to hand – J.M.W. Turner and Rowland Hilder spring
to mind.

RIGHT: High and Dry, Bosham – 29cm x 39cm
Embrace simplicity. I sometimes spend too much time looking for the complex,
overwhelmingly magnificent subjects and scenes, enjoying the challenge of the
painting process and the sense of achievement on completing them; without
checking myself down I can often ignore the beauty that lies in simplicity .
I painted this simple scene of Bosham at a time when I seemed to be stuck in
a rut of large complex paintings, extensive glazes, full sheets of stretched paper
(as much as I love those paintings and processes) and I felt exhilarated by the
fresh luminosity of the washes, painted straight onto a watercolour block, and
the simple immediate brushstrokes I used to describe the scene.

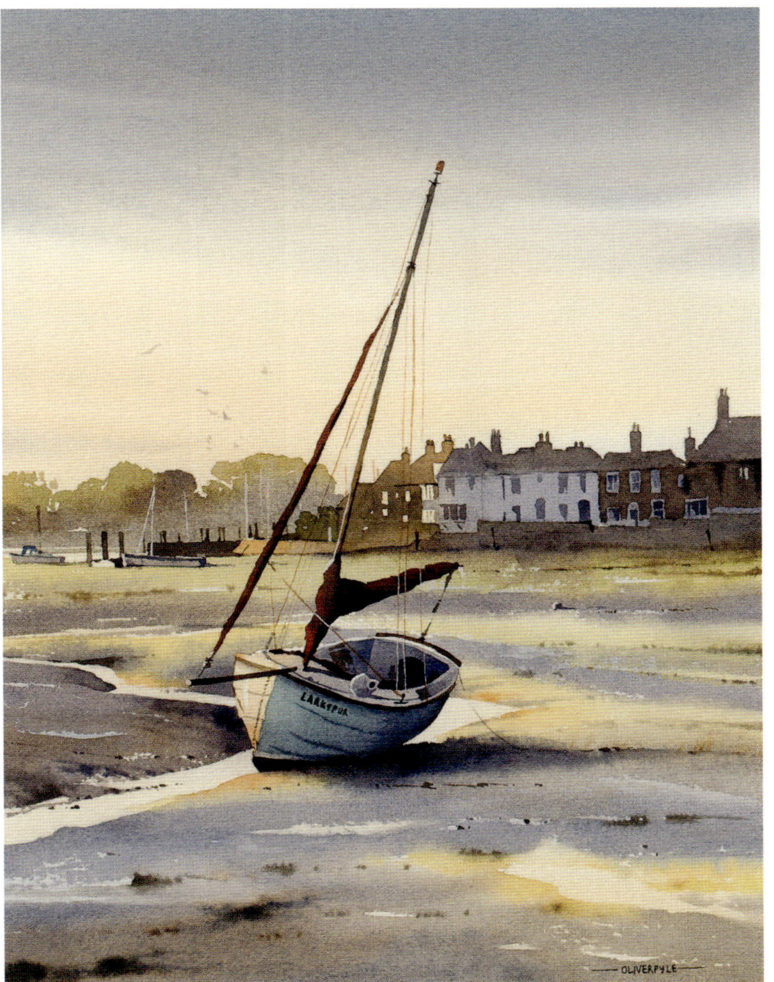

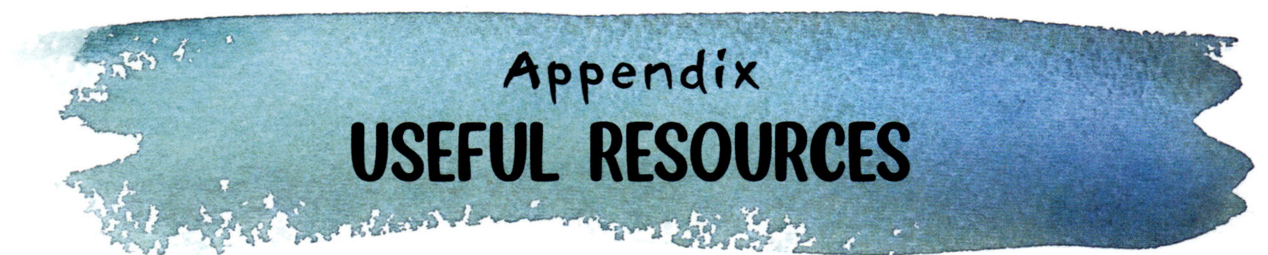

www.oliverpyle.com

My website – a gallery of recent paintings, details of the galleries that represent me in the UK and a list of the equipment used to make my paintings and for working outdoors in the landscape. The website also hosts my blog and free-to-subscribe landscape painting forum.

My tutorial content is available on the following platforms:

You Tube
Oliver Pyle – Our Landscape

Patreon
www.pateron.com/oliverpyle

Instagram
watercolour_olly

RECOMMENDED READING

Architect of Light – *Thomas W. Schaller*

Landscape Painting, The Complete Guide – *Richard Pikesley*

Pure Watercolour Painting – *Peter Cronin*

Painting on Location, and Light and Mood In Watercolour – *David Curtis*

Watercolour Painting Course – *Alwyn Crawshaw*

The Old Ways, and The Wild Places – *Robert Macfarlane*

The Making of The English Landscape – *Nicholas Crane*

Wildwood: A Journey Through Trees – *Roger Deakin*

RECOMMENDED LANDSCAPE PAINTERS

Some, but not all, of the contemporary painters mentioned here actively teach their craft through video, books and publications, and workshops and they are well worth following. Study their work, teaching, and careers and you will see that they all share the following attributes: creative integrity, insight, skills, and especially their ability to understand and express their experiences of the landscape in their own unique voices. There is no derivative work in this group:

Alwyn Crawshaw, Matthew Alexander, John Lovett, Haidee Jo Summers, Peter Cronin, David Curtis, Ann Blockley, Andy Evansen, Poppy Balser, Joseph Zbukvic, Thomas W. Schaller, Carl Purcell, Edo Hannema, Chris Robinson, Chris Forsey, Jenny Aitken, Andrew Gifford, Mark Boedges, Julia Barminova, Ian Sidaway, Richard Pikesley, Robin Mason, Helen Glassford, David Howell, Pascale Rentsch, Ray Balkwill, Sue Howells, Deborah Walker, Paul Talbot-Greaves, Jem Bowden, Tony Parsons, Dean Mitchell, Ross Paterson, Trevor Chamberlain, John Yardley, John Hoar, Nicholas Hely Hutchinson, David Atkins, Amanda Brett, Hannah Woodman, Lucy Marks, Naomi Tydeman

EQUIPMENT PROVIDERS

Daler Rowney – Art Materials
www.daler-rowney.com

Rosemary & Co – Brushes
www.rosemaryandco.com

St. Cuthbert's Mill – Paper
www.stcuthbertsmill.com

Arches – Paper
www.arches-papers.com

Etchr – outdoor painting equipment
www.etchrlab.com

Jacksons Art Supplies – online art store
www.jacksonsart.com

ACKNOWLEDGEMENTS

Although I penned the words and painted the pictures, I cannot pretend for one moment that this book is anything other than an amazing collaborative effort. Over the three years of writing and illustrating the finished book, I have drawn on the vision, knowledge and insight of others, sometimes subconsciously, to help me shape ideas, refine texts and improve formats; this is the place to consciously acknowledge those invaluable contributions.

Firstly to my publisher, Jonathan Wright at Pen & Sword and White Owl, for not only identifying the opportunity but allowing me the space to define the direction and the content of the book – thank you, a writer cannot ask for a better approach. Also, many thanks to Charlotte Mitchell, my commissioning editor and Janet Brookes, production manager, for the ease with which they have turned our ideas into print and pages. Thanks also to SJmagic Design Services, India, for their thorough work designing the book layout and all associated formatting, and Paul Wilkinson for the superb cover design.

To my wife Paula, my children Owen, Kirsten, Thom and Heidi – thank you so much for your patience as I have worked on this project, often into the early hours. Thanks also for your helpful suggestions, that you may have discounted as little more than interruptions; I certainly didn't. Countless times, simple interjections like "Why don't you…" and "Have you thought about…" or "Seriously?!" have prevented me from wandering too far off-piste. Most of all though, it is your belief in me as an artist and writer that has helped me to keep climbing when the path has seemed impassable.

My good friend and Dutch landscape painter, Edo Hannema, has been a tremendous help throughout my time working on the book. Having been able to access his deep knowledge of the watercolour medium, the worlds of online and published painting-tutorials, and a career spent working with colour and print, has been a rich resource indeed. I have enjoyed our many conversations which have often helped me to retract a paragraph here or include an illustration there. Thank you.

Some photographic credits need to be made: Paula, Kirsten, Thom and Heidi for snapping away while I have been painting and sketching outdoors (when I know you'd have preferred to be somewhere else!)

My sisters Jennifer Cassam and Chlöe Harker too, for their involvement in the Richmond-Upon-Thames field trip.

Daler Rowney, the long-established British art materials manufacturer, has been a huge support to me over the years, providing me with the equipment in my role as ambassador for the company. It was Daler Rowney pigments that I first painted with at the age of 17, long before our formal collaboration; there is still no reason to change from using their outstanding products.

Finally, many of you that read this book will have become aware of it through my presence on various social media platforms and through seeing my work in UK galleries. Over the years, I have received sack-loads of virtual mail from you, praising my work, criticising my technique, challenging my thinking, all of which have not only helped me to become a more capable artist, but have provided me with the structure and content for this book. While I haven't been able to reply to all of these, I can assure you that they have been greatly appreciated and I trust that you will be able to find some of the answers you are looking for in these pages. Most of all, I hope that it will fire your imagination and inspire a lifelong appreciation of the landscape and how to paint it. This book is a response to your invaluable correspondence and is therefore dedicated to you all.